World Wa
Aircraft

FIGHTERS • BOMBERS • GROUND ATTACK AIRCRAFT

Robert Jackson

amber
BOOKS

Printed in 2018

Published by
Amber Books Ltd
United House
London N7 9DP
United Kingdom
www.amberbooks.co.uk
Instagram: @amberbooksltd
Facebook: www.facebook.com/amberbooks
Twitter: @amberbooks

ISBN: 978-1-78274-674-4

Project Editor: Charles Catton
Editor: Helen Wilson
Picture Researcher: Tom Walker
Design: Brian Rust

Printed in China

World War II Aircraft

Contents

Arado Ar 234 Blitz

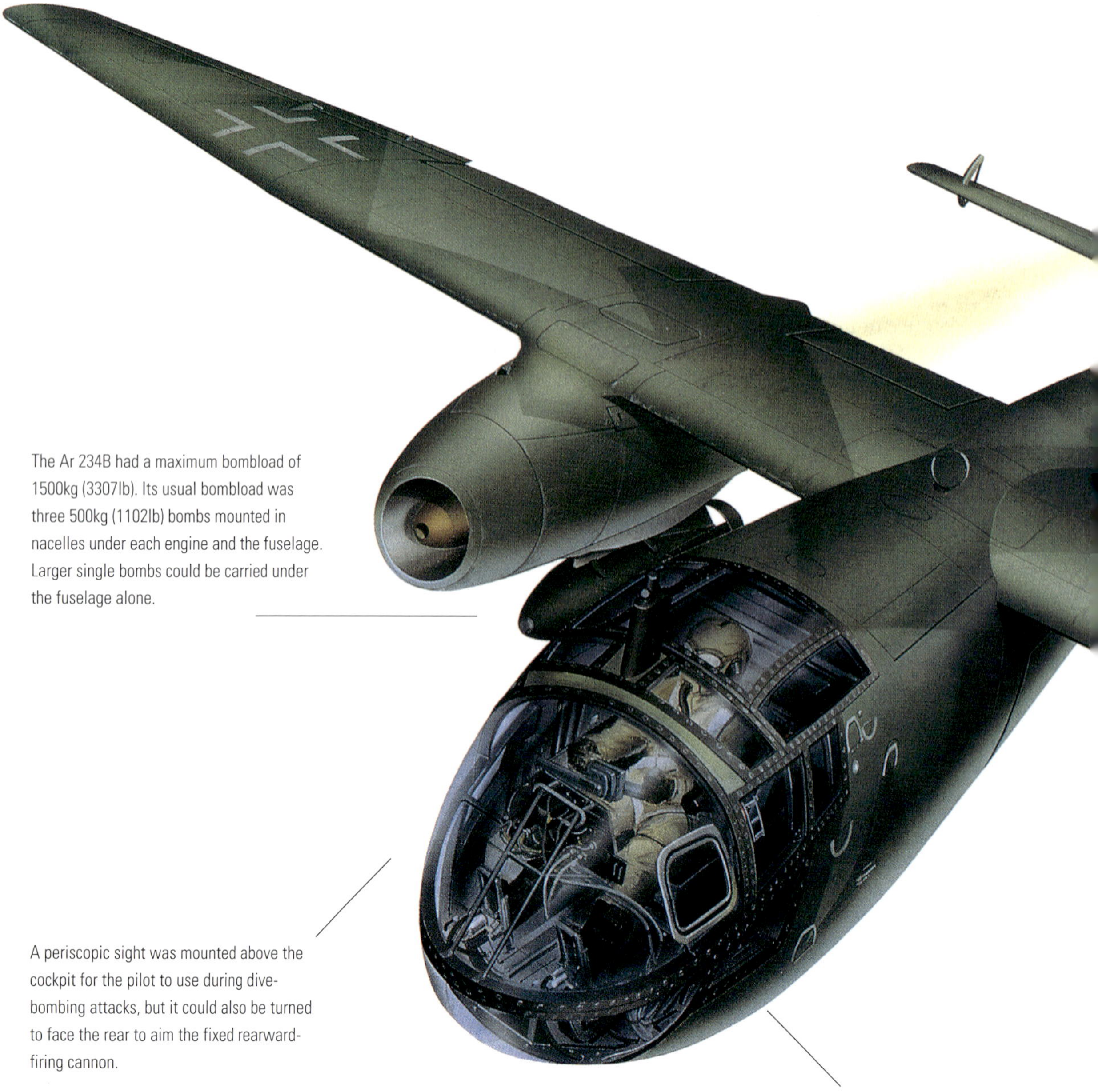

The Ar 234B had a maximum bombload of 1500kg (3307lb). Its usual bombload was three 500kg (1102lb) bombs mounted in nacelles under each engine and the fuselage. Larger single bombs could be carried under the fuselage alone.

A periscopic sight was mounted above the cockpit for the pilot to use during dive-bombing attacks, but it could also be turned to face the rear to aim the fixed rearward-firing cannon.

The pilot sat on a primitive ejection seat, with armour behind his head. A Lotfe 7K bombsight was mounted between the pilot's feet, and on a level bomb run the pilot would disconnect the control column and swing it out of the way.

This aircraft wears the markings of 9th *Staffel*, III *Gruppe*, KG 76. This unit was equipped with Ar 234s in January 1945, and was heavily involved in the attacks on Remagen bridge later that spring.

Some Ar 234Bs carried two fixed rearward-firing 20mm (0.79in) cannon mounted in the underside of the rear fuselage to protect against Allied fighters. The Ar 234 was most vulnerable when landing.

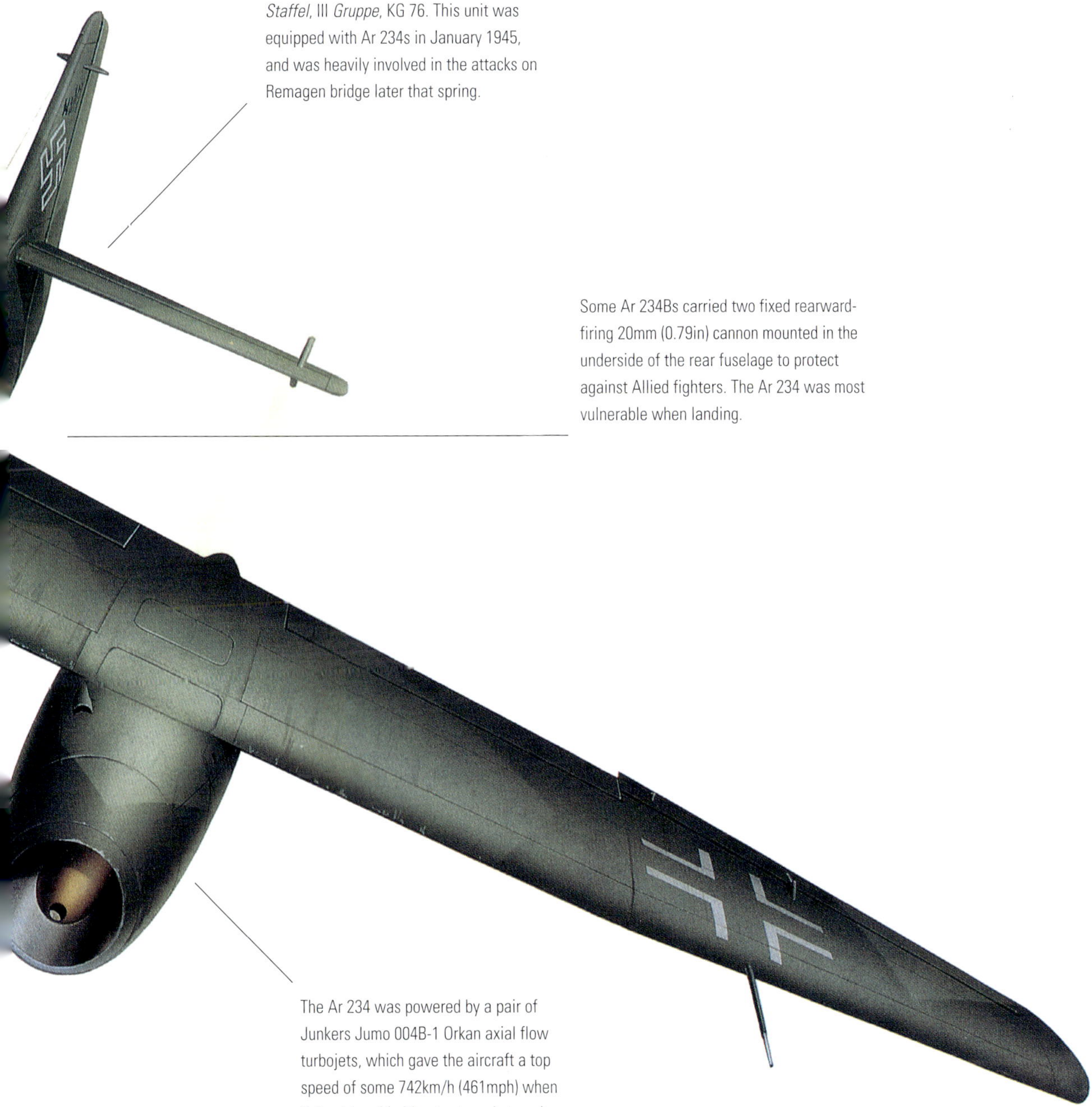

The Ar 234 was powered by a pair of Junkers Jumo 004B-1 Orkan axial flow turbojets, which gave the aircraft a top speed of some 742km/h (461mph) when flying 'clean' (without external stores).

Designed by the Arado Flugzeugwerke of Warnemünde, the Ar 234 Blitz (Lightning) was the world's first operational jet bomber. The origins of the type can be traced to a 1940 requirement issued by the German Air Ministry for a fast, turbojet-powered reconnaissance aircraft. An intensive design and development programme resulted in the construction of eight prototypes. Powered by two Junkers Jumo 004 or BMW 003 turbojets, it had provision for rocket-assisted take-off units, a single-seat cabin with or without pressurization and a pilot's ejection seat, and a clumsy combination of a jettisonable trolley for take-off and extendable skids for landing. The prototype Ar 234V-1, which flew for the first time on 15 June 1953, and the next seven aircraft (Ar 234V-2 to V-8) all used the trolley-and-skid arrangement.

The second prototype, the Ar 234V-2, was identical to the first machine. The Ar 234V-3 was fitted with an ejection seat and rocket-assisted take-off equipment, the rocket pods being installed under the wings. Both the V-4 and V-5 had the ejector seat, but the V-6 differed from earlier prototypes in that it had four BMW 003 turbojets in individual nacelles. This prototype and the similarly powered Ar 234V-8 were both tested in the spring of 1944.

Below: The Arado Ar 234V-6 was used for four-engined trials. Following these trials, it was decided to build a production version designated Ar 234C. Only a small number of Ar 234C-0 and C-1 aircraft was produced before the project was abandoned.

The Ar 234V-7 was fitted with the more powerful Jumo 004B engines scheduled for the production B-series. This prototype flew on 10 April 1944 but crashed during flight testing, killing *Flugkapitän* Selle, Arado's chief test pilot, who had conducted all the initial flight testing of the Ar 234 prototypes up to that time.

Although the launching trolley and landing skid arrangement had functioned well, this configuration was abandoned, and with it the Ar 234A-1, as the aircraft's lack of mobility on landing would be a severe disadvantage when it came to operational deployment. The design was changed and the aircraft was fitted with a conventional wheeled undercarriage. The fuselage was slightly widened to accommodate two mainwheels midway along its length, and a nosewheel was mounted under the pilot's cockpit. In this guise the aircraft was designated Ar 234B, of which 210 were built. Only two versions were used operationally; these were the Ar 234B-1 unarmed reconnaissance variant, and the Ar 234B-2 bomber. The prototypes for the B series were the V-9 to V-16. One of these, the V-13, had four BMW 003A-1 engines in two paired nacelles, while the BMW-powered V-16 featured swept wing and tail surfaces and had rocket-assisted take-off gear.

It was planned to replace the B series in production with the C series, but only 19 production Ar 234C-3 bombers had been completed by the end of the war. The prototypes for the C series were V-19 to V-30, all powered by four BMW 003 turbojets. These were virtually identical, except

Above: Arado Ar 234B-2 of KG 76, the unit that introduced the bomber version of the Ar 234 into service. On 24 February 1945 an aircraft of KG 76 became the first Ar 234 to fall into Allied hands; it was brought down by USAAF P-47s, near Segelsdorf.

for the V-21 and V-28, both of which were two-seaters, and the V-26 and V-30, which tested laminar flow aerofoils. The proposed initial production models, the Ar 234C-1 and C-2, were similar to the B-1 and B-2, with the addition of cabin pressurization and, in the case of the C-1, a pair of rearward-firing MG 151/20 cannon. However, they were abandoned in favour of the multi-role version, the C-3, which appeared in the early part of 1945 and was intended to fulfil both bomber and nightfighter roles. The C-4 was to have been a single-seat reconnaissance aircraft, while the C-5 and C-6 were two-seat bombers. The C-7 was a projected nightfighter model powered by four Heinkel-Hirth He SO11 engines; these were intended for the D series, but only two Ar 234D-1 reconnaissance aircraft were completed with this powerplant. The projected Ar 234D-2 was a bomber variant.

The first operational Ar 234 sorties were flown by the V-5 and V-7 prototypes, which were delivered to *I/Versuchsverband.Ob.d.L* (Luftwaffe High Command Trials Unit) at Juvincourt, near Reims, in July 1944. Both aircraft were fitted with Walter rocket-assisted take-off units and made their first reconnaissance sorties on 20 July, photographing harbours on the south coast of England from an altitude of 9000m (29,530ft). Several more sorties were made over the UK before the unit was transferred to Rheine in September. Other reconnaissance trials units received the Ar 234, and in January 1945 these were amalgamated into I/F.100 and I/F.123 at Rheine, and I/F.33 at Stavanger, Norway. The latter unit was responsible for flying reconnaissance sorties over the British naval base at Scapa Flow, situated in the Orkneys, until as late as mid-April 1945.

The bomber version of the Ar 234 equipped KG 76 from October 1944, flying its first operational missions during the Ardennes offensive in December. The jet bombers were very active in the early weeks of 1945, one of their most notable missions being the 10-day series of attacks on the Ludendorff bridge at Remagen, captured by the Americans in March 1945. Very few Ar 234 sorties were flown after the end of March, although an experimental Ar 234 nightfighter unit, the *Kommando* Bonow, equipped with two Ar 234s converted to carry upward-firing cannon, would continue to operate until the end of the war.

Type: Jet bomber (Ar 234B-2)	
Crew:	1
Powerplant:	two 800kg (1764lb) thrust BMW 003A-1 turbojets
Max speed:	742km/h (461mph) at 6000m (19,685ft)
Time to height:	12.8 mins to 6000m (19,685ft)
Service ceiling:	10,000m (32,810ft)
Max range:	1630km (1013 miles)
Wing span:	14.11m (46ft 3in)
Wing area:	27.3m² (293.8sq ft)
Length:	12.64m (41ft 5in)
Height:	4.30m (14ft 1in)
Weights:	5200kg (11,464lb) empty; 9850kg (21,715lb) loaded
Armament:	two fixed rearward-firing 20mm (0.79in) MG 151 cannon in underside of rear fuselage; external bomb load of 1500kg (3307lb)

Focke-Wulf FW 190

The FW 190F-2 was powered by the BMW 801D-2 14-cylinder two-row radial engine. The fuselage was the same as the FW 190A-5, which had been lengthened to accommodate the engine.

Two 7.9mm (0.31in) machine guns were mounted in front of the pilot on the upper decking of the fuselage. Each gun had a 1000 rounds of ammunition.

The FW 190 proved that radial-engined fighters could be as fast or faster than inline-engined rivals. The armoured cowling was designed to maximize airflow while minimizing drag.

The real punch of the FW 190 was in the wingroots, where two 20mm (0.79in) MG 151 cannon were mounted, each with 200 rounds of ammuntion.

The FW 190F series were intended to be close support aircraft. Either a single 500kg (1100lb) bomb or four 50kg (110lb) bombs could be carried on the centreline pylon, with optional wing racks for two 250kg (551lb) bombs.

The markings on this FW 190 show it to be from the 5th Staffel of Schlachtgeschwader 1, based at Deblin-Irena in Poland in late 1943. The Schlachtgeschwader used symbols for unit identification, in this case a black triangle. The letter identifies the aircraft, and is painted in the staffel's colour.

The pilot was protected by armour on both sides and behind him. Ground visibility was poor – later versions had a 'blown' canopy to correct this fault. The entire canopy and fairing slid backwards for entering and exiting the aircraft.

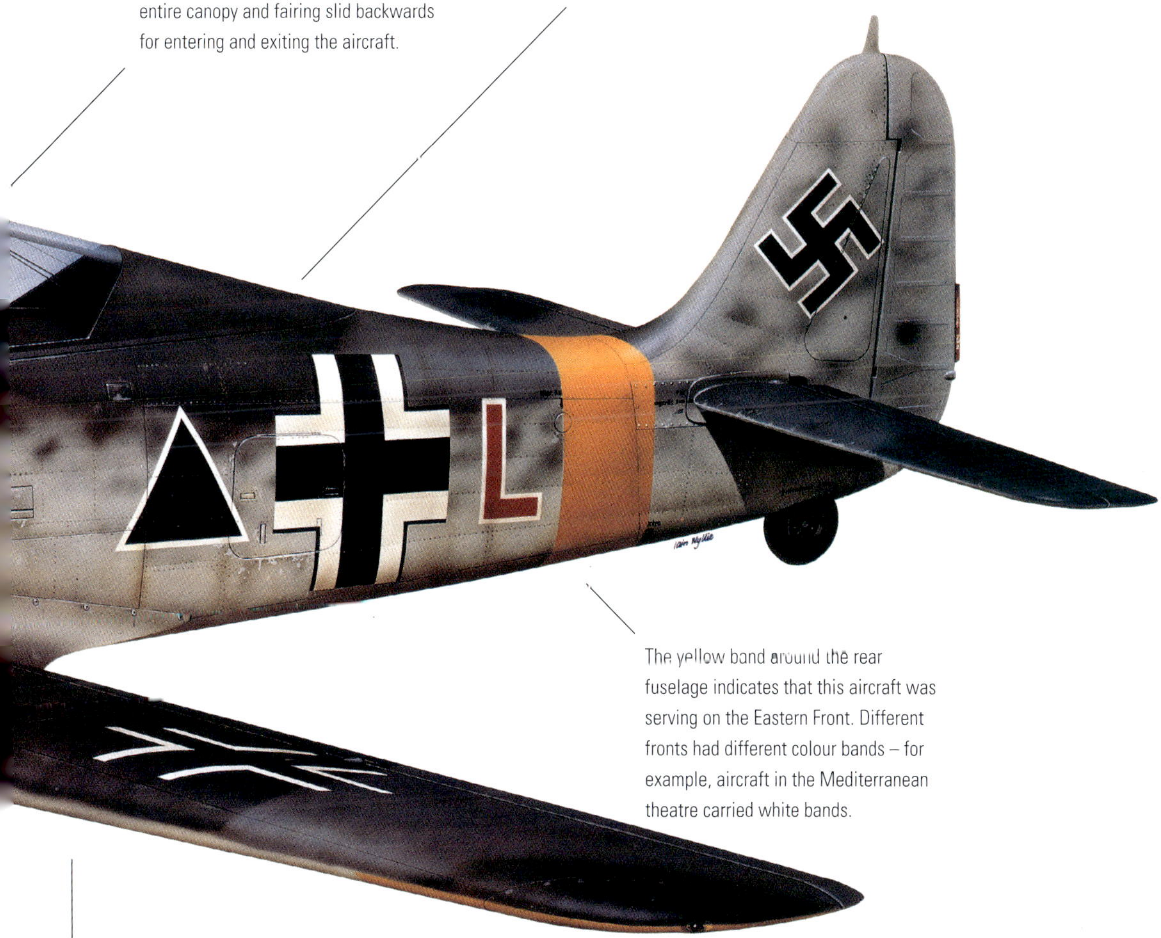

The yellow band around the rear fuselage indicates that this aircraft was serving on the Eastern Front. Different fronts had different colour bands – for example, aircraft in the Mediterranean theatre carried white bands.

The radio was located behind the pilot. In the FW 190F-2, this was a FuG16Z. The aerial wire was held taut by a spring pulley mounted behind the pilot.

The Focke-Wulf FW 190 stemmed from a suggestion by the German Air Ministry in 1937 that the company should develop an interceptor fighter to complement the Bf 109. Instead of opting for the Daimler Benz DB601 in-line engine, already in production for the Bf 109, Kurt Tank - Focke-Wulf's technical director - chose the BMW type 139 18-cylinder radial, which was still in the developmental stage. Three prototypes were built, the first of which flew on 1 June 1939. Apart from some engine overheating problems, the flight tests went very well, and construction of the other prototypes was accelerated. The fifth FW 190 was re-engined with the new 1238kW (1660hp) BMW 14-cylinder 801C-0 engine, and this met all the Luftwaffe requirements. Its success led to the construction of 30 pre-production aircraft designated FW 190A-0, these being followed by the FW 190A-1, which went into service with JG 26 at Le Bourget, Paris, in August 1941. As the FW 190 was encountered more frequently by the RAF, it became apparent that it outclassed the latest Spitfire variant, the Spitfire V, in all aspects except radius of turn. The first major operation in which the FW 190 was involved was

Type: Fighter (FW 190A-8)	
Crew:	1
Powerplant:	one 1567kW (2100hp) BMW 801D-2 radial engine with water-methanol boost
Max speed:	654km/h (406mph) at 6000m (19,685ft)
Time to height:	9 mins 6 secs to 6000m (19,685ft)
Service ceiling:	11,400m (37,402ft)
Max range:	1470km (914 miles)
Wing span:	10.50m (34ft 5in)
Wing area:	18.30m² (196.99sq ft)
Length:	8.84m (29ft)
Height:	3.96m (13ft)
Weights:	3170kg (6989lb) empty
Armament:	two 7.92mm (0.31in) MG in nose; up to four 20mm (0.79in) cannon in wings; provision for wide range of under-fuselage and under-wing bombs and rockets

Left: The FW 190 was the only German fighter to be brought into service, and to be produced in large numbers, after the outbreak of World War II. Throughout its career, this type was to be the subject of intensive engine development.

the famous 'Channel Dash' on 12 February 1942, when the German battlecruisers *Scharnhorst* and *Gneisenau*, together with the heavy cruiser *Prinz Eugen*, made a fast passage from the French Atlantic port of Brest to northern Germany via the English Channel.

The FW 190A-1 was followed into production by the A-2 (426 built), with a longer span and heavier armament, and 509 A-3 fighter-bombers. Both JG 2 and JG 26 rearmed with the A-3 in June 1942 and began attacks on targets on the south coast of England, causing serious problems for the air defences. The next variant, the FW 190A-4, of which 494 were built, had a methanol-water power boost system. The A-5 was a development of the A-4, with the engine relocated 0.15mm (0.59in) further forward, which restored the centre of gravity to the position it had occupied before it was moved by the addition of extra equipment in the rear fuselage. A total of 723 aircraft were delivered, and undertook a variety of roles including assault, nightfighting, torpedo-bomber and bomber destroyer. Some A-5s were modified as two-seat FW 190S-5 trainers, the S denoting *Schulflugzeug* (training aircraft). The FW 190A-6, of which 569 were built, was a version of the FW 190A-5/U10 fighter with a lightened wing structure and a fixed armament of four 20mm (0.79in) cannon. There were several A-6 sub-variants, one being a fighter-bomber with provision for 1000kg (2205lb) of bombs, and others being bomber destroyers, with 30mm (1.19in) cannon and extra armour to protect the pilot in head-on attacks.

The FW 190A-7, which entered production in December 1943, had a revised armament of two 20mm (0.79in) cannon in the wing roots and two 12.7mm (0.50in) machine guns in the forward fuselage. Only 80 aircraft were built before it was supplanted by the FW 190A-8, the last new-build variant of the FW 190A series. Total

Above: An FW 190A-6/R11 of I/NJG 10 flown by Oberleutnant Hans Krause from Werneuchen in August 1944. The aircraft is fitted with FuG 16ZE and FuG 25 radio equipment; note the aerials.

Below: An FW 190A-5 fighter-bomber being prepared for a mission on the Eastern Front. From the summer of 1943, German pilots found themselves facing new Soviet fighter types that they discovered were increasingly a match for their own aircraft.

production was 1334 aircraft. The A-8 was fitted with a nitrous oxide power boost system and an extra fuel tank in the rear fuselage. Some were converted to the training role with the designation FW 190S-8. The next major production version, the FW 190D, had a lengthened nose accommodating a 1324kW (1776hp) Junkers Jumo 213A-1 engine; a liquid-cooled unit fitted with an annular radiator duct that gave it a radial-engined appearance. The aircraft also had a lengthened rear fuselage. The first major production model was the FW 190D-9 interceptor, which entered service with JG 3 in 1943. Subsequent versions, equipped for ground attack, included the D-11, with two wing-mounted 30mm (1.19in) MK 108 cannon, and the D-12 and D-13, with a 1536kW (2060hp) Jumo 213F engine.

Although designed as a fighter, the FW 190 proved readily adaptable to the ground attack role, and 1942 saw the emergence of the FW 190G long-range attack variant. This interim aircraft was followed, out of sequence, by the FW 190F, which was basically a FW 190A-5 airframe with strengthened landing gear, more armour protection, and a combination of one ETC 501 bomb rack sitting under the fuselage and four ETC 50 bomb racks under the wings. A batch of 30 FW 190F-1 aircraft was followed by 271 FW 190F-2s with an improved canopy, about 250 FW 190F-3s with a revised wing structure, 385 FW 190F-7s based on the FW 190A-7, and an unknown number of FW 190F-9s produced with the powerful 1693kW (2270hp) BMW 801TS/TH turbocharged engine.

The Focke-Wulf FW 190 was so successful that the German Air Ministry (*Reichsluftministerium*) allowed its designer, Dipl Ing Kurt Tank, to use the first letters of his surname to prefix all subsequent Focke-Wulf designs. Only two, however, were used operationally in World War II; one was the Ta 154 twin-engined nightfighter, a few of which saw brief operational service; the other was the Ta 152, a long-span development of the FW 190D with increased armament and a boosted Jumo 213E/B engine that gave it a top speed of 760km/h (472mph) at 12,500m (41,010ft). The production version was the Ta 152H, which was first issued to JG 301 early in 1945, its task being to protect the Me 262 jet fighter bases. About 150 examples were completed before the collapse of Germany brought an end to further production.

Focke-Wulf FW 200 Condor

The FW 200C-1 was crewed by five men. The pilot and co-pilot usually sat side-by-side on the flight deck. The detachable nose cone in front of the cockpit covered the forward antenna for the direction-finder.

The forward-firing 7.92mm (0.31in) MG 15 machine gun in the fully-enclosed forward cupola was fired by the co-pilot when the aircraft was threatened by a frontal attack.

The FW 200C-1 was powered by four BMW 132H radial engines. Later Condors were equipped with the more powerful BMW-Bramo 323R-2 Fafnir radial.

The forward gondola gun position was manned by a crewmember who was also the navigator, radio operator and bomb-aimer. The position mounted an Oerlikon MG FF 20mm (0.79in) cannon. Behind the gun is the Lofte 7D bomb sight.

The weapons bay of the ventral gondola was sufficient in size for a 250kg (551lb) cement bomb, which was used to calculate ballistics or calibrating the bombsight before the main bombload was released. Behind it was the rear gunner position, manned by the flight engineer with a 7.92mm (0.31in) gun.

The FW 200 aircraft were painted in the standard Luftwaffe camouflage scheme of two-tone green splinter upper surfaces and light grey undersides.

The FW 200C-1 carried four 250kg (551lb) bombs on its armed reconnaissance missions. These were carried externally, two on the outboard engine nacelles and two on wing racks.

The rear dorsal gunner sat in a semi-enclosed turret position armed with a 7.92mm (0.31in) MG 15 machine gun.

This hatch in the bottom of the rear fuselage could be used for dropping small stores in flight, such as flares, light buoys or direction-finding buoys.

The markings show this FW 200C-1 to be an aircraft from I Gruppe, Kampfgeschwader 40, of IV Fliegerkorps, Luftflotte 3, based at Bordeaux-Mérignac, France, in 1940.

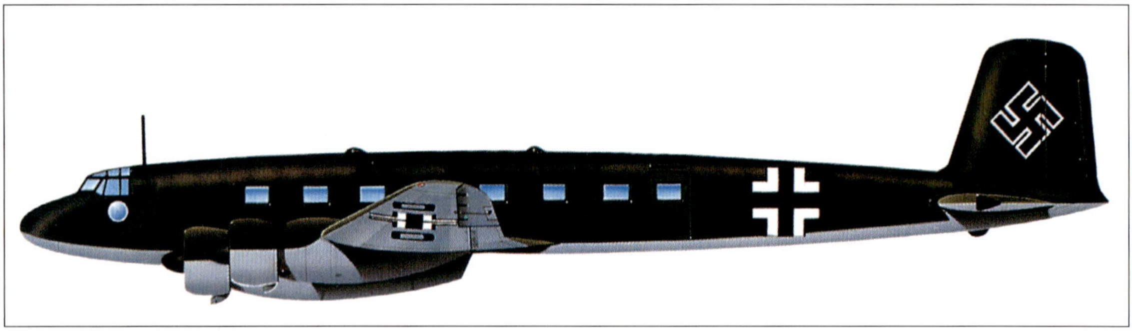

Above: Focke-Wulf FW 200 F8+BB, one of the first Condors to be fitted with a ventral pannier and full maritime and bombing equipment. The model was assigned to Stab I/KG 40, and subsequently would take part in the invasion of Norway in April 1940.

The Focke-Wulf FW 200 Condor was designed in 1936 as a 26-passenger commercial airliner and, powered by four 537kW (720hp) BMW 132G radial engines, the prototype FW 200 V-1 (D-AERE, later named *Saarland*) flew on 27 July 1937, powered by four 652kW (875hp) Pratt & Whitney Hornet radial engines. On 10 August 1938 this aircraft, now re-registered D-ACON and named *Brandenburg*, made a non-stop flight from Berlin to New York in 24 hours 36 minutes. The initial production version, designated FW 200A, was essentially similar to the prototype, but the first major production model, the FW 200B-1, had increased all-up weight and 634kW (850hp) BMW 132Dc engines, while the FW 200B-2 had the 619kW (830hp) BMW 132H-1. The FW 200B was used by Lufthansa and Danish Air Lines, while one of the three prototypes, the FW 200 V-3 Immelmann III, was allocated to Adolf Hitler as his personal transport.

Type: Long-range maritime patrol aircraft (FW 200C-3)	
Crew:	6
Powerplant:	four 895kW (1200hp) BMW-Bramo 323R-2 Fafnir nine-cylinder radial engines (FW 200C-3/U4)
Max speed:	360km/h (224mph) at 4700m (15,420ft)
Time to height:	Unknown
Service ceiling:	6000m (19,685ft)
Max range:	4440km (2759 miles)
Wing span:	32.84m (107ft 8in)
Wing area:	118.00m² (1270sq ft)
Length:	23.85m (78ft 2in)
Height:	6.30m (20ft 7in)
Weights:	12,950kg (28,549lb) empty; 22,700kg (50,044lb) max t/o
Armament:	one 7.92mm (0.31in) gun in forward dorsal turret; one 13mm (0.51in) gun in rear dorsal position; two 13mm (0.51in) guns in beam positions; one 20mm (0.79in) gun in forward position of ventral gondola; one 7.92mm (0.31in) gun in aft ventral position; maximum bomb load of 2100kg (4630lb)

Late in 1938, D-ACON *Brandenburg*, the first prototype, made a demonstration flight from Berlin to Tokyo. The Japanese Army Air Force was so impressed by the high performance of the aircraft that it ordered three examples of a bomber conversion. The Focke-Wulf design team started work on this early in 1939, the converted aircraft being designated FW 200C. The FW 200C featured a considerably strengthened structure, and was powered by four 746kW (1000hp) BMW (Bramo) 323 Fafnir radial engines. The undercarriage was also strengthened to allow for extra all-up weight, double wheels replacing the single wheels previously fitted to the main undercarriage units.

By the time the first FW 200C had been completed World War II had begun, and conversion of the Condor was taken over by the Luftwaffe, the aircraft being ordered into production for the maritime reconnaissance role. Pre-production FW 200C-0s were used as transports during the invasion of Norway in April 1940, together with FW 200Bs requisitioned from Lufthansa. The first unit to receive the maritime reconnaissance Condor was the Luftwaffe's Long-Range Reconnaissance Squadron (*Fernaufklärungsstaffel*), which began operations in April 1940 and was re-designated I/KG 40 later in the month. Production of the FW 200C-1 continued throughout 1940, 36 aircraft being produced in the course of the year, and in 1941 Focke-Wulf turned out 58 FW 200C-2s, which had two bomb racks of improved design under each wing. While the initial production version of the Condor was operationally successful, it suffered from a serious structural weakness of the rear fuselage, and some aircraft were destroyed when they literally broke in half on landing. To remedy the problem, a structurally strengthened version, the FW 200C-3, was placed in production by mid-1941, and this variant of the Condor was produced in greater numbers than its predecessors. Normal endurance was 9 hours and 45 minutes, but with internal long-range tanks fitted, the aircraft could remain airborne for as long as 18 hours, making it possible for a Condor to take off from Bordeaux, make an Atlantic reconnaissance to the west of the British Isles, and land at Stavanger in Norway. The FW 200C-3 had a maximum take-off weight of 22,650kg (49,934lb), a normal bomb load of 1495kg (3296lb), and a maximum bomb load of 5345kg (11,783lb).

KG 40's Condors presented a far more serious threat than submarines to Allied shipping in the Atlantic and North Sea between 1940 and 1941. Between August 1940 and February 1941, they claimed 368,826 tonnes (363,000 tons) sunk; most of this loss occurred in April 1941, when 116 ships, totalling 328,185 tonnes (323,000 tons), were sunk. Losses from air attack only began to diminish with the deployment of long-range Beaufighter squadrons to airfields in Cornwall and Northern Ireland, and with the adoption by the Royal Navy of the first escort carriers in 1942. From 1 January 1941, KG 40 came under the direct control of the *Fliegerführer Atlantik*, a naval command.

The armament of the FW 200 varied considerably during its operational career. The C-1 had five 7.92mm (0.31in) MG 15 machineguns, two mounted in the waist for lateral fire, one firing aft from the bomb bay gondola, one in a forward-mounted electrically operated turret, and one in a manually operated dorsal position, and a forward-firing 20mm (0.79in) MG FF cannon. The FW 200C-3/U1 differed in having a 20mm (0.79in) MG 151 cannon mounted in the forward turret, the FW 200C-3/U2 had 7.92mm (0.31in) MG 15 guns in all positions, the FW 200C-3/U3 had 12.7mm (0.5in) MG 131 machineguns in forward turret and dorsal positions, and the FW 200C-3/U4 had a 20mm (0.79in) MG 151 cannon in the front of the gondola, and MG 131 machineguns in the dorsal position and waist. Some FW 200C-3/U1 and U4 aircraft were equipped with search radar and designated FW 200C-4; these aircraft also carried an impressive array of communications equipment. The final operational version of the Condor was the FW 200C-6, developed from the C-3 to carry a Henschel Hs 293B air-to-surface missile under each outer engine nacelle, the underwing bomb racks being removed. The combination of Hs 293 and FW 200 was first used operationally on 28 December 1943.

In 1942 84 Condors were produced, followed by 76 in 1943, but by the beginning of 1944 the heyday of the FW 200 had passed. Production was terminated; the grand total of Condors produced during the war years was 252 aircraft. Many were relegated to transport duties in 1942, nine being lost during attempts to resupply the German garrison at Stalingrad.

Below: Between 1940 and 1941, with relatively few U-boats so far at sea, the Condors of KG 40 represented the biggest threat to British convoys making their way through the North Sea and the Atlantic. In April 1941 alone, these Condors sank no fewer than 116 ships.

Heinkel He 111

This aircraft, a Heinkel He 111H-22, belongs to III *Gruppe, Kampfgeschwader* 3, based in Holland in late 1944.

Most Heinkels had two 7.92mm (0.31in) MG 81 machine guns in the rear of the ventral gondola. However, here they have been removed to save weight. Another pair of machine guns would be mounted in the aircraft's beam positions.

The Fi 103 was powered by an Argus-Schmidt As 014 spring-valve pulse jet mounted above the missile's rear fuselage. The missile's cruising speed was approximately 800km/h (497mph).

The dorsal turret mounted a single 13mm (0.51in) MG 131 machine gun with 1000 rounds of ammunition. The gunner was also the radio operator.

The standard crew of a late He 111 was five: the pilot, bomb-aimer and three gunners. The pilot sat offset to port in the glazed nose section, the navigator/bomb-aimer sitting beside him on a folding seat for take-off.

The He 111H-22 was based on the earlier H-16 and H-20 airframes, which were powered by the Junkers Jumo 211F-2 12 cylinder engine. A few H-22s used H-21 airframes, which were equipped with the Junkers Jumo 213E-1 engine instead.

The Fi 103 missile is better known as the V1 which was launched from ground bases in France and the Low Countries against Britain. About 1200 operational air launches were made, the first of these in late July 1944, almost two months after D-Day.

During operations, the bomb-aimer had a pad in the extreme nose from which he could use the bombsight or fire the nose gun, an MG FF 20mm (0.79in) cannon with 180 rounds of ammunition.

Siegfried and Walter Günter designed the Heinkel He 111 early in 1934 as high-speed transport and as a bomber for the still-secret Luftwaffe. The design owed a great deal to that of the earlier He 70, retaining the latter's graceful line. The first prototype, the He 111a (later redesignated He 111 V-1) flew for the first time on 24 February 1935, powered by two 492kW (660hp) BMW VI engines, and was followed by the V-2, which made its maiden flight on 12 March 1935. This aircraft, D-ALIX, was a transport version with a reduced span and a straight trailing edge; it was delivered to Lufthansa, named *Rostock*, and was later used for secret reconnaissance missions. The He 111 V-3, D-ALES, was a bomber with a further reduced wing-span, and was the forerunner of the He 111A production model.

Following the success of the He 111 V-3, Heinkel was ordered to construct a pre-production batch of 10 He 111A-0s. Two aircraft were sent to Rechlin for trials, but were found to be unsuitable for operational use, their handling characteristics being badly affected by the extra

Right: Two LT F5b practice torpedoes being loaded beneath the fuselage of a Heinkel He 111H-6 on PVC weapon racks. The first unit to arm with the H-6 torpedo-bomber was I/KG 26, which was based at Bardufoss and Banak in northern Norway.

Type: Medium bomber (He 111H-16)	
Crew:	5
Powerplant:	two 1007kW (1350hp) Junkers Jumo 211F inverted V-12s
Max speed:	436km/h (271mph) at 6000m (19,685ft)
Time to height:	42 mins to 6000m (19,685ft)
Service ceiling:	6700m (21,982ft)
Max range:	1950km (1212 miles)
Wing span:	22.60m (74ft 1in)
Wing area:	86.50m² (931sq ft)
Length:	16.40m (53ft 8in)
Height:	3.40m (11ft 1in)
Weights:	8680kg (19,136lb) empty; 14,000kg (30,864lb) max t/o
Armament:	one 20mm (0.79in) MG FF cannon in nose; one 13mm (0.51in) MG 131 gun in dorsal position; two 7.92mm (0.31in) MG 15 guns in rear of ventral gondola; two 7.92mm (0.31in) MG 81 guns in each of two beam positions; internal bomb load of up to 2000kg (4409lb), similar external load

Above: The Heinkel He 111H, as seen in this picture, was the definitive model of the He 111 series and was in essence the He 111P fitted with two Jumo 211 engines. The He 111H entered service in 1939, and a total of 6150 examples of it were built.

weight of military equipment. All 10 were shipped to China for use against the Japanese. Meanwhile, development of the civil transport series continued with the He 111 V-4 D-AHAO, which could carry 10 passengers. It was delivered to Lufthansa in January 1936 and was followed by six production Heinkel He 111C-0s, all named after German cities. In the meantime, Heinkel had been working on a replacement for the He 111A-0. This was the He 111B, which had two 746kW (1000hp) Daimler-Benz DB 600A engines. The prototype was the He 111 V-5 D-APYS. The aircraft was ordered into production for the Luftwaffe as the He 111B-1, the first examples being delivered to I/KG 154 *Boelcke* at Hannover-Langenhagen late in 1936. In 1937 the He 111B-1 was tested under combat conditions with the German-sponsored Condor Legion in Spain and proved to be very successful, its speed alone enabling it to evade fighter interception.

The He 111D followed the 300 He 111Bs. Only a few were completed before production switched to the He 111E bomber with Junkers Jumo engines and a small number of He 111Fs similarly powered, the latter being the first to feature a wing with a straight leading edge. These variants also served in Spain, and after the civil war were taken over by the Spanish Air Force. The He 111G was another transport version, five being delivered to Lufthansa and four to Turkey. About 1000 examples of all these He 111s variants had been produced by mid-1939, by which time a new model had appeared. This was the He 111P, which was powered by two 858kW (1150hp) Daimler-Benz DB 601Aa engines and which incorporated a fully-glazed asymmetric nose, with its offset ball turret, in place of the stepped-up cockpits of the earlier variants. Relatively few He 111Ps were completed before production switched to the He 111H, powered by two 820kW (1100hp) Junkers Jumo 211 engines. Sub-variants of this series formed the backbone of the Luftwaffe's bomber force between 1940

and 1943, about 6150 being built before production ended in 1944. The series was subjected to a progressive upgrading of its powerplant, continual revision of its offensive and defensive armament, the provision of additional armour, and its adaptation to its various roles that included anti-shipping torpedo attack, pathfinding, missile carrying and launching, paratroops delivery and glider towing. The first version to carry torpedoes was the He 111H-6, followed by the He 111H-15. The He 111H-8 was fitted with a large and cumbersome balloon cable fender; the He 111H-11R2 was a glider tug for the Gotha Go 242, while the He 111H-14 and H-18 were pathfinder versions with special radio equipment. The He 111H-16 featured heavier gun armament, while the He 111H-20 included 16-paratroop transport, nightbomber and glider tug sub-variants. The He 111H-22 carried a single Fieseler Fi-103 (V-1) flying bomb under its wing, launching these weapons from over the North Sea at targets in the United Kingdom towards the end of 1944. (These operations, incidentally, cost the launcher units 77 aircraft from July 1944 to January 1945, many the victims of Mosquito nightfighters). The final variant of the Heinkel bomber was the He 111Z (*Zwilling*, or twin), built to tow the massive Me 321 *Gigant* glider. The aircraft comprised two He 111H-6 or H-16 airframes joined by a new centre section on which a fifth engine was mounted.

In the early days of World War II, during operations against Poland, the losses suffered by the He 111 units were comparatively light, but it was a different story when they encountered determined opposition during the Battle of France, and even more so in the Battle of Britain. One of the last major missions undertaken by the He 111 was on the night 21/22 June 1944, when Heinkels of KGs 4, 27, 53 and 55 attacked the Russian airfield of Poltava, where 114 USAAF B-17s and their P-51 fighter escort had landed after an attack on Berlin earlier in the day. Led by a Heinkel He 177 pathfinder aircraft, the German bombers destroyed 43 Fortresses and 15 Mustangs in the attack. The He 111 also scored some successes against the Arctic convoys to Russia, notably against the ill-fated PQ17 in July 1942, when the convoy was virtually destroyed.

Below: This study of a Heinkel He 111H gives a good overall view of the bomber's defensive armament positions, in the nose, ventral gondola and dorsal cupola. Armament was strengthened as a result of losses suffered during the Battle of Britain.

Junkers Ju 52

Three men flew the Ju 52, with a pilot and co-pilot sitting side-by-side, and a radio operator sitting on a jump-seat between them. The cockpit was raised above the cabin floor height.

The Ju 52 had a loop antenna for the direction-finding equipment, and an aerial mast mounted behind the cockpit.

The Ju 52/3mg5e was powered by three BMW 132T-2 9-cylinder radial engines. The two outboard engines faced slightly outwards to reduce yaw should one of them fail. The exhaust gas was collected by annular ducts which gave the aircraft its trademark stains.

The engine nacelles on the wings also housed the engine oil tanks above the wing leading edge.

The undercarriage was very strong to cope with repeated landings on rough fields. Spats were also issued to reduce the drag of the wheels, but these would quickly clog up with mud on operations.

When fitted with seats the Ju 52 could carry up to 18 passengers, sitting in single rows separated by an aisle.

The dorsal hatch had a mounting for a 7.92mm (0.31in) MG 15 machine gun. A transparent fairing was fixed in front of it to give the gunner some protection from the airstream in flight.

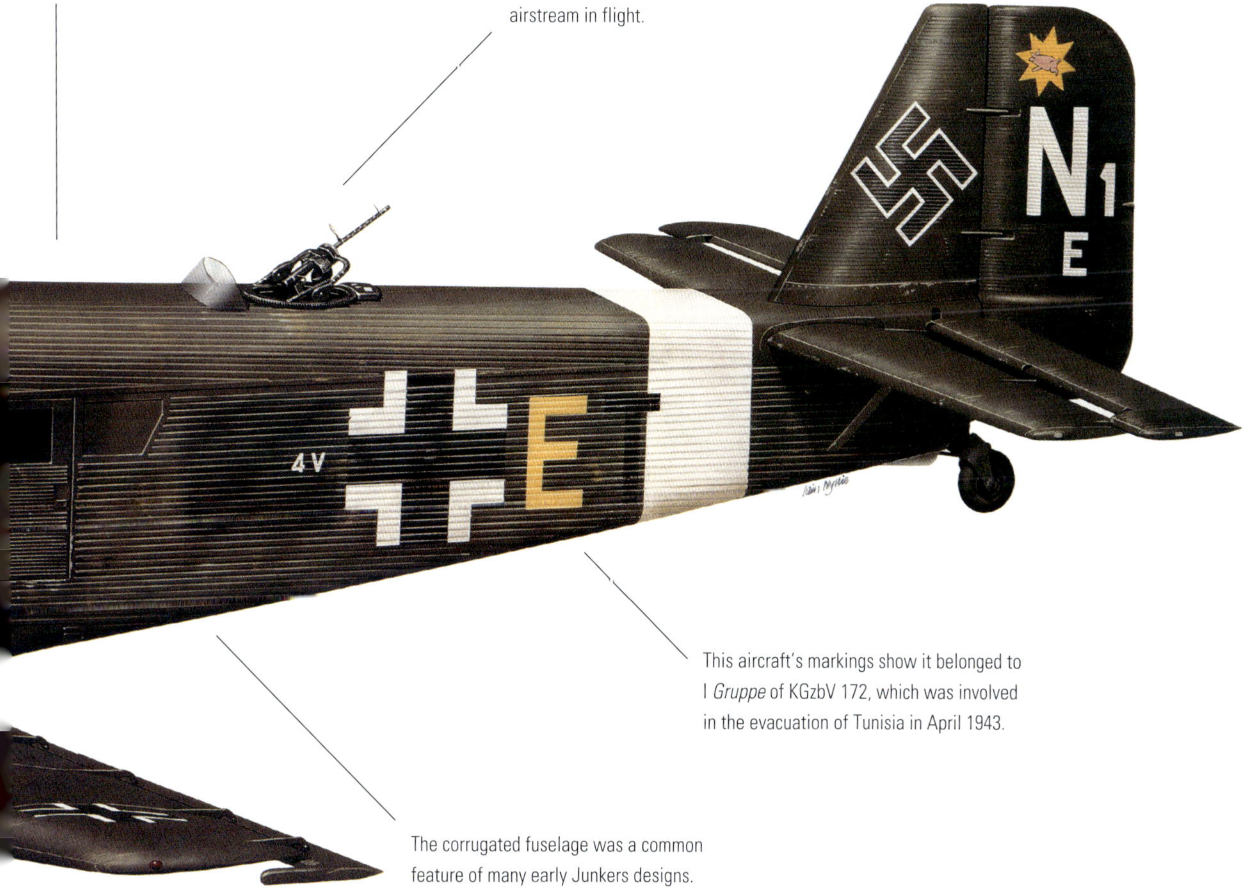

This aircraft's markings show it belonged to I *Gruppe* of KGzbV 172, which was involved in the evacuation of Tunisia in April 1943.

The corrugated fuselage was a common feature of many early Junkers designs. The metal skin was load-bearing, and the corrugation gave it immense strength for little weight penalty.

The story of the Ju 52/3m, one of the most famous transport aircraft in history, began on 13 October 1930, with the maiden flight of the single-engined Ju 52/1m commercial transport. Eighteen months later a new variant of the basic design appeared; the Ju 52/3m, fitted with three 429kW (575hp) BMW 132A radial engines (licence-built Pratt & Whitney Hornets). The modified aircraft was an immediate success. A rugged, reliable transport, capable of operating from small, rough, high-altitude airstrips, the Ju 523/m was an extremely efficient aircraft, and large numbers were ordered by Deutsche Lufthansa and other airlines around the world. The aircraft was eventually operated by 28 airlines.

In 1934 a military version of the Ju 52/3m was produced for use by the still-secret Luftwaffe. With the designation Ju 52/3mg3e, the aircraft was designed as a heavy bomber with a crew of four and armed with two MG 15 machine guns, one mounted in the dorsal position and the other in a retractable 'dustbin' suspended under the fuselage. Between 1934 and 1935, no fewer than 450 Ju 52/3ms were delivered to the Luftwaffe, the type entering service with KG 152 *Hindenburg*. In August 1936, 20 aircraft were sent to Spain where, flown by German volunteers, their first task was to transport 10,000 troops from Spanish Morocco. In the following November, about 50 Ju 52/3mg4e bombers were included in the equipment of the German Condor Legion, deployed to Spain in support of Franco's Nationalist forces. Operations included the bombing of Republican-held Mediterranean ports and the support of the land battle around Guernica, the destruction of which town brought the German bombers notoriety. The Ju 52 was also delivered to several Spanish Nationalist bomber units as the war progressed. The last sortie was made on 26 March 1939, by which time the Ju 52s had flown 5400 sorties for the loss of 8 aircraft, 5 in the air and 3 on the ground.

In Luftwaffe service the Ju 52 bomber was soon replaced by types such as the Ju 86 and Do 17, and from then on it operated purely as a military transport. In March 1938, during the 'union' with Austria, 160 Ju 52s flew 2000 airborne troops to Vienna. The following year, these aircraft took part in the German occupation of Czechoslovakia. In April 1940 the Ju 52 was at the forefront of the invasions of Denmark and Norway, 160 transports dropping paratroops to capture key airfields and a 340 aircraft flying in supplies and reinforcements.

Left: Close-up of the Ju 52/3m's engine arrangement. Essentially similar to the single-engined variant from which it was developed, the prototype flew in April 1932, powered by three Pratt & Whitney Hornet radials.

Above: Junkers Ju 52/3m in the mottled camouflage scheme which was used in the Mediterranean and Balkans between 1941 and 1943. Ju 52s suffered terrible losses to Allied fighters as they attempted to fly reinforcements to Tunisia in early 1943.

About 475 Ju 52s were available for the invasion of the Netherlands, and suffered serious losses (167 aircraft) in the opening stages of the operation.

The next large-scale airborne operation, the invasion of Crete in April/May 1941, was the last of its kind undertaken by the Luftwaffe. The force committed included 493 Ju 52s and over 80 DFS 230 gliders. The invasion – Operation Merkur – cost the Germans 7000 men killed or wounded (including 25 per cent of the paratroops dropped) and 170 Ju 52s. When the Germans invaded the Soviet Union in June 1941, their offensive was supported by six Ju 52 transport *Gruppen*. Another 150 aircraft were assigned to support Rommel's offensives in North Africa, and by the end of the year around 300 Ju 52s were operating in the Mediterranean theatre. In July, August and September 1942, Ju 52s and other transport aircraft ferried 46,000 men and 4000 tons (4064 tonnes) of equipment to North Africa, but after the Battle of El Alamein in October, severe losses were inflicted on the Ju 52s by Desert Air Force fighters, 70 aircraft being destroyed between 25 October and 1 December. The real martyrdom of the Ju 52 *Gruppen* in the Mediterranean, however, came early in 1943, when the Germans and Italians made frantic efforts to resupply the Axis forces in Tunisia. On one day alone – 7 April 1943 – American and British fighters destroyed 52 out of 77 Ju 52s near Cap Bon, most of the petrol-laden transports exploding in spectacular fashion. Between 5 and 22 April, no fewer than 432 German transport aircraft, mostly Ju 52s, were destroyed for the loss of only 35 Allied fighters.

On the Russian front, five Ju 52 *Gruppen* took part in the Stalingrad airlift. Between 24 November 1942 and 31 January 1943, 266 Ju 52s were lost, 52 of them in a 24-hour series of attacks on Sverevo airfield.

Despite the development of later transport aircraft, production of the Ju 52 continued to rise during most of World War II; 502 aircraft were delivered in 1941, a further 502 in 1942, and 887 in 1943, but by then production was being transferred to the Société Amiot in Occupied France, this firm being controlled by Junkers. Only a further 379 aircraft were delivered from German factories in 1944, when production ceased. Total production of the Ju 52/3m between 1939 and 1944 was 4845 aircraft.

Type: Bomber/transport	
Crew:	2/3, plus 18 troops or 12 stretcher cases
Powerplant:	three 619kW (830hp) BMW 132T-2 nine-cylinder radials
Max speed:	286km/h (178mph)
Time to height:	17 mins 30 secs to 3000m (9842ft)
Service ceiling:	5900m (19,357ft)
Max range:	1305km (811 miles)
Wing span:	29.20m (95ft 8in)
Wing area:	110.5m² (1189.3sq ft)
Length:	19.90m (65ft)
Height:	4.52m (14ft 8in)
Weights:	6500kg (14,330lb) empty; 11,030kg (24,317lb) loaded
Armament:	four 7.92mm (0.31in) MG, one each in forward and rear dorsal positions, one in each beam position

Junkers Ju 87 Stuka

The Ju 87's pilot sat under a sliding canopy, with armour protection surrounding him. The aircraft had an automatic dive control which would pull the aircraft out of its dive at a preset altitude when engaged by the pilot.

The Ju 87B was powered by a Junkers Jumo 211Da 12-cylinder liquid-cooled engine. The notch cut-out on the top of the fuselage is an intake for the oil cooler.

The Stuka was armed with a pair of Rheinmetall-Borsig 7.92mm (0.31in) MG 17 machine guns with 1000 rounds of ammunition each.

The large chin radiator was a characteristic of the Ju 87. The radiator itself was protected in an armoured 'bath'. Hydralically-operated cooling gills at the rear of the cowling allowed more air to flow through the radiator at low speeds.

The terror of a Stuka attack during the early years of Blitzkrieg was augmented by the use of a siren on the undercarriage. However in this case the siren is not mounted, although the fairing remains.

The Stuka's gull wing allowed the fixed undercarriage to be kept short, thus reducing drag as much as possible.

The markings show this to be a Ju 87B-2 from 7th *Staffel*, III *Gruppe*, *Stukageschwader* 77 on the Eastern Front.

The rear gunner was also the radio operator, although Ju 87Bs were also flown as single seat aircraft. The gunner had his own sliding canopy, and was armed with a MG 15 7.92mm (0.31in) machine gun.

Either two 250kg (551lb) or four 50kg (110lb) bombs could be carried on the wing pylons in addition to the single 500kg (1100lb) or 250kg (551lb) bomb carried in a cradle under the fuselage. The cradle was to ensure the bomb fell clear of the propeller during a dive attack after it was released.

The 50kg (110lb) bombs shown here have extended detonator rods to make the bomb explode above ground to maximize the blast effect of the explosion.

Although the word Stuka – an abbreviation of *Sturzkampfflugzeug*, literally 'diving combat aircraft' – was applied to all German bomber aircraft with a dive-bombing capability during World War II, it will forever be associated with the Junkers Ju 87, with its ugly lines, inverted-gull wing and, above all, the banshee howl of its wing-mounted sirens as it plummeted towards its target.

Designed by Dipl Ing Hans Pohlmann in response to a 1933 Luftwaffe requirement for a dive-bomber, the Ju 87 was developed from the K-47, a two-seat, high-performance monoplane fighter of 1928, built at Junkers' Swedish plant at Malmo-Limhamn and exported in small numbers to China. The first prototype Ju 87V-1 was flown for the first time in the late spring 1935, powered by a 477kW (640hp) Rolls-Royce Kestrel engine. An all-metal monoplane, it featured rectangular twin fins and rudders and an unusual method of construction in which its fuselage was built in two halves, joined along the centreline. The aircraft was destroyed a few weeks later when it developed tail flutter during diving trials. It was followed by the Ju 87V-2, which featured a revised engine cowling and radiator arrangement, and also a single fin and rudder.

Left: The Junkers Ju 87R (the 'R' denoting Reichweite, or range) was developed from the Ju 87B Stuka specifically for anti-ship and other missions requiring long endurance. The outer wing panels were strengthened for the carriage of wing tanks.

In March 1937 the Ju 87V-2 was sent to the Luftwaffe test centre at Rechlin for comparative trials, and was chosen in preference to the other three contenders, the Arado Ar 81, Blohm und Voss Ha 137 and Heinkel He 118. The third prototype, the Ju 87V-3, was generally similar to the V-2, but had an improved forward view and was powered by a 507kW (680hp) Junkers Jumo 210 engine.

Production began with the pre-series Ju 87A-0, powered by the Jumo 210Da engine, and continued with the Ju 87A-1, first deliveries of which were made to I/ St.G 162 *Immelmann*, the unit tasked with developing operational tactics, in 1937. The Ju 87A-1 carried an armament of one MG 17 and one MG 15. With a crew of one, a 453kg (1000lb) bomb load could be carried in a Knauth cradle-carriage between the 'trousered' main undercarriage units, but with the gunner also on board this was reduced to 250kg (550lb). In December 1937 three Ju 87A-1s were sent to Spain for operational trials with the Condor Legion, the German units flying in support of the Spanish Nationalists. The Ju 87A-2 sub-series, the next to appear, differed only in the type of propeller used. Maximum speed of the Ju 87A series was 318km/h (198mph) at 3660m (12,008ft), and loaded weight was 3402kg (7500lb). The early-model Stuka had been mainly relegated to training duties by the outbreak of World War II in September 1939, and was succeeded on the production line in 1938 by an extensively modified version, the Ju 87B, which used the more powerful 820 kW (1100hp) Jumo 211Da. The aircraft had a redesigned cockpit and a 'spatted' undercarriage. The Ju 87B-1 carried a 697kg (1536lb) bomb load and had a top speed of 373km/h (232mph) at 4117m (13,507ft). Fixed forward-firing armament was increased to two MG 17 guns, and loaded weight was 4245kg (9358lb). The Ju 87B-2 had a broad-blade propeller and internal modifications. An antishipping version of the Ju 87B-2 was known as the Ju 87R. This carried long-range fuel tanks, and the bomb load was reduced to 250kg (550lb). The undercarriage could be jettisoned for ditching. The Ju 87R-1, R-2, R-3 and R-4 differed only in equipment detail.

One of the more interesting and little-known versions of the Stuka was the Ju 87C, a shipboard dive-bomber intended for service on Germany's planned aircraft carrier, the *Graf Zeppelin*. It had hydraulically operated folding wings, deck arrester gear and a jettisonable undercarriage. The Ju 87C-0 was a conversion of the Ju 87B-1 without wingfolding mechanism. A small production batch of Ju 87C-1 aircraft was built and a unit 4 (Stuka)186 formed, but the *Graf Zeppelin* was abandoned when it was virtually complete and the aircraft were converted to Ju 87B standard. The unit 4 (Stuka) 186 took part in the Polish campaign. *Graf Zeppelin*'s air group was to have comprised 29 Stukas and 12 Bf 109 fighters.

The next production model in service was the Ju 87D, which was fitted with a 1044kW (1400hp) Jumo 211J-1

2491

Above: Junkers Ju 87D of Stuka-Geschwader 1. The various units of this Geschwader were to fight on every battlefront, and they were very active against British convoys – as well as against the warships escorting them – in the Mediterranean.

with induction cooling. The engine cowling and cockpit enclosure were redesigned and the contours of the undercarriage fairings improved. Additional armour was fitted, a bomb load of 1794kg (3955lb) could be carried, and top speed was increased to 410km/h (255mph) at 4117m (13,507ft). Several sub-series of the Ju 87D were produced in some quantity, incorporating modifications to suit the type for a variety of tasks. The Ju 87D-2, for example, had a specially strengthened tailwheel leg with a glider attachment point; the Ju 87D3 had additional armour and was intended for ground attack, with provision for a twin 20mm (0.79in) MG FF gun pack to be mounted under each; the Ju 87D-4 could carry weapons containers for the resupply of ground forces, and was used mainly on the Russian front; the Ju 87D-5 had its wing span increased from 13.8m (45ft 3in) to 15m (49ft 2in), and was primarily intended for night operations; the similar Ju 87D-7 had no dive brakes and was fitted with extra outer-wing bomb racks; and the Ju 87D-8 was similar to the D-3, but had the extended wing.

The Ju 87 E and F were proposals only, and the last Stuka variant was the Ju 87G, a standard Ju 87D-5 converted to carry two BK 37 cannon (37mm (1.46in) Flak 18 guns) under the wing. No dive brakes were fitted, and the Ju 87G proved very adept at destroying Russian armour. Its chief exponent was Colonel Hans-Ulrich Rudel, who knocked out 500 tanks on the Eastern Front. The Ju 87H was the designation given to all dualcontrol versions of the Du 87D-1, D-3, D-5, D-7 and D-8. In the final analysis, although the Stuka was a very effective weapon when under an umbrella of fighter superiority, when the latter was lacking – as was the case in the Battle of Britain, when the Stuka units suffered heavy losses – it was easy prey for its enemies.

Left: A Staffel of Ju 87s en route to their target on the Eastern Front. Although initially able to operate with impunity, as the Soviet air forces improved the Stukas found themselves fighting for survival, and requiring a heavy fighter escort.

Type: Dive-bomber/assault aircraft (Ju 87D-1)	
Crew:	2
Powerplant:	one 1044kW (1400hp) Junkers Jumo 211J inverted-Vee piston engine
Max speed:	410km/h (255mph)
Time to height:	19 mins 48 secs to 5000m (16,404ft)
Service ceiling:	7300m (23,950ft)
Max range:	1535km (954 miles)
Wing span:	13.80m (45ft 3in)
Wing area:	31.90m² (343.38sq ft)
Length:	11.50m (37ft 7in)
Height:	3.88m (12ft 7in)
Weights:	3900kg (8598lb) empty; 6600kg (14,550lb) max t/o
Armament:	two 7.92mm (0.31in) fixed forward-firing MG in wing leading edges; one 7.92mm (0.31in) trainable twin-barrel rearward-firing machinegun in rear cockpit; external bomb load of up to 1800kg (3968lb)

Junkers Ju 88

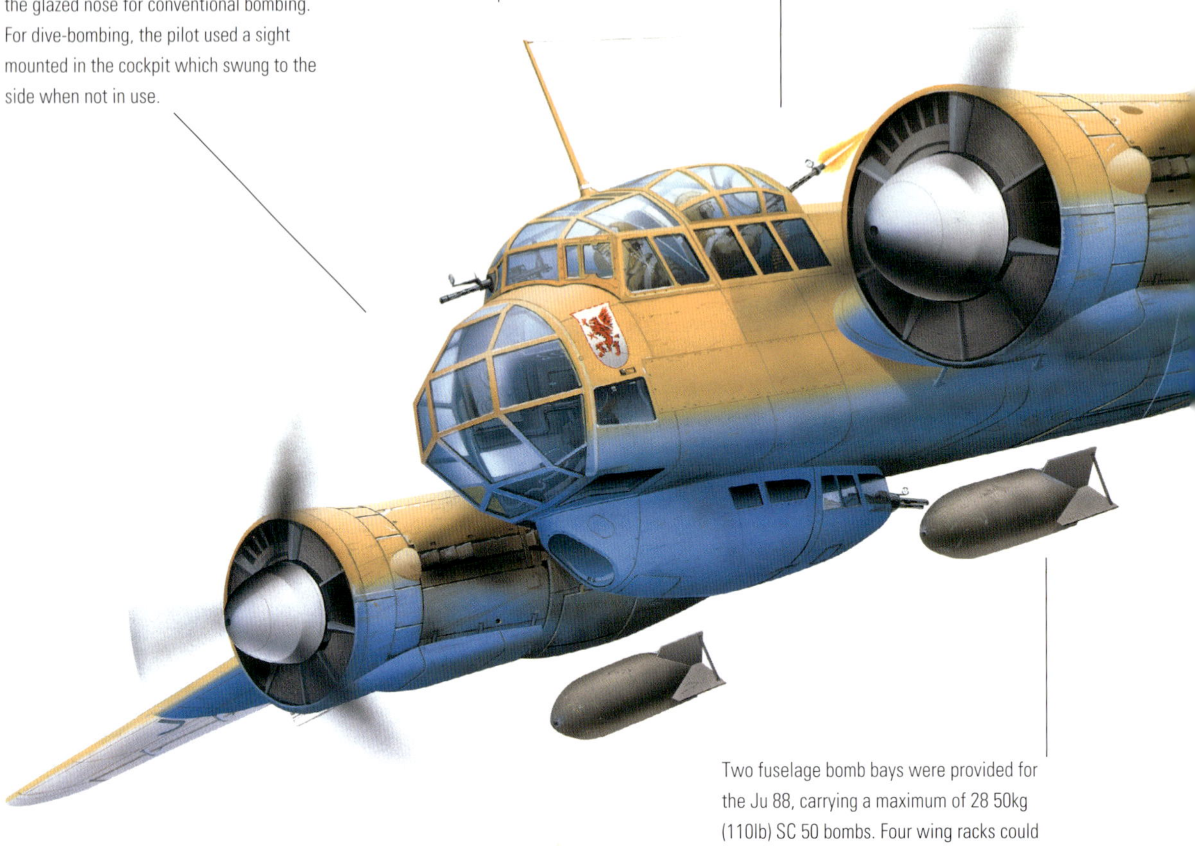

When the Ju 88 was under development, dive bombing came into vogue, and so the aircraft was fitted with slatted divebrakes under the wing's leading edge.

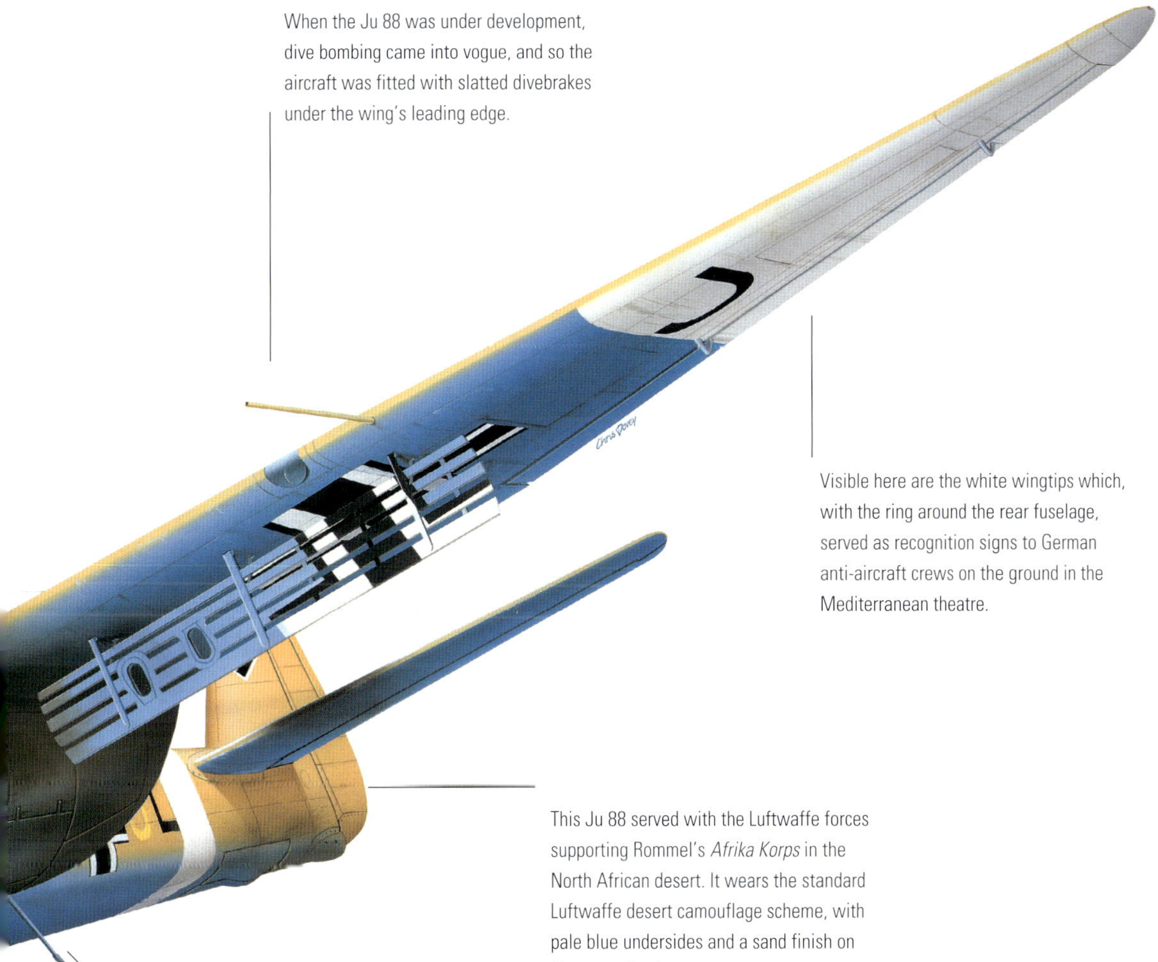

Visible here are the white wingtips which, with the ring around the rear fuselage, served as recognition signs to German anti-aircraft crews on the ground in the Mediterranean theatre.

This Ju 88 served with the Luftwaffe forces supporting Rommel's *Afrika Korps* in the North African desert. It wears the standard Luftwaffe desert camouflage scheme, with pale blue undersides and a sand finish on the upper fuselage.

The Ju 88 was equipped with the Junkers Jumo 211G-1, which was a 12-cylinder liquid-cooled engine.

Above: Used in anti-shipping as well as ground-attack roles, the Ju 88A-14 had a 20mm (0.79in) cannon which was installed within the gondola. The window of the bomb sight was faired over, and it was equipped with a shell ejection chute.

One of the most versatile and effective combat aircraft ever produced, the Junkers Ju 88, remained of vital importance to the Luftwaffe throughout World War II, serving as a bomber, dive-bomber, nightfighter, close-support aircraft, long-range heavy fighter, reconnaissance aircraft and torpedo bomber. It had its origin in a massive military aircraft expansion programme initiated by Germany's new Nazi government in 1934, before it was officially admitted that the Luftwaffe was in existence. Much emphasis was placed on the development of bombers, the re-armament programme producing such types as the Junkers Ju 86, Heinkel He 111, and Dornier Do 17. All these aircraft were originally designed as transports, partly to camouflage the fact that Germany was re-arming; the Ju 88, work on which began in 1936, was designed as a bomber from the outset, the camouflage having by this time been stripped aside. The prototype Ju 88 (D-AQEN) flew for the first time on 21 December 1936, powered by two 746kW (1000hp) DB 600A in-line engines; the second prototype was similar, except that it was fitted with Jumo 211A radials, the engines that were mostly to power the aircraft throughout its career. A pre-series batch of Ju 88A-0s was completed during the summer of 1939, the first production Ju 88A-1s being delivered to a test unit, *Erprobungskommando* 88. In August 1939 this unit was redesignated I/KG 25, and soon afterwards it became I/KG 30, carrying out its first operational mission – an attack on British warships in the Firth of Forth – in September. The same target was attacked on 16 October, when Spitfires shot down two Ju 88s. About 60 operational aircraft were in service by the end of the year. The Ju 88A was built in 17 different variants up to the Ju 88A-17, with progressively uprated engines, enhanced defensive armament and improved defensive capability.

Variants included the Ju 88A-2, which was equipped with rocket-assisted take-off gear; the Ju 88A-6, with a balloon cable fender; the Ju 88A-6U long-range maritime bomber, equipped with FuG 200 search radar; the Ju 88A-9, -10 and -11, tropicalized versions of the Ju 88A-1, A-5 and A-4 respectively; the Ju 88A-14 anti-shipping strike aircraft; the Ju 88A-15, with a bulged bomb bay for 3000kg (6614lb) of bombs; and the Ju 88A-17 torpedo-bomber. The most widely used was the Ju 88A-4, which served in Europe and North Africa, the first version to incorporate technical improvements resulting from the combat experience gained during the battles of France and Britain; it had extended-span wings, Jumo 211J engines and a heavier defensive armament. Twenty Ju 88A-4s were supplied to Finland, and some were supplied to Italy, Romania and Hungary. The Ju 88A-5 was generally similar, with some equipment changes. Some 7000 examples of the Ju 88A series were delivered.

Below: The Ju 88 was an excellent night intruder, being fast and heavily armed. Had Hitler continued night intruder operations after 1941, crippling blows might have been dealt against the Allies.

The Ju 88As saw considerable action in the Balkans, the Mediterranean, and on the Eastern Front. They operated intensively during the German invasion of Crete, and were the principal threat to the island of Malta and its supply convoys. Some of their most outstanding service, however, was in the Arctic, where aircraft of KG 26 and KG 30, based in northern Norway, carried out devastating attacks on Allied convoys to Russia. A force of never more than 120 Ju 88s sank 27 merchant ships and 7 naval vessels.

The Ju 88B was the subject of a separate development programme, and eventually evolved into the Ju 188, which made its operational debut later in the war. Chronologically, the next major production model was the Ju 88C heavy fighter; the first version was the Ju 88C-2,

which was a conversion of the Ju 88A-1 with a 'solid' nose housing three MG 17 machineguns and a 20mm (0.79in) MG forward-firing cannon, plus a single rearward-firing MG 15. It entered service with NJG 1 in the late summer of 1940 and was used for intruder operations over the British Isles. A small number of Ju 88C-4s, using the same extended span wing as the Ju 88A-4, and the C-5 followed

Type: Medium/dive bomber (Ju 88A-4)	
Crew:	4
Powerplant:	two 999kW (1340hp) Junkers Jumo 211J inverted V-12s
Max speed:	450km/h (280mph) at 6000m (19,685ft)
Time to height:	23 mins to 5400m (17,716ft)
Service ceiling:	8200m (26,903ft)
Max range:	2730km (1696 miles)
Wing span:	20m (65ft 6in)
Wing area:	54.50m² (506.63sq ft)
Length:	14.40m (47ft 2in)
Height:	4.85m (15ft 9in)
Weights:	9860kg (21,737lb) empty
Armament:	up to seven 7.92m (0.31in) MG 15 or MG 81 machineguns; maximum internal and external bomb load of 3600kg (7935lb)

it. The next variant, the Ju 88C-6, had Jumo 211J engines and two 20mm (0.79in) cannon added to its forward armament, the rear MG 15 being replaced by a MG 131. The Ju 88C-6, and the last variant in this series, the C-7, were used as nightfighters and dayfighters. In the latter role, they provided cover for U-boats in the Bay of Biscay.

The last fighter variant of the Ju 88, which made its appearance in the spring of 1944, was the Ju 88G. This version, with the angular tail unit of the Ju 188 and improved Lichtenstein AI radar, was a highly effective nightfighter. The principal sub-types were the G-1 with BMW 801D engines, the G-6a and G-6b with BMW 802Gs, the G-6c with Jumo 213As, and the G-7 with Jumo 213E-1s. Two more sub-variants, the Ju 88H-2 and the Ju 88R, brought the fighter Ju 88 line to an end.

A specialist version designed for ground attack and anti-tank work, mainly on the Russian Front, also made its appearance during World War II. This was the Ju 88P, and it was armed with either a 75mm (2.95in) gun (Ju 88P-1) or two 37mm (1.46in) cannon (Ju 88P-2). The total Ju 88 production was 14,676 aircraft; of these, about 3900 were fighter- or ground-attack variants.

Left: This curious Ju 88A-4 bears a Wellenmuster (wave pattern) camouflage on its front half, but the rear fuselage and tail are painted white with a red cross, presumably in order to denote that the aircraft has been modified for air ambulance duties.

Messerschmitt Bf 109E

The Bf 109E-3 carried two 7.92mm (0.31in) MG 17 machine guns in its upper fuselage, firing through the propeller arc. The nose, tail and the underside of the wingtips were painted yellow for ease of recognition by friendly forces. The prominent intake on the port side was for the supercharger.

The Bf 109E carried a pair of 7.92mm (0.31in) MG 17 machine guns in the wings to supplement the firepower of the fuselage-mounted armament.

An engine-mounted MG FF 20mm (0.79in) cannon fired through the propeller hub. This made the Bf 109 considerably better-armed than its machine gun-carrying RAF opponents in the Battle of Britain.

The Emil was powered by the Daimler Benz DB 601A-1 liquid-cooled V-12 inline engine. The chin intake admitted air for cooling the engine oil. A ventral fuel tank could also be carried for extra range.

The pilot sat in a cramped, narrow cockpit protected by an armoured windscreen. The canopy was hinged. The pilot's visibility was poor for the time, with thick canopy frames and limited rear vision.

This aircraft served on the Western Front in 1940 during the Battle of Britain.

The chin radiator of earlier Bf 109s was replaced by two wing intakes providing cooling air for the glycol engine coolant. The intakes had controllable flaps at the rear to increase the airflow as needed.

Above: Messerschmitt Bf 109E-4 of Erprobungsgrupppe 210, here shown armed with a 227kg (500lb) bomb. On 12 August 1940, this unit opened the main phase of the Battle of Britain by attacking several radar stations on the south coast of England.

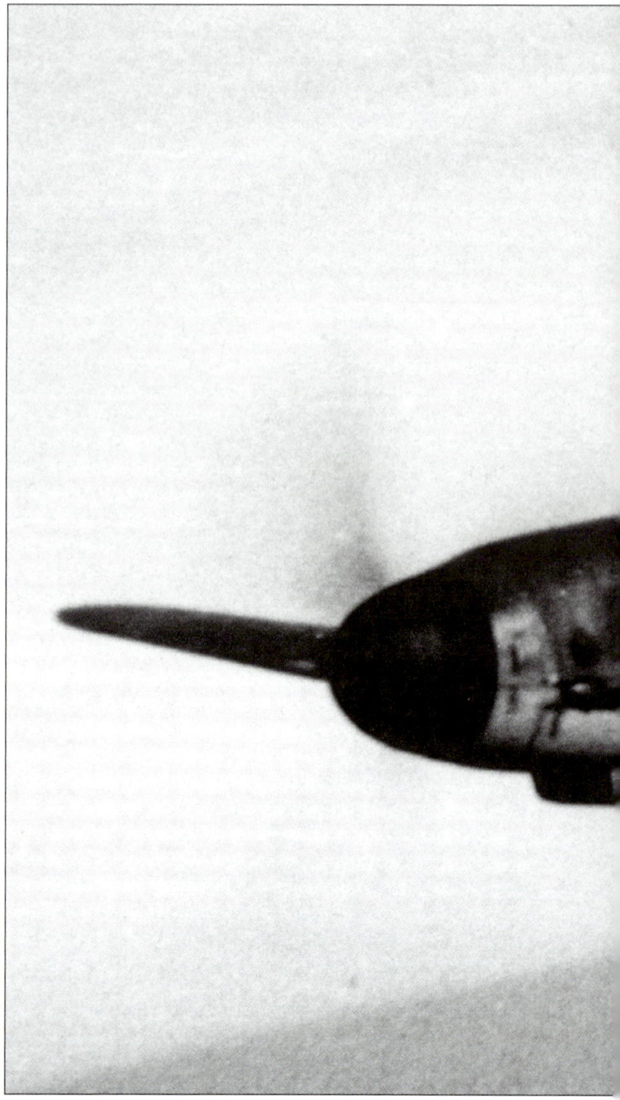

Development of Willi Messerschmitt's famous Bf 109 fighter (the prefix 'Bf', incidentally, is a company designation denoting *Bayerische Flugzeugwerke*, the Bavarian Aircraft Factory where the type was first manufactured) began in 1933, when the *Reichsluftministerium* (RLM) issued a requirement for a new monoplane fighter. The prototype Bf 109V-1 flew for the first time in September 1935, powered by a 518kW (695hp) Rolls-Royce Kestrel engine, as the 455kW (610hp) Junkers Jumo 210A intended for it was not yet available. It was installed in the second prototype, which flew in January 1936. The third aircraft, the Bf 109V-3, was intended to be the prototype for the initial production model, the Bf 109A, but its armament of only two MG 17 machineguns was rightly considered to be inadequate and was increased in subsequent aircraft. The Bf 109V-7, armed with two machine guns and a single MG FF (20mm (0.79in) Oerlikon cannon), consequently became the prototype for the first series production model, the Bf 109B, powered by a Jumo 210 engine.

Professor Messerschmitt had originally intended the 109's thin, frail wings to be left free of guns, but when the Luftwaffe High Command learned that the Spitfire and Hurricane were to be fitted with eight machineguns, they insisted that the Bf 109 was to carry wing-mounted guns too. Messerschmitt was therefore forced to design a new wing, with bulges for the ammunition boxes of the 20mm (0.79in) cannon mounted on each side. Further strain was put on the wing when the Bf 109E variant was fitted with a more powerful Daimler Benz 601A engine, as ducted radiators had to be mounted underneath. One innovation, the Bf 109's narrow-track undercarriage, was designed so that the fuselage, rather than the wings, bore the weight of the aircraft on the ground; but 5 per cent of all 109s built, some 1750 aircraft, were destroyed in landing accidents.

Three of the Bf 109 prototypes were evaluated in Spain in February and March 1937 and were followed by 24 Bf 109B-2s, which immediately proved superior to any other fighter engaged in the civil war. It was the use of the Bf 109 in Spain that enabled the Luftwaffe to develop the fighter tactics that would wreak havoc among its opponents in the early years of World War II. By the time the conflict had begun in September 1939, 1060 Bf 109s of various sub-species were in service with the Luftwaffe's fighter units. These included the Bf 109C and Bf 109D, which were already being replaced by the Bf 109E series; this model was to be the mainstay of the Luftwaffe's fighter units throughout 1940. The series extended to the E-9, including models built as fighters, fighter-bombers and reconnaissance aircraft. Ten Bf 109Es were converted for operations from Germany's planned aircraft carrier, the *Graf Zeppelin*, under the designation Bf 109T. The Bf 109E-3, the RAF's principal fighter opponent in the

Below: The Messerschmitt Bf 109G was, in numerical terms, the most important variant of the Messerschmitt fighter, and was still in production at the end of World War II. Improvements made it a heavy aircraft, at the expense of handling qualities.

Battle of France, featured four MG 17 machineguns, two mounted in the nose and two in the wings, as well as an engine-mounted forward-firing cannon firing through the propeller boss. However, complaints about this arrangement led to the deletion of the nose-mounted cannon, and two Oerlikons were installed in the wings of the Bf 109E-4 variant. It was the Bf 109E-4 variant which was to equip most German fighter units during the latter part of the Battle of Britain. A total of 19 Bf 109E-3s were exported to Bulgaria, while 40 were exported to Hungary, 2 to Japan, 69 to Romania, 16 to Slovakia, 80 to Switzerland, 5 to the USSR and 73 to Yugoslavia.

The best Bf 109 variant, the Bf 109F, began to reach Luftwaffe units in France in May 1941. It proved to be superior in most respects to the principal RAF fighter of the time, the Spitfire Mk V. The Bf 109F differed from the Bf 109E in that it had a cleaned-up airframe, re-designed engine cowling, wing, radiators and tail assembly. The first production version, the Bf 109F-1, had a 895kW (1200hp) DB 601N or 969kW (1300hp) DB 601E engine; later sub-variants had armament and other equipment changes. The Bf 109F performed well on all fronts, especially in the Western Desert, where it served principally with JG 27 and was flown by such aces as Hans-Joachim Marseille.

The Bf 109F was succeeded by the Bf 109G, which appeared late in 1942. Pre-production Bf 109G-0 aircraft retained the DB 601E of the F series, but the first production model, the Bf 109G-1, had the more powerful DB 605A engine. The G-1, G-3 and G-5 had provision for pressurized cockpits and were fitted with the GM-1 emergency power-boost system, which was lacking in the G-2 and G-4. Various armament combinations were employed, and later aircraft were fitted with wooden tail units. The fastest G model, the Bf 109G-10, without wing armament and with MW 50 power-boost equipment, reached a maximum speed of 687km/h (427mph) at 7400m (24,278ft), climbed to 6100m (20,013ft) in 6 minutes, and had an endurance of 55 minutes.

Type: Fighter (Bf 109G-6)	
Crew:	1
Powerplant:	one 1100kW (1474hp) Daimler-Benz DB 605AM 12-cylinder inverted-Vee engine
Max speed:	621km/h (386mph) at 7000m (22,966ft)
Time to height:	6 mins to 6100m (20,013ft)
Service ceiling:	11,550m (37,893ft)
Max range:	1000km (621 miles)
Wing span:	9.92m (32ft 5in)
Wing area:	16.05m² (172.75sq ft)
Length:	8.85m (29ft)
Height:	2.50m (8ft 2in)
Weights:	2673kg (5893lb) empty; 3400kg (7496lb) max t/o
Armament:	one 20mm (0.79in) or 30mm (1.19in) fixed forward-firing cannon in an engine installation; two 12.7mm (0.50in) fixed forward-firing MGs in the upper part of the forward fuselage; external bomb load of 250kg (551lb)

The last operational versions of the Bf 109 were the K-4 and K-6, which both had DB 605D engines with MW 50 power boost. The Bf 109K-4 had two 15mm (0.59in) MG 151 guns semi-externally mounted above the engine cowling and a 20mm (0.79in) MK 108 or 30mm (1.19in) MK 103 firing through the propeller hub. The Bf 109K-6 had the cowling-mounted MG 151s replaced by 12.7mm (0.50in) MG 131 machineguns and had two 30mm (1.19in) MK 103 cannon in underwing gondolas. The last variant was the Bf 109K-14, with a DB-605L engine, but only two examples saw service with JG 52.

The Bf 109G was built in both Spain (as the Hispano Ha-1109) and Czechoslovakia (as the Avia S-199). The Spanish aircraft, some re-engined with Rolls-Royce Merlins, served for many years after World War II and Israel acquired some of the Czech-built aircraft in 1948, equipping No. 101 Squadron. In all, Bf 109 production reached a total of approximately 35,000 aircraft.

Left: Messerschmitt Bf 109Fs of JG 27 streak low over the North African desert. One of the pilots with this unit was the celebrated Hans-Joachim Marseille, who gained 158 victories. Marseille was to die in 1942 as the result of an accident.

Messerschmitt Me 110

The Bf 110 was designed for a crew of three, with a pilot, radio operator and rear gunner. In practice the rear gunner also acted as radio operator. The C-4 was the first model to introduce armour protection for the crew.

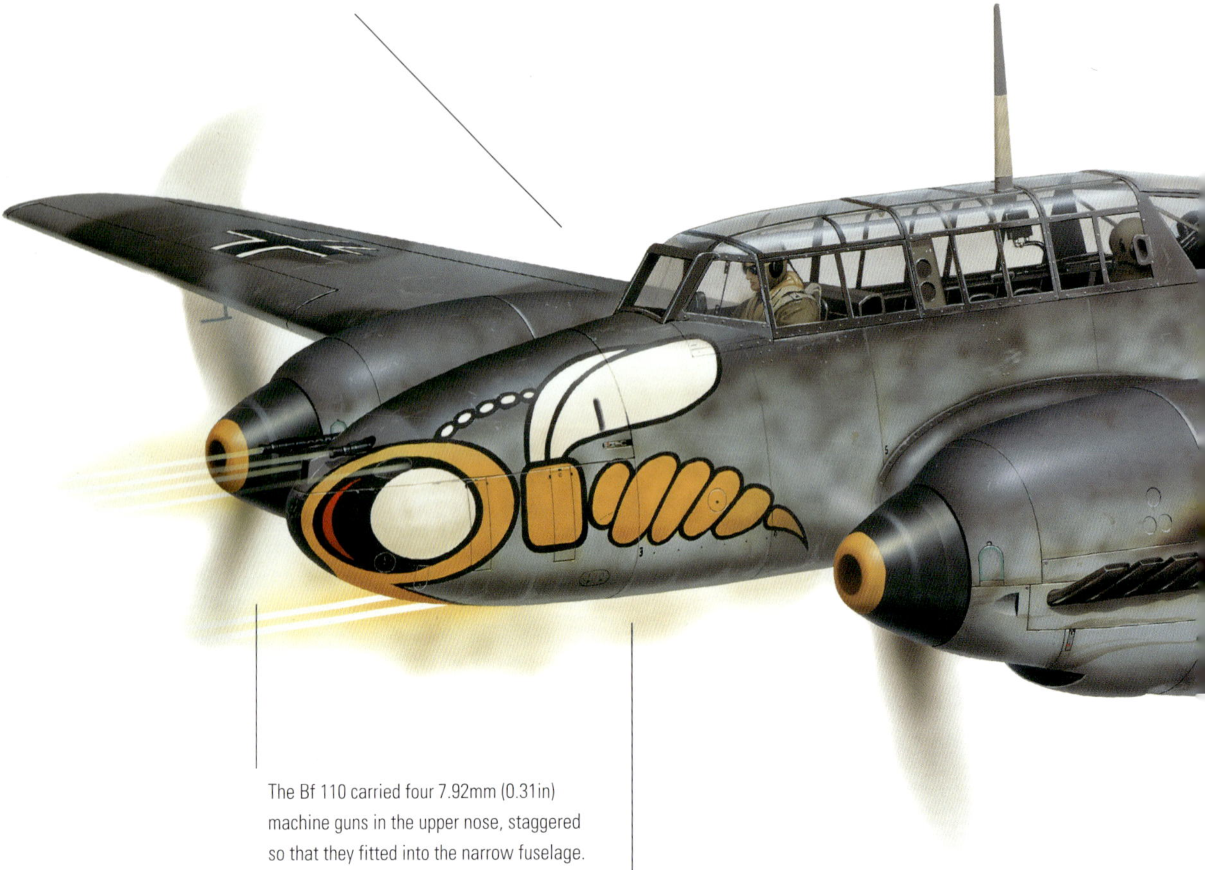

The Bf 110 carried four 7.92mm (0.31in) machine guns in the upper nose, staggered so that they fitted into the narrow fuselage. Two MG FF 20mm (0.79in) cannon were mounted in the lower fuselage beneath the pilot's seat.

The *Wespen* (Wasp) was the unofficial unit marking. Many German aircraft had some form of animal character used as an identifier in this way.

The rear gunner was armed with a single 7.92mm (0.31in) MG 15 machine gun with 750 rounds of ammunition. The hood on his portion of the cockpit could swing upwards to give a better field of fire.

The markings identify this aircraft as a Messerschmitt Bf 110C-4/B of II *Gruppe*, *Zerstörergeschwader* 1, Belgorod, in the Ukraine, in the autumn of 1942.

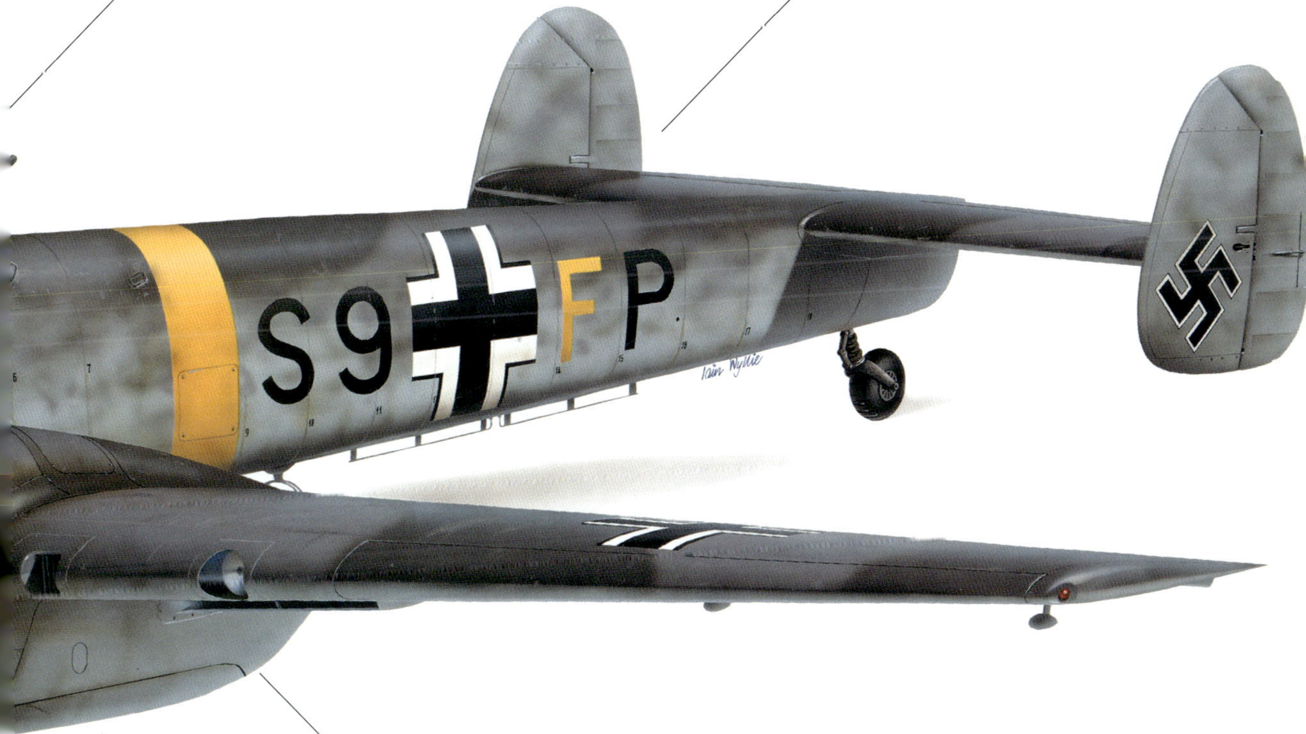

The Bf 110C-4/B was powered by the Daimler Benz DB 601A which used high octane fuel, increased compression ratio and redesigned piston heads to improve its performance over the regular Bf 110C-4.

The Bf 110C-4 was the first variant of the aircraft to be dedicated to the fighter-bomber role, and so it was equipped with a pair of hardpoints under the fuselage centresection, which carried a 250kg (551lb) bomb each.

Above: A bomb-carrying Messerschmitt Bf 110F-2. The Bf 110F was fitted with the more powerful DB 601F engines, a powerplant which made it suitable for the fighter-bomber role. Total Bf 110 production, including all variants, was 583 aircraft.

The Messerschmitt Bf 110 was designed in response to a 1934 *Reichsluftminsterium* (RLM) specification for a long-range escort fighter and *Zerstörer* (destroyer) aircraft. Three prototypes were completed with DB 600 engines, the first of these flying on 12 May 1936. Four of the pre-series Bf 110A-0s were ordered, powered by 455kW (610hp) Jumo 210B engines, while a small number of Bf 110B-0 trials aircraft were fitted with the 515kW (690hp) DB 600A. However, these were inadequate and the first production model, the Bf 110C-1, used the more powerful 820kW (1100hp) DB 601A. The aircraft also featured several aerodynamic improvements over the Bf 110A-0, such as square-cut wingtips (which increased speed but reduced manoeuvrability) and an improved cockpit canopy. Armament was four 7.92mm (0.31in) MG 17 machineguns and two 20mm (0.79in) MG FF cannon, the former in the upper half of the nose and the latter in a detachable tray attached to the fuselage belly. In addition, a manually operated MG 15 machine gun was provided in the rear cockpit. First deliveries went in 1938 to I/(*Zerstörer*) *Gruppe* of the technical development unit, *Lehrgeschwader* I.

The Bf 110C-2 differed only from the C-1 in its radio equipment (FuG 10), while the C-2/U1 was an experimental version fitted with remote-controlled rearward-firing armament, an arrangement adopted later in the Me 210 and Me 410 fighter-bombers. The C-3 and C-3 had modified 20mm (0.79in) cannon. A fighter-bomber version, the Bf 110C-4B, carried two 250kg (551lb) bombs under the centre section, and the C-5 was a special reconnaissance version with a camera replacing the 20mm (0.79in) cannon. At sea level, the Bf 110C-4 had a maximum cruising speed of 423km/h (263mph), giving a range of 772km (480 miles). At 7000m (22,965ft), top cruising speed was 484km/h (301 mph) and range 909km (565 miles).

The Bf 110C first went into action in Poland on 1 September 1939, where it was primarily used for ground attack. The RAF first encountered the Bf 110 in action on 14 December 1939, when the German fighters destroyed 5 out of 12 Vickers Wellingtons over the Heligoland Bight. However, its performance against British and French single-engined fighters during the Battle of France proved less satisfactory, and it suffered very serious losses during the Battle of Britain. Nevertheless, the aircraft continued in quantity production, and in 1940 the Messerschmitt factories turned out 1008 Bf 110 fighters and 75 reconnaissance aircraft.

Type: Nightfighter (Bf 110G)	
Crew:	2/3
Powerplant:	two 1100kW (1475hp) Daimler-Benz DB 605B-1 12-cylinder inverted-Vee-type engines
Max speed:	550km/h (342mph) at 7000m (22,966ft)
Initial climb rate:	661m (2169ft) per min
Service ceiling:	8000m (26,247ft)
Max range:	1300km (808 miles)
Wing span:	16.25m (53ft 3in)
Wing area:	38.40m^2 (413.3sq ft)
Length:	13.05m (42ft 9in) including SN-2 radar antenna
Height:	4.18m (13ft 7in)
Weights:	5094kg (11,230lb) empty; 9888kg (21,799lb) max t/o
Armament:	two 30mm (1.19in) fixed forward-firing cannon in the nose; two 20mm (0.79in) fixed forward-firing cannon in ventral tray; one twin-barrel MG in the rear cockpit position;alternatively, two upward-firing 20mm (0.79in) cannon in rear fuselage dorsal position

Right: Messerschmitt Bf 110D-3s of ZG 76 over the Mediterranean, 1941. The code 3U was adopted in July that year. The Bf 110's role in the Mediterranean air war was crucial.

Numerous variants also appeared: these included the Bf 110C-6; which resembled the C-2 but augmented its firepower with the addition of a 30mm (1.19in) MK 101 cannon mounted in a fairing beneath the fuselage; and the Bf 110C-7 specialized bomber which could carry two 500kg (110lb) bombs, making it necessary to strengthen the undercarriage.

The Bf 110D was originally intended as a long-range escort fighter, and the Bf 110D-0 pre-series aircraft featured a large ventral fuel tank, but the drag this created impaired the aircraft's performance so badly that it was deleted in the production Bf 110D-1 and replaced by external wing tanks. The D-2 could be used in either the fighter or bomber roles and could carry up to two 1000kg (2205lb) bombs, and the D-3 was a D-1 with bomb racks attached. The Bf 110E-1 and E-2 were able to carry four 50kg (110lb) bombs under the wing in addition to the larger bombs slung under the fuselage, while the E-3 was a special long-range reconnaissance model.

The Bf 110F-1 (bomber), F-2 (heavy fighter), F-3 (long-range reconnaissance aircraft) and F-4 (nightfighter) had 969kW (1300hp) DB 601F engines, but the final major production aircraft, the Bf 110G, produced in larger numbers than any other variant, adopted the 1007kW (1350hp) DB 605 engine. With this engine, the Bf 110G-1 bomber and the G-2 fighter achieved a maximum speed of 544km/h (338mph) at 6405m (21,013ft) and a range of 2079km (1292 miles). The Bf 110G2/R1 carried a 37mm (1.46in) BK cannon in addition to four 7.92mm (0.31in) MG 17 guns; the Bf 110G-2/R3 was similar but fitted with the GM1 power boost system, as was the G-2/R5; and the G-2/R4 was similar to the G-2/R1 except that the four MG 17s were replaced by two 30mm (1.19in) MK 108 cannon. The Bf 110G-3 was a long-range reconnaissance model fitted with Rb 50/30 and Rb 75/30 cameras, and the G-4 was a nightfighter.

It was as a nightfighter that the Bf 110 truly excelled. In July 1941 a prototype AI radar set, the Lichtenstein SN-2, was installed in a Messerschmitt 110 based at Leeuwarden, Holland. On 9 August this aircraft, crewed by *Oberleutnant* Ludwig Becker and *Feldwebel* Josef Staub intercepted a Wellington bomber with the aid of Lichtenstein and shot it down. Despite this success, it was not until early in 1942 that Lichtenstein-equipped aircraft began to reach the nightfighter *Geschwader* in any numbers. Once they did, the effectiveness of the German nightfighter force increased immeasurably, and some pilots began to achieve quite remarkable scores. One of them was *Hauptmann* Werner Streib, commanding I/NJG 1 at Venlo, who – accompanied by his observer, *Gefreiter* Lingen – had destroyed his first bomber, a Whitley, on the night of 20/21 July 1940 while flying an Me 110. In August 1941 Streib destroyed three more bombers, and on the night 1/2 October he intercepted and destroyed 3 Wellingtons inside 40 minutes. Streib went on to gain 66 victories; for a long time he was Germany's top-scoring nightfighter pilot. Close behind him came *Leutnant* Helmut Lent, a veteran Me 110 pilot who had fought over Poland, Norway and in the defence of Germany against the early (and disastrous) daylight raids on the north German ports by RAF Bomber Command. On 1 November 1941, Lent formed a new nightfighter *Gruppe*, II/NJG 2. Helmut Lent destroyed 102 aircraft at night and 8 by day before his death in an accident in October 1944.

Total production of the Bf 110, which only ended in 1945, was 5873 aircraft.

Messerschmitt Me 163

The pilot sat in a primitive cockpit with a reflector gun-sight for aiming the cannon. Rear visibility was limited, but this was of little importance while the rocket motor was running. Komets were vulnerable to Allied fighters when landing.

The *Komet* was armed with a pair of MK 108 30mm (1.18in) cannon in the wingroots which gave it a mighty punch, but the high closing speed of the aircraft gave the pilot approximately 3 seconds firing time.

As the main wheels were detached from the aircraft shortly after take-off, the Me 163 relied on an extending skid for landing.

This Me 163B carries the Baron von Munchhausen badge of I *Gruppe*, JG 400, based at Brandis, near Leipzig, in late 1944. It wears the original camouflage scheme of a green upper surface, but the fin and rudder have been newly painted.

The aircraft was powered by a single Walter HWK 509A-2 rocket motor, which would run for about six minutes on full throttle.

On 28 July 1944, P-51 Mustangs of the 359th Fighter Group were escorting B-17s at 7600m (25,000ft) over Merseburg when the pilots spotted two contrails at six o'clock, 8km (5 miles) away and several thousand feet higher up. The Mustang leader's combat report described the ensuing action:

'I identified them immediately as the new jet-propelled aircraft. There contrails could not be mistaken and looked very dense and white, somewhat like an elongated cumulus cloud some three quarters of a mile in length. My section turned 180 degrees back towards the enemy, which included two with jets turned on and three in a glide without jets operating at the moment. The two I had spotted made a diving turn to the left in close formation and feinted towards the bombers at six o'clock, cutting off their jets as they turned. Our flight turned for a head-on pass to get between them and the rear of the bomber formation. While still 3000 yards [2743m] from the bombers, they turned into us and left the bombers alone. In this turn they banked about 80 degrees but their course changed only about 20 degrees. Their turn radius was very large but their rate of roll appeared excellent. Their speed, I estimated, was 500 to 600mph [800 to 965km/h]. Both planes passed under us 1000 feet [305m] below while still in a close formation glide. In an attempt to follow them, I split-S'd. One continued down in a 45-degree dive, the other climbed up into the sun very steeply and I lost him. Then I looked back at the one in the dive and saw he was five miles away at 10,000 feet [3050m].'

In fact, the attackers were not jet aircraft at all, but early operational examples of the rocket-powered Messerschmitt Me 163 *Komet*. This remarkable little aircraft was based on the experimental DFS 194, designed in 1938 by Professor Alexander Lippisch and transferred, together with its design staff, to the Messerschmitt company for further development. The first two Me 163 prototypes were flown in the spring of 1941 as unpowered gliders, the Me 163V-1 being transferred to Peenemünde later in the year to be fitted with its 750kg (1653lb) thrust Walter HWK R.II rocket motor. The fuel used was a highly volatile mixture of *T-Stoff* (80 per cent hydrogen peroxide and 20 per cent water) and *C-Stoff* (hydrazine hydrate, methyl alcohol, and water). The first rocket-powered flight was made in August 1941, and during subsequent trials the Me 163 broke all existing world air speed records, reaching speeds of up to 1000km/h (621mph). On one occasion, on 6 July 1944, one of the Me 163 development aircraft, the Me 163V-18, attained the remarkable speed of 1130km/h (702mph) at low altitude, but although a safe landing was made, the rudder was torn away when flutter developed. Because of the need for secrecy, these achievements remained unpublicized until after the war. Development of the Me 163 was accelerated, the first 70 pre-production airframes being allocated to various trials under the designation Me 163B-a1, but the programme became protracted because of delays with the production version of the rocket motor, the HWK 509A. The programme entered a new phase early in 1943, when some Me 163s powered by early examples of the HWK 509A were each fitted with two MG 151 20mm (0.79in) cannon and assigned to a new unit, *Erprobungskommando* 16 (EK16) based at Peenemünde West under the command of Major Wolfgang Späte. EK16's principal function was to pioneer the Me 163B (the fully operational version) into Luftwaffe use, and to train a cadre of experienced pilots. Later, the unit was transferred to Bad Zwischenahn. Halfway through the training programme Späte was inexplicably transferred to command a fighter group on the Eastern Front, his place being taken by Captain Toni Thaler.

In May 1944 an operational *Komet* unit, JG 400, began forming at Wittmundhaven

Left: A pre-production Me 163 on its launching trolley. About 30 pre-production *Komets* were issued with V-numbers (for *Versuchs*, or experimental) and these were to be used in a test and evaluation programme during 1942.

Above: An operational Komet of KG 400. At least one fuelled Komet and its pilot were always kept in standby for instant action in case of any enemy bombers coming within range. The Me 163 was an extremely dangerous aircraft for pilots to fly.

and Venlo, and in June all three *Staffeln* of this unit moved to Brandis near Leipzig, together with EK16. The task of the *Komets* at Brandis was to defend the Leuna oil refinery, which lay 90km (56 miles) to the south. Taking off on its jettisonable trolley, the *Komet* would climb initially at 3600m/min (11,811ft/min), this rate rising to 10,200m/min (33,465ft/min) at 9760m (32,021ft). Time to the *Komet*'s operational ceiling of 12,100m (39,698ft) was a mere 3.35 minutes; maximum powered endurance was 8 minutes. With its fuel exhausted, the Me 163 would make high-speed gliding attacks on its targets, using its two MK 108 30mm (1.19in) cannon and Revi 16B gunsight. With its 120 rounds of ammunition used up and its speed starting to drop, the *Komet* would then dive steeply away from the combat area and glide back to base, landing on a skid.

This in itself was a hazardous procedure, as there was always a risk of explosion if any unburnt rocket fuel remained in the aircraft's tanks. Many Me 163s were lost in landing accidents. About 300 *Komets* were built, but JG 400 remained the only operational unit and the rocket fighter recorded only nine kills during its brief career. The Me 163C, the last version to be built for operational use, had a pressurized cockpit, an improved Walter 109-509C motor, and featured a bubble canopy on a slightly lengthened fuselage. Only a few examples were produced, and these were not issued to units. The Me 163C was to have been fitted with a novel armament arrangement developed by Dr Langweiler (inventor of the *Panzerfaust* one-man anti-tank weapon) comprising five vertically mounted tubes in each wing, each tube containing a 50mm (1.97in) shell. The equipment was activated by a photoelectric cell as the rocket fighter passed under an enemy bomber.

The final development of the *Komet* was the Me 163D, which incorporated substantial re-design, including a retractable undercarriage. The aircraft was re-designated Me 263, a single prototype being built in 1944.

Type: Rocket-powered fighter	
Crew:	1
Powerplant:	one 1700kg (3748lb) thrust Walter 109-509A-2 rocket motor
Max speed:	955km/h (593mph) normal operational
Time to height:	2 mins 36 secs to 9145m (30,003ft)
Service ceiling:	12,000m (39,370ft)
Max range:	35.5km (22 miles) combat radius
Wing span:	9.33m (30ft 6in)
Wing area:	19.62m^2 (211.2sq ft)
Length:	5.85m (19ft 2in)
Height:	2.76m (9ft)
Weights:	1908kg (4206lb) empty; 4310kg (9502lb) loaded
Armament:	two 30mm (1.19in) MK 108 cannon in wing roots

Messerschmitt Me 262

Although the pilot's cockpit was narrow, the canopy gave him excellent visibility. He was protected by an armoured backplate and a thick armoured windscreen.

The aircraft carried four 30mm (1.18in) MK 108 cannon in the nose, with 100 rounds per gun for the upper guns, and 80 rounds per gun for the lower pair.

The Me 262 was initially equipped with a reflector sight, but this was later replaced by the Askania EZ42 gyroscopic sight.

This Me 262A-1a wears the markings of 9th *Staffel* of *Jagdgeschwader* 7, based at Parchim in March 1945. It is now on display at the National Air and Space Museum, Washington, DC.

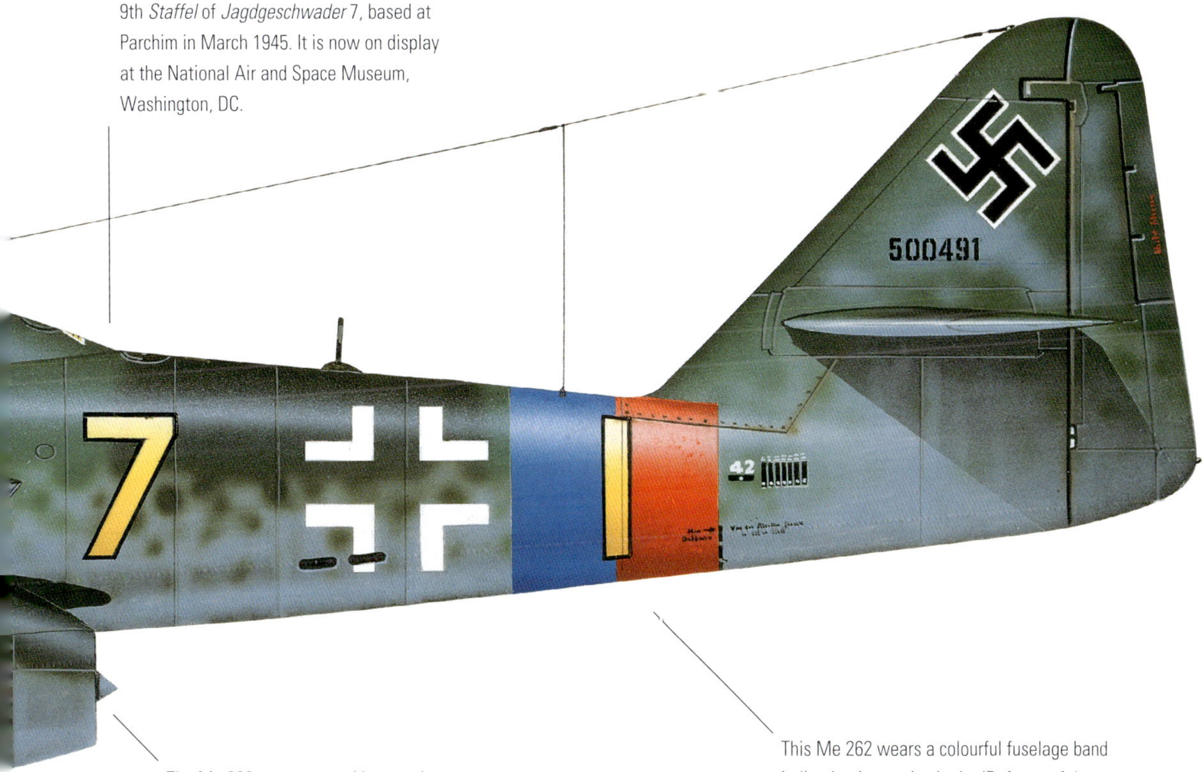

The Me 262 was powered by two Jumo 004B turbojets which used axial-flow compressors. They were very unreliable and short-lived, reducing the availability of Me 262s for front-line units.

This Me 262 wears a colourful fuselage band indicating its service in the 'Defence of the Reich' campaign.

Above: A Messerschmitt Me 262A-1a fighter-bomber with two 500kg (1102lb) bombs under the forward fuselage. Adapting the Me 262 to the fast bomber role was to set back production of the fighter version. This would prove to be a costly error for the Germans.

Design work on the Me 262, the world's first operational jet fighter, began in September 1939, a month after the successful flight of the world's first jet aircraft, the Heinkel He 178. However, due to delays in the development of satisfactory engines, the massive damage caused by Allied air attacks and Hitler's later obsession with using the aircraft as a bomber rather than a fighter, six years would elapse between the 262 taking shape on Messerschmitt's drawing board and its entry into Luftwaffe service. Because of the lack of jet engines, the prototype Me 262V-1 flew on 18 April 1941 under the power of a Jumo 210G piston engine, and it was not until 18 July 1942 that the Me 262V-3 made a flight under turbojet power. December 1943 saw the first flight of the Me 262V-8, the first of the type to carry a full armament of four 30mm (1.19in) MK 108 cannon. Despite numerous snags, production of the Me 262 began to get into its stride in April 1944, with widely dispersed airframe factories and assembly plants being set up at various locations. The end of 1944 had completed 730 Me 262s, and 564 more were built in the early months of 1945, making a total of 1294 aircraft. Notwithstanding Hitler's obsession with turning the aircraft into a fast bomber, the Me 262 initially went into production as a pure fighter, entering service with a trials unit known as *Erprobungskommando* 262 (EK262) at Lechfeld, near Augsburg, in August 1944. It was originally commanded by Captain Tierfelder – later killed when his aircraft crashed in flames during one of the unit's first operational missions – and his successor was Major Walter Nowotny, at the age of 23 one of the Luftwaffe's top fighter pilots with a score of 258 kills, 255 of them achieved on the

Eastern Front. By the end of October the *Kommando* Nowotny, as the unit had come to be known, had reached full operational status and was deployed to the airfields of Achmer and Hesepe near Osnabruck, astride the main American daylight bomber approach route. Because of a shortage of adequately trained pilots and technical problems, the *Kommando* Nowotny was usually able to fly only three or four sorties a day against the enemy formations, yet in November 1944 the 262s destroyed 22 aircraft. By the end of the month, however, the unit had only 13 serviceable aircraft out of an established total of 30, a rate of attrition accounted for mainly by accidents rather than enemy action.

The Me 262 presented a serious threat to Allied air superiority during the closing weeks of 1944. Two versions were now being developed in parallel: the Me 262A-2a *Sturmvogel* (Stormbird) bomber variant and the Me 262A-1a fighter. The *Sturmvogel* was issued to *Kampfgeschwader* 51 *Edelweiss* in September 1944; other bomber units that armed with the type at a later date were KG 6, 27 and 54. Problems encountered during operational training delayed

Below: A Messerschmitt Me 262 in a forest clearing. In the last months of the war, the Germans dispersed many of their jet fighters in forests bordering the Autobahnen (freeways/motorways), as the airfields with suitable runways had been pulverized by Allied bombing.

the aircraft's combat debut, but in the autumn of 1944 the 262s began to appear in growing numbers, carrying out low-level attacks on Allied targets, mainly moving columns. There were also two reconnaissance versions, the Me 262A-1a/U3 and Me 262A-5a. For weeks, these aircraft roved almost at will over the entire battlefront, photographing installations and troop movements deep behind the Allied lines. The Allies resorted to mounting heavy attacks on the 262s' bases, an extremely hazardous procedure. Not only had the Germans organized 'flak lanes', consisting of strings of 20mm (0.79in) batteries extending for 3.2km (2 miles) along the approach to an airfield's runways, but a group of Focke-Wulf 190s (JG 54) was assigned to defend the two principal bases at Achmer and Hesepe.

Nevertheless, attacks on their airfields began to take an increasing toll. During one such attack, on 8 November 1944, Walter Nowotny was shot down and killed by Mustangs while approaching to land at Achmer. Shortly after his death, one of the *Kommando*'s groups was used to form the nucleus of a new jet fighter unit, *Jagdgeschwader* JG 7 *Hindenburg*, under the command of Major Johannes

Type: Jet fighter (Me 262A-1a interceptor)	
Crew:	1
Powerplant:	two 900kg (1984lb) thrust Junkers Jumo 109-004B 4 turbojets
Max speed:	870km/h (541mph) at 7000m (26,966ft)
Time to height:	6 mins 48 secs to 6000m (19,685ft)
Service ceiling:	11,450m (37,566ft)
Max range:	1050km (652 miles)
Wing span:	12.51m (41ft)
Wing area:	21.68m² (233.3sq ft)
Length:	10.60m (34ft 7in)
Height:	3.83m (11ft 6in)
Weights:	4420kg (9744lb) empty; 7130kg(15,719lb) max t/o
Armament:	four 30mm (1.19in) MK108 cannon in nose

Left: This view of the Me 262 Schwalbe (Swallow) shows off the aircraft's clean lines to good advantage. Although the airframe was a superb piece of design, the Swallow's engines were a constant source of trouble and had a life of only 25 hours.

Steinhoff. Although this unit eventually comprised three *Gruppen*, only one of these, III/JG 7, made real and continual contact with the enemy, moving in turn to bases at Brandenburg-Briest, Oranienburg and Parchim. In the middle of February 1945, III/JG 7 took delivery of the first consignment of R4M 5cm (1.9in) air-to-air rockets; the Me 262 could carry 24 of these missiles mounted on simple wooden racks beneath the wings, and when the salvo was fired towards an enemy bomber formation it spread out rather like the charge from a shotgun, increasing the chances of hitting one or more targets. During their first series of operations in the last week of February 1945, using a combination of R4Ms, 30mm (1.19in) cannon and Revi gunsights, the pilots of III/JG 7 destroyed no fewer than 45 four-engined American bombers and 15 of their escorting fighters for the loss of only four Me 262s. Meanwhile, authority had been given for the formation of a second Me 262 jet fighter unit. Known as *Jagdverband* 44, and commanded by Lieutenant-General Adolf Galland, it comprised 45 highly experienced pilots, many of them Germany's top-scoring aces. Its main operating base was Munchen-Riem, where its main targets were the bombers of the Fifteenth Army Air Force, coming up from the south, while JG 7 continued to operate from bases in northern and central Germany before the jets were grounded through lack of fuel or engine spares, the Jumo 004 having a life of only 25 hours. Their ground crews destroyed most of the 262s shortly before the airfield was overrun by American tanks on 3 May.

Several variants of the Me 262 were proposed, including the radar-equipped Me 262B-1a/U1 two-seat nightfighter, which saw brief operational service from March 1945 with 10/NJG 11 under *Leutnant* Welter, who on the night 30/31 March destroyed four RAF Mosquitoes near Berlin.

Mistel

The bomber used in this Mistel 2 'Vater und Sohn' combination was a Ju 88G-1 airframe.

The undercarriage of the bomber was not strengthened in any way despite the added weight of the fighter. Ground crews would sweep runways before take-off to reduce the risk of a tyre blow-out.

The upper component in this Mistel combination is a Focke Wulf Fw 190A-8 fighter. Many fighters used in Mistel attacks had their wing guns removed to save weight, leaving only their fuselage guns for self-defence.

The Mistel combination was controlled by a single pilot in the upper aircraft, either a Fw 190 or a Bf 109 fighter. Duplicate controls for the lower aircraft were provided in the fighter's cockpit.

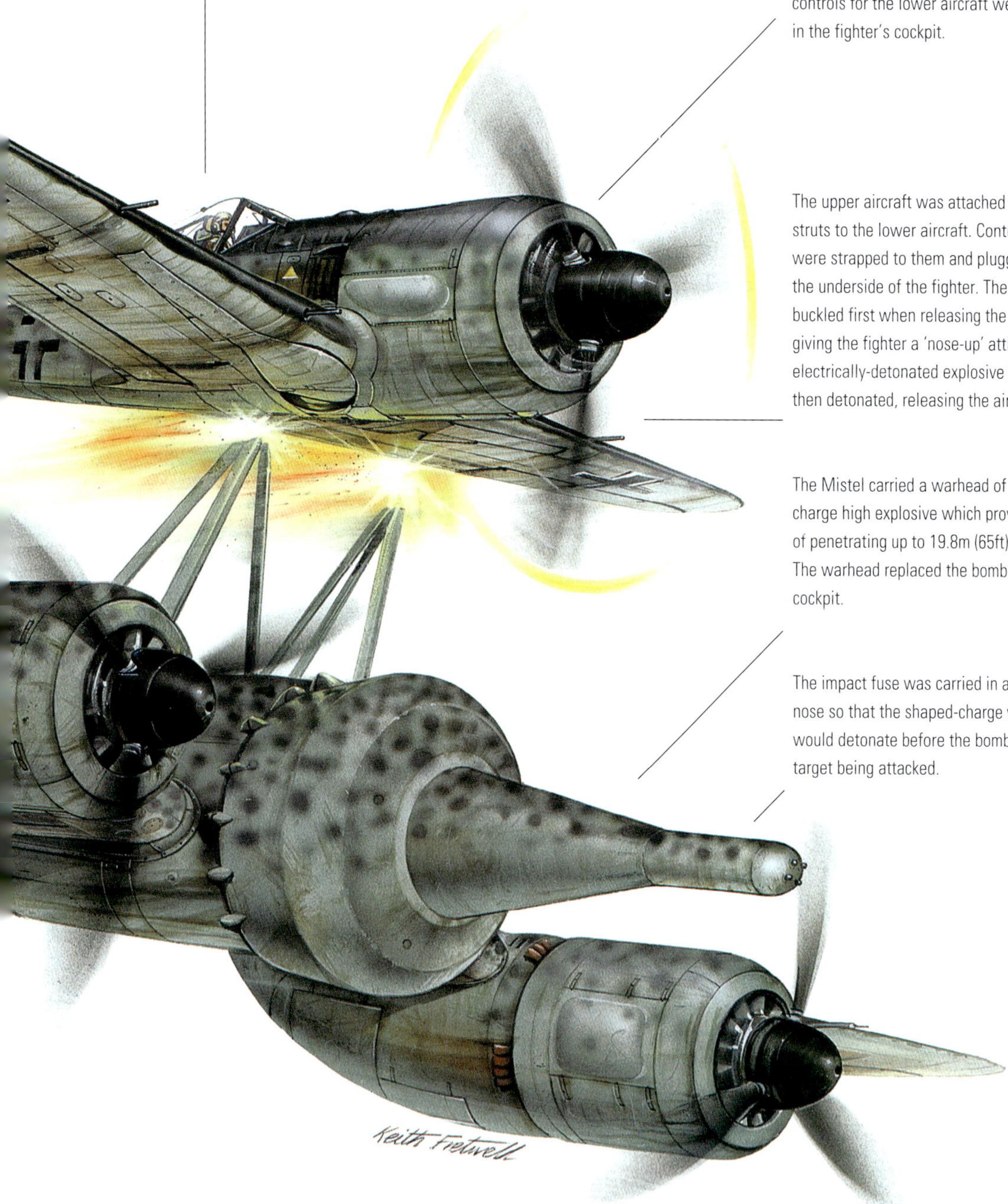

The upper aircraft was attached by three struts to the lower aircraft. Control cables were strapped to them and plugged into the underside of the fighter. The rear strut buckled first when releasing the Mistel, giving the fighter a 'nose-up' attitude. The electrically-detonated explosive ball joints then detonated, releasing the aircraft.

The Mistel carried a warhead of a shaped-charge high explosive which proved capable of penetrating up to 19.8m (65ft) of concrete. The warhead replaced the bomber crew's cockpit.

The impact fuse was carried in an extended nose so that the shaped-charge warhead would detonate before the bomber hit the target being attacked.

The concept of packing a discarded bomber with high explosives and guiding it to its target by means of a piloted fighter aircraft which would be coupled to it during the outward flight, was pioneered by the *Deutsches Forschungsinstitut für Segelflug* (DFS), the German Glider Research Institute. DFS had begun studying the problem of how to couple one aircraft with another in 1940, the incentive being to find a means of providing fighter escort on long-range missions. The idea was that if the bomber component came under attack, the fighter would detach itself, engage the enemy and, after the action, recouple and refuel. This idea was resurrected in the late 1940s in American experiments with fighter protection for the very long-range Convair B-36 strategic bomber.

As an offshoot of its research, DFS projected the *Mistel* (Mistletoe) idea. It was supported by Junkers test pilot *Flugkapitän* Siegfried Holzbauer, who proposed that old Ju 88 bombers should be converted into stand-off bombs and guided to their objective by a coupled fighter. Despite an initial lack of official interest, practical experiments began in 1942, using a DFS 230 assault glider as the lower component and a Klemm Kl 35 light aircraft as the upper. The success of these early trials gave the *Reichsluftministerium* (RLM) food for thought, and early in 1943 the ministry ordered a prototype combination of a Ju 88A-4 and a Bf 109F to investigate the possibility of using this combination in the attack role. The composite aircraft assembly was known unofficially as *Vater und Sohn* (Father and Son), the lower component being named *Mistel.* Testing of the prototype began in July and was completed in October 1943, by which time 15 similar combinations were on order.

Above: This Mistel combination involves a Ju 88A-4 lower component and a Bf 109F-4 'parent' aircraft. These two components were known as Vater und Sohn (Father and Son). An ambitious plan to attack Scapa Flow naval base came to nothing.

As part of the steering control system, a master compass, S-compass and a three-axes autopilot were installed in the rear of the bomber. This equipment steered the combination in normal flight, leaving the fighter's controls free. The fighter pilot was connected to the

Type: Flying bomb (Mistel 3C)	
Crew:	1
Powerplant:	As original aircraft
Max speed:	550km/h (342mph)
Time to height:	not applicable
Service ceiling:	not applicable
Max range:	4100km (2548 miles)
Wing span:	Ju 88: 20m (65ft 6in)
Wing area: combined:	72.8m² (783.5sq ft)
Length:	18.53m (61ft 10in) including warhead nose
Height:	not known
Weights:	23,600kg (52,028lb) maximum t/o
Armament:	1725kg (3803lb) Hexogen/TNT warhead

bomber's controls by two thumb-operated buttons, one on the control column operating the bomber's rudder and ailerons simultaneously, and one on a new centre panel operating the elevators. By operating a switch, the pilot could elect to fly the combination by using the fighter's stick and rudder, the control surfaces of both components working in unison. Apart from some strengthening of the rear fuselage, the fighter needed little conversion work. In the case of the bomber, the nose section was replaced by a 3500kg (7716lb) hollow-charge warhead containing 1725kg (3803lb) of high explosive and an impact fuse which primed about three seconds after the aircraft separated. The final *Mistel* warhead tests were completed in April 1944, by which time it had been established that the warhead's 1000kg (2205lb) steel core was capable of penetrating 7.5m (24ft 6in) of concrete.

The completion of the warhead trials coincided with the formation of the first *Mistel* unit, 2/KG 101, with five pilots under the command of *Hauptmann* Horst Rudat. Training took place at the Junkers plant, Nordhausen, with Ju 88A-4/Bf 109F-4 combinations from the prototype batch, these having the designation *Mistel* S1; operational combinations were designated *Mistel* 1. The original operational plan envisaged a *Mistel* attack, launched from Denmark, on units of the British fleet at Scapa Flow in the Orkneys, but when the Allies landed in Normandy the *Mistel* were hurriedly transferred to St Dizier. From there, on the night 24/25 June 1944, they made their first operational sortie, an attack on invasion shipping in the Seine Bay. Four *Mistel* found targets; a fifth malfunctioned and had to be jettisoned. On 9/10 August *Mistel* made an unsuccessful attack on shipping in the English Channel; one Ju 88 component crashed and exploded at Binley, in Hampshire. In October, five *Mistel* took off from Grove in Denmark for the long-planned Scapa Flow attack, which ended in disaster; three crashed and exploded, and two failed to find the target.

In November 1944 the *Mistel* assets were concentrated under the umbrella of II/KG 200, the Luftwaffe's special duties unit. The *Mistel* 1 had now been joined by the *Mistel* 2, a combination of Ju 88G-1 and FW 190A-6 or F-8. The focus of *Mistel* operations now shifted to the Eastern Front, with bridge targets being given priority. On 8 March 1945, four *Mistel* attacked the Oder bridges at Görlitz; two bridges were hit and one *Mistel* was shot down. On 25/26 March, four *Mistel* attacked the Oder bridges with unknown results; other *Mistel* were despatched to attack bridges over the Vistula. Meanwhile, an ambitious plan (Operation Eisenhammer) had been hatched to use the *Mistel* to destroy power stations in the Soviet Union. About 82 *Mistel* were prepared for the operation, which was to take place on 28/29 March, but many of these were expended in bridge attacks and the operation was abandoned. The final attack against Soviet bridgeheads took place on 16 April 1945, the composites being used in conjunction with Henschel Hs 293 missiles. New versions of the *Mistel* which appeared before the end of hostilities were the *Mistel* 3A (Ju 88A-4/FW 190A-8), Mistel 3B (Ju 88H-4/FW 190A8) and *Mistel* 3C (Ju 88G-10 and FW 190F-8). Many more *Mistel* projects involving combinations of jet aircraft and missiles remained on the drawing board.

Right: In service from the summer of 1944, the Mistel stand-off bomb was a devastating weapon – that was, provided it could reach its target. Most Mistels failed to get where they had intended, instead falling victim to Allied fighters, as well as ground fire.

Boeing B-17

Two pilots sat side-by-side on the flight deck, with the dorsal turret just behind them. In front of the cockpit was a domed observation window for the navigator to take sextant readings from.

Defence of the upper side of the aircraft was largely entrusted to the dorsal turret which mounted two 12.7mm (0.5in) machine guns. It was positioned well forward on the fuselage so that it could augment the forward defence of the aircraft.

The bombardier's station was in the extreme nose. The aircraft was equipped with the Norden bombsight, which compensated for drift and windage. Behind the bombardier sat the navigator.

The remotely-controlled chin turret was a new feature on the B-17G, and mounted two 12.7mm (0.5in) machine guns. Two 12.7mm (0.5in) cheek guns were also mounted in the nose for forward defence, and were operated by the navigator.

The B-17 carried a small bombload for its size compared to the B-24 or Lancaster. The bombs were stacked either side of the bay, allowing the crew to pass through it to the rear fuselage.

The triangle on the tail reveals this aircraft to be part of the 1st Bomb Wing. The letter identifies it as part of the 91st Bomb Group. The red band is a further aid to identification. On the waist the aircraft has its squadron markings in yellow, which follow the RAF style with two letter codes. This aircraft belongs to the 322nd Bomber Squadron based at RAF Bassingbourn.

A single trainable gun could be fired upwards from a hatch on the upper fuselage when the aircraft was under severe attack. Between this position and the dorsal turret was stored a dinghy, to be used if the aircraft ditched into the sea.

The tailgunner was situated in a cramped rear turret below the rudder. Two 12.7mm (0.5in) guns were mounted in the tailcone.

A 12.7mm (0.5in) machine gun was mounted either side of the aircraft in the waist for lateral defence against fighters. A Sperry ball turret was mounted below the aircraft for defending its underside, mounting two 12.7mm (0.5in) guns.

The B-17G was powered by four Wright R-1820-97 Cyclone engines, each rated at 897kW (1200hp), and equipped with turbochargers for improved performance.

The B-17 Flying Fortress was designed in response to a United States Army Air Corps requirement, issued in 1934, for a long-range, high-altitude daylight bomber. The prototype, bearing the company designation Boeing Model 299, was powered by four 559kW (750hp) Pratt & Whitney Hornet engines and flew for the first time on 28 July 1935. Although the prototype was later destroyed in an accident, the cause was attributed to human error and the project went ahead. Thirteen Y1B-17s and one Y1B-17A were ordered for evaluation, and after the trials period, these were designated B-17 and B-17A respectively. The first production batch of 39 B-17Bs, featuring a modified nose, enlarged rudder and various other modifications, were all delivered by the end of March 1940; meanwhile a further order had been placed for 38 B-17Cs, which were powered by four Wright 895kW (1200hp) Cyclone engines and featured some minor changes. Twenty of these were supplied to the RAF as the Fortress I in 1941, but after sustaining several losses on bombing operations the remainder were diverted to Coastal Command or the Middle East.

By the time the Pacific war began, the B-17D, 42 of which had been ordered in 1940, was in service. This was generally similar to the C model, and the Cs in service were subsequently modified to D standard. About half the early-model B-17s in the Pacific Theatre were destroyed

Above: Boeing B-17G 'A Bit o'Lace' of the 711th Bombardment Squadron, 447th Bombardment Group, based at Rattlesden in Suffolk. During its combat career, the 447th Bombardment Group flew 7605 sorties and dropped 17,273 tonnes (17,000 tons) of bombs.

Left: A B-17G formation releases its bombs over a German target. The white trail is a smoke marker, which has been released by the lead aircraft as a signal for the other aircraft in the group to bomb in unison. This technique proved very effective.

by Japanese air attack in the first days of the far eastern war. A new tail design, the main recognition feature of all subsequent Fortresses, was introduced with the B-17E, together with improved armament that for the first time included a tail gun position. The B-17E was the first version of the Flying Fortress to see combat in the European Theatre of Operations, operating initially with the 97th Bombardment Group. All B-17s in the Pacific Theatre were eventually transferred to Europe to reinforce the British-based US Eighth Army Air Force. The RAF received 42 B-17Es in 1942 under the designation Fortress IIA: one E was converted as the 38-passenger XC-108 transport for General Douglas MacArthur, C-in-C Pacific Theatre; another as the XC-108A freighter; and one, the XB-38, was experimentally fitted with Allison engines. A total of 512 B-17Es was produced, this variant being followed into service by the further refined B-17F, which entered production in April 1942. Total production of the B-17F was 3400, including 61 examples that were converted to the long-range reconnaissance role as the F-9. Another 19 were delivered to RAF Coastal Command as the Fortress II.

The early B-17 variants had a single hand-held flexible 7.62mm (0.3in) nose gun that could be fired by either the bombardier or the navigator. This inadequate weapon was replaced by two 12.7mm (0.5in) guns, one mounted on either side of the nose in the B-17F, but hand-held weapons

Right: A fine study of a B-17G of the 91st Bombardment Group. Based at Bassingbourn, near Cambridge, the 91st Bombardment Group was the first Eighth Army Air Force group to complete 100 missions, and it completed 340 missions (9591 sorties) in total.

of this kind had a poor degree of accuracy and their field of fire was limited. The last 86 B-17Fs were consequently fitted with a chin-mounted power-operated Bendix turret mounting a pair of 12.7mm (0.5in) guns, which proved invaluable as the Luftwaffe increasingly adopted frontal fighter attacks. This became standard on the B-17G, the major production model, which mounted 13 12.7mm (0.5in) machineguns; against this formidable weight of firepower, the Germans were forced to add extra armour to their fighters. In a further attempt to increase the defensive firepower of the B-17 formations which, in the summer of 1943, suffered appalling losses, a number of Fortresses were modified as YB-40 'escort fighters', mounting up to 30 12.7mm (0.50in) machineguns. The YB-40s proved to be slower than the bombers it was supposed to escort, and only a few missions were flown before the idea was dropped. The real answer was to provide a genuine fighter aircraft which could effectively escort the bombers all the way to the target and back. One eventually came along in the shape of the P-51 Mustang.

The RAF received 85 B-17Gs as the Fortress III, some of these for electronic countermeasures. Ten B-17Gs were converted for reconnaissance as the F-9C, while the US Navy and Coast Guard used 24 PB-1Ws and 16 PB-1Gs for maritime surveillance and aerial survey. About 130 were modified for air-sea rescue duties as the B-17H or TB-17H. These were fitted with a lifeboat – which was carried under the fuselage – and other rescue equipment. Production of the Fortress, from the B-17F onwards, was shared between Boeing, Douglas and Lockheed-Vega, who between them produced 8680 B-17Gs.

Type: Medium/heavy bomber (B-17G)	
Crew:	10
Powerplant:	four 895kW (1200 hp) Wright Cyclone R-1820-97 radials
Max speed:	462km/h (28.6 mph)
Time to height:	37 mins to 6096m (20,000ft)
Service ceiling:	10,850m (35,600ft)
Max range:	3220km (2000 miles) with 2722kg (6000lb) bomb load
Wing span:	31.62m (103ft 7in)
Wing area:	131.92m² (1420sq ft)
Length:	22.78m (74ft 7in)
Height:	5.82m (19ft 1in)
Weights:	16,391kg (36,135lb) empty; 32,660kg (72,000lb) max t/o
Armament:	twin 12.7mm (0.5in) MG under nose, aft of cockpit, under centre fuselage and in tail; single-gun mountings in side of nose, in radio operator's hatch and waist positions; maximum bomb load 7983kg (17,600lb)

The Free French Air Force would use a small number of B-17Fs in Indo-China during the closing stages of the war against Japan, and also used modified B-17Gs in the transport and survey roles. Thirteen B-17Gs in all were acquired between 1947 and 1955, all from surplus USAAF or US Government sources, and one of the B-17Fs already in French Air Force service was retained for spares. The aircraft were operated by the *Institut Geographique National* (IGN), whose main base was at Creil, near Paris, and the last of them, F-BEEA, continued to serve until the late 1980s. This Fortress, which was named *Chateau de Verneuil*, previously carried the USAAF serial 44-85643. A number of B-17s, forced down on German territory, were used operationally by KG200, the Luftwaffe's clandestine special duties unit.

During World War II, B-17s flew 291,508 sorties over Europe, dropping 650,308 tonnes (640,036 tons) of bombs. Combat losses amounted to 4688 aircraft.

Boeing B-29 Superfortress

The B-29 Superfortress was crewed by no less than 11 men, 5 of whom were officers: the pilot (the aircraft's commander), co-pilot, bombardier, navigator and flight engineer. Enlisted crew were the radio operator, radar operator, central fire control gunner, left and right gunners and the tail gunner.

For forward defence the B-29 had two turrets, mounted above and below each other and equipped with two 12.7mm (0.5in) guns each. They were remotely controlled.

The Superfortress was powered by four Wright R-3350-23 Duplex Cyclones, each with two turbochargers. Initially the engines were prone to fires, but this problem was later ironed out.

The B-29 was the world's first pressurized bomber. It had two pressurized cabins either side of the bomb bay, connected by a sealed tunnel which allowed crew members to pass between them. In the front cabin, the bombardier sat in the extreme nose, with the pilots behind him followed by the flight engineer, the radio and radar operators and the navigator at the rear.

The B-29 was equipped with the AN/APQ-13 bombing radar located between the two bomb bays. It was often retouched out of wartime photographs of the aircraft.

This aircraft is shown dropping M-47 incendiary bombs on Japan. They were bundled together for loading, but broke free from each other when released. The aircraft had two bomb bays, with bombs dropped from each alternately to preserve the centre of gravity during a bomb run.

The markings reveal this B-29 to be an aircraft from the 504th Bomb Group of the 313th Bomb Wing, based at Tinian on the Marianas Islands. The fuselage stripes reveal it to be a lead ship, responsible for the main navigation tasks of the formation.

The rear pressurized cabin stretched from the rear of the second bomb bay to the start of the dorsal fin. It contained the gunners, who used an analogue computer-controlled fire system. Four bunks were also provided for relief crews or rest during long flights.

A gunner sitting in a pressurized rear turret with armoured windscreens controlled a 20mm (0.79in) cannon and two 12.7mm (0.5in) machine guns. There was no access to the turret during flight.

Famous as the heavy bomber that brought strategic air warfare to the Japanese home islands during the last year of the Pacific war, and above all as the aircraft that carried out the nuclear attacks on Hiroshima and Nagasaki, the Boeing B-29 Superfortress was the outcome of design studies that started in 1937. The definitive design, to meet a US Army Air Corps requirement for a 'Hemisphere Defense Weapon', an aircraft capable of carrying 907kg (2000lb) of bombs for 8582km (5333 miles) at 644km/h (400 mph), was prepared in 1940. Three prototypes were ordered in that year, the first XB-29 flying on 21 September 1942. By that time orders for 1500 aircraft had already been placed, the B-29 programme having been given maximum priority following the Japanese attack on Pearl Harbor. While the 14 pre-series models (YB-29s) were being built, Boeing and the US Government set up a massive production programme which also involved the Bell Aircraft Company and the Glenn L. Martin Company. The first YB-29 evaluation aircraft were delivered to the 58th Bombardment Wing in July 1943, B-29-BW production aircraft following three months later. The other main versions of the B-29 that made their appearance during the war were the B-29A-BN with a four-gun forward upper turret and increased wing span, and the B-29B-BA with a reduced gun armament and increased bomb load. A reconnaissance version was designated F-13A (and later RB-29). The B-29 had many technical innovations, including the installation of remotely controlled gun turrets, which were periscopically sighted by gunners seated within the fuselage.

At the end of 1943 the decision was taken to utilize the B-29 exclusively in the Pacific theatre, two bombardment wings, the 58th and 73rd, being assigned to XX Bomber Command. The first units to be equipped with the B-29 were deployed to bases in India and south-west China in the spring of 1944, the first combat mission being flown on 5 June against Bangkok in Japanese-held Thailand before attacks on the Japanese mainland were initiated 10 days later. Early high-altitude missions showed poor results, mainly because of adverse weather conditions in the target areas, but also because the technical complexity of the Superfortress resulted in a large number of equipment failures. The establishment of five operational bases in the Marianas in March 1944 brought the B-29s much closer to Japan, and four bombardment wings, the 73rd, 313th, 314th and 315th, were quickly redeployed there from their bases in India and China, being followed a little later by the 58th BW. All the B-29 wings were now under the control of XXI Bomber Command, with its HQ on Guam. The move was followed by a complete revision of tactics, the B-29s now carrying out large-scale night incendiary area attacks on Japan's principal cities, with devastating results; for example, on the night 9/10 March 1945, 279 B-29s dropped 1693 tones (1667 tons) of bombs on Tokyo, killing more than 80,000 people. The B-29s that

Below: B-29s of XXI Bomber Command dropping clusters of incendiary bombers over a Japanese city. Long before the atomic bombs signalled that the war in the Pacific would soon be over, B-29 attacks had devastated the Japanese homeland.

Above: The B-29 carried a very heavy armament, as is shown in this illustration. It was only in the closing months of the war that the Japanese managed to develop fighters which were capable of inflicting real punishment on the Superfortress.

dropped the atomic bombs on Hiroshima and Nagasaki on 6 and 9 August 1945, named *Enola Gay* and *Bock's Car*, belonged to the 509th Bombardment Wing (Provisional), which was to become the principal US nuclear weapons trials unit.

The B-29 continued to be the mainstay of the USAF Strategic Air Command for several years after 1945, and saw almost continual action during the three years of the Korean War. The first B-29 strike of that conflict was carried out by the Guam-based bombers of the 20th Air Force's 19th Bombardment Wing on 13 July 1950, and the offensive was maintained against North Korean troop concentrations, communications and industrial targets throughout August, September and October. During that period, the B-29s dropped more than 30,480 tonnes (30,000 tons) of bombs on North Korean targets, thus surpassing the total dropped on Japan in World War II. From November 1950, however, the B-29s operating over North Korea – particularly lone RB-29 reconnaissance aircraft – suffered heavy losses at the hands of MiG-15 jet fighters, and it became clear that the day of the piston-engined heavy bomber was over.

Production of the B-29 ended in May 1946, after 3970 aircraft had been built, but the basic design subsequently underwent several modifications. These included the SB-29 (search and rescue), TB-29 (trainer), WB-29 (weather reconnaissance) and KB-29 (tanker). The KB-29M had British 'probe and drogue' flight refuelling equipment, while the KB-29P used the Boeing 'flying boom' method, which became standard in the USAF. One-off modifications were the XB-29G, which was adapted as a jet engine test bed and loaned to the General Electric Company, and the XB-29H, which was assigned to special armament trials. Two production variants, the B-29C and B-29D, were cancelled at the end of the war, but the design of the B-29 underwent substantial changes and became the B-50, which began to replace the B-29 in Strategic Air Command's first-line units in 1947.

Neither the B-29 nor the B-50 was exported outside the USA, but 87 B-29s were loaned to the Royal Air Force in 1951 to provide a short-term strategic capability. Known as the Washington in RAF service, the aircraft equipped eight squadrons of Bomber Command, while four were equipped for the electronic intelligence role. The Russian Tupolev Tu-4 was based on B-29s which had force-landed in the USSR after attacking targets in Manchuria.

Type: Strategic heavy bomber	
Crew:	10
Powerplant:	four 1641kW (2200hp) Wright R-3350-57 radial engines
Max speed:	576km/h (358mph) at 7620m (25,000ft)
Time to height:	38 mins to 6095m (20,000ft)
Service ceiling:	9695m (31,807ft)
Max range:	6598km (4098 miles)
Wing span:	43.36m (142ft 3in)
Wing area:	161.27m² (1736sq ft)
Length:	30.18m (99ft)
Height:	9.01m (29ft 6in)
Weights:	32,369kg (71,360lb) empty; 64,003kg (141,100lb) max t/o
Armament:	four-gun turret over nose; two-gun turrets under nose, over and under rear fuselage, all with guns of 12.7mm (0.5in) calibre; one 20mm (0.79in) and two 12.7mm (0.5in) guns in tail; up to 9072kg (20,000lb) of bombs

Consolidated B-24 Liberator

The B-24H Liberator was powered by four Pratt & Whitney R-1830-43 engines, which were turbosupercharged. The oil coolers either side of each engine gave the cowlings an unmistakeable ellipitical look.

The dorsal turret behind the flight deck was crewed by the radio operator and was equipped with two 12.7mm (0.5in) machine guns for defending the aircraft from enemy attack from above.

The nose of the B-24H sported a Consolidated or Emerson turret armed with two 12.7mm (0.5in) machine guns. Below that was the bombardier's position, where the crewman lay prone looking through an optically-flat windscreen. Behind him sat the aircraft's navigator.

The B-24H was crewed by 10 men. The pilot and co-pilot sat side-by-side on the flight deck, with the radio operator behind them. Other crew members were the bombardier, nose gunner, navigator, two beam gunners, a ventral ball turret gunner, and a tail gunner.

A conventional high-explosive bombload is released over the target. The bomb bay could carry a maximum of 5806kg (12,800lb) stowed vertically in racks.

This aircraft carries markings revealing it to be from the 726th Bombardment Squadron of the 451st Bombardment Group of the 15th Air Force of the USAAF. It was one of the 1580 B-24H Liberators built by Ford at Willow Run, Michigan.

A single 12.7mm (0.5in) machine gun was mounted each side of the fuselage in the waist positions for lateral defence against enemy fighters.

A Briggs-Sperry ventral ball turret provided defence for the aircraft's underside, armed with a pair of 12.7mm (0.5in) machine guns.

The rear gunner sat in a Consolidated or Motor Products tail turret mounting two 12.7mm (0.5in) machine guns. These were fed from a magazine situated amidships.

Produced in a number of variants for a host of operational and training tasks, the Consolidated B-24 Liberator was built in larger numbers than any other US warplane of World War II, 18,431 being produced in total, and was delivered in greater quantities than any other bomber in aviation history. It had its origin in US Army Air Corps Specification C-212, issued in 1935 and calling for a new four-engined heavy bomber with a top speed of 483km/h (300mph), a range of 4830km (3000 miles), a service ceiling of 10,675m (35,022ft) and a maximum bomb load of 3624kg (8000lb). Consolidated responded with their Model 32 bomber proposal, designed on the basis of tests flown with the Consolidated Model 31 flying boat. The fuselage of the new bomber was very deep, in order to accommodate the required bomb load, and to facilitate ground handling and produce shorter take-off runs, a tricycle undercarriage with a steerable nosewheel was adopted. The most important item 'borrowed' from the Model 31, however, was the 33.5m (110ft) span high aspect ratio wing, with its retractable Fowler flaps. The

Left: A B-24 Liberator in flight. The Liberator was a popular aircraft with its crews, and served in the RAF and RAF Coastal Command as well as the USAAF, performing sterling service in the battle of the Atlantic against the U-boats.

Type: Long range heavy bomber (B-24J)	
Crew:	8/10
Powerplant:	four 895kW (1200hp) Pratt & Whitney R-1830-65 radials
Max speed:	467km/h (290mph)
Time to height:	25 mins to 6096m (20,000ft)
Service ceiling:	8535m (28,000ft)
Max range:	32,220km (20,021 miles) with a 3992kg (8800lb) bomb load
Wing span:	33.53m (110ft)
Wing area:	97.36m² (1048sq ft)
Length:	20.47m (67ft 2in)
Height:	5.49m (18ft)
Weights:	16,556kg (36,500lb) empty; 29,484kg (65,000lb) max t/o
Armament:	two-gun turrets in nose, tail, upper fuselage aft of cockpit and under centre fuselage, single manual guns in waist (beam) positions, totalling 10 12.7mm (0.5in) MG; normal bomb load of 3992kg (8800lb)

new wing design would enable the Model 32 to carry the same payload as its rival, the Boeing B-17C Flying Fortress, but at a much greater speed and range. Also in common with the Model 31 design was the use of twin fins and rudders.

A contract for one prototype, designated XB-24, was approved on 30 March 1939. This aircraft (39-556) took off on its maiden flight from Lindberg Field, California, on 29 December 1939. It was followed by seven YB-24 service evaluation aircraft, and while these were under construction, a number of changes were made to the XB-24, including the replacement of the 895kW (1200hp) Pratt & Whitney R-1830-33 engines with R-1830-41s, which were equipped with General Electric B-2 turbo superchargers for high altitude flight. The tail span was also increased by 0.6m (2ft). Along with other modifications the aircraft was re-designated XB-24B and given the new serial 39-680.

The first Liberators to come off Consolidated's San Diego production line were six LB-30As, part of an order placed by the French Government in September 1939. With France overrun, the aircraft were diverted to the RAF, which found them unacceptable for combat over Europe (for one thing, they lacked self-sealing fuel tanks). The aircraft were taken on RAF charge in November 1940 and relegated to ferry duties. The production model for the USAAC was the B-24A, the first of nine being delivered in May 1941. A further development batch of nine B-24Cs was also delivered, leading to the first major production models, the B-24D (2738 aircraft), the generally similar B-24E (791 aircraft) and B-24G (430 aircraft) with a power-operated nose turret. Further Liberator developments were the B-24H; 738 were built by Consolidated with a Consolidated nose turret, and 2362 were produced by Douglas and Ford with an Emerson turret; the B-24J, an improved B-24H with an autopilot and other operational upgrades, including a more effective bomb sight (6678 built by Consolidated, Douglas, Ford and North American); the B-24L with two manually operated tail guns rather than a turret (1667 from Consolidated and Ford); and the B-24M, an improved version of the B-24J (2593 aircraft

Above: One of the last B-24s to go into action, this B-24J was given a flamboyant paint job by the 43rd Bomb Group, operating from the island of Ie Shima in the spring of 1945. With the threat from Japanese fighters diminished, the dorsal turret was deleted.

Below: A formation of B-24 Liberators setting out on a sortie. The B-24 was extremely vulnerable to fighter attack, catching fire readily. It was produced in greater numbers than any other bomber.

from Consoldiated and Ford). Other Liberator variants included the C-87 and RY transport, AT-22 trainer, F-7 long-range photo-reconnaissance and PB4Y-1 maritime reconnaissance versions.

The six unarmed LB-30 transport Liberators initially used by the RAF were soon followed by armed variants, beginning with 20 Liberator Mk I aircraft that were equivalents of the B-24A. Some of these were used for maritime reconnaissance, equipped with ASV (Air to Surface Vessel) radar and a ventral gun tray. These were in turn followed, from August 1941, by 139 Liberator Mk II and 260 Liberator Mk III aircraft, also for the maritime reconnaissance role, and 112 B-24Gs for service as Liberator B Mk V bombers and GR Mk V maritime reconnaissance aircraft. The numbers of later Liberator variants delivered to the RAF and Commonwealth air forces were 1302 B-24J, 437 B-24L and 47 B-24M aircraft. The B-24J machines served as Liberator B Mk VI bombers with a ball turret or as Liberator GR Mk VI long-range maritime reconnaissance aircraft, with ASV radar replacing the ball turret, while the equivalent marks based on the B-24L and B-24M were the Liberator B Mk VIII and the Liberator GR Mk VIII. The Liberator bombers served mainly in South-East Asia, where they equipped 14 squadrons, while their maritime reconnaissance counterparts succeeded in closing the 'mid-Atlantic gap', where air cover for the vital Atlantic convoys had hitherto been absent. Also delivered to the RAF were 24 Liberators C Mk VII based on the C-87 transport derivative of the B-24D. One of these, AL504 *Commando*, was the personal transport of Prime Minister Winston Churchill. It was converted from a Mk II for VIP use early in 1941, and in late 1943 was returned to Convair for modification to RY-3 standard.

The B-24 made its operational debut in June 1942 with long-range raids from Egypt against the Romanian oilfields. Although the Boeing B-29 prosecuted the offensive against the Japanese home islands, the Liberator was the principal strategic bomber elsewhere in the Pacific theatre.

Consolidated PBY Catalina

The wingtips on the Catalina would become floats for landing, giving the aircraft stability on water.

This Catalina Mk IVA is fitted with ASV Mk II radar to spot surfaced U-boats. There were two dipole antennae for this system, one under each wing.

The PBY-5/Catalina Mk IVA was powered by a pair of Pratt & Whitney R-1830-82 or -92 Twin Wasp radials. The fairing under the engine nacelle housed the oil cooler.

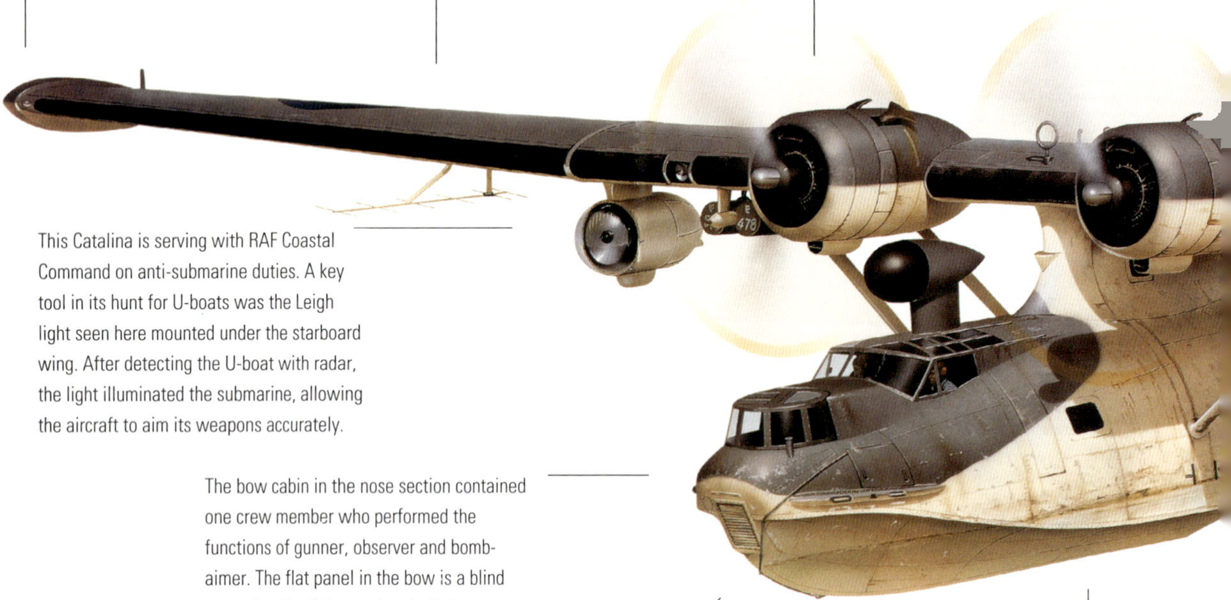

This Catalina is serving with RAF Coastal Command on anti-submarine duties. A key tool in its hunt for U-boats was the Leigh light seen here mounted under the starboard wing. After detecting the U-boat with radar, the light illuminated the submarine, allowing the aircraft to aim its weapons accurately.

The bow cabin in the nose section contained one crew member who performed the functions of gunner, observer and bomb-aimer. The flat panel in the bow is a blind protecting the flat pane bomb-aiming window. The turret is unarmed due to the lack of an air threat at this stage of the war.

The flight deck was occupied by the pilot and co-pilot sitting side-by-side. Directly above them is a teardrop radome housing a surveillance radar.

Behind the flight deck in the central cabin sat the radio operator and navigator. The latter had a table to spread out his charts. Behind them was the rear cabin, extending up into the wing root, which housed the flight engineer. There was also a wardroom complete with crew rest bunks.

The aircraft's markings reveal it to be a Catalina Mk IVA from No. 202 Squadron, RAF Coastal Command, based in Northern Ireland in 1945.

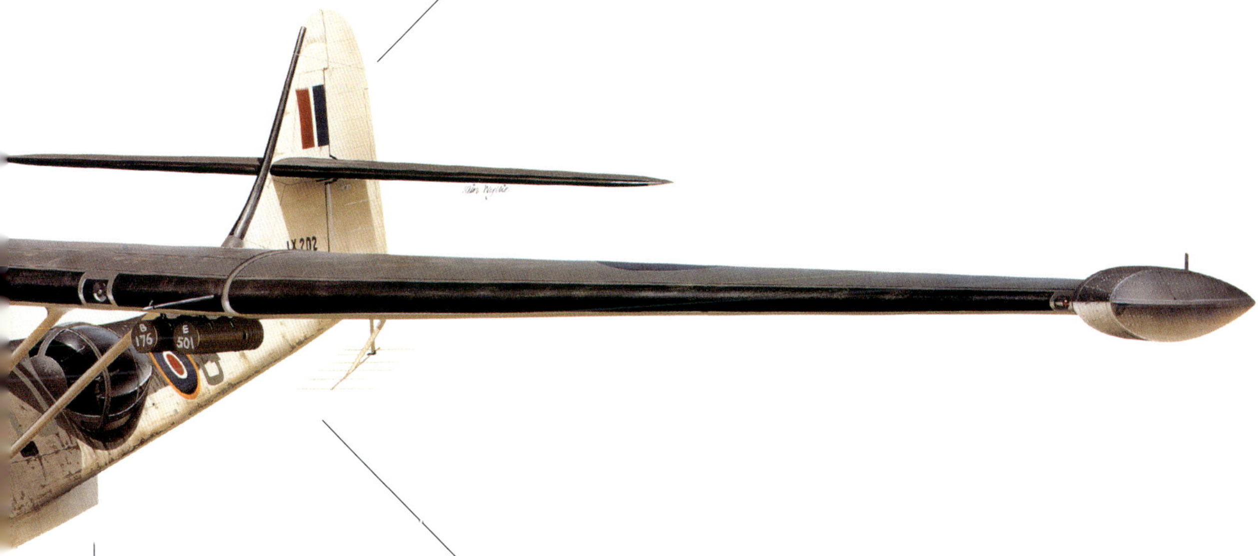

The aircraft is armed with four depth charges. Each hardpoint was stressed for up to 454kg (1000lb), and as well as depth charges the aircraft could carry bombs, torpedoes, and smoke-generators.

A central walkway from the flight deck led to the aft cabin, where the gunner/observers worked. A semi-circular platform allowed them to swing guns through a wide arc. The bulged waist blisters gave them excellent visual coverage of the surrounding area.

On 28 February 1928, the US Navy issued a contract for a prototype flying boat, the XPY-1, to the Consolidated Aircraft Corporation. This aircraft, which was designed for an alternative installation of two or three engines, was the first large monoplane flying boat procured by the USN, and was the initial configuration which eventually evolved into the most outstanding parasol monoplane flying boat of all time, the PBY Catalina. A contract for the construction of the prototype PBY, then known as the XP3Y-1, was issued to Consolidated on 28 October 1933. The aircraft flew for the first time on 21 March 1935, operational deliveries being made to Patrol Squadron VP11F in October 1936. The initial version, the PBY-1, demonstrated its long-range capability when 12 aircraft of Patrol Squadron VP-3 flew from San Diego to Coco Solo in the Panama Canal Zone, a distance of 5297km (3292 miles) in 27 hours and 58 minutes.

The PBY-1, which was fitted with 634kW (850hp) Pratt & Whitney R-1830-64 engines, was followed into service in

Right: The Consoldiated PBY Catalina was one of the most versatile flying boats of all time. It is seen here being pulled up the slipway. Some Catalinas served in a commercial capacity after World War II, and operated successfully in South America.

Type: Maritime reconnaissance amphibious flying boat (PBY-5A)

Crew:	7/9
Powerplant:	two 895kW (1200hp) Pratt & Whitney R-1830-92 Twin Wasp 14-cylinder radial engines
Max speed:	288km/h (179mph) at 2135mph (7000ft)
Time to height:	19 mins 18 secs to 3050m (10,000ft)
Service ceiling:	4480m (14,700ft)
Max range:	4095km (2545 miles)
Wing span:	31.70m (104ft)
Wing area:	130.06m² (1400sq ft)
Length:	19.45m (63ft 8in)
Height:	6.15m (20ft 2in)
Weights:	9485kg (20,910lb) empty; 16,067kg(35,420lb) max t/o
Armament:	two 12.7mm (0.5in) MG in bow turret and one in each beam blister; one 7.7mm (0.303in) MG in ventral tunnel; war load of up to 1814kg (4000lb) of bombs, mines or depth charges, or two torpedoes

9

Above: One of the 18 Consolidated PBY-5 Catalinas which was supplied to the Royal Australian Air Force and assigned to No 11 Squadron. The Catalina aircraft was manufactured in larger numbers than all other flying boats combined.

1937 by 50 PBY-2s, with 746kW (1000hp) Pratt & Whitney engines. Three examples of the next variant, named the PBY-3, were delivered to the USSR in 1938, along with a manufacturing licence. The Soviet version, designated GST and powered by Russian-built 708kW (950hp) M87 engines, was used in the transport role.

The PBY-4, which appeared in 1938, featured the large midships 'blister' observation and gun positions that were to become a well-known characteristic of the PBY. In April 1939 the US Navy ordered an amphibious version, and this became the prototype for the PBY-5A, which was to be widely used in World War II. In July 1939 the RAF received a PBY for evaluation, and this resulted in an order for 50 aircraft similar to the USN's PBY-5. The RAF named them Catalina Mk I, and the US Navy subsequently adopted the name Catalina. The RAF doubled its original order during 1940, and orders also began to flow in from other countries; Australia ordered 18, Canada 50, France 30 and the Netherlands East Indies 36. The variant that fulfilled this initial orders – and ongoing orders for the US Navy – was the PBY-5, with 895kW (1200hp) R-1830-92 radials. The last 33 aircraft of an order for 200 PBY-5s were completed as amphibians to PBY-5A standard. Total production of the PBY-5 was 750, and this was followed by 794 PBY-5As, 56 of which went to the USAF as OA-10s.

On 21 September 1939 the US Navy's Patrol Squadron 21, with 14 PBYs, deployed to the Philippines, becoming the first patrol unit in the Asiatic Fleet since 1932. This squadron, and another that arrived later in the year, formed the nucleus of Patrol Wing 10, formed in the Philippines in December 1940. A few weeks later, in the spring of 1941, the first Catalina Mk I aircraft became operational with RAF Coastal Command, and in May they played a key part in hunting down the German battleship *Bismarck*. On 30 May 1941, the US Navy Patrol Squadron VP-52 began operational patrols over the North Atlantic convoy

routes in the western Atlantic, the US Government having declared a 'neutrality zone', and on 10 December, following America's entry into the war, VP-52 also initiated anti-submarine patrols over the South Atlantic, its Catalinas operating from Natal, Brazil.

In 1942 the RAF and US Navy's Catalina squadrons combined to destroy several U-boats. In June 1942, on the other side of the world, it was reconnaissance by Catalinas that detected the whereabouts of a Japanese carrier task force approaching Midway Island, enabling the Japanese aircraft carriers to be destroyed by strike aircraft, and Catalinas subsequently carried out offensive operations against Japanese forces in the Aleutian Islands.

Lend-Lease supplies to Britain included 225 PBY-5Bs (Catalina IA) and 97 Catalina IVAs, the latter fitted with ASV (Air to Surface Vessel) radar. Further development of the Catalina resulted in the PBY-6A (235 aircraft) with revised armament, an enlarged tail and a search radar scanner mounted over the cockpit, and the Naval Aircraft Factory PBN-1 Nomad (156 aircraft), built to PBY-5A standard but featuring improvements such as a larger tail unit, greater fuel capacity and better armament. Most of these aircraft were shipped to the USSR. The PBY-5A was also built in Canada as the Canadian Vickers PVB-1A. Production of the Catalina, which ended in April 1945, included 2398 by Consolidated as well as 892 by other manufacturers, plus an unknown number which were built in the USSR as the GST.

Many Catalinas found their way into civil use in the years after the end of World War II. Although the aircraft was not a particularly economical type for commercial use, it proved to be an excellent transport vehicle in such areas as the Amazon basin and the island groups off South-East Asia. The six aircraft which were owned by Panair do Brasil operated very successfully as 22-passenger transports along the Amazon River, until the company was dissolved in 1965.

Below: PBY Catalinas pictured in the Pacific Theatre in the early months of the war with Japan. It was a Catalina that detected the Japanese task force approaching Midway Island in June 1942, with disastrous results for the enemy.

Curtiss P-40 Warhawk

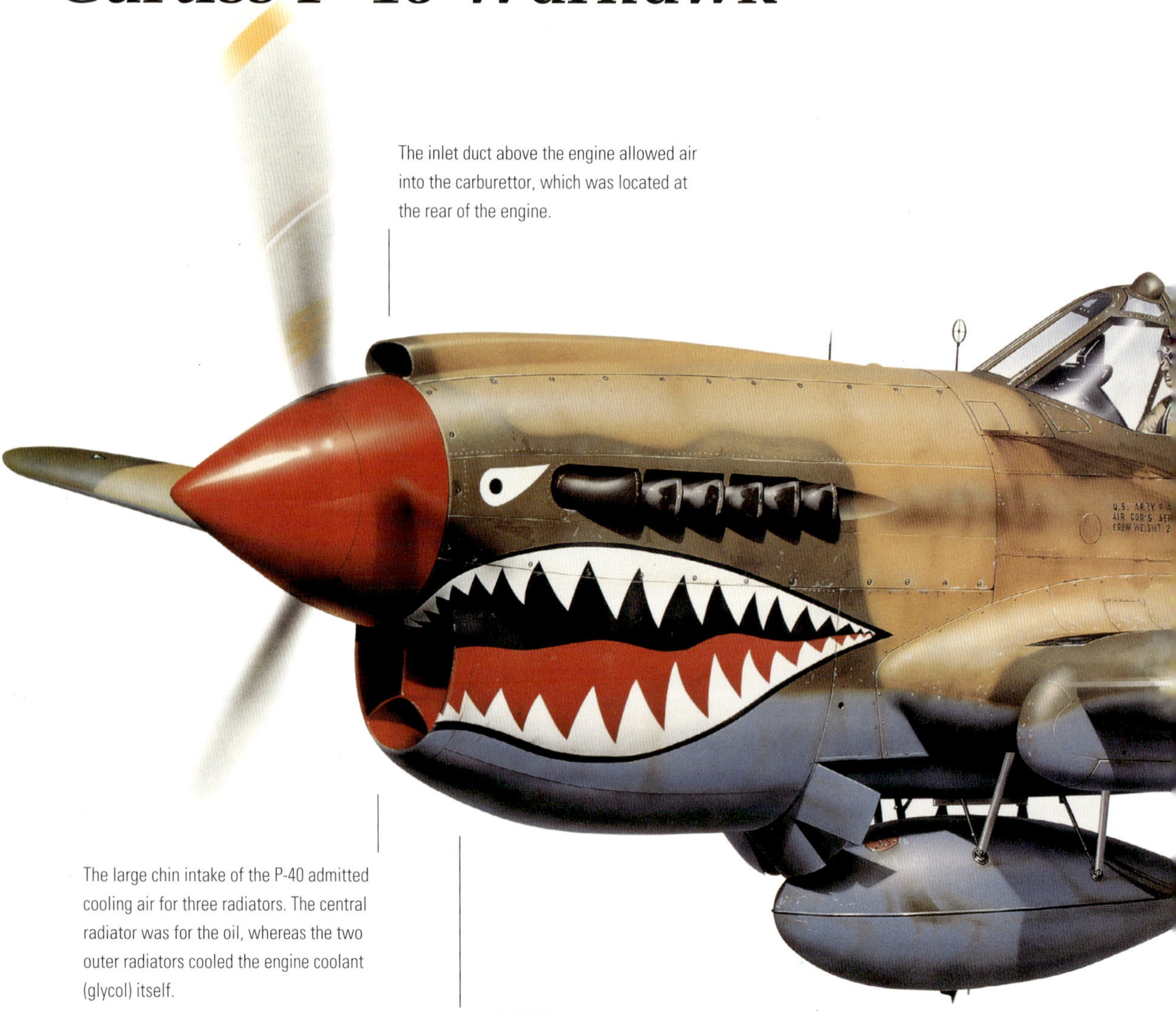

The inlet duct above the engine allowed air into the carburettor, which was located at the rear of the engine.

The large chin intake of the P-40 admitted cooling air for three radiators. The central radiator was for the oil, whereas the two outer radiators cooled the engine coolant (glycol) itself.

The P-40E Warhawk was powered by an Allison V-1710-39 12-cylinder inline engine. Most P-40 variants were Allison powered, apart from the P-40F, which used the Packard V-1650 licence-built Merlin.

A drop tank was often carried by P-40s in the Chinese theater to increase range. In front of the tank are the aircraft's cooling gills, which could be controlled to allow greater amounts of air to pass through at low speeds or when the engine was hot.

The pilot sat in a heavily-framed cockpit with glazed rear-vision panels behind him. A mirror was mounted on the cockpit frame to check the aircraft's rear. He had a reflector gunsight, but an emergency ring and bead sight was also provided.

A typical example of the tail art used by the USAF pilots in the theatre.

The markings show this P-40E to belong to the 76th Fighter Squadron of the 23rd Fighter Group serving in China and flying against the Japanese.

The P-40E was armed with six 12.7mm (0.5in) machine guns, three in each wing. Each gun was provided with 235 rounds.

Although never an outstanding combat aircraft, the Curtiss P-40 served in every theatre of war. Moreover, it was available in quantity at a critical period of World War II, when more advanced combat aircraft that would eventually take up its many roles were still at the testing stage. The P-40 originated as a development of the radial-engined Curtiss P-36A Hawk, 210 examples of which had been ordered from the Curtiss-Wright Corporation's Airplane Division by the US Army Air Corps. In July 1937 the USAAC ordered the prototype of a possible variant, designated XP-40 and powered by the new liquid-cooled Allison V-1710 12-cylinder Vee-type engine. The tenth production P-36A was fitted with the new powerplant on the assembly line, and this aircraft flew for the first time in October 1938. The prototype XP-40 proved to be some 48km/h (30mph) faster than the P-36A, and although it lacked some of the latter's manoeuvrability, its handling characteristics were praised by the USAAC test pilots who flew it. On 27 April 1939 the USAAC awarded Curtiss-Wright a contract for 524 production P-40s, the largest order ever placed for an American fighter up to that time; this was subsequently scaled down to 200, all of which were delivered to the Air Corps by September 1940. Production aircraft differed only in minor detail from the prototype, being fitted with the 776kW (1040hp) Allison V-1710-33 engine. One major shortcoming was that the aircraft totally lacked armoured protection for the pilot and the main fuel tank, situated directly behind his seat. In short, the early model P-40 was a death trap.

Despite this, France's Armée de l'Air – which, during the 'phoney war' period of 1939–40 was already operating the nimble Curtiss Hawk 75A (P-36A) – placed an order for 140 P-40s, these being given the export designation Hawk 81A-1. The French machines were to have various items of French equipment, but the most important change was that the standard armament of two Colt-Browning 12.7mm (0.5in) machineguns, mounted in the nose decking of the USAAC machines, were to be supplemented by four wing-mounted 7.62mm (0.3in) FN-Browning machineguns, housed in the inboard wing panels outboard of the wheel wells. Before the first Hawk 81A-1 could be delivered, however, France fell, and the full order was taken over by the British Purchasing Commission on behalf of the RAF. Although considered unsuitable for operational use by Fighter Command, the P-40s were fitted with four wing-mounted Browning 7.7mm (0.303in) machineguns and allocated to Army Co-operation Command as the Tomahawk I, for use in the tactical reconnaissance role. They served until 1942, when they were replaced by another American type, the North American Mustang I.

Deliveries of P-40s to the USAAC resumed in February 1941, the armament now having been brought up to the standard of the batch intended for France by the addition of four 7.62mm (0.303in) machineguns in the wings. An armoured windscreen and armour plating for the pilot were also fitted. The modified aircraft, with the designation P-40B and 130, were delivered to the USAAC, together with 110 identical aircraft which went to the RAF as the Hawk 81A-2, to be known as the Tomahawk IIA in RAF service. Since it used the same powerplant as the original production version, the P-40B, with its extra equipment, was somewhat heavier, empty weight having risen from 2435kg (5368lb) to 2532kg (5582lb). Inevitably, this had an adverse effect on the aircraft's handling characteristics and on its maximum speed, which fell from 574 to 566km/h (357 to 352mph) at 4575m (15,000ft).

Below: Curtiss P-40 of the American Volunteer Group, China-Burma, 1942. The AVG and the RAF joined forces in a gallant but vain attempt to stem the Japanese onslaught in Burma, the AVG in particular inflicting heavy losses on the enemy bombers.

The next P-40 variant was the P-40C, which was fitted with larger, self-sealing fuel tanks and two more wing guns; 193 went to the USAAF (as the USAAC had now become) and 930 to the RAF as the Tomahawk IIB, although 146 of these were diverted to the Soviet Union following the German invasion of June 1941 and another 100 to the American Volunteer Group (AVG), operating in China. In all, 2430 P-40s were allocated to the USSR in World War II, of which 2097 were actually delivered; many were lost in transit. The RAF's Tomahawk IIBs had the fuselage-mounted armament deleted, retaining only the four wing guns. These aircraft performed sterling work in the tactical support role in the Western Desert, serving with Nos 94, 112, 208, 250 and 260 Squadrons of the RAF, and Nos 2 and 4 (South African) and No 3 (Australian) Squadrons of the Desert Air Force. P-40Cs saw action with the 15th Pursuit Group, the 24th Pursuit Group, and with the American Volunteer Group, the 'Flying Tigers', which began operations in 1941 from Kunming, China and Mingaladon, Burma in defence of the Burma Road and the Sino-Burmese border. On 20 December, the AVG's Warhawks destroyed 6 out of 10 Japanese bombers which were attacking Kunming.

The P-40D's four wing guns were upgraded to 12.7mm (0.5in) calibre and the nose armament removed. Provision was also made for the carriage of bombs under the wings or fuselage. Only 22 P-40Ds went to the USAAF as the Hawk 87A Warhawk, but 560 were allocated to the RAF, which renamed them Kittyhawk I. The USAAF preferred the P-40E, with six wing guns. It ordered 820 of this model; another 1500 became Kittyhawk IAs. Installation of the Packard-Merlin engine produced the P-40F, and 1311 were built. The RAF received 21 P-40Ks as well as 600 P-40Ms (Kittyhawk III) and 586 P-40Ns (Kittyhawk IV). US production – which included 1300 P-40Ks, with increased fin area, 700 P-40Ls (with only four guns), and 4219 P-40Ns with a 1014kW (1360hp) V-1710-81 engine – would end in December 1944, after a total of 13,738 aircraft had been built.

Above: The Curtiss P-40 suffered from the temperament of its Allison engine, which could be unreliable. In fighter-versus-fighter combat, it was outclassed by contemporary enemy types, but performed well in the ground attack role.

Type: Fighter/fighter-bomber (P-40N)	
Crew:	1
Powerplant:	one 1014kW (1360hp) Allison V-1710-81 V-12 engine
Max speed:	609km/h (378mph) at 3200m (10,500ft)
Time to height:	6 mins 42 secs to 4570m (14,993ft)
Service ceiling:	11,580m (38,000ft)
Max range:	386km (240 miles)
Wing span:	11.38m (37ft 3in)
Wing area:	21.92m² (236sq ft)
Length:	10.16m (33ft 3in)
Height:	3.76m (12ft 3in)
Weights:	2722kg (6000lb) empty; 5171kg (11,400lb) max t/o
Armament:	six 12.7mm (0.5in) MG in the wings; bomb load of up to three 227kg (500lb) bombs

Douglas SBD-1 Dauntless

In front of the pilot were two 12.7mm (0.5in) fixed forward-firing machine guns. The breeches extended into the cockpit, allowing the pilot to clear any blockages and recock the guns.

The pilot sat high in the cockpit with an armoured backplate, but no bulletproof windscreen. A telescopic sight was used for aiming both bombs and guns.

The Dauntless was powered by a Wright R-1820-32 Cyclone. The oil was cooled by an undernose intake, while the large intake on top of the engine cowl fed air into the carburettor. Underneath the fuselage was the large bomb cradle, which swung the central bomb clear of the aircraft's propellor during a dive attack.

The underwing pylons of the Dauntless could carry a 454kg (1000lb) bomb each. The main weapon (either a bomb or torpedo) was carried under the centre section.

The observer/gunner faced to the rear, and could pull the aft section of the canopy to the rear to cover him after stowing his gun. The gun was a 7.62mm (0.3in) machine gun with 600 rounds.

The markings reveal this aircraft to be the commanding officer's of Marine Bombing Squadron VMB-1, the second unit to receive the Dauntless. The squadron was renumbered VMSB-132 later in 1941.

Although equipped with a functioning tailhook for carrier landings, the Dauntless was not considered carrier-capable, and was delivered to the Marine Corps.

Above: The Douglas SBD Dauntless, despite giving an indifferent performance, made an enormous contribution to the eventual Allied victory in the Pacific. During this conflict, it was accredited with sinking a greater tonnage of shipping than any other type.

The evolution of the Douglas SBD Dauntless began in November 1934, when a Northrop design team based a proposal for a new Navy dive-bomber on the Northrop A-17, a light attack bomber about to enter production for the US Army Air Corps. A protoype was ordered and flew in July 1935 with the designation XBT-1. In February 1936 an order was placed for 54 production BT-1s with 615kW (825hp) Wright R-1535-94 engines. The last aircraft of this batch was fitted with a 746kW (1000hp) R-1820-32 engine and completed as the XBT-2. Further modifications were carried out, mainly to the landing gear and vertical tail surfaces, and when the Northrop Corporation became a division of Douglas on 31 August 1937 the aircraft was re-designated XSBD-1. Delivery of 57 SBD-1s to the US Marine Corps began in mid-1940, the aircraft now having been fitted with the large, perforated dive flaps that were a distinctive feature of the Dauntless. At the same time, the US Navy ordered 87 SBD-2s with extra fuel tankage, protective armour and autopilots. Both variants were armed with two 7.62mm (0.3in) machineguns in the upper engine cowling and one in the rear cockpit. Bombs up to 454kg (1000lb) could be carried in a cradle beneath the fuselage; maximum bomb load was 544kg (1200lb).

Delivery of the SBD-2 began in November 1940, the aircraft being followed into service by the SBD-3, which had a forward-firing armament of two 12.7mm (0.5in) guns and R-1820-52 engines. Delivery of the first 174 SBD-3s began in March 1941, the US Navy subsequently receiving a further 410. The Dauntless formed the attack element of the Navy's carrier air groups at the time of the Japanese strike on Pearl Harbor, and in the early months of 1942 the SBDs, operating from the carriers *Lexington* and *Yorktown*, carried out a number of offensive operations against enemy shore installations and shipping. In May 1942, during the Battle of the Coral Sea, SBDs joined with TBD Devastator torpedo aircraft to sink the Japanese light carrier *Shoho* and damage the fleet carrier *Shokaku*, forcing the Japanese to abandon plans to occupy Port Moresby, New Guinea. In June 1942, during the Battle of Midway, the two aircraft types again joined forces for co-ordinated dive-bombing and torpedo attacks on units of the Japanese fleet, and it was the SBDs from the carriers *Enterprise*, *Hornet* and *Yorktown* that scored the major successes, sinking the Japanese carriers *Akagi*, *Kaga* and *Soryu* and damaging the *Hiryu* so badly that she had to be sunk by her own forces. During this battle, the Devastator squadrons suffered appalling attrition, losing 35 out of 41 aircraft. Torpedo Squadron 8 lost all 15.

The attrition rate of the Dauntless squadrons, on the other hand, was the lowest of any US carrier aircraft in the Pacific, thanks to the SBD's ability to absorb an amazing amount of battle damage. Later in the war, when the Curtiss SB2C Helldiver had replaced them in the dive-bombing role, they were assigned to escort carriers, carrying out anti-submarine warfare or close support missions. In October 1942 a new version, the SBD-4, made its appearance; 780 were delivered, fitted with radar and radio-navigation equipment. They were followed by the major production variant, the SBD-5, which had a more powerful 895kW (1200hp) engine. The US Navy took delivery of 2965 SBD-5s, while 65 SBD-5As, originally built to a Navy contract, were delivered to the US Marine Corps instead. One SBD-5, fitted with a 1007kW (1350hp) R-1820-66 engine, was used as the prototype for 450 SBD-6 aircraft, with which Douglas ended its Dauntless production in July 1944.

Overall production of the Dauntless was 5936 aircraft, including 178 for the USAAC, as the A-24, the A-24A and the A-24B. The main difference between these and their naval counterparts was the deletion of the arrester hook; in general, they corresponded to the SBD-3, SBD-4 and SBD-5. The Army craft saw little action in the Pacific War, most being deployed with units responsible for the protection of the Panama Canal Zone, and in due course they were relegated to training and communications duties. Eighteen SBD-3s were also issued to the Royal New Zealand Air Force, followed by 27 SBD-4s and 23 SBD-5s. Thirty-two SBD-5s were also supplied to the French Navy, and 40 A-24Bs to the Armée de l'Air, but they were all employed in training and other second-line duties. Nine SBD-5s were also delivered to the Royal Navy.

The SBD Dauntless helped turn the tide of the conflict, in Midway and in the American victory in the battle for Guadalcanal. Ultimately, it sank a greater tonnage of Japanese shipping than any other aircraft.

Type: Carrier- and land-based dive bomber (SBD-5)	
Crew:	2
Powerplant:	one 895kW (1200hp) Wright R-1820-60 Cyclone nine-cylinder radial engine
Max speed:	410km/h (255mph)
Time to height:	8 mins to 3050m (10,000ft)
Service ceiling:	7780m (25,530ft)
Max range:	2519km (1565 miles)
Wing span:	12.66m (41ft 5in)
Wing area:	30.19m² (325sq ft)
Length:	10.09m (33ft 1in)
Height:	4.14m (13ft 6in)
Weights:	2905kg (6404lb) empty; 4853kg (10,700lb) max t/o
Armament:	two 12.7mm (0.5in) fixed forward-firing MG in the upper part of the forward fuselage; two trainable 7.62mm (0.3in) MG in rear cockpit; external bomb or depth charge load of 1021kg (2250lb)

Below: A SBD-3 Dauntless of the 'Scouting Six', VB-6, aboard the USS Enterprise, seen in approximately March 1942. A few months later the dive-bombers of VB-6 would be involved in the sinking of four Japanese carriers at the Battle of Midway.

Grumman Wildcat

Grumman F4Fs were powered by a Pratt & Whitney R-1830-86 Twin Wasp two-row 14-cylinder radial engine. Gills on the rear of the engine cowling could be moved to control the amount of air entering the engine housing.

The F4F was initially designed with fixed undercarriage, but at the last moment this was changed to a retractable version. However, to retract or extend the wheels required the pilot to wind a wheel in the cockpit 28 times, while flying with the joystick in his left hand.

Early F4Fs had two Browning 12.7mm (0.5in) machine guns in the fuselage, but these were later deleted in favour of six guns mounted in the wings.

The pilot had good forward vision, but the cockpit fairing hampered any attempt to check his tail. The F4F was equipped with a reflector gunsight.

This aircraft is a F4F-3 Wildcat from Marine Fighting Squadron 121 flying from Tafuna in Samoa. These early Wildcats did not have folding wings due to their short wingspan.

Above: The Grumman F4F Wildcat was the US Navy's most important fighter at the time of the Japanese attack on Pearl Harbor, and it quite literally held the line for the Allies in the Pacific, especially at the battles for Midway and Guadalcanal.

In March 1936, the Grumman Aircraft Corporation was awarded a development contract to build an all-metal biplane fighter, the XF4F-1, for the US Navy. However, the biplane configuration was quickly shelved in favour of a monoplane design, the XF4F-2. This flew on 2 September 1937, powered by a 783kW (1050hp) Pratt & Whitney R-1830-66 Twin Wasp radial engine. The US Navy decided to develop the aircraft still further by installing a supercharged XR-1830-76 engine in a much re-designed airframe. The revamped machine, designated XF4F-3, flew for the first time on 12 February 1939. In August, the Navy issued its first production contract for 53 Grumman F4F-3 Wildcats, as the fighter had been named. The first production aircraft flew in February 1940, but deliveries were slow. By the end of 1940 only 22 Wildcats had been handed over to Navy fighter squadrons VF-4 and VF-7, these units embarking on the USS *Ranger* and USS *Wasp* respectively.

In 1939, meanwhile, France – which had one aircraft carrier in commission and two more under construction – had expressed an interest in acquiring 100 Wildcats under the export designation G-36A. Since the Twin Wasp engine was in short supply, the French machines were to be powered by the 895kW (1200hp) R-1820-G205A Cyclone. The order was later reduced to 81, and flight testing of the first of these aircraft was still in progress when France was overrun, so the order was taken over by the British Purchasing Commission on behalf of the Royal Navy, in whose service the F4F-3 was named Martlet I. The first of these aircraft was delivered on 27 July 1940, a month before the US Navy received its first Wildcat. In October No 804 Squadron began re-arming with the Martlet at Hatson, in the Orkey Islands, and scored an early success when two of its aircraft shot down a Junkers Ju 88 over the naval base at Scapa Flow. In April 1941 30 G-36As ordered by Greece were also diverted to Britain as Martlet IIIs, these aircraft having been offloaded at Gibraltar when the Germans invaded the Balkans. Neither the F4F-3 nor the Martlet I had folding wings, but these were incorporated in all but 10 of an order for 100 Martlet IIs (G-36As) placed by Britain in 1940. The total number of Martlets of all marks supplied to Britain reached 1191, including 220 Martlet IVs (F4F-4Bs with Cyclone engines), 311 as Martlet Vs and 370 Wildcat VIs, the American name having by then been adopted by the Fleet Air Arm. This was the British equivalent of the F4F-8, with a 895kW (1200hp) R-1820-56 Cyclone engine and taller fin and rudder.

In American service, the Wildcat with folding wings received the designation F4F-4, the first example flying on 14 April 1941 and going to fighter squadron VF-42 in May

Above: A Grumman F4F-3 Wildcat from VF-7 flying from USS Wasp in December 1940. In April 1942 Wasp took part in the relief of Malta, flying off fighters to the island. The ship was lost during the battle for Guadalcanal in September 1942.

for trials on the USS *Yorktown*. As 1941 drew to a close, the Wildcat was rapidly replacing all other US carrier-borne fighters. At the time of the Japanese attack on Pearl Harbor, Wildcats belonging to Marine fighter squadron VMF-211 were divided between Oahu, where nine were destroyed or damaged on the ground during the attack, and Wake Island, where seven of eight aircraft on the ground suffered a similar fate. Four survivors put up a desperate, heroic defence before they were overwhelmed.

Type: Naval fighter	
Crew:	1
Powerplant:	one 895kW (1200hp) Pratt & Whitney R-1830-66 radial
Max speed:	512km/h (318mph) at 5913m (19,400ft)
Initial climb rate:	594m (1950ft) per minute
Service ceiling:	10,638m (34,900ft)
Max range:	1239km (770 miles)
Wing span:	11.58m (38ft)
Wing area:	24.15m² (260sq ft)
Length:	8.76m (28ft 7in)
Height:	3.61m (11ft 8in)
Weights:	2612kg (5758lb) empty; 3607kg (7952lb) max t/o
Armament:	six 12.7mm (0.5in) MG in wing; external bomb load up to 91kg (200lb)

The first encounters between the Wildcat and the Zero showed that the F4F was inferior to the Japanese fighter on almost every count. An extract from an official US Navy comparison between the two types stated that:

'The Zeke [Zero] is superior to the F4F-4 in speed and climb at all altitudes above 1000ft [305m] and is superior in service ceiling and range. Close to sea level, with the Wildcat in neutral blower, the two aircraft are equal in level speed. During dives the two aircraft are also equal with the exception that the Zeke's engine cuts out during pushovers. There is no comparison between the turning circles of the two aircraft due to the relative wing loading and low stalling speed of the Zeke. In view of the foregoing, the F4F type in combat with the Zeke is basically dependent on mutual support, internal protection, and pullouts and turns at high speed where minimum radius is limited by structural or physiological effects of acceleration.'

Although very robust and capable of withstanding a huge amount of battle damage, it needed a highly experienced pilot at the controls to give the Wildcat a fighting chance of survival in combat with the Japanese fighters. Nevertheless, a number of US Navy pilots scored several noteworthy victories flying the Wildcat; on 20 February 1942, flying from the carrier USS *Lexington*, Lieutenant Edward H. O'Hare destroyed five Japanese bombers over Rabaul. As American pilots gained experience during 1942, their superior tactics and teamwork began to have a telling effect on the course of the Pacific air war. In US Marine Corps hands, the Wildcat will be remembered for its defence of Guadalcanal in the latter half of 1942.

The total number of Wildcats built, including 21 examples of the F4F-7, an unarmed reconnaissance version, was 7885.

Grumman Hellcat

This Hellcat wears the all-over midnight blue camouflage which replaced the standard Pacific colour scheme of sea blue and pale undersides later in the war.

The markings show that this Hellcat is an F6F-5P serving with Fighter Squadron VF-84, attached to USS *Bunker Hill*, in February 1945. The yellow cowling markings were adopted for attacks on Tokyo, and were removed shortly afterwards.

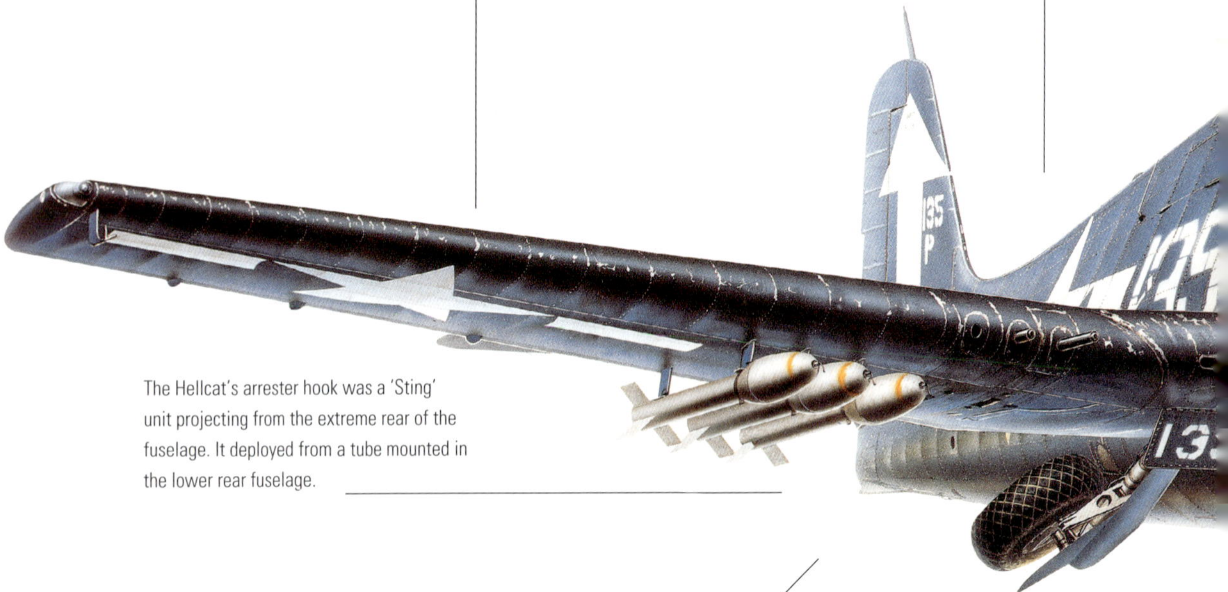

The Hellcat's arrester hook was a 'Sting' unit projecting from the extreme rear of the fuselage. It deployed from a tube mounted in the lower rear fuselage.

Almost all Hellcats were armed with six Browning 12.7mm (0.5in) machine guns in the wings, slightly staggered and armed with 400 rounds per gun.

The Hellcat's undercarriage was reinforced for carrier operations, and rotated through 90° to lie flat within the wing space when retracted during flight. The tailwheel was also fully retractable.

The pilot sat under a sliding canopy surrounded by armour, particularly to the rear. However, rearwards visibility was lacking, with no rear-view mirror. The pilot was equipped with a reflector gunsight.

The Hellcat was powered by a Pratt & Whitney R-2800-10W Double Wasp radial, with two rows of nine cylinders.

Three auxiliary intakes under the engine cowl fed cooling air for the engine oil (centre) and supercharger (two side intakes). Cooling gills on the engine cowling could be opened to increase the airflow over the cylinders themselves.

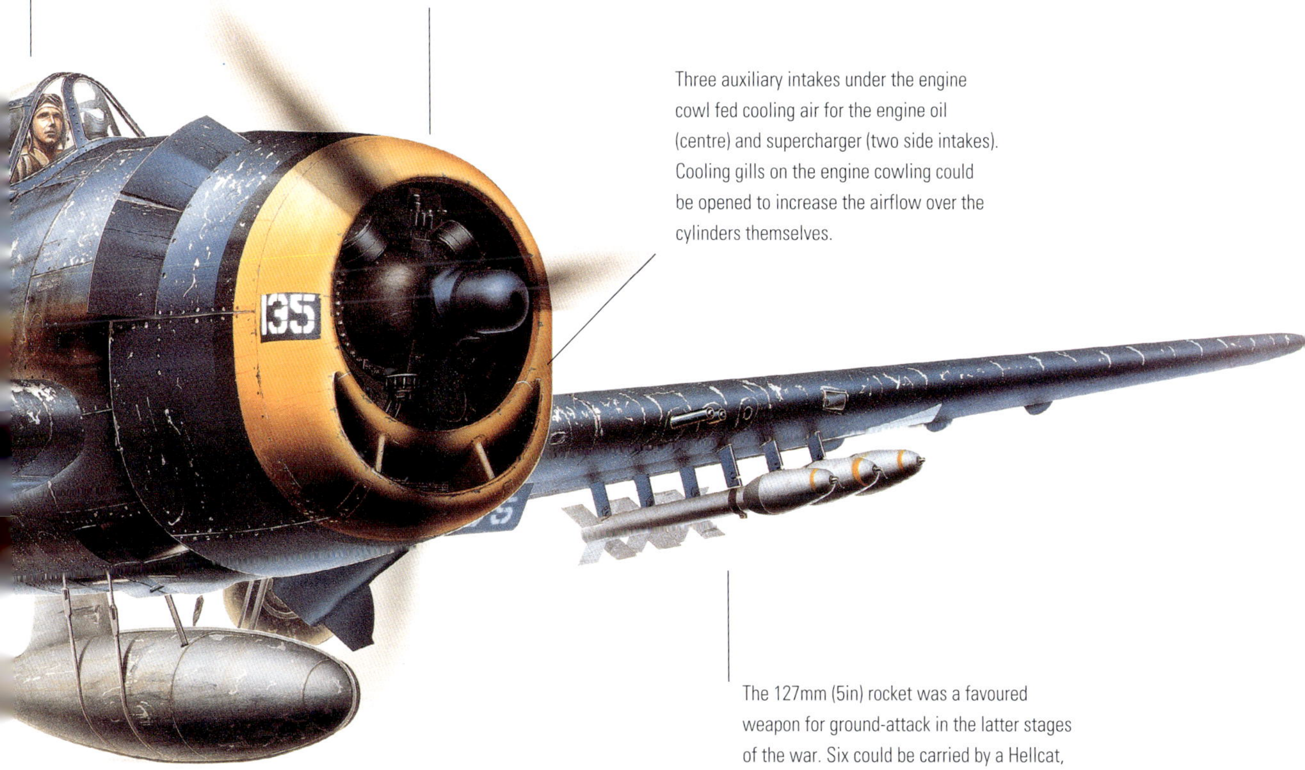

The 127mm (5in) rocket was a favoured weapon for ground-attack in the latter stages of the war. Six could be carried by a Hellcat, and these rockets were much used during the attacks on Iwo Jima and Okinawa.

Carrier fighters often carried drop tanks during operations in the Pacific to lengthen their patrol times, and this Hellcat is no exception. The tanks could be jettisoned in case of combat.

The Grumman Hellcat has an assured place in history as the fighter that changed the course of the Pacific air war. Before the Hellcat made its operational debut over Marcus Island on 31 August 1943, operating with Navy Fighter Squadron VF-5 from the USS *Yorktown*, it was the Mitsubishi Zero that had ruled the Pacific sky. The appearance of the Hellcat – the robust American fighter establishing a kill ratio in the region of 19:1 – was to change the picture completely.

Above: A Grumman Hellcat of the Royal Navy, pictured in 'invasion stripes', in June 1944. Hellcats operating from the Royal Navy's escort carriers were responsible for helping to provide air cover during the D-Day landings in Normandy.

Below: The F6F-5 Hellcat, here in 'midnite blue', was the largest production version, 7868 examples being built. The Royal Navy received a total of 932. Some F6F-5s were equipped for nightfighting.

On 30 June 1941, less than six months before the Japanese attack on Pearl Harbor, the US Navy placed an order with the Grumman Aircraft Engineering Corporation for a prototype shipboard fighter to be designated XF6F-1. The aircraft was intended to be a replacement for the Grumman F4F Wildcat, which had begun to enter service with the USN at the end of 1940. The Grumman design team was already engaged in design study work for a successor to the F4F, but early combat experience against the Zero fighter led to some important changes being made to the basic concept, and it was as the XF6F-3 that the definitive prototype was rolled out to make its first flight on 26 June 1942. The aircraft's engine was a very powerful 1491kW (2000hp) Pratt & Whitney R-2800-10 Double Wasp 18-cylinder radial, and its fuselage was an immensely strong all-metal monocoque structure with two vertical keels positioned either side of the centreline. The pressed flange aluminium alloy frames were riveted to these keel members, extruding aluminium alloy stringers completing the basic structure. Mounted in low-mid position, the threespar, all-metal wing, with flush riveted alloy skinning, comprised five principal assemblies; the section traversing the fuselage beneath the cockpit and housing the self-sealing fuel tanks, two stub centre sections providing the attachment points and accommodation for the main undercarriage members, and detachable outer panels arranged to swivel at the forward spar and fold aft along the fuselage sides. All control surfaces were of

metal construction, the rudder and elevators themselves being fabric covered; split flaps were fitted between the ailerons and the fuselage, and the fully retractable main undercarriage units retracted aft, turning through 90 degrees to lie flush within the centre-section wells. The craft's armament comprised six 12.7mm (0.50in) Colt-Browning machineguns with 400 rounds per gun, three guns being mounted outboard of each wing fold point; a total of 96kg (212lb) of armour protection was provided for the cockpit and other vital points.

First deliveries of the Grumman F6F-3 Hellcat, as the fighter was now known, were made to VF-9 aboard the USS *Essex* on 16 January 1943 and, as already mentioned, the aircraft saw its first combat over Marcus, one of the Caroline Islands, on 31 August. From the summer of 1943 the replacement of the Wildcat by the Hellcat in the USN's fighter squadrons was rapid, and by the end of the year 2545 F6F-3s had been delivered. Britain was to receive 252 F6F-3s under the terms of Lend-Lease; the first examples entered service with No 800 Squadron of the Fleet Air Arm in July 1943. In the following December, operating from the light escort carrier HMS *Emperor*, the squadron carried out anti-shipping operations off the Norwegian coast.

In the Pacific, the Hellcat played a prominent role in all US naval operations, in particular the Battle of the Philippine Sea (19/20 June 1944). In this action, naval aircraft from nine Japanese aircraft carriers, together with shore-based aircraft, launched a massive air attack against the US Task Force 58. In a battle that became known as the 'Marianas Turkey Shoot', American combat air patrols and AA fire destroyed 325 enemy aircraft, including 220 of the 328 launched by the carriers. American losses were 16 Hellcats in combat and 7 other aircraft destroyed by Japanese fighters or ground fire.

Nightfighter variants of the F6F-3 were the F6F-3E with APS-4 radar which was housed in a pod beneath the starboard wing, and the F6F-3N with the APS-6. In total, 18 F6F-3Es and 205 F6F-3Ns were built, and these aircraft became part of the total number of F6F-3s which were manufactured before production switched to the improved F6F-5 in April 1944.

The F6F-5 was fitted with a Pratt & Whitney R-2800-10W engine, capable of developing an emergency power of 1491kW (2200hp) by using water injection. The F6F-5 had a re-designed engine cowling, an improved windshield, additional armour behind the pilot (which increased the total armour weight to 110kg/242lb), new ailerons, a strengthened tail assembly, and provision for two 454kg (1000lb) bombs beneath the centre section. Provision was also made for six 12.7cm (5in) rocket projectiles, and late production F6F-5s had 20mm (0.9in) cannon in place of the two inboard 12.7mm (0.5in) guns.

The F6F-5 began to reach the Pacific task forces in the summer of 1944, and 6436 examples of this variant had been built when production ended in November 1945; about one-sixth were F6F-5N nightfighters. The Royal Navy took delivery of 930 F6F-5s as Hellcat IIs, and two squadrons, Nos 891 and 892, were armed with the nightfighter version. Two examples of an experimental version, the XF6F-6, powered by a 1566kW (2100hp) R-2800-18W engine, were built and flown, and some Hellcats (designated F6F-5K) were converted for use as attack drones during the Korean War. In all, 12,272 Hellcats were built.

Right: An F-6F-5 Hellcat is waved off the deck of a US carrier at the start of a sortie. The F6F's finest hours came during what would become known as the 'Marianas Turkey Shoot' in 1944, during which it decimated waves of Japanese attack aircraft.

Type: Naval fighter	
Crew:	1
Powerplant:	one 1491kW (2000hp) Pratt & Whitney R-2800-10W radial engine
Max Speed:	612km/h (380mph) at 7132m (23,400ft)
Initial climb rate:	908m (2980ft) per minute
Service ceiling:	11,369m (37,300ft)
Max range:	1521km (945 miles)
Wing span:	13.05m (42ft 8in)
Wing area:	31.03m² (334sq ft)
Length:	10.24m (33ft 6in)
Height:	3.99m (13ft 1in)
Weights:	4190kg (9238lb) empty
Armament:	six 12.7mm (0.5in) MG in wings, or two 20mm (0.79in) cannon and four 12.7mm (0.5in), plus provision for two 453kg (1000lb) bombs or six 12.7cm (5in) RPs

Lockheed A-29 Hudson

The main defence against enemy fighters was provided by the dorsal turret, a Boulton Paul 'C' Mk II mounting a pair of Browning 7.7mm (0.303in) machine guns.

The markings show this to be a Hudson Mk VI in service with No 48 Squadron, RAF Coastal Command. The squadron was based at Gibraltar, flying missions in support of the 'Torch' landings in North Africa.

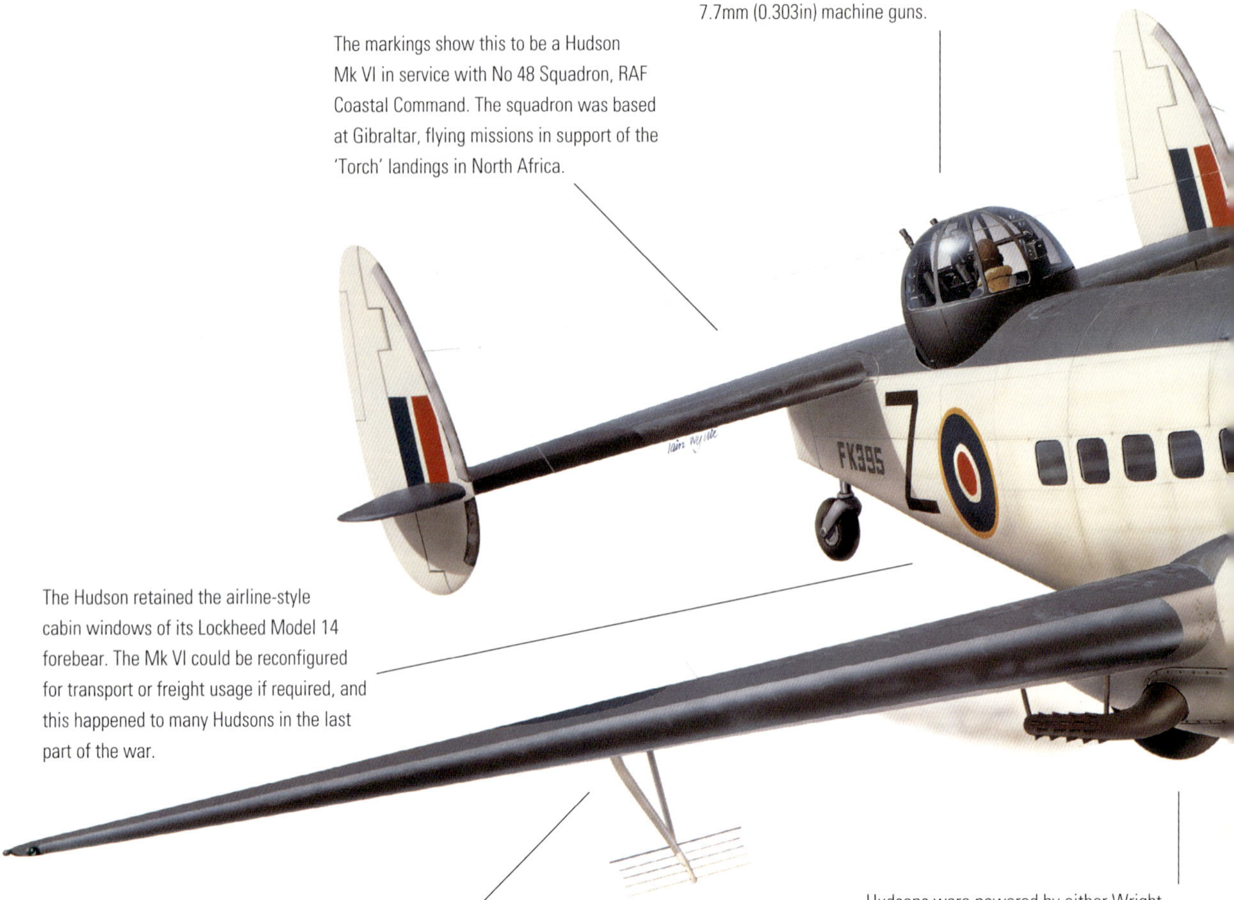

The Hudson retained the airline-style cabin windows of its Lockheed Model 14 forebear. The Mk VI could be reconfigured for transport or freight usage if required, and this happened to many Hudsons in the last part of the war.

Hudsons were powered by either Wright Cyclone or Pratt & Whitney Twin Wasp radial engines. The Mk VI used the Twin Wasps. The scoop above the engine is for the carburettor, while the intake under the engine is for air to cool the oil.

One of the three antennae for the ASV radar system fitted to the Hudsons from 1940 onwards. The radar could detect surfaced U-boats in bad weather or at night.

A loop antenna on the top of the fuselage was used for the direction-finder. Behind this was an astrodome used for taking sextant readings.

The flight deck contained the pilot and co-pilot sitting side-by-side. The co-pilot's seat could fold down to give access to the nose section during flight. The radio operator sat directly behind the pilot.

In the roof of the glazed section were two 7.7mm (0.303in) machine guns which were fired by the pilot. The Mk VI also had provision for rockets to be mounted under the wings.

The glazed nose section was occupied by the navigator, who had a seat and table for his charts. Under his seat was a flat pane window for bomb-aiming.

The Mk VI could carry 454kg (1000lb) of bombs or other stores in the bomb bay. The anti-submarine bomb was the most common weapon, but other stores include float markers (seen here) used to indicate the position of U-boats.

Above: Lockheed Hudson Mk VI in RAF Coastal Command colours in 1944. The aircraft has ASV radar and eight rockets as armament. By this time the Hudson was being phased out in the Atlantic, but it served in the Mediterranean until the end of the war.

The Lockheed Hudson was a military version of the Lockheed Model 14 twin-engined commercial airliner, one of the success stories of the late 1930s. It was developed at short notice in 1938 to meet a British requirement for a maritime reconnaissance aircraft to replace the Avro Anson in the squadrons of RAF Coastal Command, the Anson's range and offensive payload being insufficient for anything other than short-range coastal operations. The RAF placed an initial order for 200 aircraft, the first of which were delivered to No 224 Squadron at Leuchars, Scotland, in May 1939. The first batch of Hudsons came by sea (later aircraft were flown to the UK via Iceland once that island was secured by Allied forces after the outbreak of World War II) and, on arrival, were fitted with Boulton Paul dorsal turrets mounting twin 7.7mm (0.303in) machineguns. On 8 October 1939, by which time 78 aircraft had been delivered to Coastal Command and four squadrons were operational with the Hudson Mk I, an aircraft of No 224 Squadron shot down a Dornier Do 18 reconnaissance seaplane off Jutland. This was the first German aircraft destroyed by a RAF aircraft operating from the British mainland in World War II.

Type: Maritime reconnaissance aircraft (Mk I)	
Crew:	6
Powerplant:	two 820kW (1100hp) Wright GR-1820-G102A Cyclone radial engines
Max speed:	357km/h (222mph)
Time to height:	10 mins to 3050m (10,00ft)
Service ceiling:	6400m (21,000ft)
Max range:	3154km (1960 miles)
Wing span:	19.96m (65ft 5in)
Wing area:	51.19m² (551sq ft)
Length:	13.50m (44ft 3in)
Height:	3.32m (10ft 9in)
Weights:	5484kg (12,090lb) empty; 8845kg (19,500lb) max t/o
Armament:	two 7.7mm (0.303in) fixed forward-firing MG in upper part of forward fuselage; two 7.7mm (0.303in) MG in dorsal turret, two in beam positions, and one in ventral position; internal bomb load of 612kg (1350lb)

Lockheed supplied 350 Hudson Is and 20 Hudson IIs (the same as the Mk I except for different propellers) before introducing the Mk III, an improved version of the Mk I with 895kW (1200hp) Wright GR-1820-G205A Cyclone engines, ventral and beam gun positions. The RAF received 428 of this version, all purchased direct, but subsequent aircraft were supplied under Lend-Lease, the only other direct purchases being 309 Hudson Vs with 895kW (1200hp) Pratt & Whitney Twin Wasp engines. Lend-Lease aircraft included 382 Cyclone-engined Mk IIIAs, 30 Mk IVs and 450 Mk VIs with Twin Wasp engines.

During 1940, the RAF's Hudsons were employed mainly on maritime reconnaissance over the Norwegian coast, following the German invasion in April, in patrolling the English Channel during the evacuation of the British Expeditionary Force from France in May, and surveillance of the French Atlantic ports following their capture by the enemy. In January 1941 the first 14 Hudsons were fitted with ASV (Air to Surface Vessel) Mk I radar, after which the type was increasingly employed in anti-submarine operations. In the far east, the Hudson was operated by Nos 1 and 8 Squadrons RAAF in Malaya, and in December 1941, following the Japanese invasion, their aircraft were involved in a series of fierce attacks on enemy vessels landing troops at Kota Bharu on the Malayan coast. As a result of these determined attacks, it was later revealed that 15,000 Japanese troops had been killed at the beachhead, many of them following when the freighter *Awagisan Mary* exploded. No 1 Squadron lost eight aircraft in the attacks, the remaining five being evacuated to Kuantan, 240km (150 miles) to the south. In February 1942, the Australian Hudson squadrons were in action against Japanese convoys en route to invade Sumatra and Java. During these operations, reports persisted that the Japanese were using captured Hudsons to drop paratroops. In fact, the aircraft involved were Kawasaki Ki 56s, a transport which, like the Hudson, was developed from the Lockheed 14. The Ki 56 was codenamed 'Thalia' by the Allies and was first used in Sumatra.

In the North Atlantic, one of the Hudson's most famous actions occurred on 27 August 1941, when the German submarine *U-570* was attacked and damaged by an aircraft of No 269 Squadron (Sqn Ldr J. Thompson) off Iceland. The Hudson circled the U-boat, which was unable to dive, until its crew indicated that they wished to surrender. A Catalina relieved the Hudson and the submarine was towed to Iceland by an armed trawler.

The Hudson also served in USAAC/USAAF colours as the A-28 (the Twin Wasp version) and A-28 (the Cyclone version). The USAAC took delivery of a total of 82 A-28s and 418 A-29s between 1941 and 1942, 20 A-28s subsequently being transferred to the US Navy as the PBO-1. On 1 March 1942, a PBO-1 Hudson of VP-82 (Ensign William Tepuni, USNR) attacked and sank the submarine *U-656* south-west of Newfoundland; this was the first German U-boat sunk to US forces during World War II. In July 1942, a Hudson of the same squadron sank the *U-701* off the eastern coast of the United States. RAF Hudsons accounted for at least five U-boats between 1942 and 1943, during the height of the Battle of the Atlantic.

Hudsons were also used for clandestine operations, landing parties of agents in France and bringing them out again. No 161 (Special Duties) Squadron used several Hudsons in this capacity until the end of the war, latterly dropping supplies to agents in Germany itself. Three Hudsons were shot down on the night 20/21 March 1945, possibly destroyed in error by Allied nightfighters. Hudsons were also used for similar missions over Burma by No 357 (Special Duties) Squadron, which flew many successful sorties for comparatively small loss. The Hudsons operated mainly from Dum Dum in India.

Below: A Lockheed A-28, belonging to the US Army Air Corps, in 1941. Although the A-28/29 performed well in the light bombing role, it would be as the maritime patrol Hudson that this type was most effective, when it really came into its own.

Martin B-26 Marauder

Two pilots sat side-by-side on the flight deck, although sometimes the co-pilot's seat was removed to reduce weight. The fuselage below the cockpit shows that this aircraft has performed no less than 88 combat missions.

The radio room was situated behind the flight deck. It was considered to be the strongest part of the aircraft, and the crew would congregate there in an emergency.

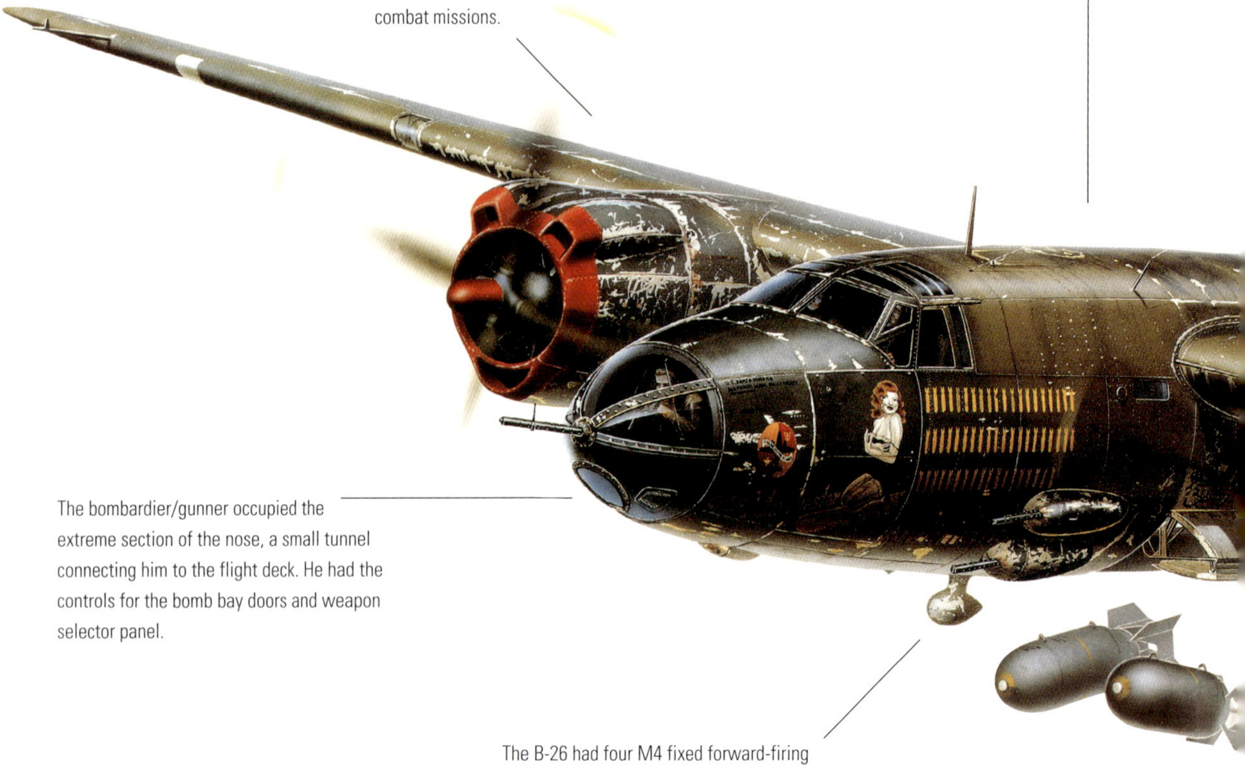

The bombardier/gunner occupied the extreme section of the nose, a small tunnel connecting him to the flight deck. He had the controls for the bomb bay doors and weapon selector panel.

The B-26 had four M4 fixed forward-firing 12.7mm (0.5in) machine guns attached to the fuselage, with 200 rounds per gun. These were fired by the pilot, who pressed a button on his control wheel.

The B-26 was the first aircraft to have an all-electrical release system. The usual bomb load of the aircraft was 1360–1815kg (3000–4000lb).

The B-26's dorsal turret was a Martin 250CE mounting a pair of 12.7mm (0.5in) machine guns. The waist positions were also equipped with a single machine gun each.

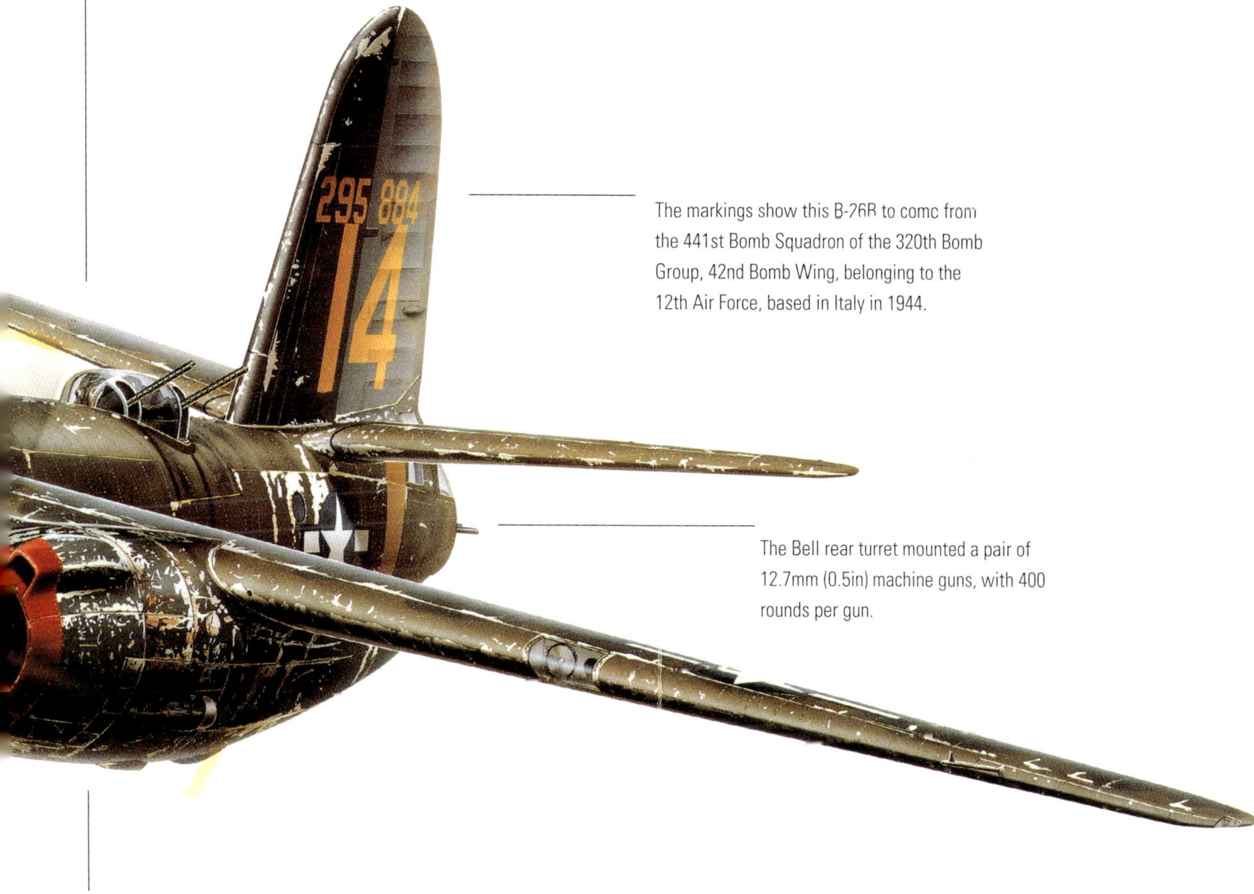

The markings show this B-26B to come from the 441st Bomb Squadron of the 320th Bomb Group, 42nd Bomb Wing, belonging to the 12th Air Force, based in Italy in 1944.

The Bell rear turret mounted a pair of 12.7mm (0.5in) machine guns, with 400 rounds per gun.

The B-26B was powered by a pair of Pratt & Whitney R-2800-43 radial engines. The top intakes on the cowling are for the carburettor, while the chin intake is for cooling the engine oil.

One of the most controversial Allied medium bombers of World War II, at least in the early stages of its career, the Glenn L. Martin 179 was entered in a US Army light- and medium-bomber competition of 1939. Its designer, Peyton M. Magruder, placed the emphasis on high speed, producing an aircraft with a torpedolike fuselage, two massive radial engines, tricycle undercarriage and stubby wings. The advanced nature of the aircraft's design proved so impressive that an immediate order was placed for 201 examples off the drawing board, even without a prototype. It was a configuration that was to result in an exceptionally high accident rate, created in the main by inexperienced pilots handling a fast, unfamiliar and unusually heavy aeroplane, which had dangerously high wing loading and rather vicious single-engined flying characteristics.

The first B-26 flew on 25 November 1940, powered by two Pratt & Whitney R-2800-5 engines; by this time, orders for 1131 B-26A and B-26B bombers had been received. The first unit to rearm with a mixture of B-26s and B-26As was the 22nd Bombardment Group at

Right: The Martin B-26 Marauder was one of the most important tactical bombers of World War II. In the Pacific, because of its high speed and ability to make surprise low-level attacks on Japanese island bases, it was a constant thorn in the enemy's side.

Type: Medium bomber	
Crew:	7
Powerplant:	two 1491kW (2000hp) Pratt & Whitney R-2800-41 radials
Max speed:	510km/h (317mph)
Time to height:	12 mins to 4750m (15,584ft)
Service ceiling:	7165m (23,507ft)
Max range:	1850km (1150 miles)
Wing span:	19.81m (65ft)
Wing area:	55.93m² (602sq ft)
Length:	17.75m (58ft 3in)
Height:	6.04m (19ft 8in)
Weights:	10,152kg (22,380lb) empty; 15,513kg (34,200lb) max t/o
Armament:	two 7.7mm (0.303in) MG (one each in nose and ventral positions), or two 12.7mm (0.5in) MG in beam positions instead of ventral gun; two 12.7mm (0.5in) MG in dorsal and two in tail turrets; maximum bomb load of 2359kg (5200lb)

Above: A number of Martin B-26s line up at the start of a sortie from an English airfield. The Martin B-26 would suffer serious losses to enemy ground fire during the early low-level attacks which it conducted on targets in the Low Countries.

Langley Field in February 1941. The 22nd BG was still the only B-26 unit when war broke out in the Pacific, and between December 1941 and January 1942 it moved to Muroc, California, to carry out anti-submarine patrols off the west coast of the USA. It then moved to Australia, where it became part of the US Fifth Air Force, attacking enemy shipping, airfields and installations in New Guinea and New Britain. It carried out its first attack, a raid on Rabaul, on 5 April 1942. During the Battle of Midway, four B-26As of the 22nd and 38th BG attacked units of the Japanese fleet with torpedoes. The 22nd BG used B-26s exclusively until October 1943, when some B-25s were added. In February 1944 it became a heavy bombardment group, equipped with B-24s.

The next variant, the B-26B, had uprated engines and increased armament. Of the 1883 built, all but the first 641 aircraft featured a new extended-span wing and taller tail fin. The B-26B made its debut in the European Theatre in March 1943, when the 322nd Bombardment Group deployed to Great Saling, Essex, and began training for low-level attack missions. The group flew its first combat mission, an attack on a power station near Ijmuiden, Holland, on 14 May 1943; this was unsuccessful, either because the delayed-action bombs were defective or because the enemy was able to disarm them in time, so a second low-level attack on the same objective was mounted on 17 May. The raid was a disaster; of the 11 Marauders that set out, 10 were lost to flak and fighters. As a result, it was decided that the B-26 was unsuitable for low-level attacks against strongly defended targets. Following additional training, all B-26 units in the European Theatre were reassigned to the medium-level bombing role, which they fulfilled magnificently until the end of the war in both north-west Europe and Italy.

The B-26C, of which 1210 were built, was essentially similar to the later B-26B models. These were succeeded by the B-26F (300 built), in which the angle of incidence (i.e.

Below: A Martin B-26B-40 of the 320th Bombardment Group which was based at Decimomannu, Sardinia, in the summer of 1944. The Marauder was widely used in Italy, since its high speed and agility made it suitable for medium-level attacks.

the angle at which the wing is married to the fuselage) was increased in order to improve take-off performance and reduce the accident rate, which was still unacceptably high. The final model to be produced was the B-26G, which differed from the F model in only minor detail; 950 of these were built.

The B-26 saw service in the Aleutians in 1942, and in the Western Desert, where it served with the RAF Middle East Command as the Marauder Mk I (B-26A), Marauder Mk IA (B-26B), Marauder Mk II (B-26F) and Marauder Mk III (B-26G). Only two RAF squadrons, Nos 14 and 39, used the Marauder; No 14 Squadron exchanged its Blenheims for Marauder Mk Is in August 1942 and used all variants until September 1944, while No 39 Squadron equipped with Marauder IIIs in February 1945 and retained them until September 1946. The total number of Marauders delivered to the RAF included 52 Marauder Is and IAs, 250 Marauder IIs and 150 Marauder IIIs. The Marauder was also used extensively by the Free French Air Force and the South African Air Force. The Free French B-26 squadrons played a prominent part in the Allied invasion of southern France in August 1944, subsequently providing tactical support for French units of the US Seventh Army on its drive into Germany. The Marauder's high speed and agility made it an excellent aircraft for penetrating heavy enemy defences, and although its unwanted reputation as a 'widow maker' clung to it throughout its operational career, its combat loss rate was less than 1 per cent.

Many Marauders were completed or converted as AT-23 or TB-26 trainers for the USAAF and JM-1s for the US Navy, some being used as target tugs. Total production was 4708 aircraft.

North American B-25 Mitchell

The B-25 was flown by a crew of two, with the co-pilot doubling up as a navigator. Later versions of the B-25 with fuselage guns had a reflector sight fitted in the cockpit.

The extensively-glazed nose was home to the bombardier/gunner, who was equipped with a Norden bombsight. There were also two machine guns, one fixed to fire directly forward, the other on a flexible mount and aimed by the bombardier.

The B-25C and B-25D were powered by a pair of Wright R-2600-13 14-cylinder, two-row radial engines.

The bomb bay was short and narrow, but reached nearly the full height of the fuselage. Bombs were held in side-by-side vertical racks.

Rear protection for the B-25 was provided by a Bendix turret mounting two 12.7mm (0.5in) machine guns. The later B-25J had the dorsal turret moved forward, and a separate tail turret added.

Mitchells operating in the desert had a sand-coloured camouflage scheme to match their surroundings.

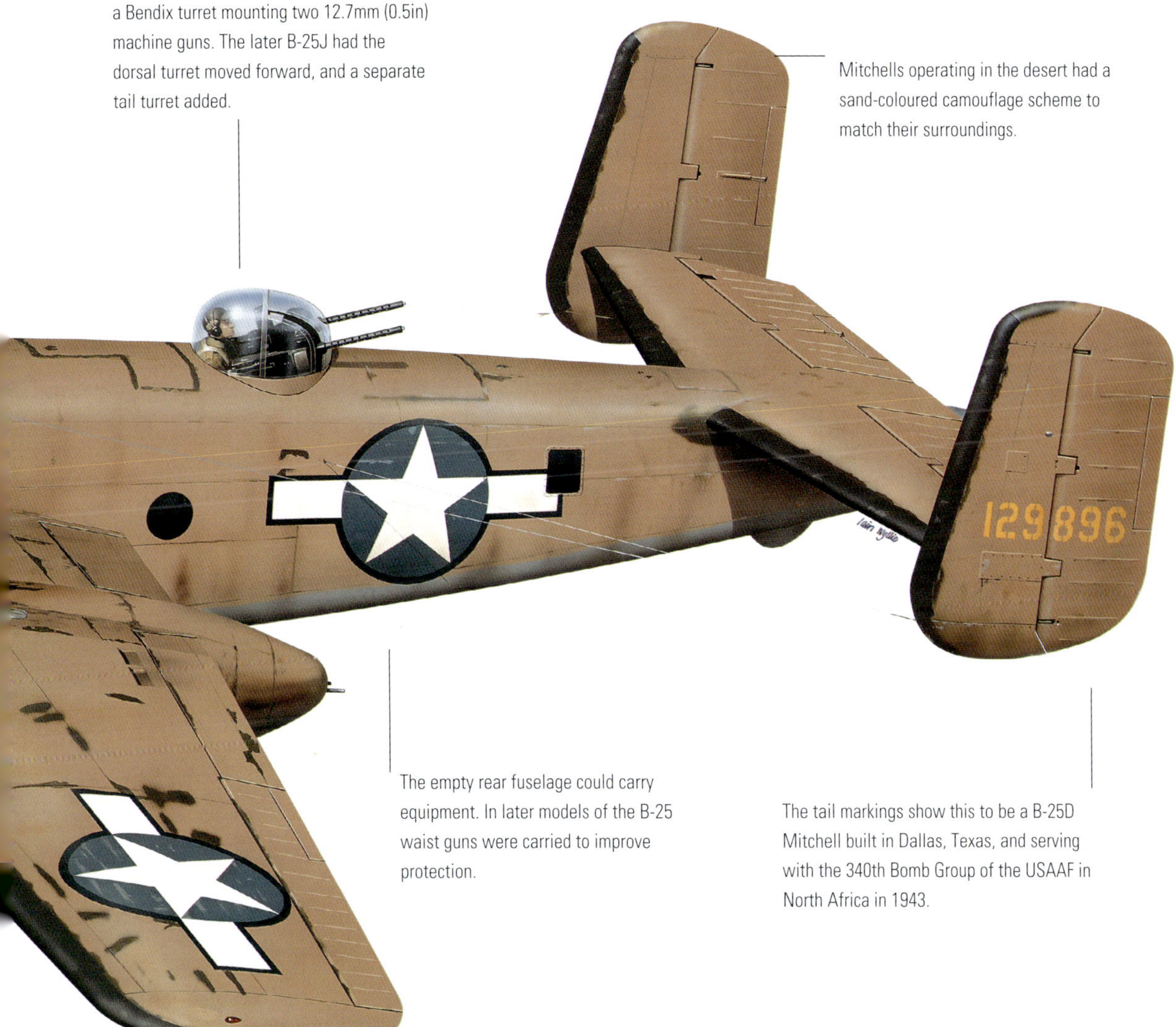

The empty rear fuselage could carry equipment. In later models of the B-25 waist guns were carried to improve protection.

The tail markings show this to be a B-25D Mitchell built in Dallas, Texas, and serving with the 340th Bomb Group of the USAAF in North Africa in 1943.

Above: A North American B-25 Mitchell aircraft decked out in a curious mixture of markings. The aircraft is carrying a Royal Air Force fin flash, while also retaining the insignia of the USAAF. The B-25 was used by both the RAF and the USAAF.

One of the most important US tactical warplanes of World War II, the North American B-25 was designed as a tactical bomber, but found a valuable second role as a potent anti-shipping aircraft in the Pacific Theatre. The type was begun as a private venture in 1938, when North America reasoned that the USAAC would soon need a new, modern attack bomber. The prototype, bearing the company designation NA-40, flew for the first time in January 1939, in the same month that the USAAC issued a definitive requirement; this resulted in the NA-40B, a modified version which in turn was developed into the NA-62. This version was ordered into production as the B-25. The NA-62 flew on 19 August 1940 and the first batch of 24 initial production aircraft was delivered from February 1941, further deliveries comprising 40 B-25As and 120 B-25Bs, the former with self-sealing tanks and the latter with dorsal and ventral turrets but no tail gun position. Some early concerns were expressed by pilots regarding the type's often tricky handling qualities, but these were soon dispelled and the B-25 began to have a notable impact on the air war.

On 16 April 1942, the Mitchell leapt into the headlines when the aircraft carrier USS *Hornet*, from a position at sea 1075km (668 miles) from Tokyo, launched 16 B-25Bs of the 17th AAF Air Group, led by Lt Col J.H. Doolittle, for the first attack on the Japanese homeland. All the B-25 crews bombed their assigned targets in the Tokyo, Yokosuka and Osaka-Kobe areas and then diverted to China, where they planned to land; this was frustrated by bad weather, and most baled out. Of the 80 aircrew members who took part, 10 were killed, either accidentally or as a result of falling into enemy hands in China, and 15 were injured. The Tokyo raid had far-reaching consequences; as a direct result, Admiral Yamamoto, the Japanese Naval Commander-in-Chief, launched an ambitious plan to extend the eastern perimeter of the Japanese conquests in the Pacific and bring the US Pacific Fleet to battle. It was a policy that was to have disastrous consequences for the Japanese a few weeks later, in June 1942. USAAF Mitchells operated effectively against Japanese forces in New Guinea, carrying out low-level strafing attacks in the wake of Allied bombing operations.

The B-25B was followed into service by the virtually identical B-25C, 1619 of which were built at North American's Inglewood plant, and B-25D, with uprated engines, an autopilot, external hardpoints for one 907kg (2000lb) torpedo or eight 113kg (250lb) bombs, provision

Type: Medium bomber (B-25D)	
Crew:	5
Powerplant:	two 1268kW (1700hp) Wright R-2600-13 18-cylinder two-row radial engines
Max speed:	457km/h (284mph)
Time to height:	16 mins 30 secs to 4570m (14,993ft)
Service ceiling:	6460m (21,200ft)
Max range:	2454km (1525 miles) with a 1452kg (3200lb) bomb load
Wing span:	20.60m (67ft 6in)
Wing area:	56.67m^2 (610 sq ft)
Length:	16.12m (52ft 9in)
Height:	4.82m (15ft 10in)
Weights:	9208kg (20,300lb) empty
Armament:	two 12.7mm (0.5in) trainable forward-firing guns in nose position, two 12.7mm (0.5in) trainable MG each in dorsal and tail turrets; internal and external bomb/torpedo load of 1361kg (3000lb)

Above: B-25 Mitchells bombing a target in Italy. In the tactical bomber role, the B-25 was superb, but it was found that the B-25H version, with a heavy nose armament and rocket projectiles, was equally as effective in the anti-shipping role.

for forward-firing machineguns in packs attached to the sides of the forward fuselage and, in later aircraft, increased fuel capacity. North American's Kansas City factory produced 2290 B-25Ds. The two variants were used in most theatres of war, and 533 B-25C/D aircraft were delivered to the RAF as Mitchell Mk IIs to supplement an earlier delivery of 23 Mitchell Mk I (B-25B) aircraft. Eight squadrons of the RAF's No 2 Group, including two Dutch and one Free French, used the Mitchell. Their first operational use by the RAF was on 22 February 1943, when Nos 90 and 108 Squadrons attacked oil installations at Terneuzen, Holland.

The dedicated anti-shipping version of the Mitchell was the B-25G, 405 of which (including five B-25C conversions) were produced. Developed for use in the Pacific Theatre, the B-25G had a four-man crew and was fitted with a 75mm (2.95in) M4 gun in the nose, adding to its already powerful nose armament of four 12.7mm (0.5in) guns. The follow-on variant, the B-25H (1000 built) had a lighter 75mm (2.95in) gun, eight 12.7mm (0.5in) fixed forward-firing machineguns, six 12.7mm (0.5in) machineguns (two each in the dorsal and tail positions and one in each of the two new beam positions), and provision for eight 127mm (5in) rockets under the wings. The 4318 examples of the next variant, the B-25J, featured either a glazed B-25D nose or, in later aircraft, a 'solid' nose with eight 12.7mm (0.5in) machineguns. The RAF took delivery of 313 B-25Js as the Mitchell III, and 458 B-25Js were transferred to the US Navy from 1943, these aircraft being designated PBJ-1H. They were used primarily by the US Marine Corps, taking part in many air attacks on stubborn Japanese targets such as Rabaul, which held out until the end of the war. The first attack by USMC Mitchells (Marine Bombing Squadron 413) was made on 15 March 1944, marking the type's combat debut in Marine Corps hands and the last on 9 August 1945.

The Soviet Union also took delivery of 862 Mitchells under Lend-Lease, eight more being destroyed in accidents during their delivery flights. Total production of all Mitchell variants was 9816 aircraft. Surplus B-25s were widely exported after World War II and the type continued to serve for many years. Customers included Brazil (29), China (131), and the Netherlands (249). The USAF used converted Mitchells as staff transports, the last one being retired in May 1960.

North American P-51 Mustang

The markings show that these aircraft are P-51B-5s belonging to the 334th Squadron of the 4th Fighter Group.

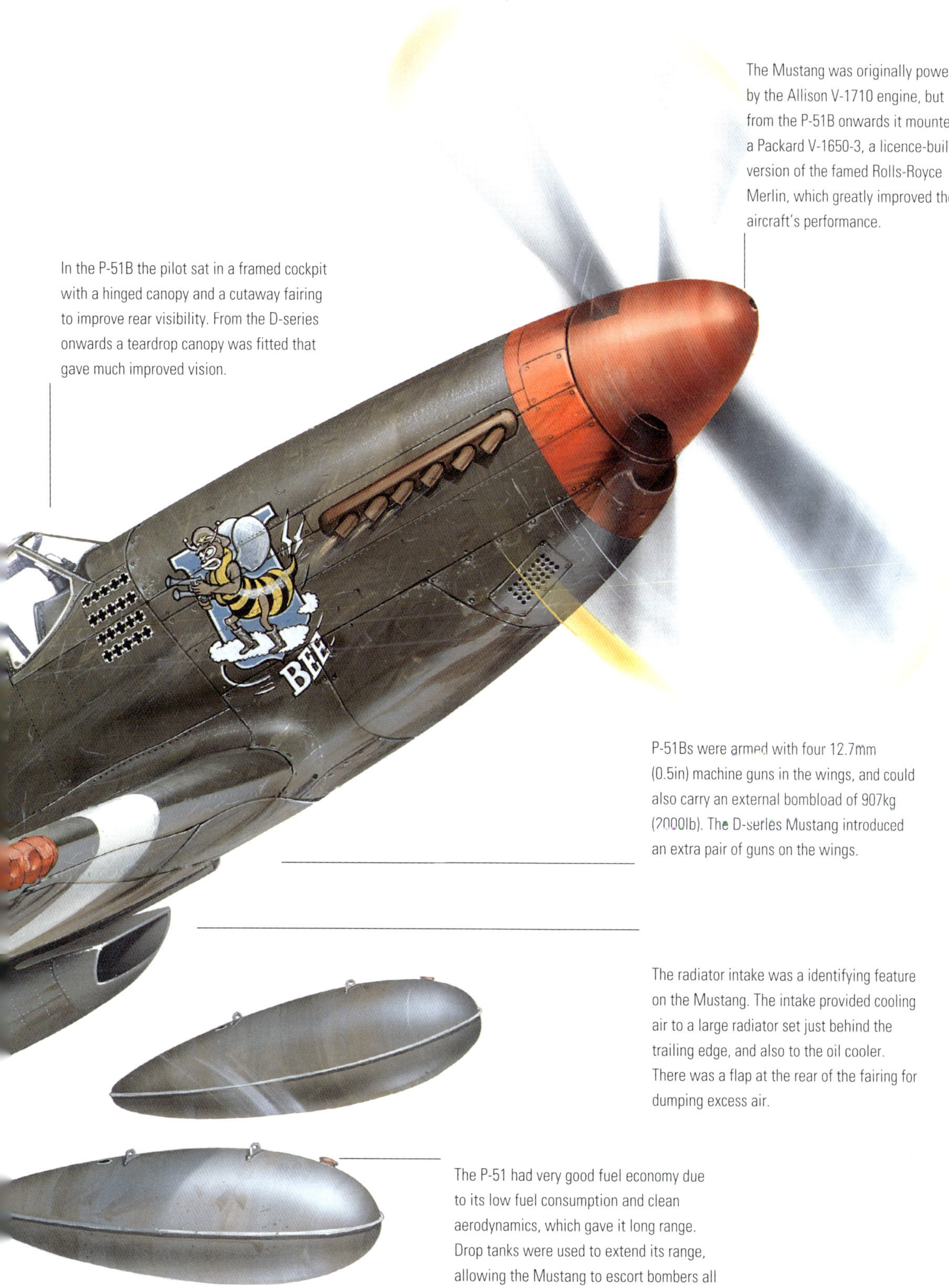

The Mustang was originally powered by the Allison V-1710 engine, but from the P-51B onwards it mounted a Packard V-1650-3, a licence-built version of the famed Rolls-Royce Merlin, which greatly improved the aircraft's performance.

In the P-51B the pilot sat in a framed cockpit with a hinged canopy and a cutaway fairing to improve rear visibility. From the D-series onwards a teardrop canopy was fitted that gave much improved vision.

P-51Bs were armed with four 12.7mm (0.5in) machine guns in the wings, and could also carry an external bombload of 907kg (2000lb). The D-series Mustang introduced an extra pair of guns on the wings.

The radiator intake was a identifying feature on the Mustang. The intake provided cooling air to a large radiator set just behind the trailing edge, and also to the oil cooler. There was a flap at the rear of the fairing for dumping excess air.

The P-51 had very good fuel economy due to its low fuel consumption and clean aerodynamics, which gave it long range. Drop tanks were used to extend its range, allowing the Mustang to escort bombers all the way to Berlin.

The North American P-51 Mustang was initially produced in response to a 1940 RAF requirement for a fast, heavily-armed fighter which was able to operate effectively at altitudes in excess of 6100m (20,000ft). North American built the prototype in 117 days, and the aircraft, which was designated NA-73X, flew on 26 October 1940. The first of 320 production Mustang Is for the RAF flew on 1 May 1941, powered by an 820kW (1100hp) Allison V-1710-39 engine. RAF test pilots soon found that with this powerplant, the aircraft did not perform well at high altitude, but that its low-level performance was excellent. It was therefore decided to use the type as a high-speed ground attack and tactical reconnaissance fighter, and it was in this role that it entered service with Army Co-operation Command in July 1942. The RAF also used its Mustangs in the night-intruder role, a task to which the aircraft, with its long endurance, was well suited. Somewhat belatedly, the USAAF realized the fighter's potential and evaluated two early production Mustang Is under the designation P-51. The RAF suggested that the P-51 would perform much better as a high-altitude interceptor if it were re-engined with the Rolls-Royce Merlin. However, this suggestion was initially ignored and the first two USAAF Mustang variants, optimized for ground attack and designated A-36A and P-51A, were fitted with Allison engines. The USAAF went on to order A-36As, which were delivered between September 1942 and March 1943, and 310 P-51As, deliveries of which started in the spring of 1943. Trials with Mustangs fitted with Packard-built Rolls-Royce Merlin 61 engines showed a dramatic improvement in performance, maximum speed being raised from 627km/h (390mph) to 710km/h (441mph), and thus production of the Merlin-powered P-51B finally got under way in the autumn of 1942. North American's Inglewood factory manufactured 1988 P-51Bs, while the 1750 aircraft built at the new Dallas plant were designated P-51C. Had the decision been taken to install the Merlin engine in a high-altitude interceptor version of the P-51 six months earlier, then the American daylight bombers would have had the benefit of effective long-range escort virtually from the start of their offensive against Germany. As things

Above: A CP-51B Mustang of the 325th Fighter Group, Fifteenth Army Air Force. Known as the 'Checkertail Clan', the 325th Fighter Group operated from bases in Italy and was responsible for escorting B-17s on deep-penetration missions into Germany.

were, it was not until December 1943 that P-51Bs of the 354th Fighter Group flew their first operational escort mission from England, in which they escorted B-17s to Kiel and back, a round trip of 1600km (1000 miles).

The RAF, which had ordered 1000 P-51Bs under the designation Mustang Mk III, began to receive its first aircraft early in 1944, the first 36 having been diverted to the US Eighth AAF to alleviate the critical shortage of escort fighters. The RAF was not happy with the very poor visibility from the Mustang's cockpit, and replaced the existing canopy with a streamlined, frameless bubble-type hood designed by Malcolm Aircraft Ltd. The canopy was also fitted to some of the USAAF's P-51Cs. North American, who tested two P-51Bs with a one-piece sliding canopy and cut-down rear fuselage, however, found the real solution to the problem. Whereas the P-51B/C had been armed with four 12.7mm (0.5in) machineguns with 1260rpg, the conversions, designated XP-51D-NA, had six 12.7mm (0.5in) calibre Browning air-cooled machineguns with 1880 rounds in a strengthened wing. The aircraft were also later fitted with a dorsal fin to compensate for the loss of keel surface after the removal of the upper rear fuselage. Other refinements in the course of production included the addition of two sets of stub rocket launchers under each wing to carry 127mm (5in) rockets. The first production P-51Ds began to arrive in England in the late spring of 1944 and quickly became the standard equipment of the USAAF Eighth Fighter Command.

There is no doubt at all that the Mustang won the daylight battle over Germany. Operating from bases in England and Italy, it provided not only fighter escort for the bombers engaged in a two-pronged assault on Hitler's Reich; it also hunted the Luftwaffe on its own airfields. In the Pacific,

Left: The P-51D Mustang, fitted with its excellent Packard-built Merlin engine, was the escort fighter the US Eighth AAF had badly needed for so long. Sweeping ahead of the daylight bombers, it brought the Luftwaffe's fighters to battle.

"Mrs. Virginia

Type: Long-range fighter	
Crew:	1
Powerplant:	one 1111kW (1490hp) Packard Rolls-Royce Merlin V-1650-7
Max speed:	704km/h (437mph) at 7620m (25,000ft)
Time to height:	13 mins to 9145m (30,000ft)
Service ceiling:	12,770m (41,900ft)
Max range:	3347km (2080 miles)
Wing span:	11.28m (37ft)
Wing area:	21.65m^2 (233.2sq ft)
Length:	9.85m (32ft 3in)
Height:	3.71m (12ft 2in)
Weights:	3232kg (7125lb) empty
Armament:	six 12.7mm (0.5in) MG in the wings; provision for up to two 454kg (1000lb) bombs or six 12.7cm (5in) rockets

Left: Two P-51C Mustangs on a mission over Burma in 1943. Although the P-51C retained the troublesome Allison engine, it was an adequate performer in combat at medium and low level, heights at which most of the air action over Burma took place.

Mustangs operating from the captured Japanese islands of Iwo Jima and Okinawa were to adopt similar tactics from April 1945, when they escorted B-29s to their targets and succeeded in neutralizing the Japanese air force on the ground. Production totalled 7956 P-51Ds and 1337 basically similar P-51K (which had an Aeroproducts propeller instead of the Hamilton Standard unit). Of these aircraft, 876 became Mustang IVs with the RAF, and a total of 299 became reconnaissance F-6Ds or F-6Ks.

The fastest Mustang version, which saw service in the Pacific towards the end of the war, was the P-51H, with a top speed of 784km/h (487mph). The P-51H owed its origins to the XP-51F, XP-51G and XP-51J, all of which were experimental lightweight versions of the Mustang with a laminar flow wing designed to a British requirement. The P-51H was the production lightweight Mustang, and a total of 555 were built.

The Mustang continued to serve with some 20 air forces around the world for years after the end of World War II, and gave valiant service during the early months of the Korean War with US, Australian, South African and South Korean air units.

Northrop P-61

The radar operator sat in the upper forward position. An oscilloscope display was mounted in the cockpit for the SCR-720 radar. He also controlled the forward firing of the gun turret, and his seat could swivel through 360°.

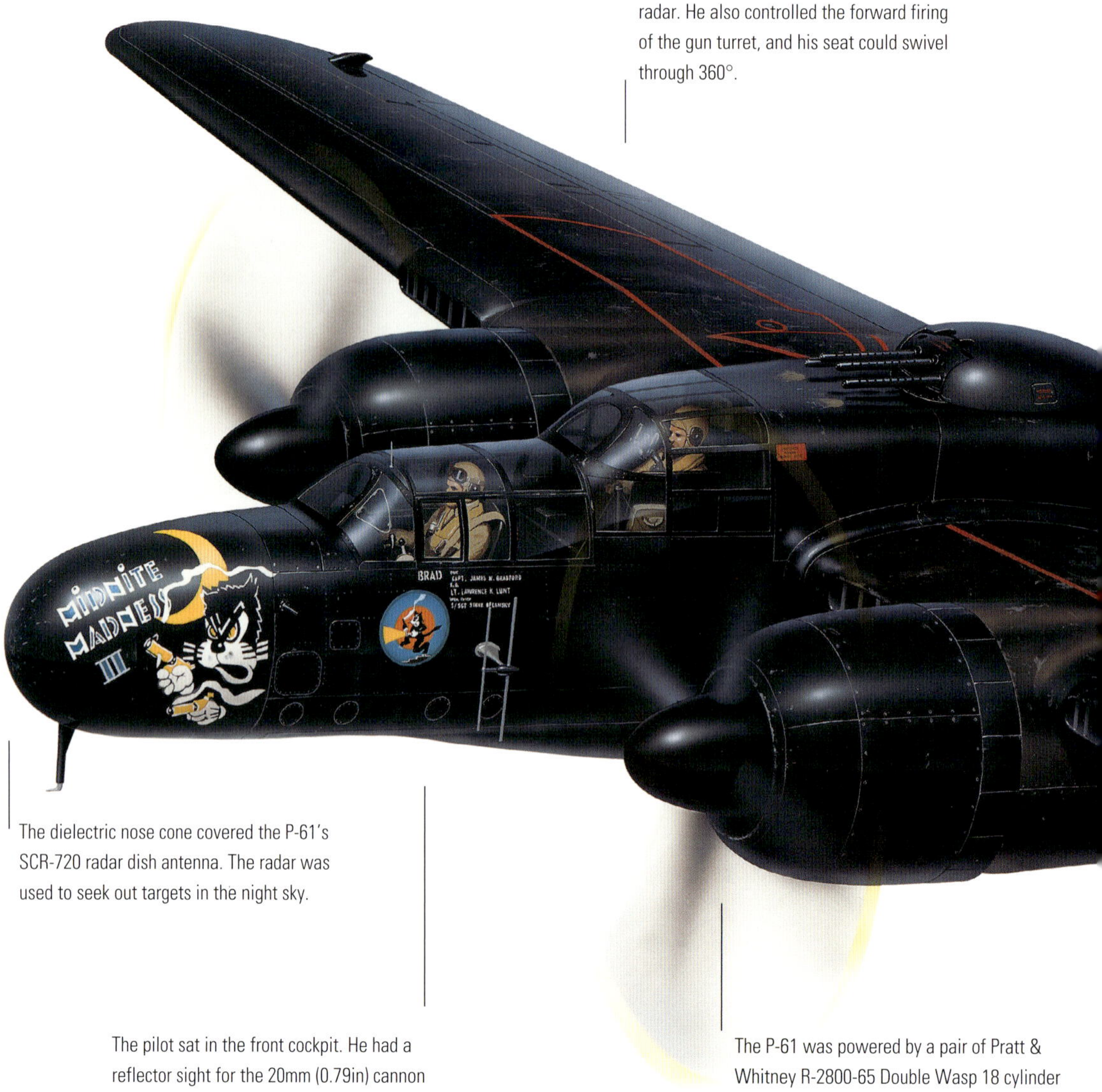

The dielectric nose cone covered the P-61's SCR-720 radar dish antenna. The radar was used to seek out targets in the night sky.

The pilot sat in the front cockpit. He had a reflector sight for the 20mm (0.79in) cannon in the ventral bulge under the fuselage. On the outside of his cockpit are radar receivers for picking up the radar return.

The P-61 was powered by a pair of Pratt & Whitney R-2800-65 Double Wasp 18 cylinder two row radial engines. Air intakes either side of the engines provided air for the heater (inner intakes) and the intercooler and supercharger (outboard intakes).

The dorsal turret mounted four 12.7mm (0.5in) Colt-Browning machine guns, each with 560 rounds. It could rotate through 360° and the guns could be elevated. However it was usually locked in a forward-firing position.

The rear gunner was located in a separate, heavily-glazed compartment to the rear of the turret. He was responsible for protection of the rear hemisphere, and like the radar operator was equipped with a swivelling seat. He was also responsible for the radios.

The markings show this aircraft to be a P-61B Black Widow of the 548th Night Fighter Squadron of the 7th Air Force, operating in the Pacific in 1945.

The Black Widow had four forward-firing 20mm (0.79in) cannon in a ventral bulge under the fuselage. Each gun had 200 rounds of ammunition. The P-61 could also carry 2904kg (6400lb) of stores on four underwing hardpoints.

At the time of the Japanese attack in December 1941, the United States Army Air Corps had no specialized nightfighter. In fact, scant thought had been given to nightfighting at all until the late summer of 1940, when Lt Gen Delos C. Emmons, commanding general of GHQ Air Corps, visited Britain and saw at first hand the threat posed by night bombers. As a result of his recommendations, the USAAC drew up preliminary specifications for a nightfighter and passed them to the Northrop Company, which at that time was working on a nightfighter design on behalf of the British Purchasing Commission in the USA. The design then taking shape involved a radar-equipped aircraft with a crew of two, heavy armament and long endurance, so that incoming bombers could be intercepted long before they reached their targets. Before negotiations could begin with the British on construction of a prototype, the USAAC stepped in and virtually commandeered the project, although British involvement was maintained for the time being; the RAF relinquished its interest when the Bristol Beaufighter began to prove its worth in the night-defence role.

In January 1941 Northrop was contracted to construct two protypes under the designation XP-61, and production contracts totalling 573 aircraft were issued within the next 13 months. The first prototype flew on 21 May 1942, but it was to be another 18 months before the first production P-61A Black Widow aircraft appeared. The first 37 aircraft featured a remotely controlled dorsal turret with four 12.7mm (0.5in) guns in addition to four fixed 20mm (0.79in) cannon in the belly, but airflow instability caused its deletion from the 38th aircraft onwards. The P-61 was fitted with a Westinghouse SCR-270 AI radar, which had a British magnetron. The 421st NFS (18th Fighter Group) was the first to rearm with the new type, operating from Mokmer in New Guinea, and on 7 July 1944 one of its aircraft scored the first P-61 victory in the South-west Pacific by shooting down a Mitsubishi Ki 46 Dinah over Japan island. Early P-61A operations were plagued by unserviceability of the aircraft's Pratt & Whitney R-2800-65 engines, and after 200 P-61As had been built, production switched to the P-51B, of which 450 were built. This version was modified for night-intruder operations, being capable of carrying up to four 726kg (1600lb) bombs or four 1136-litre (300 US gal) drop tanks under the wings. Some units adapted their aircraft locally to carry eight 127mm (5in) rockets in order to carry out night attacks on Japanese shipping.

The 421st NFS, which was joined in the theatre at later dates by the 418th and 547th NFS, moved to Tacloban, Leyte, on 25 October 1944, and on 29 November the Black Widows were ordered to make a night attack on a Japanese convoy in Leyte Gulf. The convoy, consisting of two escort destroyers and a number of smaller vessels, was heading

Below: Although it did not possess the performance or the firepower of the German He 219 Uhu, the P-61 Black Widow was nevertheless still an immensely potent and impressive nightfighter. This aircraft was also to prove very effective as an intruder.

Above: In addition to its primary role, the P-61 was widely used to conduct night attacks against enemy shipping which was stationed in the Pacific Theatre. Post-war, the P-61 Black Widow would be replaced by the F-82 Twin Mustang.

towards Ormoc to land reinforcement troops and supplies. The convoy was duly harassed throughout the night, preventing the landing of its troops, and US surface forces sank one of the destroyers at daybreak. In the Central Pacific, the US Seventh Air Force had three Black Widow squadrons, the 6th, 548th and 549th. The last two arrived in the theatre on 7 and 24 March 1945 respectively, being based on Iwo Jima. The 548th NFS soon moved up to Iwo Jima to provide forward air defence and also to carry out night-intruder operations over Kyushu, scoring five kills during these operations; the 549th remained on Iwo Jima, sending detachments to Saipan and Guam as required.

There were two Black Widow squadrons in the China-Burma-India (CBI) Theatre. The first was the 426th NFS, which was activated on 1 January 1944 at Hammer Field, California, and arrived at Chengtu, China, under Fourteenth Air Force command on 5 November 1944. It operated from a number of bases thereafter, mostly in the night ground-attack role, as there was virtually no air opposition. The other was the 427th NFS, which was activated on 1 February 1944 and deployed to Myitkyina, Burma, in December by way of Italy and India. During the next few months, under the command of the Tenth and later the Fourteenth Air Force, the 427th flew 73 defensive patrols without encountering a single enemy aircraft and so its aircraft were modified to carry bombs and rockets for intruder operations against Japanese troop concentrations and supply dumps. A detachment at Kunming, China, carried out similar work.

In the European Theatre, P-61As were issued to the 422nd NFS at Scorton, Yorkshire, in May 1944, followed by the 425th at Charmy Down. Their task was to provide night protection for the American sectors of the Normandy invasion, which took place on 6 June 1944. Before departing for the continent the two squadrons flew some sorties against V-1 flying bombs, shooting down nine of the pilotless aircraft. During night operations over northwest Europe, three of the 422nd NFS's crews achieved 'ace' status by destroying five enemy aircraft each. In Italy, the P-61 was flown by the 414th, 415th, 416th and 417th NFS, assigned to the Twelfth Air Force, but although the 414th managed to claim five victories at night, operational flying was severely curtailed by a lack of spare parts.

The last production version of the Black Widow was the P-61C, which had 2088kW (2800hp) R-2800-73 engines; 41 were built. In the immediate post-war years, P-61s were replaced by the North American P-82 Twin Mustang.

Type: Nightfighter	
Crew:	3
Powerplant:	two 1491kW (2000hp) Pratt & Whitney R-2800-65 18-cylinder radial engines
Max speed:	589km/h (366mph) at 6095m (20,000ft)
Time to height:	12 mins to 6095m (20,000ft)
Service ceiling:	10,090m (33,100ft)
Max range:	4506km (2800 miles)
Wing span:	20.12m (66ft)
Wing area:	61.69m² (664sq ft)
Length:	15.11m (49ft 6in)
Height:	4.46m (14ft 6in)
Weights:	9979kg (22,000lb) empty; 13,472kg (29,700lb) max t/o
Armament:	four 20mm (0.79in) cannon in fuselage belly, fixed to fire forward; provision for four 726kg (1600lb) bombs under wings; last 250 aircraft armed with four 12.7mm (0.5in) MG in remotely controlled dorsal turret

Republic P-47 Thunderbolt

The P-47C and -D both had lengthened fuselage to provide space for a 114 litre (30 US gal) water tank added behind the engine to provide water for water injection.

The size of the Thunderbolt's engine required a large propeller. The P-47 was the first US fighter to use a four-bladed propeller. It had a diameter of 3.71m (12ft 2in) and required the aircraft to have telescoping undercarriage to provide sufficient ground clearance.

This P-47D was powered by the same engine as the P-47C, the Pratt & Whitney R-2800-21 or -59 which was equipped with water injection.

Like many US fighters, the P-47 had controllable cooling gills at the rear of the engine cowling to allow more air into the engine at low speeds or when the engine was running hot.

This is an early production P-47D built by Republic at Farmingdale, New York. The aircraft served with 334th Fighter Squadron, 4th Fighter Group of the 8th Air Force based at Debden in England in 1943.

The pilot sat in a heavily-framed cockpit protected by a bullet-resistant windscreen and an armour plate in front of and behind him. Later Thunderbolts were fitted with a teardrop canopy for improved visibility.

The supercharger was mounted in the rear of the fuselage, giving the P-47 a bulky appearance. The exhaust gases were vented behind the supercharger.

This P-47 was armed with eight 12.7mm (0.5in) machine guns, four in each wing, with 425 rounds each. Later Thunderbolts had underwing pylons added at the cost of a pair of guns and reduced ammunition.

One of the truly great fighter aircraft of all time, the Republic P-47 Thunderbolt represented the culmination of a line of aircraft which had its origin in two 1936 designs, the Seversky P-35 and P-43. Soon after starting the latter project, Alexander Kartveli, chief designer of the Republic Aviation Corporation (as the Seversky Aviation Corporation became known after Alexander P. de Seversky was forced to step down in 1939) also started work on two other aircraft derived from it, the AP-4 and the AP-10. The former was fitted with a very poweful radial engine, while the latter was designed around the V-12 liquid-cooled Allison engine and was conceived as a lightweight fighter.

Below: Known to its pilots as the 'Jug', the Republic P-47 Thunderbolt carved out a name for itself as an escort fighter over Europe, and also distinguished itself in the ground attack role.

Oddly enough, it was from this aircraft that the P-47 Thunderbolt, the largest, heaviest single-seat fighter of its day, was to evolve.

Kartveli submitted the AP-10 project to the technical branch of the USSAC on 1 August 1939 only to have it turned down, with a request that he should develop a larger and more powerful version. Kartveli accordingly drew up a proposal for two re-designed prototypes, the XP-47 and XP-47A, both of which were to be powered by the Allison engine. A thorough study of the air combats that took place over western Europe in the first months of World War II, however, quickly led to a re-appraisal of what was required in a modern fighter aircraft in terms of performance, armament and armour. As far as the former was concerned, Kartveli realized that the Allison engine, with its mediocre performance at high altitude, would not be suitable. He therefore drew up an alternative design around the most powerful engine then available, the new 1491kW (2000hp) Pratt & Whitney Double Wasp radial. The new proposal was submitted to the USAAC in June 1940 as the XP-47B and was immediately accepted, orders being placed in September for 171 production P-47Bs and 602 P-47Cs. Basically the two were similar, but the P-47C had a slightly longer fuselage to improve stability.

Above: From the first operational sortie over Europe in April 1943 until the end of the Pacific war, Thunderbolts were to fly a staggering number of combat sorties: 546,000. During these sorties, they were responsible for dropping 134,118 tonnes (132,000 tons) of bombs.

Type: Fighter/fighter-bomber (P-47D)	
Crew:	1
Powerplant:	one 1715kW (2300hp) Pratt & Whitney R-2800-59 radial
Max speed:	689km/h (428mph) at 9145m (30,000ft)
Time to height:	9 mins to 6095m (20,000ft)
Service ceiling:	12,800m (42,000ft)
Max range:	2028km (1260 miles)
Wing span:	12.43m (40ft 8in)
Wing area:	27.87m² (300sq ft)
Length:	11.01m (36ft 1in)
Height:	4.32m (14ft 2in)
Weights:	4536kg (10,000lb) empty; 8800kg (19,400lb) max t/o
Armament:	six or eight 12.7mm (0.5in) MG in the wings; two 454kg (1000lb) bombs or 10 rockets

The XP-47B, therefore, was the true Thunderbolt prototype, and it flew for the first time on 6 May 1941. Numerous teething troubles manifested themselves, some examples being the 'snatching and freezing' of the ailerons at altitudes above 9150m (30,000ft), excessive control loads and the jamming of the cockpit canopy at high altitudes, but these were progressively eradicated, and in March 1942 the first production P-47B came off the assembly line, with a production type R-2800-21 engine, metal-covered control surfaces instead of the fabric-covered surfaces of the prototype, a sliding hood instead of the original hinged canopy, and several other refinements.

In June 1942 the 56th Fighter Group began to rearm with the P-47, and between December 1942 and January 1943 it deployed to England, flying its first combat mission – a fighter sweep over St Omer – on 13 April 1943. During the next two years the 56th Fighter Group was to destroy more enemy aircraft than any other fighter group of the Eighth USAAF. The 56th's fearsome motto, *Cave Tonitrum*

459

(Beware the Thunderbolt) from this point of view seems to have been well justified.

From that first operational sortie over Europe until the end of the fighting in the Pacific in August 1945, Thunderbolts flew 546,000 combat sorties, dropped 134,118 tonnes (132,000 tons) of bombs, launched 60,000 rockets and expended more than 135 million rounds of ammunition. In the European Theatre along, from D-Day (6 June 1943) to VE Day (8 May 1945), the Thunderbolt was credited with destroying 9000 locomotives, 86,000 railway wagons, and 6000 armoured vehicles. In all theatres of war, its pilots claimed the destruction of 3752 enemy aircraft in the air and a further 3315 on the ground. By the time the 56th Fighter Wing flew its first operational sortie in the spring of 1943, huge orders had been placed for the P-47D, which was – at first – externally almost identical to the P-47C. As time went by, however, so many changes were introduced in the P-47D that it differed as much from the original P-47D as did that fighter from the XP-47B prototype.

In all, 12,602 P-47Ds were built by Republic in four batches, a further 354 being built by Curtiss-Wright with the designation P-47Gs. The RAF acquired 354 early-model P-47Ds as the Thunderbolt I, while a further 590 later-model P-47Ds were supplied as the Thunderbolt II. All the RAF's Thunderbolts were assigned to squadrons in South-East Asia Command (India and Burma), where they replaced the Hawker Hurricane in the ground-attack role.

The next production version was the P-47M, 130 being completed with the 2088kW (2800hp) R-2800-57 engine. It was built specifically to help combat the V-1 flying bomb attacks on Britain. The last variant was the P-47N, a very long-range escort and fighter bomber, of which Republic built 1816. Overall P-47 production, which ended in December 1945, was 15,660 aircraft. About two-thirds of these, almost all P-47Ds, survived the war and found their way into the air forces of Brazil, Chile, Colombia, Dominica, Ecuador, Mexico, Peru, Turkey and Yugoslavia.

France also used the P-47D in its operations against dissidents in Algeria during the 1950s, since the Armée de l'Air had discovered that jet aircraft were unsuitable for close support in that particular environment. During World War II, the Soviet Union flew 195 P-47s out of the 203 allocated to her, some having been lost en route.

Left: This photograph clearly demonstrates how rotund was the shape of the P-47. Because of its weight, the aircraft had the capability of building up a phenomenal acceleration in a dive, a feature which was extremely useful during combat.

Vought Corsair

The pilot sat in a high position with a bulged clear-view canopy. Early Corsairs had limited visibility, with the engine blocking the view over the nose. In the F4U the engine was drooped by 2.5° to improve the pilot's forward vision.

The markings of this F4U-5N Corsair show that it served with VMF(N) 513 in the Korean War. The midnight blue finish was later replaced by a matt black with deep red code markings to reduce visibility.

This aircraft is armed with eight HVAR air-to-ground rockets for interdicting enemy ground movements. Napalm was also used by the Corsair pilots in Korea.

The F4U-5 and F4U-5N were powered by the Pratt & Whitney R-2800 Double Wasp two-row 18-cylinder radial engine, which dramatically improved their performance over earlier, World War II-era Corsairs.

The Corsair had two intakes either side of the engine cowling which collected air for a two-stage supercharger.

The gun armament of the F4U was four 20mm (0.79in) cannon in the wings, which gave it a heavy punch.

The F4U-5N had a APS-19A radar mounted on the starboard leading edge. This had a 130km (80 mile) range for ground mapping, but could only pick up an aircraft within five kilometres (three miles).

In February 1936, the US Navy invited the Chance Vought Division of United Aircraft to take part in a design contest for a new single-seat, single-engined carrier-borne fighter. Under the leadership of Rex B. Beisel, the Vought design team presented two proposals: the V-166A, designed around the most powerful production engine then available, the Pratt & Whitney R-1830 Twin Wasp, and the V-166B, powered by the still experimental Pratt & Whitney XR-2800-2 Double Wasp. Two months after the proposals had been submitted, the US Navy placed a contract for one prototype of the V-166B under the designation XF4U-1.

The Double Wasp engine was fitted with a two-stage two-speed supercharger and developed 1342kW (1800hp). To make the maximum use of this power, Hamilton Standard designed what was at that time the

Type: naval fighter (F4U-1)	
Crew:	1
Powerplant:	one 1491kW (2000hp) Pratt & Whitney R-2800-8 radial
Max speed:	671km/h (417mph) at 6066m (19,900ft)
Initial climb rate:	1180m (3870ft) per minute
Service ceiling:	11,247m (36,900ft)
Max range:	1633km (1015 miles)
Wing span:	12.50m (41ft)
Wing area:	29.17m² (314sq ft)
Length:	10.17m (33ft 4in)
Height:	4.9m (16ft 1in)
Weights:	4074kg (8982lb) empty; 6350kg (14,000lb) max t/o
Armament:	six 12.7mm (0.5in) MG in wings

Below: The pilot of an F4U Corsair runs up his aircraft's powerful Pratt & Whitney radial engine in preparation for take-off. The F4U Corsair experienced more than its fair share of troubles in the design stage, but went on to become an excellent fighter-bomber.

Above: Although it had been designed as a carrier-borne fighter, the Corsair operated mainly from bases ashore. Its long nose had the disadvantage of obstructing the pilot's forward view and making operations from aircraft carriers extremely difficult.

largest propeller ever used by a fighter. This in itself caused some problems, because if it were fitted to a low-wing design, a very long undercarriage would be needed to provide the required 45cm (18in) ground clearance. Vought solved the problem by adopting the inverted gull-wing platform that was to be the F4U's main recognition feature. This permitted the use of an undercarriage of normal dimensions and also improved visibility for the pilot, which was restricted forward by the huge engine. The rearward-retracting main undercarriage members rotated through 90 degrees to lie flush with the wing surfaces.

The prototype XF4U-1 flew for the first time on 29 May 1940. This aircraft carried an armament of one 12.7mm (0.5in) machinegun in each wing, plus another 12.7mm (0.5in) and a 7.62mm (0.3in) machine gun in the upper decking of the forward fuselage. This was soon assessed as inadequate, so the two fuselage-mounted guns were removed and two (later four) 12.7mm (0.5in) guns installed in each outer wing. This meant that the wing centre section integral fuel tanks had to be removed, together with those built into the leading edges of the outer wing panels, and all fuel stowed in a self-sealing fuselage tank. As this had to located as near as possible to the centre of gravity to avoid changes in trim as the fuel was used up, the Vought design team had no option but to move the cockpit 91cm (3ft) aft, which restricted the pilot's vision even further. One consequence of this was that the F4U spent more than half its operational career operating from land bases, as the restricted cockpit vision made flight deck operations hazardous. Other modifications included the provision of extra armour for the pilot and oil tanks, and the addition of transparent panels aft of the pilot's headrest to improve the rearward view. Aileron span was increased to improve the rate of roll, IFF (Identification Friend or Foe) equipment was fitted, and the 1491kW (2000hp) R-2800-8 engine was installed. At an early production stage, the armament was upgraded to six 12.7mm (0.5in) machine guns.

On 2 April 1941, Vought received a contract for 584 aircraft, the type to be named Corsair in US Navy service. Because of all the required modifications, however, the first production aircraft did not fly until 25 June 1942, by which time the Brewster and Goodyear companies had been designated associated Corsair constructors. The former subsequently built 735 aircraft under the designation F3A-1 (its contract was cancelled in 1944 because of shoddy working practices and other misdemeanours) and the latter 3808, designated FG-1. The first Vought-built F4U-1 was delivered to the USN on 31 July 1944. Carrier trials began in September 1942, and the first Corsair unit, Marine Fighting Squadron VMF-

89-F-7
89-F-26
89-F13
89-F34

214, was declared combat-ready in December, deploying to Guadalcanal in February 1943. After trials with VF-12, the Corsair became operational with Navy Fighting Squadron VF-17 in April 1943, deploying to a land base in New Georgia in September.

The Corsair's combat career got away to a rather inauspicious start. However, as pilots became experienced in flying their powerful new fighter-bombers, they started to become formidable opponents. One pilot in particular achieved spectacular successes while flying the Corsair; he was Lieutenant Bob Hanson, a member of Marine Squadron VMF-215, and he rose to fame in the embattled sky over Rabaul. On 14 January 1944 Hanson fought the first of a series of combats that would set a record, destroying 5 out of a formation of 70 Zeros that were engaged in trying to intercept American bombers. His next five sorties over Rabaul netted him one Zero, three Zeros, four Zeros, three Zeros and four Zeros. This achievement was to bring his score to the impressive total of over 20 enemy aircraft, destroyed in a period of only 17 days.

Of the 12,681 Corsairs built during World War II, 2012 were supplied to the Royal Navy, equipping 19 squadrons of the Fleet Air Arm; some of these aircraft were diverted to equip three squadrons of the Royal New Zealand Air Force, operating in the Solomons. The first RN squadron to arm with the Corsair I (F4U-1) was No 1830, on 1 June 1943. RN Corsair squadrons provided cover for Fleet Air Arm attacks on the German battleship *Tirpitz* in 1944, and subsequently deployed to the Pacific with a British carrier task force in 1945, taking part in the final offensives against Japan. Corsair variants used by the RN were the Corsair II (F4U-1A), Corsair III (F3A-1) and Corsair IV (FG-1).

Variants of the Corsair included the F4U-1C cannon-armed fighter, F4U-1D fighter-bomber, F4U-2 night-fighter, F4U-3 high altitude research version, and F4U-4 fighter. Post-war developments included the F4U-5 fighter-bomber, F4U-5N nightfighter and F4U-5P photo reconnaissance aircraft, all of which gave tremendous service during the Korean War of 1950–53, the F4U-6 (later A-1) attack aircraft and the F4U-7, also supplied to the French Navy. French Corsairs saw combat during the Anglo-French Suez operation of 1956.

Left: During its combat career, the Corsair was to fulfil a wide variety of roles. Post-war developments of the aircraft included the F4U-5 fighter-bomber, the F4U-5N nightfighter and the F4U-5P photo-recce versions, all of which were active in the Korean War.

Avro 683 Lancaster

The Lancaster carried a standard crew of seven: pilot, flight engineer, navigator, wireless operator, bomb-aimer, mid-upper gunner, and a rear gunner. There was only one set of flight controls. Aircrew were always in short supply – 47,000 were lost on Lancaster raids.

This aircraft was one of the third production batch of Lancaster B Mk Is built by Armstrong Whitworth at Coventry. It operated with No 9 Squadron from June 1944 to the end of the war. It flew attacks on the *Tirpitz* and shuttle bombing missions landing in the Soviet Union. It was retired in November 1946.

The mid-upper turret has been removed from this aircraft to accomodate the weight of its Tallboy bomb. It was also removed for very long range missions.

The bomb-aimer lay on the padded emergency escape hatch. He used the Mk XIV bombsight which had a mechanical computer to allow for drift, looking through an optically flat panel in the nose cone. When not bomb-aiming, the crew member manned the front turret.

The Tallboy bomb was designed by Barnes Wallis, inventor of the 'bouncing bomb' used by the Dambuster squadron. The bomb weighed 12,000lb (5443kg) and was designed to spin on the way to the ground to ensure accuracy. The bomb would penetrate far into the ground before exploding, making it the ideal weapon to attack the concrete U-boat pens.

The original Frazer-Nash tail turret had four 7.7mm (0.303in) machine guns with 10,000 rounds of ammunition. The 12.7mm (0.5in) Rose turret shown here gave the gunner greater range, but a lower rate of fire. Late production aircraft had automatic gun laying using centrimetric radar.

Code letters were used by the RAF to identify the aircraft and its squadron. Each squadron had a two-letter code (in this case WS) and the aircraft were known by single letters – here, the letter Y.

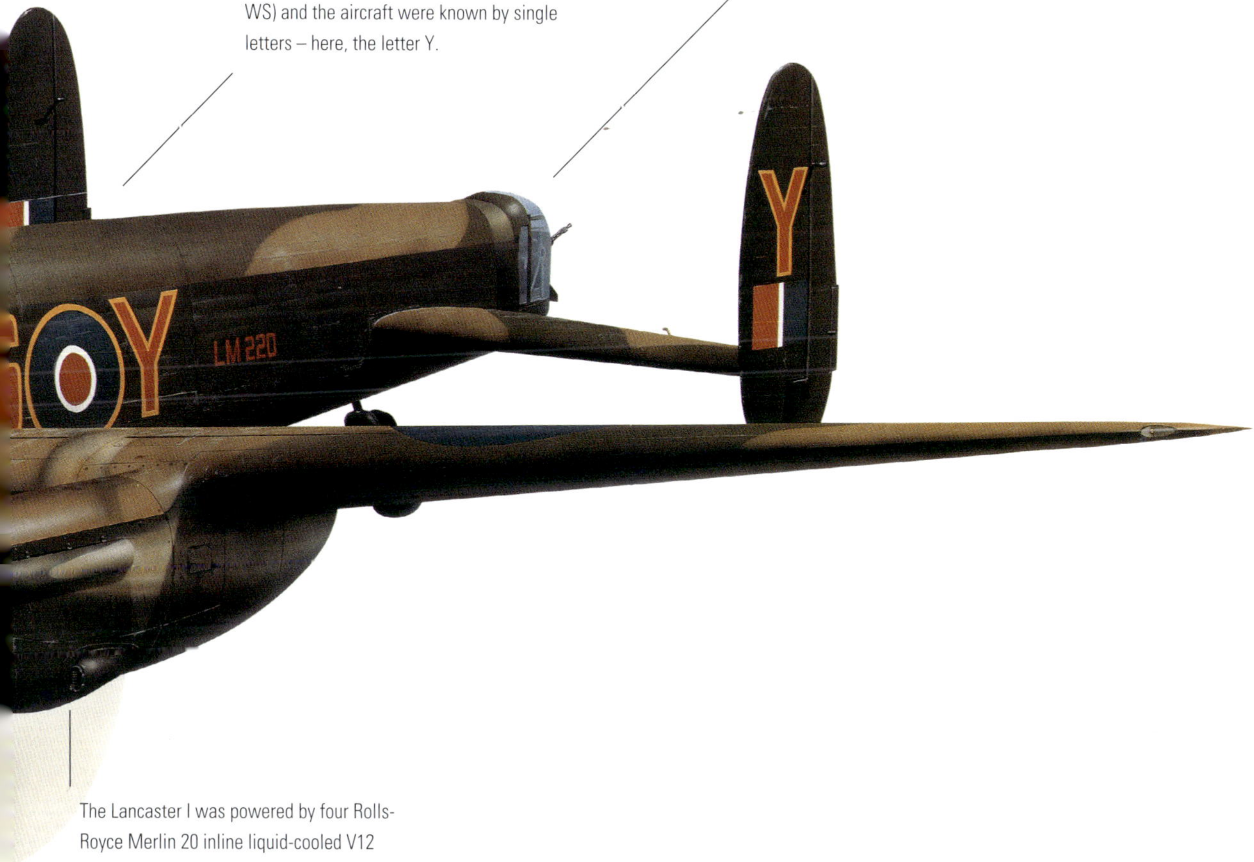

The Lancaster I was powered by four Rolls-Royce Merlin 20 inline liquid-cooled V12 engines. The Lancaster II was equipped with 14-cylinder Bristol Hercules VI or XVI radial engines, to relieve pressure on Merlin production. The Lancaster III was powered by licence-built Merlin 20/22 engines built by Packard Motor Corporation in the USA as the Merlin 28.

Above: Lancaster Mk III 'S for Sugar' of No 467 Squadron, an Australian unit operating with RAF Bomber Command. Note the H_2S radar blister under the fuselage and the tally of missions on the nose.

One of the most famous bomber aircraft of all time, the Avro Lancaster was developed from the Avro Manchester, a design that suffered from the unreliability of its two Rolls-Royce Vulture engines. While production of the Manchester was in progress, one airframe, BT308, was designated a 'four-engined Manchester' and fitted with four Rolls-Royce Merlin XX engines. This was the first prototype Lancaster, which first flew on 9 January 1941 with triple fins and without ventral or dorsal turrets. (A ventral turret was to have been a feature of the Lancaster, but was eliminated to provide extra bomb bay space.) Before the full test programme was initiated, the aircraft was fitted with twin fins on a tailplane spanning 10m (33ft), which improved flight characteristics considerably. All Manchesters were similarly retrofitted, being designated Manchester Mk 1As. The designation Manchester Mk 3 was to have been allotted to the four-engined variant, but the name Lancaster was adopted instead. A further Manchester, L7527, was allocated to the Lancaster development programme, and this became the first production Avro Type 683 Lancaster I. All-up weight had by this time risen to 29,445kg (65,000lb), while maximum speed was 443km/h (275mph) at 4575m (15,010ft), initial rate of climb 76m (250ft) min, and maximum range 4070km (2530 miles) carrying 3170kg (6988lb) of bombs. The new bomber was to be manufactured for the RAF by a consortium of companies comprising Avro, Austin Motors, Vickers-Armstrong, Metropolitan Vickers and Armstrong Whitworth.

The first Lancaster, BT308, was delivered to No 44 (Rhodesia) Squadron at Waddington, Lincolnshire in September 1941 for familiarization, and by January 1942 the squadron had begun to replace its Handley Page Hampdens with the type. First operational sortie with Lancasters was on 3 March 1942, when four aircraft laid mines in the Heligoland Bight. The second squadron to be equipped with Lancasters was No 97, and in company with No 44, it carried out a low-level daylight raid on the MAN factory at Augsburg, Bavaria, which at that time was manufacturing U-boat diesel engines. Out of the 12 Lancasters involved in the attack, 7 were lost. Sqn Ldr J.D. Nettleton, one of 44 Squadron's flight commanders, was awarded the VC.

As an insurance against possible interruption in supplies of Merlins, it was decided to equip some Lancasters with four 1230kW (1650hp) Bristol Hercules 6 (or 16) radials in place of the Merlin XX, these aircraft becoming the Lancaster Mk II. First prototype Mk II was DT810. Production of this variant was turned over to Armstrong Whitworth, who produced 300. Several Mks I and II were used for experimental work, particularly as engine test-beds. One of the Mk I experimental aircraft, ED817, had its fuselage underside modified to accommodate development rounds of the special mine used in the famous raid by No 617 Squadron on the Ruhr dams in May 1943. Little modification was made during its life to the basic Lancaster airframe, a testimonial to its sturdiness and reliability, and so very little extra work was necessary when the Mk III with Packard-built Merlin engines superseded the Mk 1 on the production lines. By this time new navigational and radar aids were becoming standard, and the familiar H_2S blister appeared under the fuselage. Deployment of the Lancaster III enabled Bomber Command to use first the 3624kg (8000lb) bomb, then the 5436kg (12,000lb) Tallboy, and finally the 9966kg (22,000lb) Grand Slam, recessed in the doorless bomb bay. The last Lancaster raid of the war was carried out against an SS barracks at Berchtesgaden on 25 April 1945. During the war, Lancasters flew a total of 156,192 sorties, dropping 618,380 tonnes (608,612 tons) of bombs. Losses in action were 3431 aircraft, a further 246 being destroyed in operational accidents. At its peak strength in August 1944, no fewer than 42 Bomber Command squadrons were armed with the Lancaster.

Towards the end of the war in Europe plans were made for the large-scale use of Lancasters and Lincolns against Japan, with some Lancasters converted to flight refuelling tankers.

Below: Lancaster Mk I of No 44 (Rhodesia) Squadron which, together with No 97 Squadron, was responsible for carrying out the famous low-level daylight attack on the MAN Diesel engine factory situated at Augsburg, in Bavaria, on 17 April 1943.

RE172

Left: A fine study of a Lancaster in flight. The grand total of Lancaster production was 7374 aircraft, and many of these aircraft continued to serve on air-sea rescue and maritime reconnaissance duties long after World War II had come to an end.

Flight Refuelling Ltd carried out extensive trials, and a great deal of equipment had already been manufactured when the war ended and the project was abandoned.

The much-modified Lancasters IV and V became the Lincoln Mks I and II. The Mk VI, nine of which were converted from Mks I and III, was equipped for electronic countermeasures. The last production Lancaster was the Mk VII, of which Austin Motors built 180. The Mks VIII and IX were never built, and the Mk X was a licence-built Mk III, 422 being produced by the Victory Aircraft Co of Canada. Some Lancasters were converted as RAF and later BOAC transports, with faired-over turrets.

Lancasters remained in service with RAF Bomber Command after World War II, until replaced by the Avro Lincoln, and RAF Coastal Command used the GR.3 maritime patrol version until the Avro Shackleton replaced this. Avro refurbished 54 Mk 1s and 7s and converted them to the maritime patrol role for use by France's Aéronavale. Total Lancaster production, including all variants, was 7374 aircraft.

Type: Heavy bomber (Mk III)	
Crew:	7
Powerplant:	four 1223kW (1640hp) Rolls-Royce Merlin 28 or 38 12-cylinder V-type engines
Max speed:	462km/h (287mph)
Initial climb rate:	76m (250ft) per minute
Service ceiling:	5790m (19,000ft)
Max range:	2784km (1730 miles) with a 5443kg (12,000lb) bomb load
Wing span:	31.09m (102ft)
Wing area:	120.49m² (1297sq ft)
Length:	21.18m (69ft 5in)
Height:	6.25m (20ft 5in)
Weights:	16,783kg (37,000lb) empty; 29,484kg (65,000lb) max t/o
Armament:	two 7.7mm (0.303in) MG in nose turret; two 7.7mm (0.303in) MG in dorsal turret; four 7.7mm (0.303in) MG in tail turret; maximum internal bomb load of 8165kg (18,000lb)

Bristol Blenheim

The flight deck had the pilots' seat on the port side. The seat on his right was occupied by the navigator when not working in the nose. A ring and bead sight gave the pilot an rudimentary aiming system for the sole forward firing gun.

The rear gunner had a emergency exit hatch behind him in the roof of the fuselage. The pilot and navigator had sliding panels in the cockpit roof, or an escape hatch in the floor of the nose section.

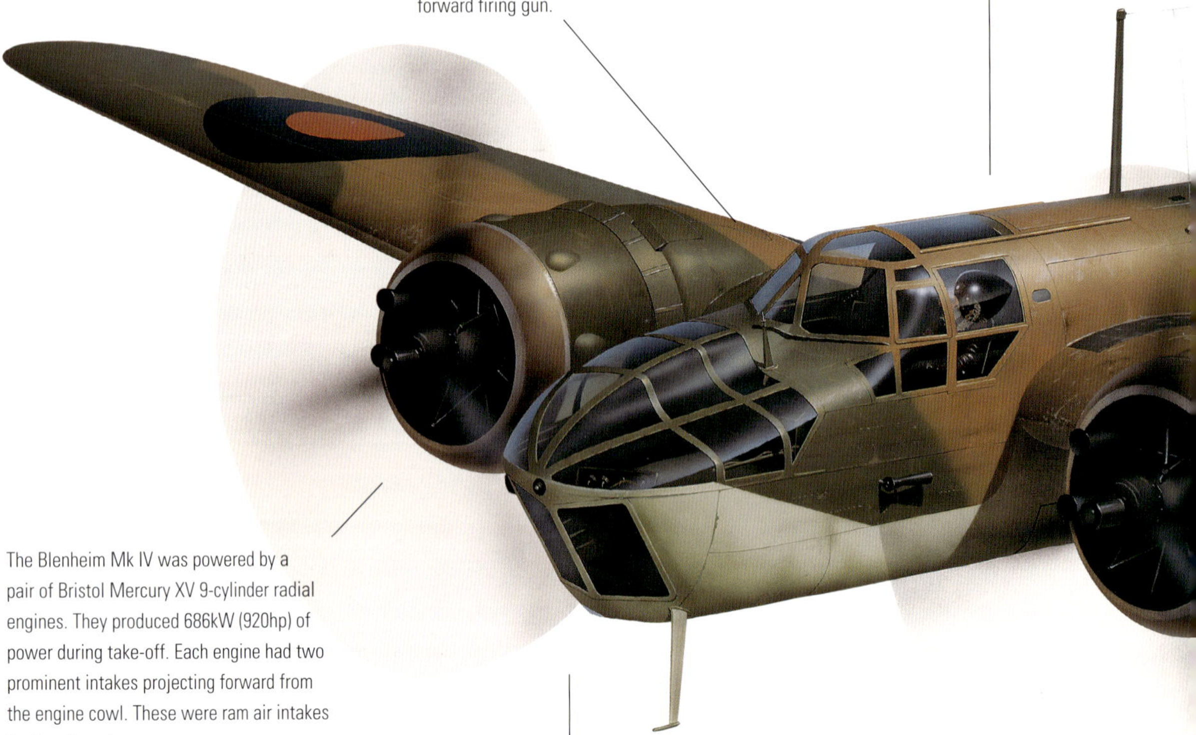

The Blenheim Mk IV was powered by a pair of Bristol Mercury XV 9-cylinder radial engines. They produced 686kW (920hp) of power during take-off. Each engine had two prominent intakes projecting forward from the engine cowl. These were ram air intakes for the oil cooler.

The navigator had a chart table and instrument panel on the port side of his station in the glazed nose. Below this were two flat-pane windows for bomb-aiming, which the navigator would also perform.

The rear gunner had two 7.7mm (0.303in) Browning machine guns in his turret. He was also responsible for aiming the ventral gun in the gondola below him.

Only a small section of the Blenheim's tail fin was fixed, and it had a large full-height rudder controlled by cables running through the fuselage to the controls in the cockpit.

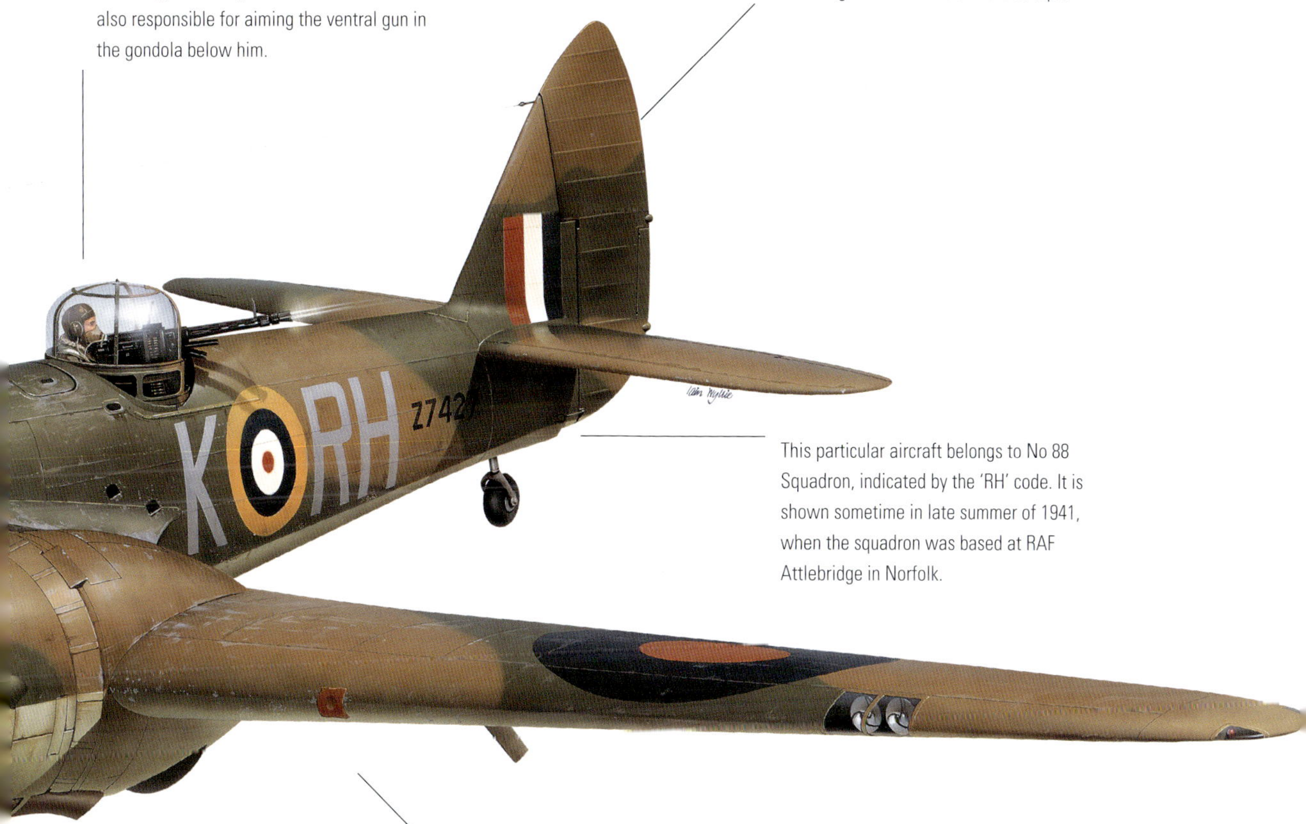

This particular aircraft belongs to No 88 Squadron, indicated by the 'RH' code. It is shown sometime in late summer of 1941, when the squadron was based at RAF Attlebridge in Norfolk.

As a result of the losses in France in 1940, the Blenheim was fitted with a 7.7mm (0.303in) machine gun in its ventral gondola to give added protection against fighters.

The port wing carried a single fixed-firing 7.7mm (0.303in) Browning machine gun. The ammunition for the gun was housed in a tank in the wing. Fuel was also carried in the wing, either side of the engine nacelles.

In 1933 Frank Barnwell, Chief Designer with the Bristol Aeroplane Company, announced a proposal for a light high-speed passenger aircraft, the Bristol Type 135. The machine would carry up to eight passengers inside an all-metal cantilever stressed skin fuselage, power being provided by two 500hp nine-cylinder Bristol Aquila I radial engines. The proposal was supported by Lord Rothermere, owner of the Daily Mail newspaper, who saw the Type 135 as an ideal means of transporting business executives rapidly between the major cities of Europe. The only real snag was that the Type 135 lacked sufficient range to meet Lord Rothermere's requirements, so Bristol re-engined the design with 640hp Bristol Mercury VI radials. Detailed design work on the prototype, now designated Bristol Type 142, began in April 1934, funded by Lord Rothermere, and the aircraft flew for the first time on 12 April 1935.

The prototype's performance proved to be even better than expected, prompting the RAF to ask if they could borrow it for evaluation. The Type 142, named *Britain First*, duly arrived at Martlesham Heath, the Aeroplane and Armament Experimental Establishment, in June 1935, and in July the RAF serial number K7557 was applied to it. A civil registration, G-ADCZ, had been allocated, but was never used. During flight testing, the Type 142 reached a speed of 458km/h (285mph) fully laden, and achieved a top speed of 494km/h (307mph). It was an impressive performance, and in August 1935 the Air Ministry issued Specification B28/35, covering the conversion of the aircraft to the bomber role under the designation Type 142M. Major modifications were necessary, including raising the wing from the low- to mid-wing position to make room for an internal bomb bay, and widening the nose section to accommodate both pilot and observer/bomb aimer. Defensive armament comprised a single 7.7mm (0.303in) Lewis machine gun in a power-operated dorsal turret; the thinking was that the aircraft was fast enough to out-run any contemporary fighter. A Browning 7.7mm (0.303in) was also installed in the port wing leading edge and fired by the pilot. The modified aircraft was designated Bristol Type 142M.

In September 1935 the Air Ministry placed an initial order for 150 aircraft under the service designation Blenheim Mk I, to be powered by 626kW (840hp) Mercury VIII radial engines. The first of these, K7033, went to Martlesham Heath in June 1936 to serve as the development prototype. When the test programme ended in December 1936 the RAF ordered full-scale production of the Blenheim Mk I and awarded Bristol a contract for another 434 aircraft. The first Blenheims were delivered to No 114 Squadron in March 1937; 1280 Mk Is were built in total, and of these 1007 were on RAF charge at the outbreak of World War II. These included 147 completed as Mk IF fighters, fitted with a ventral gun pack with four Browning machineguns; some were later equipped with AI radar and served as interim nightfighters in the autumn of 1940. By the time war broke out, however, most of the Mk I bombers were serving in the Middle and Far East, the home-based squadrons having rearmed with the improved Blenheim Mk IV. Twelve Blenheims were supplied to Finland (which built an additional 55 between 1941 and 1944), 13 to Romania and 22 to Yugoslavia, where a further 48 were built under licence by Ikarus.

Below: Bristol Blenheims flying in formation. Although it was fast and effective when it first entered service, the Blenheim was outclassed as a day bomber by the outbreak of World War II, and it would suffer heavy losses during the Battle of France.

Above: Bristol Blenheim Mk I of No 84 Squadron, 1941. This unit fought in the Greek campaign and was afterwards deployed to the Middle East and then India. It used Blenheims until June 1942, when it re-armed with the Vultee Vengeance.

The Blenheim Mk IV evolved from the Bristol Type 149, developed to Air Ministry Specification 11/36, which called for an interim reconnaissance bomber for RAF Coastal Command in order to bridge the gap between the obsolescent Avro Anson and the Bristol Beaufort torpedo-bomber. In the event, the Lockheed Hudson filled the gap, so the Type 149 prototype, K7072, was released to the RAF. The aircraft was basically a Mk I airframe with two 742kW (995hp) Mercury XV radials driving de Havilland three blade variable pitch propellers, extra fuel tankage and a much re-designed, lengthened nose. By 3 September 1939 the RAF had 197 Blenheim IVs on strength, and on the second day of the war, aircraft of Nos 107 and 110 Squadrons from Marham, Norfolk, carried out the RAF's first offensive operation when they attacked units of the German Navy in the Elbe Estuary. The attack was unsuccessful, many of the bombs failing to explode, and 5 of the 10 Blenheims involved were shot down.

The total inadequacy of the Blenheim's defensive armament became apparent in the battles of Norway and France, when both the UK-based Blenheim squadrons engaged in anti-shipping operations in the North Sea and those deployed to France suffered appalling losses. The armament was subsequently increased to five machineguns. In 1941 most of the RAF's home-based Blenheim IVs were under the control of No 2 Group, based in East Anglia, from where they carried out ongoing anti-shipping patrols (Operation Channel Stop) and attacks on targets in France and the Low Countries. Channel Stop cost the Blenheim squadrons dearly; about 25 per cent of all aircraft despatched failed to return. Nevertheless, the Blenheims carried out some spectacular low-level missions, notably an attack on enemy power stations near Cologne. The Douglas Boston and the De Havilland Mosquito eventually replaced the Blenheims in No 2 Group. In all, 1930 Mk IVs were built. From the 81st aircraft onward they were designated Blenheim IVL, the suffix indicating longer range by virtue of extra fuel tanks.

One final version of the Blenheim, the Mk V, was built in Britain to Specification B.6/40. Rootes Securities Ltd built 942, mostly the VD tropical version. Combat losses were very heavy and it was soon replaced by US Baltimores and Venturas. In Canada, Fairchile built 676 Blenheims for the RCAF, who designated them Bolingbroke Mks I to IV.

Type: Light day bomber	
Crew:	3
Powerplant:	two 686kW (920hp) Bristol Mercury XV radial engines
Max speed:	428km/h (266mph) at 3595m (11,795ft)
Initial climb rate:	457m (1500ft) per minute
Service ceiling:	6705m (22,000ft)
Max range:	2340m (1460 miles)
Wing span:	17.7m (58ft)
Wing area:	43.57m² (469sq ft)
Length:	12.98m (42ft 6in)
Height:	2.99m (9ft 8in)
Weights:	4445kg (9799lb) empty; 6537kg (14,411lb) max t/o
Armament:	one 7.7mm (0.303in) Browning MG in leading edge of port wing; two 7.7mm (0.303in) MG in dorsal turret; two 7.7mm (0.303in) rearward-firing blister position under nose; max internal bomb load of 454kg (1000lb)

Bristol Beaufighter

British Beaufighters had six 7.7mm (0.303in) guns in the wings, but the Australian Mk XXI had four 12.7mm (0.5in) guns, two in each wing, with the barrels slightly protruding.

The single-seat cockpit housed the pilot. He has a large reflector sight in front of him for aiming his cannon. The bulge in front of the cockpit houses the Sperry autopilot, while the ring antenna behind him, inside a transparent radome, is for the direction-finding equipment.

The Mk XXI could carry underwing armament – usually either two 113kg (250lb) bombs or eight rocket projectiles.

The Australian Mk XXI Beaufighters were powered by a pair of Bristol Hercules Mk XVIII 14-cylinder radial engines, capable of 1295kW (1735hp) each. The sleeves made a whistling sound which inspired the Japanese nickname for the aircraft, 'Whispering Death'.

The Beaufighter's main armament was its four 20mm (0.79in) cannon mounted in its lower fuselage and firing from below the cockpit, just behind the pilot.

In the rear fuselage blister sat the observer/radio operator, who faced the rear. In some Beaufighters he was given a single machine gun to give an added measure of protection against enemy aircraft.

The squadron markings on this aircraft show that it belongs to No 22 Squadron of the Royal Australian Air Force. The serial code indicates that this particular Beaufighter Mk XXI was built in Australia at the Fisherman's Bend factory.

Early Beaufighters had a straight tailplane, but as a result of longitudinal stability problems later aircraft were fitted with a 12° dihedral which resolved the issue.

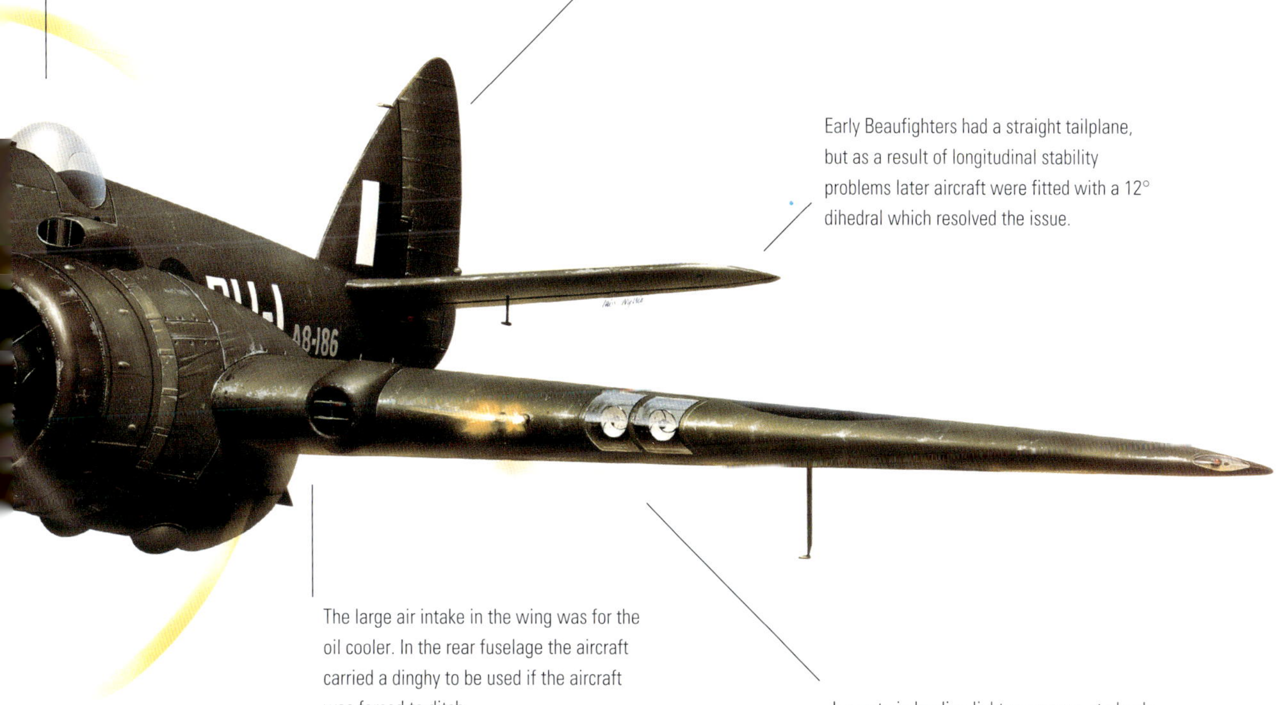

The large air intake in the wing was for the oil cooler. In the rear fuselage the aircraft carried a dinghy to be used if the aircraft was forced to ditch.

Large twin landing lights were mounted only in the port wing. The Beaufighter's large flap sections gave it good control at low speeds, and enabled it to operate out of rough jungle strips on operations.

Above: A Bristol Beaufighter TF Mk X of No 455 Squadron, RAAF. This squadron originally formed as a No 5 Group bomber unit, until being transferred to RAF Coastal Command, where it would take on the role of an anti-shipping strike squadron.

In October 1938, the Bristol Aeroplane Company submitted a proposal for a twin-engined nightfighter, heavily armed with a mixture of cannon and machineguns and equipped with AI (artificial intelligence) radar, to the RAF Air Staff. The proposal was based on the design of the Beaufort torpedo-bomber, which had just made its first flight, and was initially called the Beaufort Fighter. The Air Staff's reaction was enthusiastic and prompt; Specification F.17/39 was written around the proposal and an order placed for 300 Beaufighters, as the aircraft would be named. The first of four Beaufighter prototypes (R2052) flew for the first time on 17 July 1939 powered by two Bristol Hercules I-SM engines (forerunners of the Hercules III). By mid-1940 Bristol had received a second contract for 918 Beaufighters. Two variants were now to be produced, the Mk I with Hercules III engines and the Mk II with Rolls-Royce Merlins, the Hercules being in short supply. The Beaufighter I was cleared for delivery to the RAF on 26 July 1940 and, after evaluation by the Fighter Interception Unit, deliveries to operational squadrons began in September. Delays in the production of AI Mk IV radar equipment prevented the full complement of five Beaufighter units (Nos 25, 29, 219, 600 and 604 Squadrons) from becoming operational until the spring of 1941, but despite early teething troubles, those that were operational enjoyed some success. The first AI-assisted Beaufighter kill was claimed on the night 19/20 November 1940, when Flt Lt John Cunningham and Sgt Phillipson of No 604 Squadron were credited with the destruction of a Junkers 88, and by the time all five Beaufighter squadrons reached operational status their efficiency was greatly enhanced by the commissioning of six GCI (Ground Controlled Interception) radar stations on the south and east coasts of England. These could provide wide coverage, and controllers could bring the fighter to within 4.8km (3 miles) of the target aircraft, at which point the AI Mk IV radar took over. The first GCI-controlled interception was

Type: Nightfighter (Mks I, II and VI); anti-ship strike aircraft (TF Mk X)	
Crew:	2 (Mks I, II and VI); 2-3 (TF Mk X)
Powerplant:	two 1220kW (1636hp) Bristol Hercules VI 14-cylinder radials (Mk VI); two 1320kW (1770hp) Hercules XVII 14-cylinder radials (TF Mk X)
Max speed:	Mk VI, 536km/h (333mph); TF Mk X, 512km/h (318mph)
Time to height:	Mk VI, 4570m (14,996) in 7 mins 48 secs; TF Mk X, 1524m (5000ft) in 3 mins 30 secs
Service ceiling:	Mk VI, 8075m (26,493ft); TF Mk X, 4572m (15,000ft)
Normal range:	Mk V, 2382km (1480 miles); TF Mk X, 2366km (1470 miles)
Wing span:	17.63m (57ft 8in)
Wing area:	46.73m² (503sq ft)
Length:	12.70m (41ft 6in)
Height:	4.82m (15ft 8in)
Weights:	Mk VI: 6623kg (14,600lb) empty; 9798kg (21,600lb) max t/o. TF Mk X: 7076kg (15,600lb) empty; 11,431kg (25,200lb) max t/o
Armament:	Mk VI: four Hispano 20mm (0.79in) fixed cannon in underside of forward fuselage; six 7.7mm (0.303in) MG in leading edges of wing (two to port and four to starboard). TF Mk X: four 20mm (0.79in) fixed forward-firing cannon in underside of forward fuselage; one trainable rearward-firing 7.7mm (0.303in) MG in dorsal position; one 748kg (1649lb) or 965kg (2127lb torpedo, two 227kg (500lb) bombs, eight 76.2mm (3in) rockets

made by John Cunningham on 12 January 1941, but was unsuccessful, as the Beaufighter's guns jammed. Then, on 10 May 1941 – the last major Luftwaffe attack on London – GCI-controlled Beaufighters destroyed 14 German bombers, the highest loss sustained by the Luftwaffe on any one night since the Blitz began. Thirteen more Beaufighter squadrons were assigned to the night defence of Great Britain between 1941 and 1942, and many of the RAF's nightfighter aces scored their early kills while flying the heavy twin-engined fighter. Total Mk I production was 914, and 450 Mk IIs were built.

In December 1941 No 89 Squadron deployed at Abu Sueir, Egypt, with Beaufighter Mk Is, and in May 1941 No 46 Squadron began reforming as a nightfighter unit at Idku, initially using some of 89 Squadron's aircraft. These two squadrons remained responsible for the night defence of the Canal Zone and for protection of coastal shipping throughout 1942, providing occasional detachments to Malta and, in 1943, carrying out intruder patrols over the Greek islands and Sicily. No 89 Squadron left for Ceylon in October 1943, while No 46 Squadron continued to provide air defence detachments around the eastern Mediterranean. In December 1942, meanwhile, another RAF Beaufighter nightfighter squadron, No 153, had arrived in North Africa; based at Maison Blanche in Algeria, its task was to protect the North African ports following the Allied invasion of November 1942 (Operation Torch). In March 1943 No 108 Squadron, which had been operating in the night-bombing role from various locations in North Africa, reformed as a nightfighter unit at Shandur with Beaufighter VIs (the Mk VI being a variant fitted with Hercules VI engines), flying night patrols over Egypt and Libya before moving to Malta in June. Early in 1943 four USAAF nightfighter units also arrived in North Africa; these were the 414th, 415th, 416th and 417th FS, whose crews had trained with RAF units in the UK. All four were armed with the Beaufighter VIF; they subsequently moved to Sicily and Italy, and were the only nightfighter units operating with the US Twelfth Air Force.

The Beaufighter Mk IC – 300 were produced – was a long range fighter variant for RAF Coastal Command. Operated initially by Nos 252 and 272 Squadrons in Malta and North Africa, it was used successfully as a strike aircraft against enemy shipping and, modified locally to carry two 113kg (250lb) or 227kg (500lb) bombs under the fuselage, it was used equally as effectively as a ground-attack aircraft in the Western Desert. It was supplanted by the Mk VI (the Mks III, IV and V being experimental aircraft); Mk VIs for Fighter Command were designated Mk VIF (879 aircraft), and those for Coastal Command Mk VIC (693 aircraft). Sixty Mk VIs on the production line were completed as Interim Torpedo Fighters, but two new variants for Coastal Command soon appeared. These were the TF Mk X torpedo bomber and the Mk XIC. Both were fitted with 1320kW (1770hp) Hercules XVII engines and had a dorsal cupola containing a rearward-firing 7.7mm (0.303 in) machine gun. Production of the TF Mk X, the most important British anti-shipping aircraft from 1944 to the war's end, totalled 2205 aircraft, while 163 aircraft were completed to Mk XIC standard. The Beaufighter TF Mk X was also built in Australia; the RAAF used it to good effect in the south-west Pacific. British production of the Beaufighter (all variants) was 5562.

Below: A Beaufighter TF Mk X pictured with its crew. The Beaufighter was the most important British anti-shipping strike aircraft from 1944 to the end of the war, and during this period it was responsible for inflicting serious damage on enemy convoys.

De Havilland Mosquito

The cockpit in the PR.34A Mosquito was a two-man side-by-side, with the pilot on the left. The rear of the seats were armoured, and the sides of the cockpit were bulged to aid rear vision. The navigator had an astrodome above his seat in order to take sextant readings.

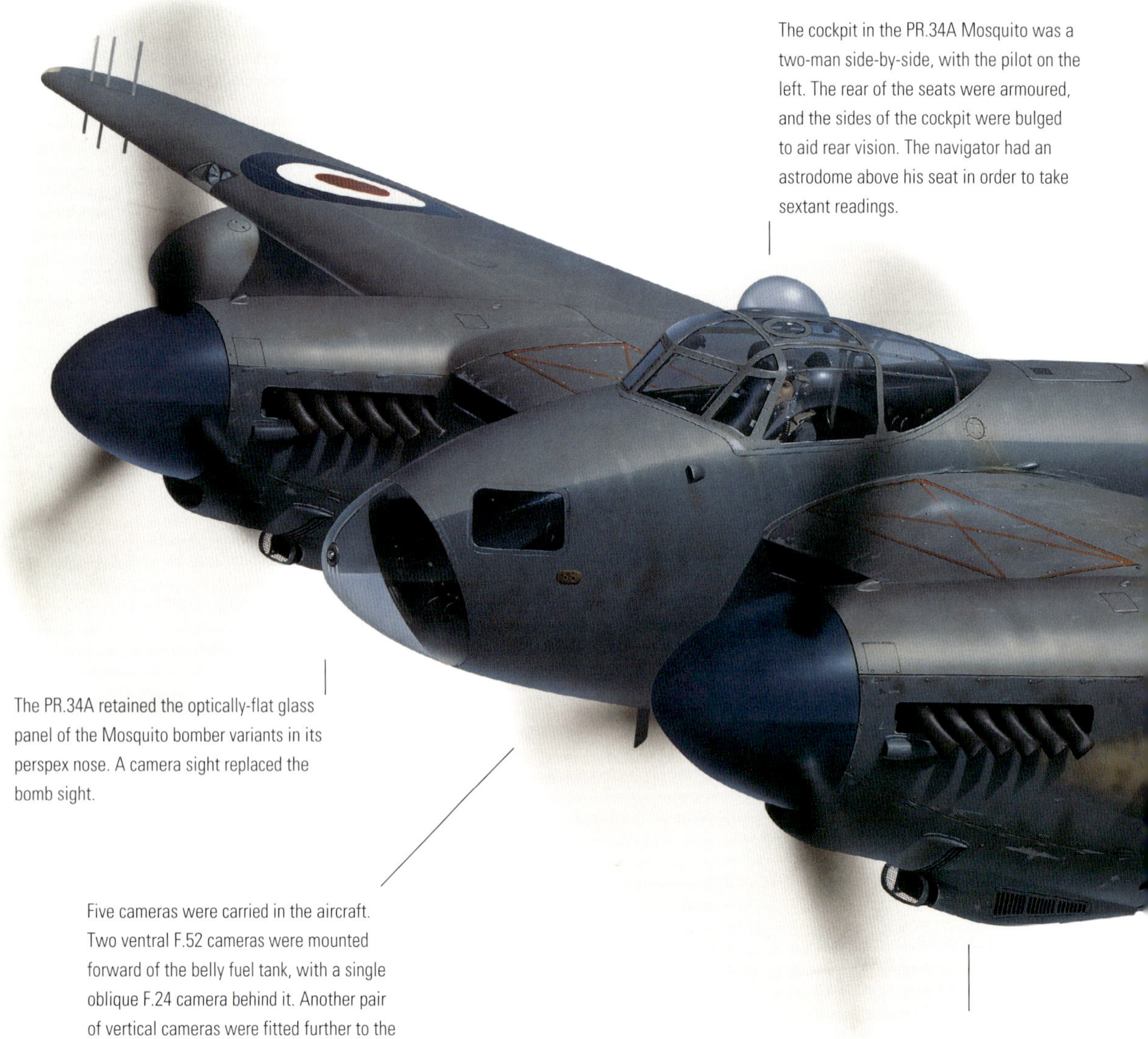

The PR.34A retained the optically-flat glass panel of the Mosquito bomber variants in its perspex nose. A camera sight replaced the bomb sight.

Five cameras were carried in the aircraft. Two ventral F.52 cameras were mounted forward of the belly fuel tank, with a single oblique F.24 camera behind it. Another pair of vertical cameras were fitted further to the rear of the aircraft.

The PR.34A was equipped with two Rolls-Royce Merlin two-stage turbo-charged piston engines. A Merlin 113 was fitted on the starboard side, and a Merlin 114 on the port side. The intakes below each engine are for the carburettor. The intakes for the oil and coolant radiators were in the wing roots between the engine and the fuselage.

The wooden fuselage of the Mosquito carried a large amount of internal fuel on the PR.34A for its long range missions. The aircraft is wearing the standard post-war reconaissance colour scheme of a medium sea grey upper fuselage with cerulean (or PRU blue) undersides.

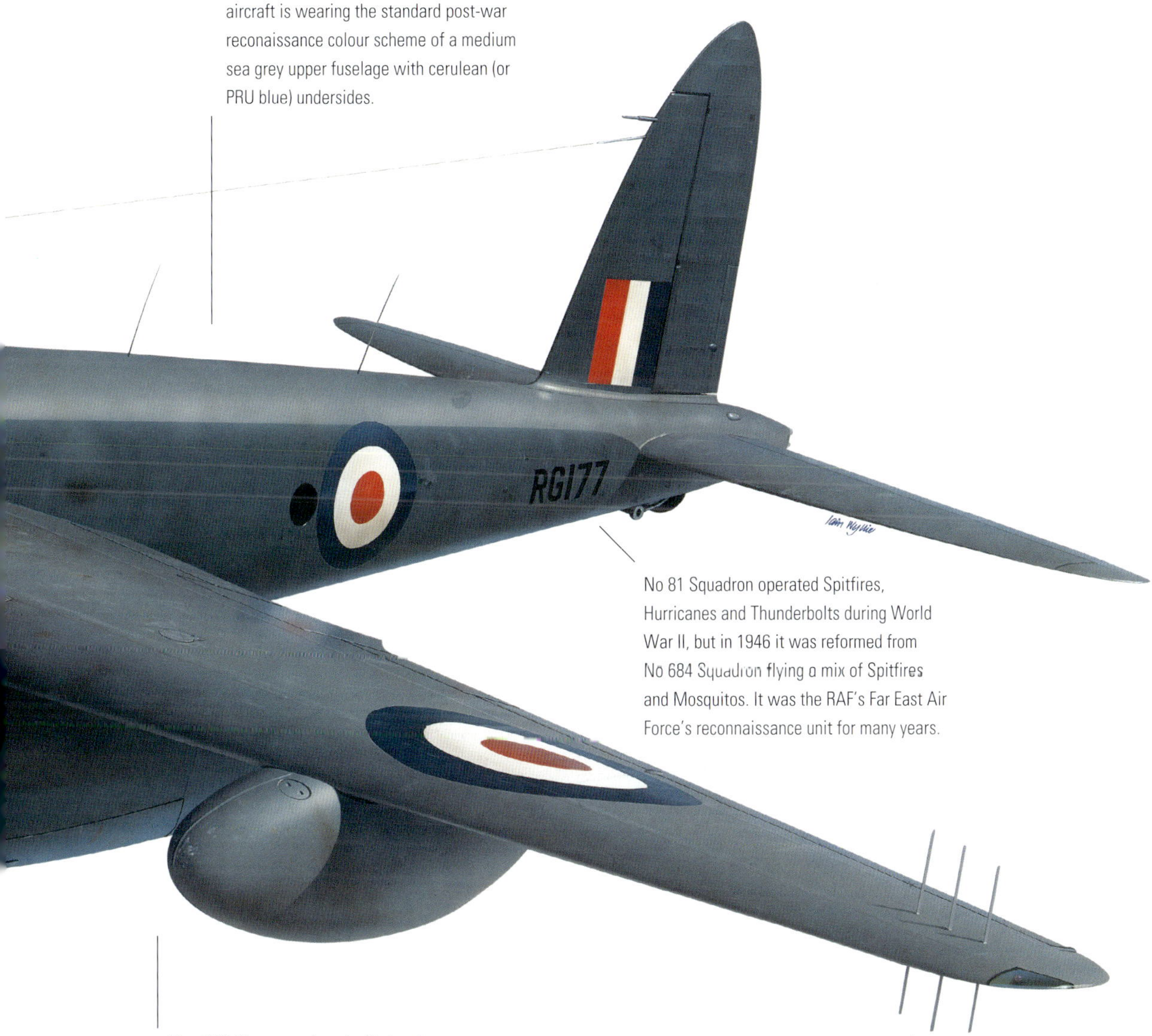

No 81 Squadron operated Spitfires, Hurricanes and Thunderbolts during World War II, but in 1946 it was reformed from No 684 Squadron flying a mix of Spitfires and Mosquitos. It was the RAF's Far East Air Force's reconnaissance unit for many years.

The PR.34A was equipped with two large slip tanks housing 1820 litres (400 gallons) of fuel. However they had a significant drag effect, and were rarely used operationally.

The wingtip aerials were for the IFF (Identification Friend or Foe) transmitter/receiver. Earlier Mosquitos had their air intercept radar aerials in this position on the wingtips.

The de Havilland DH.98 Mosquito was, without doubt, one of the most versatile and successful aircraft of World War II. It saw service throughout the world as a day and nightfighter, fighter-bomber, high altitude bomber, pathfinder, anti-shipping strike aircraft, reconnaissance aircraft and trainer. Conceived in 1938 as a private venture, its designers opted for all-wood construction; not only would this produce a relatively light aircraft with a high speed, but it would also alleviate the problem of strategic metals shortages in time of war. They also opted for two Merlin engines. Official interest in the Mosquito was slow to awaken, but in March 1940 the Air Ministry issued Specification B.1/40, covering the building of three prototypes and an initial production batch of 50 aircraft. The first prototype, originally bearing the maker's serial E0234 (it was changed to W4050 after two flights) and completed in bomber configuration, flew for the first time on 25 November 1940. The second prototype, W4051, was completed as a photo-reconnaissance aircraft and flew on 10 June 1941, while the third, W4052, was equipped as a nightfighter and made its first flight a few weeks earlier, on 15 May 1941.

The initial production batch of 50 aircraft included 9 PR Mk I and 10 B Mk IV aircraft. The latter was the definitive

Above: A Mosquito Mk XVI of No 571 Squadron. Formed in April 1944, this unit was part of the Light Night Striking Force and used its Mosquitoes until it disbanded in September 1945. Mainly, its aircraft carried a single 1812kg (4000lb) bomb.

light bomber version. The PR Mosquito was the first into service, being issued to No 1 Photographic Reconnaissance Unit at RAF Benson, Oxfordshire in September 1941. The first operational sortie was flown on 20 September. The first Mosquito B IV bombers went to No 105 Squadron at Marham, Norfolk, in May 1942, and made their first operational sortie on the 31st. Five aircraft were sent to Cologne to photograph the damage caused by the previous night's 1000-bomber raid and to drop a few bombs. One Mosquito was hit by flak and crashed in the North Sea. Total production of the B IV, which eventually equipped 12 squadrons, was 273 aircraft.

The Mosquito nightfighter prototype was completed with AI Mk IV radar in a 'solid' nose and a powerful armament of four 20mm (0.79in) cannon and four machine guns. The first Mosquito fighter squadron, No 157, formed at Debden in Essex on 13 December 1941, its first aircraft, a dual-control Mk II, arriving at Debden's satellite airfield, Castle Camps, on 26 January 1942. Seventeen Mk IIs were delivered to Maintenance Units for the fitting of AI Mk V, and by mid-April No 157 Squadron had 19 NF Mk IIs on its inventory, 3 of them without radar. By this time, No 151 Squadron at Wittering had also begun to rearm with the NF Mk II, with 16 aircraft on strength at the end of April. Seventeen squadrons were eventually armed with the NF II, 466 of which were built. A total of 97 Mk IIs were later converted to NF Mk XII standard with AI

Left: Mosquitoes of No 13 Operational Training Unit formed up in a neat line prior to the day's flying. No 13 Operational Training Unit retained its Mosquitoes until well after the war, when it merged with No 54 Operational Training Unit in May 1947.

Type: Fighter-bomber (FB.Mk VI)	
Crew:	2
Powerplant:	two 1104kW (1480hp) Rolls-Royce Merlin 21 or 23 12-cylinder V-type engines
Max speed:	595km/h (370mph)
Time to height:	6 mins 45 secs to 4570m (15,000ft)
Service ceiling:	10,515m (34,500ft)
Max range:	2744km (1705 miles)
Wing span:	16.51m (54ft 2in)
Wing area:	40.41m^2 (435sq ft)
Length:	13.08m (42ft 9in)
Height:	5.31m (17ft 4in)
Weights:	6429kg (14,173lb) empty; 9072kg (20,000lb) max t/o
Armament:	four 20mm (0.79in) fixed forward-firing cannon; four 7.7mm (0.303in) fixed forward-firing MG in the nose; internal and external load of bombs, RPs or drop tanks of up to 907kg (2000lb)

Mk VIII with centimetric radar, followed by 270 NF Mk XIIIs, the production counterpart of the Mk XII. These and subsequent nightfighter Mosquitoes retained only the 20mm (0.79in) cannon armament. Other specialist nightfighter Mosquitoes were the Mk XVs and XVIIs, 100 of which were converted from Mk IIs, and the NF Mk XIX. The latter aircraft, and the Mk XVII, were equipped with the US-made AI Mk X.

It was the Mosquito NF Mk II that provided the basis for the major production version, the FB Mk VI fighter-bomber, of which 2718 were built during and after the war. The first Mk VI was a converted Mk II (HJ662), and flew for the first time in February 1943. The standard NF II gun armament was retained, and the aircraft could carry two 113kg or 227kg (250lb or 500lb) bombs in the rear of the bomb bay, with two additional bombs or auxiliary fuel tanks beneath the outer wing sections. In late spring 1943, Mk VI HJ719 carried out trials with rocket projectiles. These proved very successful, and RAF Coastal Command equipped some of its strike wings with Mk VI Mosquitoes armed with eight 27kg (60lb) rockets under each wing.

The Mosquito Mk VI entered service with No 418 Squadron in the spring of 1943 and subsequently armed several squadrons of No 2 Group, replacing such aircraft as the Lockheed Ventura. These squadrons carried out some daring low-level precision attacks during the last year of the war, including the raid on Amiens prison in February 1944 and attacks on Gestapo headquarters buildings in Norway and the Low Countries.

Right: Armourers bombing up a Mosquito before a sortie to Germany. The Mosquito was one of the most versatile aircraft ever built, although problems were experienced with its wooden construction in the heat and humidity of the Far East.

Mosquito FB Mk XVIII (27 built) carried eight rockets and two 227kg (500lb) bombs, and was armed with a single 57mm (6pdr) gun in the nose. Known as the Mosquito 'Tsetse', this variant was used by only two squadrons, Nos 248 and 254. The first high-altitude bomber version was the B IX, and this was followed by 387 examples of the B XVI, fitted with a pressurized cabin. Its successor was the B 35, which did not become operational before the war's end. The photoreconnaissance equivalents were the PR IX, XVI and 34. The last nightfighter variant was the NF 30, with improved Merlins. Canadian Mosquito production, which ran to 1134 aircraft powered by Packard-built Merlins, included the Mk XXs and 25s bombers, Mk 26 fighter-bomber and Mk 22s and 27s trainers. Total Mosquito production reached 7781 aircraft, 6710 of which were built during the war years.

Fairey Swordfish

The Swordfish's pilot flew, like the rest of the crew, in an open cockpit. A sight bar was mounted just below the wing for aiming torpedoes when attacking shipping.

The Mk II was powered by a Bristol Pegasus 30 radial piston engine.

This Mk II carries a standard 457mm (18in) torpedo, but mines, rockets or bombs were alternative combat loads used by the Fleet Air Arm.

The fixed undercarriage of the Swordfish was testament to its relative age, the first examples going into service in 1936. Despite its ungainly appearance, the 'Stringbag' outlasted its supposed replacement, the Fairey Albacore, in production.

Although this aircraft does not carry squadron markings, the colour scheme is consistent with that in use in 1940/1, around the time of the famous attack on the Italian Fleet in Taranto.

The rear gunner was equipped with a 7.7mm (0.303in) Lewis machine gun which is shown here in its stowed position. The pilot had a fixed, forward-firing Vickers mounted on the starboard side of the cockpit.

The arrester hook was a vital part of the aircraft's fittings for service on carriers. The Swordfish's wings were also hinged to fold back against the fuselage to reduce the amount of space needed by each aircraft on board a carrier.

The Fairey Swordfish, known universally as the 'Stringbag', appeared to be an anachronism from the moment of its conception; a slow, lumbering biplane that seemed to have no place in the increasingly streamlined world of 1930s aviation. Yet the design of the Swordfish was exactly right for the principal tasks it had to perform, and its rugged structure made it ideal for aircraft carrier operations. It was to serve with great distinction throughout World War II, from the North Atlantic to the Indian Ocean, and in so doing, performed feats of arms that became legendary.

The Swordfish was derived from the private-venture Fairey TSR 1, whose prototype was lost in an accident in September 1933. Undeterred, the Fairey Aviation Company's design team followed up with a larger development, the TSR II (for Torpedo-Spotter-Reconnaissance II). The prototype, K4190, flew for the first time on 17 April 1934, and a contract for 86 production Swordfish Mk I aircraft was placed in April 1935. The aircraft entered service with No 825 Squadron of the Fleet Air Arm in July 1936. Production models were built to Specification S.38/34, featuring a slightly swept-back upper wing, all-metal construction with a fabric covering, and a Bristol Pegasus IIIM 3 engine. The Swordfish I was designed to carry a 730kg (1610lb) torpedo under the fuselage, but it could carry a mine in that position, or an equivalent weight of bombs under the fuselage and lower wings.

Below: Although it was somewhat antiquated in appearance, the Fairey Swordfish was nonetheless very effective in all the roles it was called upon to perform, from general reconnaissance to torpedo attack. Later versions would carry ASV radar.

By the outbreak of World War II 689 Swordfish had been delivered or were on order. Thirteen squadrons were equipped with the type, and a further 12 were formed during the war years. Early war roles for the Swordfish included fleet escort and convoy protection, the first offensive missions being flown during the Norwegian campaign, which took place between April and June 1940. It was in the Mediterranean Theatre that the Swordfish really proved its worth. On 3/4 July, during the tragic but necessary attack on the French fleet at Mers-el-Kebir, Swordfish from HMS *Ark Royal* disabled the French flagship *Dunkerque*. The following day, shore-based Swordfish from Egypt attacked Axis shipping in Tobruk harbour, sinking one Italian destroyer and damaging another, and also sinking a large freighter and damaging the troopship *Liguria*.

In the months following, Swordfish inflicted considerable damage on Italian shipping, culminating in the spectacular night attack on the Italian fleet at Taranto on 11 November 1940 by 21 Swordfish of Nos 815 and 819 Squadrons from HMS *Illustrious*. Of the Swordfish, 12 carried torpedoes; the others carried flares for target illumination, and bombs for use against oil installations on shore. The attack was brilliantly successful. The Italian battleship *Conte di Cavour* was so badly damaged that she took no further part in hostilities; her sister ship, the *Caio Duilio*, had to be beached and was out of action for six months; while the *Littorio* was disabled for four months. At one stroke, the Italian battle fleet had been reduced from six to three capital ships at a crucial period of the Mediterranean war, and for the loss of only two Swordfish.

It was the first real demonstration of the aircraft carrier as a means of exercising flexible, mobile sea power, and the lesson was not lost on the Japanese Admiral Isoroku Yamamoto, whose carrier aircraft attacked Pearl Harbor just over a year later.

Other notable Swordfish actions included the Battle of Cape Matapan in March 1941, the crippling of the German battleship *Bismarck* in May, and the gallant action against the *Scharnhorst*, *Gneisenau* and *Prinz Eugen* during the famous 'Channel Dash' of February 1942, when all six Swordfish of No 825 Squadron involved were shot down and their commander, Lt Cdr Eugene Esmonde, was awarded a posthumous Victoria Cross.

The Swordfish Mk II, which appeared in 1943, had metal-covered lower wings, enabling it to transport rocket projectiles. Rocket-armed Swordfish carried out many attacks on small enemy vessels in the North Sea during the closing months of the war. Swordfish registered some success against German submarines, too, as on 21 November 1942, when carrier-based aircraft attacked and sank the *U-517* in the North Atlantic, as well as on 23 May 1943, when Swordfish of No 819 Squadron from the escort carrier HMS *Archer* attacked and consequently sank the *U-752* with rockets.

Later Mk II Swordfish were fitted with the 611kW (820hp) Pegasus XXX engine, and this also powered the Swordfish Mk III, which carried ASV radar in a housing between the main landing gear legs. All three Swordfish variants were converted as Mk IVs for service with the Royal Canadian Air Force, and many Mk Is were converted as twin-float seaplanes for service aboard catapult-equipped warships. Swordfish production ended on 18 August 1944, by which time 2391 aircraft had been built. Of these, 692 were produced by Fairey and 1699 by Blackburn.

Above: The Swordfish Mk II, pictured here, was built by Blackburn. The aircraft was fitted with a strengthened lower wing, skinned with metal rather than fabric, and this feature permitted the craft to carry up to a maximum of eight air-to-surface rockets.

The Swordfish was still operational as an aircraft in the final moments of the war in Europe, seeing active service on the last day. However, its retirement was rapid from that point onwards. The last Swordfish squadron would be disbanded on 21 May 1945, only two weeks after the final surrender of Germany.

Type: Torpedo/ASW/reconnaissance aircraft	
Crew:	3
Powerplant:	one 611kW (820hp) Bristol Pegasus XXX radial engine
Max speed:	222km/h (138mph)
Initial climb rate:	372m (1220ft) per minute
Service ceiling:	5867m (19,248ft)
Max range:	879km (546 miles)
Wing span:	12.97m (42ft 5in)
Wing area:	56.39m² (607sq ft)
Length:	10.87m (35ft 7in)
Height:	3.76m (12ft 3in)
Weights:	2132kg (4700lb) empty; 3406kg(7508lb) max t/o
Armament:	one fixed forward-firing 7.7mm (0.303in) MG; one trainable 7.7mm (0.303in) gun in rear cockpit; offensive load of one 457mm (18in) torpedo or eight 27.2kg (60lb) rocket projectiles

Handley Page Halifax

The Halifax had a crew of seven. The pilot was on the flight deck, with the flight engineer behind him. The bomb-aimer/gunner was in the nose, with the navigator and wireless operator behind him. Two gunners were carried in the mid-upper and rear turrets.

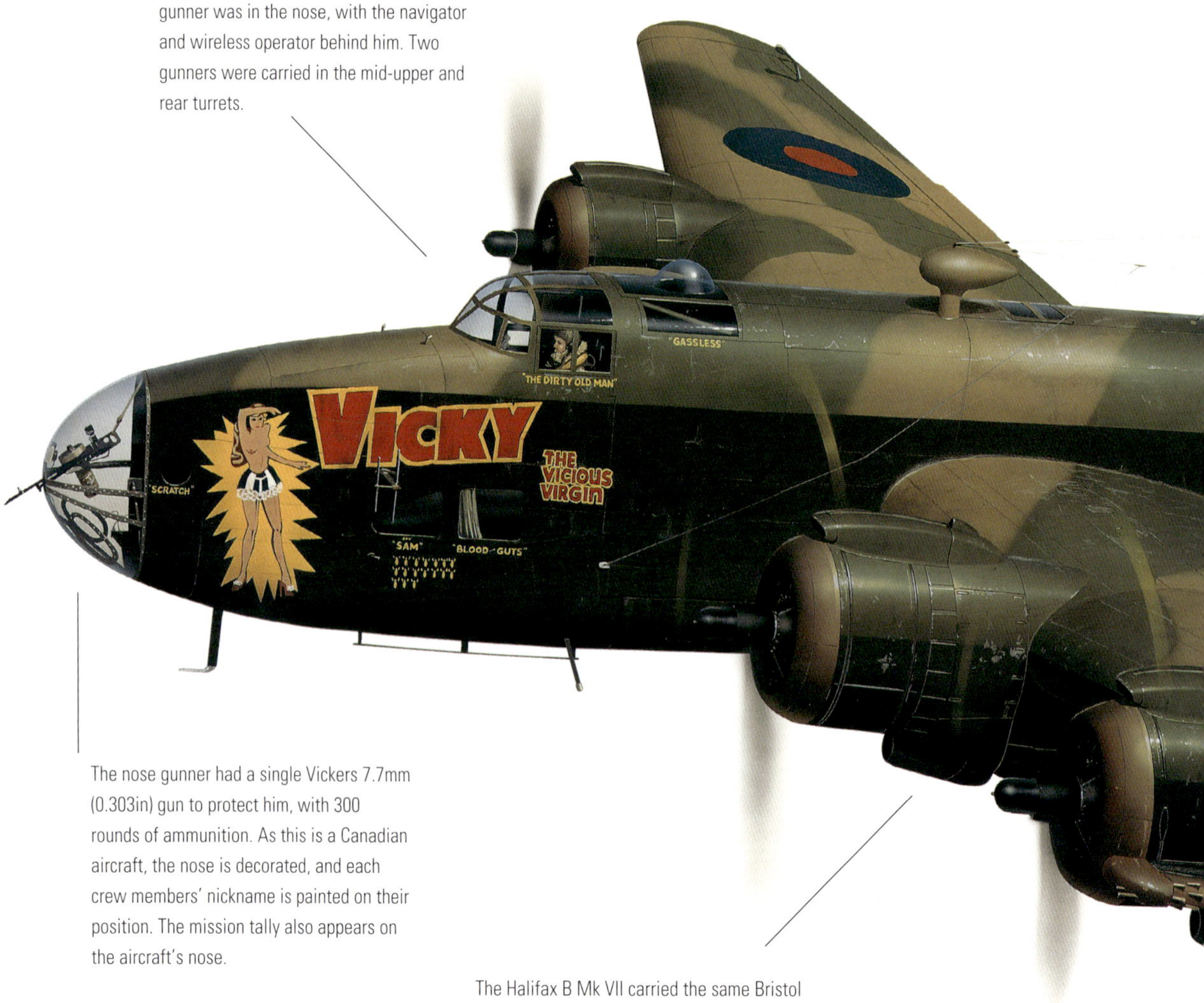

The nose gunner had a single Vickers 7.7mm (0.303in) gun to protect him, with 300 rounds of ammunition. As this is a Canadian aircraft, the nose is decorated, and each crew members' nickname is painted on their position. The mission tally also appears on the aircraft's nose.

The Halifax B Mk VII carried the same Bristol Hercules XVI 14 cylinder radial engines as the B Mk III. They drove a de Havilland constant-speed propellor and were each rated at 1204kW (1615hp) for take off.

The dorsal turret was a Boulton Paul A Mk III mid-upper turret, armed with four 7.7mm (0.303in) guns with 1160 rounds each. The teardrop fairing in front of the turret houses the direction finder aerial.

This Halifax belongs to No 408 Squadron of the Royal Canadian Air Force. It operated Halifaxes from July 1944 to May 1945. It was known as the Goose squadron thanks to its unit badge, which featured a Canada Goose in its design.

Late model Halifaxes were equipped with two types of rear turret: either the Type D with twin 12.7mm (0.5in) machine guns (as shown) or the Type E with four 7.7mm (0.303in) guns.

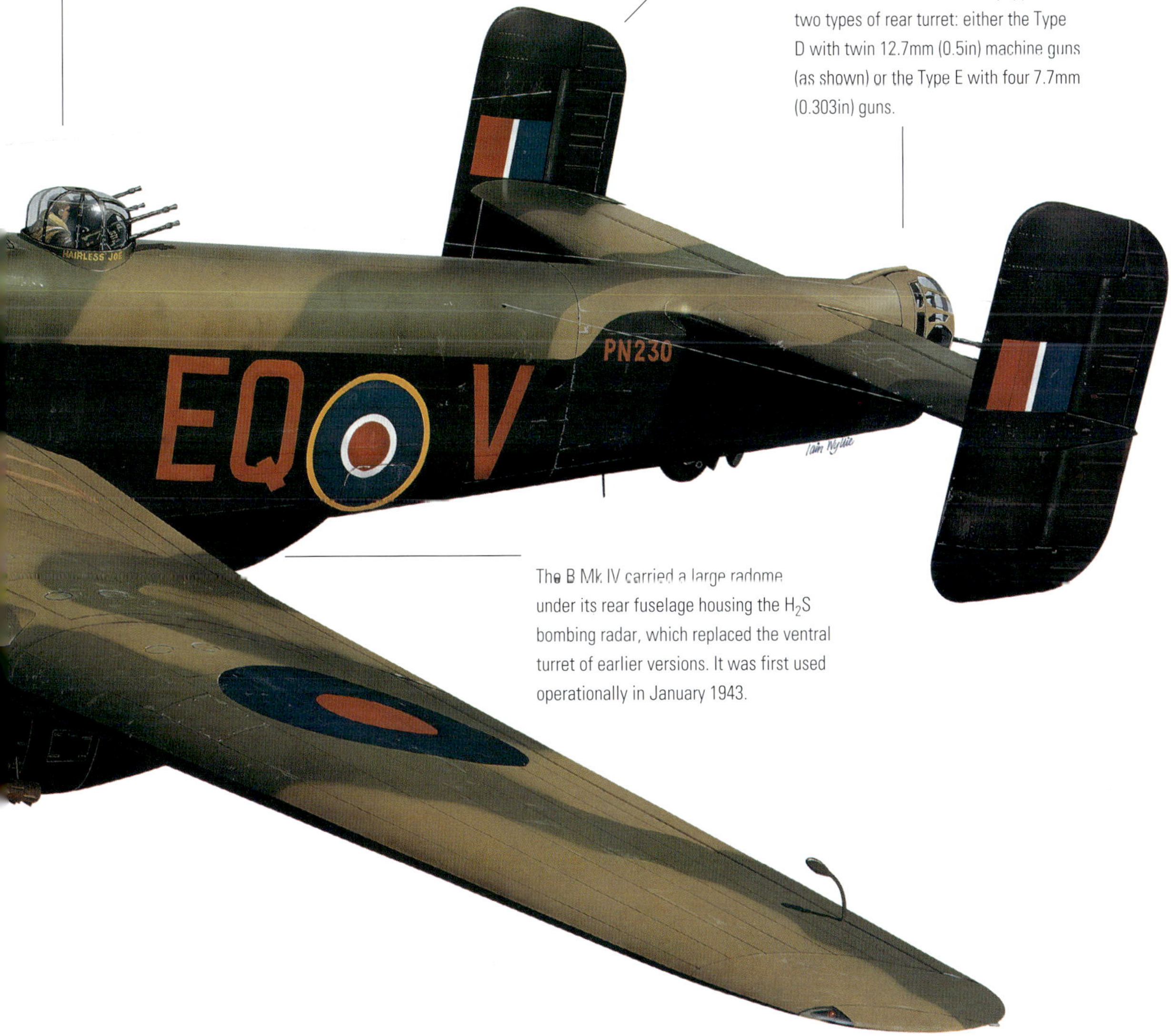

The B Mk IV carried a large radome under its rear fuselage housing the H_2S bombing radar, which replaced the ventral turret of earlier versions. It was first used operationally in January 1943.

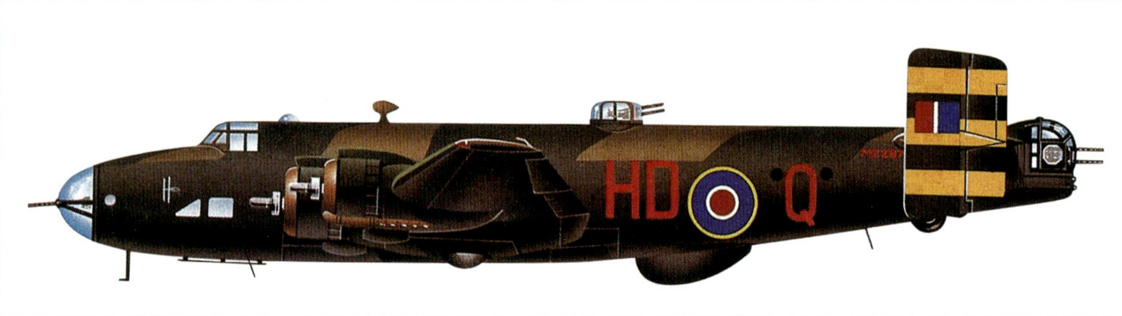

Above: A Handley Page Halifax Mk III of No 466 Squadron Royal Canada Air Force. The tail markings shown here denote that the aircraft is carrying G-H equipment, which would enable it to operate as a lead bomber in the target-marking role.

One of the truly famous bomber aircraft of World War II, the Handley Page Halifax had its origin in Air Ministry Specification P.13/36, which called for an all-metal, mid-wing cantilever monoplane bomber powered by two 24-cylinder Rolls-Royce Vulture engines, then still under development. An earlier design to B.1/35, powered by two Rolls-Royce Merlin engines, was rejected; a mock-up, however, was built. Two prototypes of the HP.56, as the Vulture-powered proposal was designated, were ordered in April 1937, but as the Vulture featured prominently in the RAF's hurried re-armament programme, the Air Ministry was concerned that not enough engines of this type would be available, and so on 3 September 1937 two prototypes of a version powered by four Rolls-Royce Merlins were ordered instead. The basic design of the aircraft, which was re-designated HP.57, was unchanged, although the fuselage length and wing span were increased and the estimated all-up weight went from 11,914kg (26,265lb) to 18,120kg (39,947lb). In fact, loaded weight at 24,915kg (54,927lb) was well above the estimate, but it was still low in relation to the aircraft's size and horsepower.

Type: Heavy bomber/transport/maritime patrol (Halifax III)	
Crew:	7
Powerplant:	four 1204kW (1615hp) Bristol Hercules VI or XVI 14-cylinder two-row radial engines
Max speed:	454km/h (282mph)
Time to height:	37 mins 30 secs to 6095m (20,000ft)
Service ceiling:	7315m (24,000ft)
Max range:	3194km (1985 miles) with a 3175kg (7000lb) bomb load
Wing span:	30.07m (98ft 6in)
Wing area:	118.45m^2 (1275sq ft)
Length:	21.82m (71ft 6in)
Height:	6.32m (20ft 7in)
Weights:	17690kg (39,000lb) empty; 30,845kg (68,000lb) max t/o
Armament:	one 7.7mm (0.303in) MG in nose position; four 7.7mm (0.303in) MG each in dorsal and tail turrets; internal bomb load of 6577kg (14,500lb)

The prototype HP.57, L7244 (the bomber was not given the name Halifax until 12 September 1940) flew for the first time on 25 October 1939, followed by a second aircraft in August 1939. In November 1940 L7244 was borrowed from the Ministry of Aircraft Production and flown to RAF Leeming in Yorkshire to be used for training by No 35 Squadron, which was forming as the first Halifax Mk I squadron in Bomber Command. In December the squadron moved to Linton-on-Ouse, near York, and it was from there, on the night 10/11 March 1941, that six of its Halifaxes made the type's first operational sortie. One Halifax was lost, shot down in error by a RAF nightfighter while on its way home.

Early production aircraft became known as the Halifax Mk I Series I, which was followed by the Mk I Series II with a higher gross weight and the Series III, with increased fuel tankage. The first major modification appeared in the Mk II Series I, which had a two-gun dorsal turret and uprated 1037kW (1390hp) Merlin XX engines. The Mk II Series I (Special) had a fairing in place of the nose turret, and the engine exhaust muffs were omitted, while the Mk II Series IA was the first variant to introduce the drag-reducing moulded Perspex nose that was a feature of all subsequent Halifaxes, a four-gun dorsal turret, and Merlin 22 engines. The Mk II Series IA also had large, rectangular vertical tail surfaces, as serious control difficulties had been experienced with the original tail configuration. Variants of the Mk II Series I (Special) and Series IA, with Dowty landing gear instead of the standard Messier gear, were designated Mk V Series I (Special) and Mk V Series IA. Production of the Halifax increased substantially through 1941, and satellite factories included English Electric, who built 2145 aircraft, Rootes (1070), Fairey (661) and the London Aircraft Production Group (710). As more modifications crept into the basic airframe the aircraft gradually became heavier and consequently underpowered, and in 1943 the Merlin engines were replaced by four 1204kW (1615hp) Bristol Hercules XVI radial engines in the Halifax Mk III. Merlin-engined Halifaxes were, however, retained by the RAF's special duties squadrons, which used them to drop agents and supplies to resistance groups throughout occupied Europe, as these aircraft had a longer range than the Mk III did. The latter, however, had considerably improved flight characteristics as well as performance, and remained in the front line up to the end of the war.

The Halifax Mk IV was a project only. The next operational variants were the Mks VI and VII, the former powered by the 1249kW (1675hp) Hercules 100 and the latter using the MK III's Hercules XVI. These were the ultimate bomber versions, and were produced in relatively small numbers. Some Halifax IIIs, Vs and VIIs were converted to paratroop dropping and glider towing; in fact, the Halifax was the only aircraft capable of towing the massive Hamilcar glider, used to deliver heavy vehicles to the battlefront. The Halifax MK VIII, which entered service just before the end of the war, was a transport version with faired-over gun positions and a detachable 3624kg (8000lb) freight panner under the fuselage, and the final version, produced after the war, was another transport, the Mk IX. Various marks of Halifax also served with some squadrons of RAF Coastal Command as a long-range maritime patrol aircraft, supplementing very long-range (VLR) aircraft such as the Liberator and Fortress.

Although overshadowed by the Lancaster, the Halifax proved to be a far more versatile aircraft in that it could be adapted to many different roles, including electronic countermeasures. The total Halifax production figure of 6176 aircraft included 2050 Mks I and II, 2060 Mk III, 916 Mk V, 480 Mk VI, 395 Mk VII, 100 Mk VIII and the rest Mk IX. During World War II, Halifaxes flew a total of 75,532 sorties, dropping altogether 231,263 tonnes (227,610 tons) of bombs.

Below: A Halifax Mk I of No 35 Squadron. This squadron, which was based initially at Leeming in Yorkshire, was the first to arm with the Halifax, and its early operations were flown against enemy capital ships in the French Atlantic ports.

Hawker Hurricane

The Hurricane MK II was powered by a Rolls-Royce Merlin XX with two-stage supercharging, which required a slightly longer nose than the Hurricane Mk I. The engine's rear-facing exhausts also added slightly to its thrust.

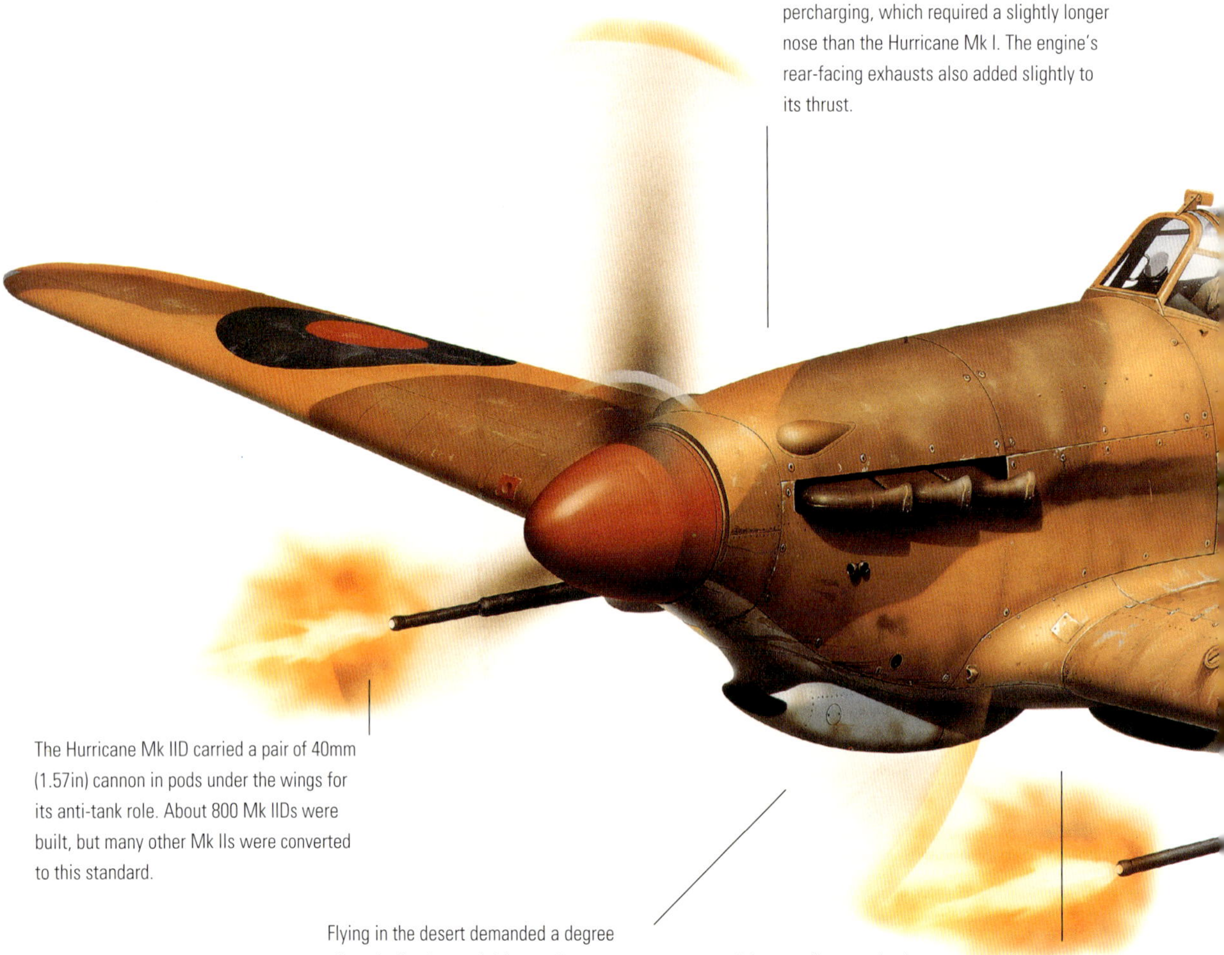

The Hurricane Mk IID carried a pair of 40mm (1.57in) cannon in pods under the wings for its anti-tank role. About 800 Mk IIDs were built, but many other Mk IIs were converted to this standard.

Flying in the desert demanded a degree of tropicalization, and this prominent chin air intake was the result. A Vokes air filter purified the air entering the engine, but performance was degraded by approximately eight per cent.

A large radiator under the centre section of the fuselage cooled both oil and coolant for the engine.

The pilot was protected by a full-length armour plate behind him. The flat-pane windscreen was also bulletproof. A rear view mirror was mounted on top of the canopy framing.

During early spin testing the Hurricane was found to be slightly unstable, so a ventral fin was fitted fore and aft of the tailwheel.

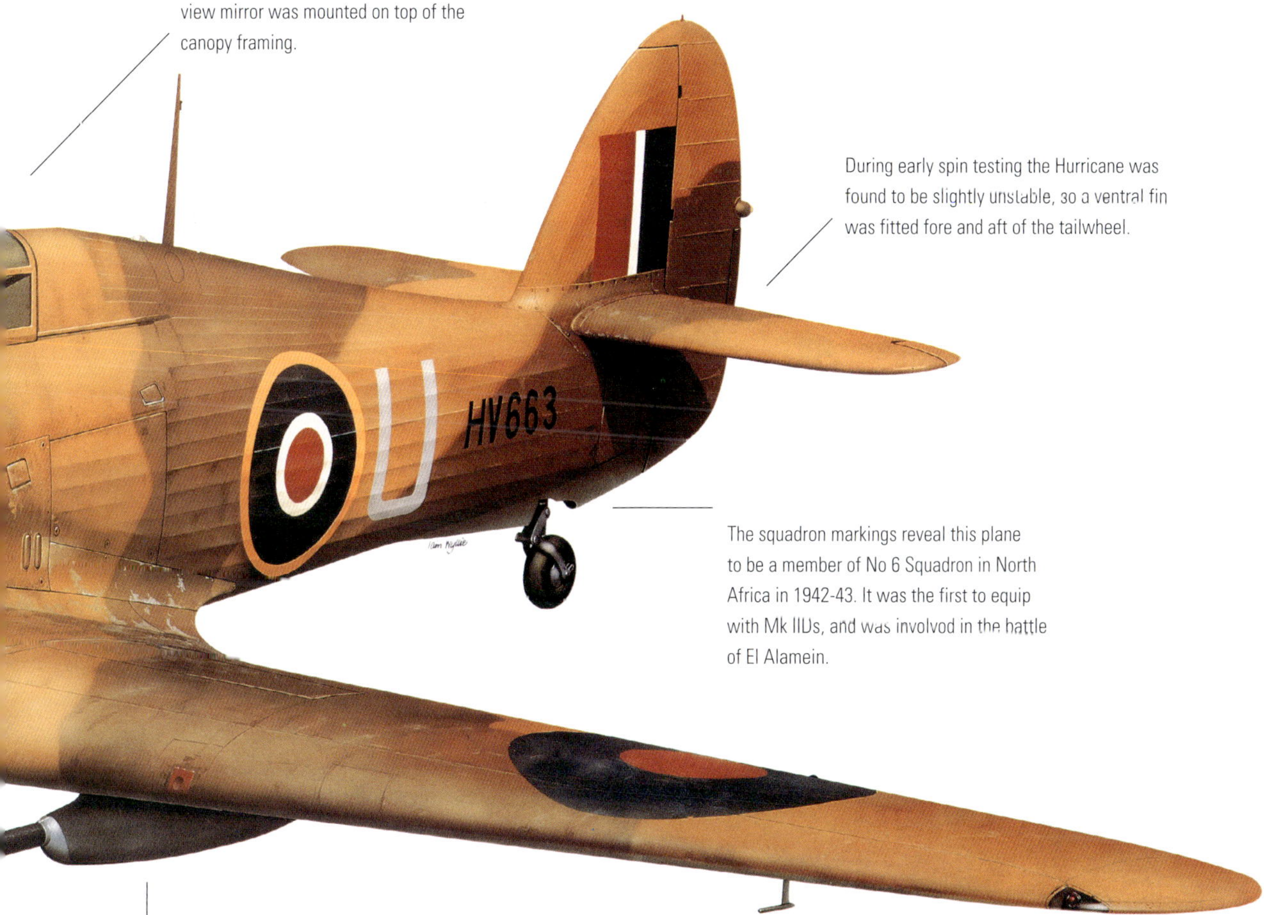

The squadron markings reveal this plane to be a member of No 6 Squadron in North Africa in 1942-43. It was the first to equip with Mk IIDs, and was involved in the battle of El Alamein.

The Mk IID retained a pair of Browning 7.7mm (0.303in) guns, one mounted in each wing. The muzzle was taped over to prevent foreign objects entering the gun before it was first fired.

To match its surroundings, this Hurricane Mk IID is wearing desert markings, a two-tone sand and brown scheme.

The Hawker Hurricane was the first of Britain's new monoplane fighters, powered by the Rolls-Royce Merlin engine and given an armament of eight 7.7mm (0.303in) Colt-Browning machineguns. Developed from the Hawker Fury biplane (it was originally known as the Fury Monoplane) under the design leadership of Sydney Camm to meet Air Ministry Specification F.36/34, the prototype (K5083) flew on 6 November 1935. It was powered by a Merlin 'C' engine of 738kW (990hp), and began Service trials at Martlesham Heath in March 1936. Hawkers, confident of the success of their design, began preparations for the production of 1000 examples before the first Air Ministry order was forthcoming. An order for 600 machines eventually materialized in June 1936, and the first – after some delay caused by the decision to install the 768kW (1030hp) Merlin II engine – flew on 12 October 1937, an initial batch being delivered to No 111 Squadron at Northolt in November. At a later date, the Merlin II was replaced by the Merlin III, driving a three-blade Rotol or de Havilland propeller; these propellers were tested on a

civil-registered Hurricane, G-AFKX, and one Hurricane Mk I was used to test a six-blade contra-rotating propeller. In 1938 the first deliveries were made to foreign customers (Portugal, Yugoslavia, Persia and Belgium); Hurricanes were also exported to Romania and Turkey.

When the Hurricane first encountered German aircraft in combat during the 'Phoney War' period of 1939–40, the wisdom of arming the fighter with eight machineguns instead of four, as had originally been intended, was quickly appreciated. It was thought that the eight guns would throw out a large bullet pattern, rather like the pellets from a shotgun cartridge, so that the average pilot would stand some chance of striking the enemy. However, experience showed that this was a waste of hitting power and eventually the guns were harmonized so that their bullets converged 229m (250yd) in front of the fighter's nose and then spread out again to a width of a few yards within a distance of 457m (500yd). In the few seconds available to destroy or disable an enemy aircraft, the concentration of eight guns firing 8000 rounds per minute (or 400 per three-second burst, representing a weight of metal of about 4.5kg/10lb) was frequently enough to knock a fatal hole in the wings, fuselage, tail or engine, assuming that the vital cockpit area was not hit.

Eventual production of the Hurricane Mk I, shared between the Hawker and Gloster factories in the UK and the Canadian Car and Foundry Co. of Montreal, amounted to 3954. On 11 June 1940 Hurricane P3269 flew with a 884kW (1185hp) supercharged Merlin XX engine, serving as prototype for the Hurricane Mk II, and as more Mk IIs reached the squadrons, many Mk Is were fitted with Vokes sand filters and sent to the Middle East. Early Mk IIs, which retained the eight-gun

Left: Armourers pictured at work on a Hawker Hurricane, loading the aircraft's machine guns with fresh ammunition. The aircraft carries no squadron code letters, and is probably an instructional airframe or used for testing purposes.

Type: Anti-tank aircraft (Mk IID)	
Crew:	1
Powerplant:	one 884kW (1185hp) Rolls-Royce Merlin XX 12-cylinder V-type
Max speed:	518km/h (322mph)
Time to height:	12 mins 24 secs to 6095m (19,997ft)
Service ceiling:	9785m (32,103ft)
Max range:	1448km (900 miles)
Wing span:	12.19m (40ft)
Wing area:	23.93m² (257.5 sq. ft)
Length:	9.81m (32ft 2in)
Height:	3.98m (13ft 1in)
Weights:	2596kg (5723lb) empty; 3674kg (8100lb) max t/o
Armament:	two fixed 40mm (1.58in) Vickers 'S' guns under each wing; two Browning 7.7mm (0.303in) MG in each wing

armament, were designated Mk IIAs; with 12 machine guns the designation became Mk IIB, while the Mk IIC had a wing armament of four 20mm (0.79in) Hispano cannon. The Mk IID was a special anti-tank version, armed with two underwing 40mm (1.58in) Vickers 'S' guns and two 7.7mm (0.303in) Brownings in the wings. Both IIBs and IICs were fitted with cameras and used for reconnaissance as the Mks PR IIB and PR IIC, which special IICs used for meteorological work were designated Met 2Cs. In 1942, Hurricane Is and IIAs operated in Singapore, the Netherlands East Indies, Ceylon and Burma, and it was during the Burma Campaign that the Hurricane really came into its own as a tactical support aircraft, armed with a pair of 226kg (500lb) bombs. The only other British production model, the Mk IV, was also a ground-attack type, armed principally with eight 27kg (60lb) rocket projectiles and fitted with a 1620hp Merlin 24 or 27 engine. Alternative payloads included two 113kg (250lb) or 226kg (500lb) bombs, or two Vickers 'S' guns. The Hurricane Mk V was designed to take the higher-powered Merlin 27 or 32 engine, but only two were built.

In 1941 the Hurricane was adopted by the Royal Navy for fleet protection duties, the first Sea Hurricane Mk IAs being deployed on escort carriers (converted merchant vessels, known as Catapult Aircraft Merchantmen, or CAM ships, in 1941). As Hurricanes were progressively withdrawn from first-line RAF squadrons, they were converted for naval use as Sea Hurricanes Mks IB, IIC and XIIA. Although envisaged as an interim aircraft, the Sea Hurricane gave excellent service on the Arctic and Mediterranean convoy routes between 1942 and 1943. It was eventually replaced by more modern equipment.

One major user of the Hurricane was the Soviet Union, the first batch to be delivered comprising 24 Mk IIBs turned over to the Soviet Navy's 72nd Fighter Air Regiment by No 141 Wing RAF, which operated in North Russia in the late summer of 1941. The eventual total of Hurricane IIBs delivered to the USSR reached 1542, including some Canadian-built Hurricane Xs that were re-categorized as Mk IIBs. A total of 786 Mk IIC fighter-bombers were also despatched between 1943 and 1944, together with 223 Mk IIC fighters. These included a few Mk IIBs converted to IIC standard, and the Russians fitted some of them with rocket rails to carry 82mm (3.2in) RS-82 rocket projectiles. Another Hurricane variant shipped to Russia during 1943 was the Mk IID, with 40mm (1.58in) Vickers 'S' guns. A total of 60 were delivered from RAF stocks in the Middle East and were followed by 30 Hurricane IVs with similar armament. Tank-busting Hurricanes were used to good effect in the battles of Kuban and Kursk in 1943. Some of the Hurricanes underwent interesting modifications in Russian service, some fitted with 12.7mm (0.5in) machineguns instead of the more usual 7.7mm (0.303in). Other Hurricanes were adapted as two-seat trainers, and at least one such aircraft was fitted with a rear gun position. Altogether, 2952 Hurricanes – over 20 per cent of the total number built in the UK – were delivered to the UK.

Overall Hurricane production in the UK was 13,080 by Hawker, Gloster and Austin Motors. Another 1451 Mks X, XI, XII and XIIA, which were fitted with various armament combinations and Packard-built Rolls-Royce Merlins, were produced by the Canadian Car and Foundry Co.

Above: A Hawker Hurricane Mk I of No 111 Squadron, RAF Fighter Command. 'Treble One' was the first squadron to arm with the Hurricane. The squadron numbers seen on the fuselage were soon dropped in favour of code letters.

Right: Hurricane Mk IIs of No 601 Squadron flying in echelon formation. Formations such as this, which were regularly used in combat by Fighter Command in the early phase of the war, were in fact tactically useless, and were to cost the RAF dearly.

UFOP
UFOW
UFOY
UFOD

Hawker Sea Hurricane

Like the land-based version of the aircraft, the pilot was protected by a full-length armour plate behind him and a flat-pane bulletproof windscreen. A rear view mirror was mounted on top of the canopy framing for checking the pilot's 'six' (rear).

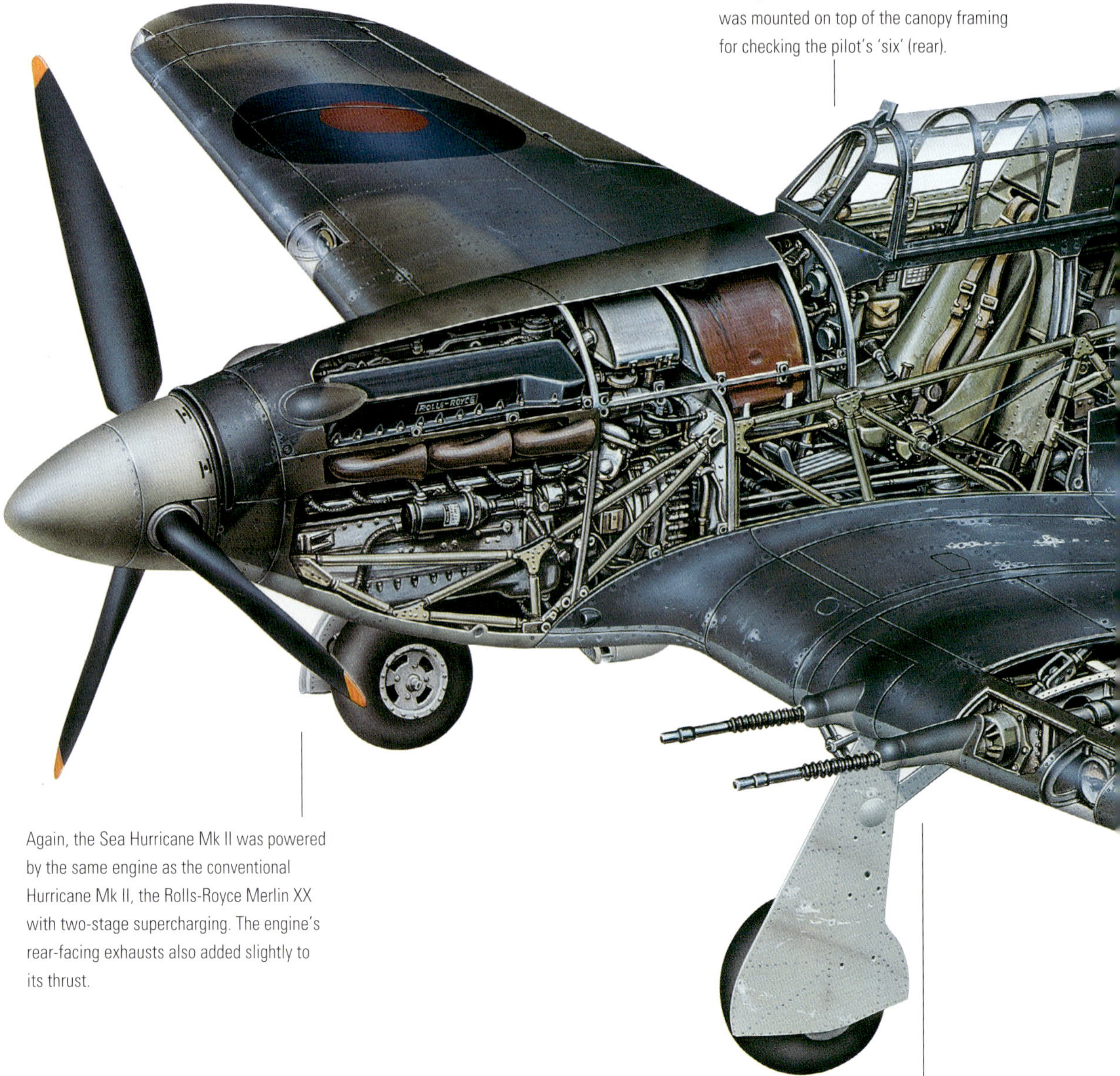

Again, the Sea Hurricane Mk II was powered by the same engine as the conventional Hurricane Mk II, the Rolls-Royce Merlin XX with two-stage supercharging. The engine's rear-facing exhausts also added slightly to its thrust.

The wide-track undercarriage of the Hurricane made it more suitable for navalization than its more famous counterpart, the Spitfire.

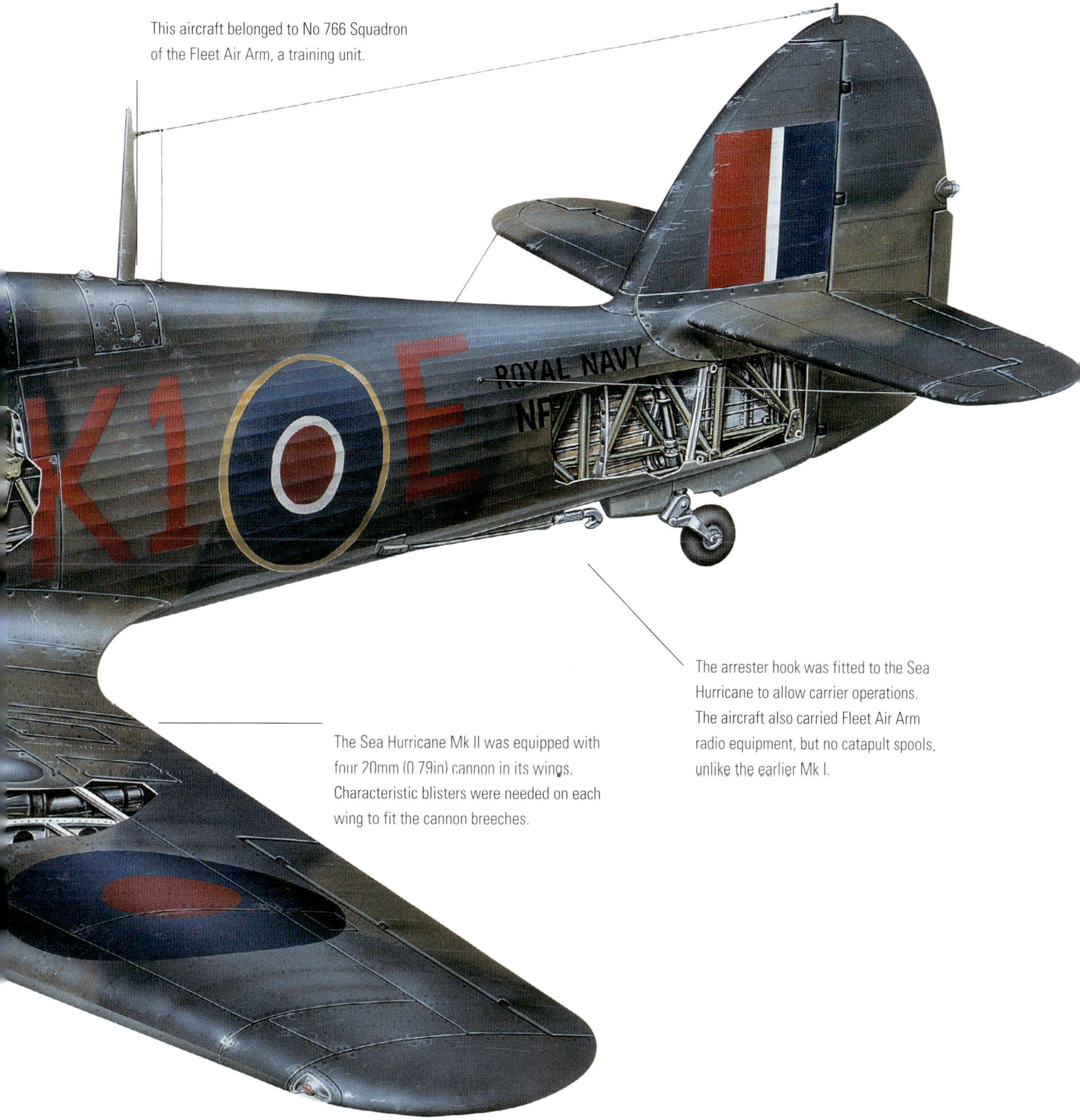

This aircraft belonged to No 766 Squadron of the Fleet Air Arm, a training unit.

The arrester hook was fitted to the Sea Hurricane to allow carrier operations. The aircraft also carried Fleet Air Arm radio equipment, but no catapult spools, unlike the earlier Mk I.

The Sea Hurricane Mk II was equipped with four 20mm (0.79in) cannon in its wings. Characteristic blisters were needed on each wing to fit the cannon breeches.

In November 1941, 25 Mk IIA Hurricanes were allocated to the Admiralty for conversion to Sea Hurricanes. These aircraft were fitted with both v-frame arrester hooks and catapult spools, so that they could be operated from CAM ships (merchant vessels fitted with catapult gear for launching either a Hurricane or a Fairey Fulmar) as well as from conventional aircraft carriers. The decision to convert the Hurricane to naval use followed successful operational trials in the summer of 1941, when four aircraft – fitted with arrester hooks only – were deployed on the carrier HMS *Furious* for operations off Norway. The converted aircraft were designated Sea Hurricane Mk IB, and were followed by the cannon-armed Sea Hurricane Mk IC. When further conversions were re-engined with the Rolls-Royce Merlin XX engine, they were designated Sea Hurricane MK IIB when fitted with machineguns, and Sea Hurricane Mk IIC with cannon.

By the end of 1941, Sea Hurricane Mk IBs were operational with two flights of No 801 Squadron, embarked in HMS *Argus* and HMS *Eagle*; No 806 Squadron in HMS *Formidable*; No 880 Squadron in HMS *Avenger*; and No 885 Squadron in HMS *Victorious*. Early in 1942, No 880 Squadron transferred to the newly commissioned carrier HMS *Indomitable*, and in May the squadron took part in an operation to seize the Vichy French naval base of Diego Suarez on the island of Madagascar to prevent its possible capture and use by the Japanese as a submarine base in the Indian Ocean. In June 1942 Sea Hurricanes were active in providing air cover for Harpoon, the vital convoy that sailed from Gibraltar with supplies for Malta, and on 10 August five Sea Hurricane squadrons accompanied the naval force assigned to protect a second convoy, Pedestal – which comprised 13 freighters and an oil tanker – in what was literally a do-or-die attempt to relieve the besieged island.

During a desperate three-day battle, only four of the freighters and the vital tanker got through, but the picture would have been far worse had it not been for the Sea Hurricanes, which – assisted by a squadron of Grumman Martlets and one of Fulmars – claimed the destruction of 38 Italian and German bombers and torpedo-bombers for the loss of 13 British fighters, some of which ran out of fuel and had to ditch.

Below: Hawker Sea Hurricane being made ready for a sortie from a Royal Navy escort carrier. The Sea Hurricane made a massive difference to the Royal Navy, enhancing its ability to push vital convoys through 'bomber alley' to the island of Malta.

Above: A Catapult Aircraft Merchantman (CAM) ship, here shown with a Hurricane mounted on the launching apparatus. This was a desperate stop-gap measure designed to combat the Focke-Wulf Condor maritime reconnaissance aircraft.

In the Arctic, Sea Hurricanes on board the escort carrier HMS *Avenger* provided fighter cover for Convoy PQ18, outward bound for Russia in September 1942. Three months earlier, Convoy PQ17 had suffered disastrous losses, mainly to air attack, but this time the fighters successfully broke up many attacks by torpedo-carrying Heinkel 111s and Ju 88 dive-bombers and drove them inside the convoy's anti aircraft screen, where they suffered heavy losses. Between them, the Sea Hurricanes and the AA (mainly the latter which, because of the fighters' efforts, was able to concentrate on individual aircraft) accounting for 41 enemy bombers. Four Sea Hurricanes were lost, three of them, ironically, shot down by the convoy's AA gunners.

During Operation Torch, the North Africa landings in November 1942, Sea Hurricanes of Nos 800 and 891 Squadrons operated from the escort carrier HMS *Biter*, while those of No 835 Squadron were embarked in another escort carrier, HMS *Dasher*. During these operations, five Vichy French Dewoitine D.520 fighters were shot down by No 800 Squadron. At Oran, the main Fleet Air Arm operations were directed against the airfields of La Senia and Tafaraoui, and at the former, HMS *Biter*'s Sea Hurricanes combined with Fairey Albacores in destroying 47 Vichy aircraft on the ground.

By 1943 the day of the Sea Hurricane was over, and the squadrons with which it had served were being re-armed with more modern naval fighters, many of them American. Nevertheless, the Sea Hurricane continued to serve afloat until 1944 with Nos 824 and 835 Squadrons, operating in turn from the escort carrier HMS *Nairana*, which was mainly employed in escorting convoys to and from Gibraltar. Early in the year, on one such run, Sea Hurricanes of No 835 Squadron came across and shot down two four-engined Junkers Ju 290 maritime reconnaissance aircraft over the Bay of Biscay.

The re-equipment of No 824 Squadron with Grumman Hellcats in April 1944 left No 835 as the last Sea Hurricane squadron afloat. The last operational sortie was flown on 26 September 1944, while Nairana was escorting a Gibraltar convoy. Sea Hurricanes served ashore with Nos 895 and 897 Squadrons at Stretton, Cheshire, and with No 877 Squadron, formed in April 1943. The total number of Sea Hurricanes built or converted was about 800.

Type: Carrier-borne fighter	
Crew:	1
Powerplant:	one 955kW (1280hp) Rolls-Royce Merlin XX 12-cylinder V-type
Max speed:	505km/h (314mph)
Time to height:	12 mins 24 secs to 6095m (20,000ft)
Service ceiling:	10,516m (34,500ft)
Max range:	1207km (750 miles)
Wing span:	12.19m (40ft)
Wing area:	23.92m^2 (257.5 sq. ft)
Length:	9.81m (32ft 2in)
Height:	3.98m (13ft)
Weights:	2617kg (5770lb) empty; 3511kg (7740lb) max t/o
Armament:	four 20mm (0.79in) Hispano cannon

Hawker Tempest

The Tempest Mk II was powered by the Bristol Centaurus V 18 cylinder two row radial engine. Delays in the engine's development meant that the Mk II entered service after the Tempest Mk V.

To aim his cannon the pilot was equipped with a reflector gunsight. The windscreen of the cockpit was of sufficent thickness to protect the pilot from small calibre rounds.

The Mk II was armed with four fixed forward-firing 20mm (0.79in) cannon in the wings in addition to the stores carried under the wings.

Although this Tempest is armed with eight rockets, the aircraft could also carry bombs up to a maximum load of 907kg (2000lb).

The pilot sat in a raised position under a one-piece sliding canopy with excellent all-round vision. He was protected by an armoured backplate.

This aircraft has the markings of No 16 Squadron RAF, based at Lüneberg in northern Germany in 1946/7. The squadron only flew Mk IIs for about two years, before converting to the de Havilland Vampire. Its unit badge is painted on the tail.

Above: The Centaurus-engined Tempest II was to have been the first model to enter service, but engine development problems delayed its debut until after World War II had finished. It was originally intended for service in the Pacific theatre.

Late in 1941, it became clear to the Hawker design team, armed with the growing volume of information on the Typhoon's inadequacies – fed back to them by the RAF Air Fighting Development Unit and No 56 Squadron, which had pioneered the type's entry into service – that a number of radical improvements to the basic design would be necessary if the aircraft were to fulfil its primary role, which was still considered to be interception at all altitudes. Three main areas were isolated. First, cockpit visibility required drastic improvement; secondly, the wing would have to be re-designed to improve performance at altitudes above 6100m (20,013ft) and in high-speed dives; and thirdly, increased fuel tankage would have to be provided to improve the Typhoon's endurance, which was restricted to about an hour and a half.

The problem with the Typhoon's wing section – with its thickness/chord ratio of 19.5 per cent at the root, 12 per cent at the tip and its maximum thickness at 30 per cent chord – was that although it performed well at all level speeds within the aircraft's flight envelope, it proved aerodynamically poor in a high-speed dive, producing severe buffeting and aileron reversal tendencies. The Hawker team had recognized this shortcoming at an early stage and in September 1940 had begun the design of an entirely new wing, semi-elliptical in plan form and with a vastly improved thickness/chord ratio: 10.5 per cent at the tip, 14.5 per cent at the root and with its maximum thickness at 35 per cent chord. Compared with the Typhoon's wing, the new design effectively reduced the thickness at the root by some 12.7cm (5in). The new wing design also generated other changes, including the lengthening of the fuselage to accommodate the fuel tanks that could no longer be fitted into the wing, the re-design of the undercarriage, and the development of new Hispano Mk V cannon.

The modified design, designated Hawker P.1012, was tendered to Air Ministry Specification F.10/41, and on 18 November 1941 Hawker Aircraft Ltd received a contract to build two prototypes, to be known as the Typhoon Mk II. However, such were the differences, particularly in external appearance, between the Typhoon and the new design that, before the prototype had flown, the type was renamed Tempest in August 1942. By this time there were four F.10/41 prototypes on order; two (Tempest Mks I and V) with Napier Sabre engines and two (Tempest Mks III and IV) with Rolls-Royce Griffons, the intention being also to order to further aircraft (Tempest Mk II) powered by the Bristol Centaurus radial engine when development of this powerplant had progressed further.

The prototype Tempest I (HM595) flew on 2 September 1942 but an initial contract, calling for 400 Tempest Is powered by the Napier Sabre IV engine, was cancelled and the contract amended in favour of the Centaurus-

Type: Fighter-bomber	
Crew:	1
Powerplant:	one 1685kW (2260hp) Napier Sabre IIA, IIB or IIC 24-cylinder H-type engine
Max speed:	700km/h (435mph)
Time to height:	6 mins 6 secs to 6100m (20,000ft)
Service ceiling:	10,975m (36,000ft)
Max range:	2092km (1300 miles)
Wing span:	12.50m (41ft)
Wing area:	28m² (302sq ft)
Length:	10.26m (33ft 7in)
Height:	4.90m (16ft 1in)
Weights:	4854kg (10,700lb) empty; 6187kg (13,640lb) loaded
Armament:	four 20mm (0.79in) Hispano Mk V cannon; external stores up to 907kg (2000lb)

powered Tempest Mk II. Delays in the production of this engine, however, and the cancellation of the projected Tempest Mks III and IV, meant that the first variant to enter production was the Tempest Mk V, powered by the Napier Sabre II. This gave it an impressive acceleration. The first 100 production aircraft had the Sabre IIA engine and long-barrelled British Hispano Mk II 20mm (0.79in) cannon, and were designated Mk V Series I. Subsequent production aircraft had the Sabre IIB or 'C', the short-barrelled Hispano Mk V cannon fully recessed in the wing leading edge and spring-tab ailerons, and were designated Mk V Series II. At the time it entered service with No 3 Squadron RAF and No 486 Squadron RNZAF (the two squadrons combining to form No 150 Wing) in April 1944 the Tempest was the fastest and most powerful fighter in the world. Below 3000m (10,000ft) it could be dived at up to 869km/h (540mph), far in excess of the speed attainable by any other piston-engined fighter, and its maximum speed, straight and level, was 708km/h (440mph). Combat radius was 800km (500 miles) with external tanks and its ammunition magazines held 800 20mm (0.79in) shells, enough for 20 seconds of firing time. The two initial Tempest squadrons flew many cross-Channel sorties before and during the invasion of Normandy, and in their first encounter with the Luftwaffe, on 8 June 1944, they destroyed four Messerschmitt Bf 109s, with two more damaged, in exchange for two Tempests damaged.

Soon afterwards, however, the Tempest squadrons were assigned to the air defence of Great Britain, operating against the V-1 flying bombs now being launched against London. The Tempest's high speed made it the ideal interceptor; No 3 Squadron was the top-scoring unit, with 258 V-1s destroyed; No 486 claimed 223. Anti-flying bomb operations, however, revealed some snags with the Tempests' Sabre engines, and the fighters were withdrawn from front-line service for some weeks while the troubles were rectified. The Tempest squadrons subsequently moved to the Continent with 2nd TAF and became a potent addition to the Allies' striking power during the closing months of the war. Eventually, 11 squadrons were armed with the Tempest Mk V and 5 with the Mk VI, with its 2013kW (2700hp) Sabre VA engine. Total numbers built were 805 Mk Vs, 142 Tempest VIs, and 472 Tempest IIs. Tempest IIs were also supplied to India (89) and Pakistan (24).

Below: Hawker Tempest V of No 274 Squadron. This squadron received its first Tempests in August 1944 and subsequently used them against the V-1 flying bombs, before moving to the continent as part of the 2nd Tactical Air Force.

Hawker Typhoon

The Typhoon was powered by the Napier Sabre IIA engine, which had four rows of six cylinders arranged in an 'H' formation. It was started by a Coffman starter, a large explosive cartridge which made the engine literally explode into life.

No 175 Squadron first began using rockets in the spring of 1944. Eight rockets could be carried by a Typhoon. Each rocket was 76mm (3in) in diameter and was equipped with a 27kg (60lb) warhead capable of knocking out tanks and trains.

All but a handful of the early Typhoons were equipped with four 20mm (0.79in) Hispano cannon in the wings, each gun having 140 rounds of ammunition.

Early Typhoons had a framed canopy with a 'car door' allowing access to the cockpit, but this was later changed to the one-piece teardrop sliding canopy seen here to improve the pilot's vision. To the same end, a whip aerial replaced its solid predecessor on the rear fuselage.

No 175 Squadron transferred to the Typhoon in April 1943. This example of the Mk IB flew in support of the Normandy landings and was based at Le Fresne-Camilly in France in August 1944.

Early Typhoons had a number of fatal crashes due to their tailplanes falling off in flight. After a lengthy diagnosis, small fishplate strengtheners were added, which cured the problem.

Allied aircraft flying in support of the Normandy landings wore black-and-white markings to show their allegiance to ground troops below, and prevent friendly fire incidents. Some aircraft also wore the stripes on their wings.

A cantilever low-wing monoplane of basically all-metal stressed-skin construction with a retractable tailwheel, the Hawker Typhoon was designed in response to a 1937 Air Staff requirement, leading to Air Ministry Specification F.18/37, for an aircraft capable of taking on heavily armed and armoured escort fighters like the Messerschmitt Bf 110. In fact, two separate designs were submitted, the Type R and Type N. The Type R was powered by a Rolls-Royce Vulture engine; it flew in prototype form as the Tornado, but was abandoned when production of the Vulture was curtailed. A 2100hp Napier Sabre H-type in-line engine powered the Type N, and the first of two prototypes, P.5212, flew for the first time on 24 February 1940 , named Typhoon. The first production aircraft, however, did not fly until May 1941. Delays in production were blamed on the unreliability of the massive Sabre engine, but there were other problems, including structural failures of the rear fuselage. These had still not been cured when No 56 Squadron at Duxford was issued with the Typhoon in September 1941, and several pilots were lost in accidents. Although the aircraft was fast and handled well at medium and low altitudes, at high altitude its performance was inferior to that of both the Focke-Wulf 190 and the Messerschmitt Bf 109F, and its rate of climb was poor. Teething troubles with the type kept the squadron non-operational until the end of May 1942, and at one time there was even talk of cancelling the Typhoon programme altogether.

It was a change in enemy tactics that brought about the aircraft's reprieve. In the summer of 1942, FW 190s of JG 2 and JG 26, based on the Channel coast, began carrying out sporadic hit-and-run attacks on coastal targets in south-east England. The Luftwaffe pilots made full use of the contours of the South Downs, flying that would nowadays be called 'nap of the earth', to pop up and attack coastal targets from the rear. Only the Typhoon was fast enough to catch the elusive intruders, and at low level it was in its element. Two more, Nos 609 and 266 Squadrons, had now joined the original Typhoon squadron, No 56, and together these formed the Duxford Typhoon Wing. During the summer months of 1942, still suffering from technical problems, they were engaged in air defence duties, but No 609 Squadron, having received the appropriate authority, began to carry out a series of

Above: Hawker Typhoon IB of No 440 (RCAF) Squadron. Formed in February 1944, this Canadian unit originally flew Hurricanes, which were soon replaced by Typhoons. The squadron operated in support of the 1st (Canadian) Army's advance.

Below: Hawker Typhoon Mk IA of No 609 Squadron, which pioneered the type into service through a succession of accidents, leading to a number of changes that eventually turned the Typhoon into the world's most effective fighter-bomber.

operational trials to investigate the aircraft's usefulness in other roles. These included night interception and, most important of all for the Typhoon's future, ground attack by both day and night. The Typhoon Mk IA, which was armed with 12 7.7mm (0.303) machineguns, was now giving way to the Mk IB, whose four 20mm (0.79in) cannon proved highly effective in the ground-attack role and which was powered by a somewhat more reliable Sabre IIA engine with 1626kW (2180hp).

The Duxford Wing's cannon-armed Typhoon IBs went into action for the first time in August 1942, when they carried out an uneventful sweep from Dunkirk to Calais as a preliminary to the disastrous Anglo-Canadian landing at Dieppe, which took place the next day. Thirty-six Typhoons took part in the operation, but claimed only two 'probables' and three enemy aircraft damaged. One Typhoon was lost through engine failure and a Spitfire shot another down. The operation served only to underline the complete inadequacy of the Mk I's cockpit canopy design, with its extremely poor pilot visibility, for air superiority fighting. Later production Typhoons had a clear bubble-type sliding canopy, a vast improvement.

Although the Typhoon continued to have problems well into 1943 when they were finally rectified, and its future still hung in the balance, its prowess against the Luftwaffe's low-level intruders had begun to tip the scales in its favour. Since June 1942 the fighter-bomber attacks had been assuming greater proportions, more Focke-Wulf fighter-bombers having been allocated to JG 2 and 26. It was soon apparent that the main line of defence, the Spitfire, was unable to cope with the faster FW 190A-4, with which the *Jagdgeschwader* were now equipped. But on 20 January 1943 the Typhoon at last showed what it could do as an interceptor. On that day, 28 enemy fighter-bombers, escorted by single-engined fighters, made a daylight attack on London, causing much damage and many casualties. Little warning had been

Type: Low-level interceptor and ground-attack aircraft	
Crew:	1
Powerplant:	one 1566kW (2100hp) Napier Sabre I 24-cylinder in-line (Mk IA); one 1626kW (2180hp) Sabre IIA, 1640kW (2200hp) Sabre IIB or 1685kW (2260hp) Sabre IIC Mk IB)
Max speed:	663km/h (412mph)
Time to height:	5 mins 50 secs to 4570m (15,000ft)
Service ceiling:	10,730m (35,200ft)
Max range:	1577km (980 miles) with external tanks
Wing span:	12.67m (41ft 6in)
Wing area:	25.92m² (257.5 sq.ft)
Length:	9.73m (31ft 9in)
Height:	4.67m (15ft 3in)
Weights:	4445kg (9800lb) empty; 5171kg (11,400lb) max t/o
Armament:	12 7.7mm (0.303in) fixed forward-firing MG with 500rpg in wing (Mk IA); four 20mm (0.79in) fixed forward-firing cannon in wing; external bomb load up to 907kg (2000lb) or eight 60lb RPs

received of the attack, but as the raiders were making their exit from the target area, they were intercepted by the Typhoons of No 609 Squadron. In the ensuing fight, Flying Officer J. Baldwin, later to become the top-scoring Typhoon pilot with 15 victories, destroyed three Bf 109Gs, while four FW 190s were shot down by other pilots. No 609 Squadron achieved several more successes against the enemy fighter-bombers in the weeks that followed, and during this period the squadron continued to expand its offensive operations against targets on the Continent. There was no longer any doubt about the aircraft's effectiveness at low level, and 609 Squadron's performance effectively killed a last-ditch attempt by the Engineering Branch of Fighter Command, early in 1943, to have the fighter axed in favour of the American P-47 Thunderbolt. By the end of the year, the aircraft's technical problems were cured. Now the growing number of Typhoon squadrons, carrying a pair of 226kg (500lb) bombs or eight underwing rocket projectiles on their aircraft, in addition to the built-in cannon armament struck hard at the enemy's communications, shipping and airfields, and the Typhoon was heading for its place in history as the most potent Allied fighter-bomber. After the Allied landings in Normandy, the name of the rocket-armed Typhoon would become synonymous with

Right: Hawker Typhoon armed with eight 27kg (60lb) rocket projectiles. A salvo of these missiles was the equivalent of a broadside from a 15cm (6in) gun cruiser; therefore rocket-armed Typhoons could cause awesome damage to enemy armour.

the break-up of an enemy armoured counter-attack at Mortain and the destruction of the retreating German Army at Falaise. During the last days of the World War II, having supported the Canadian 1st and British 2nd Armies in their drive through north-west Europe, its final actions were against enemy shipping in the Baltic.

In all, 3330 Typhoons were built, all by Gloster except for the two prototypes, five Mk 1As and ten Mk 1Bs. The Mk IB was the major production version, over 3000 being completed. About 60 per cent of these had bubble-type canopies in place of the original frame-type cockpit hood and car-type access door.

Short Sunderland

Two pilots sat side-by-side with full dual controls on the flight deck. Behind them were the navigator and wireless operator, with a flight engineer behind them. The windscreen and canopies were flat Triplex panels for better vision.

The guns of the Sunderland led it to be nicknamed the 'Flying Porcupine'. The front turret in the Mk II had a single machine gun, but this was later changed to twin guns, and fixed forward-firing guns were added for the pilot's use.

Inside the Sunderland's hull was space for a dinghy, the bomb-aimer's compartment, a wardroom with tables and folding bunks, a small workshop and a galley.

A Frazer Nash F.N.7 mid-upper turret offset to starboard was mounted in the upper fuselage. It contained a pair of 7.7mm (0.303in) machine guns.

Most Mk II Sunderlands were equipped with ASV. Mk II radar, of which these four dipole antennae were part. The Germans later learned to detect the radar's emissions, and it was replaced with the ASV. Mk III.

Early Mk IIs had an F.N. 13 turret with four 7.7mm (0.303in) machine guns and 500 rounds per gun.

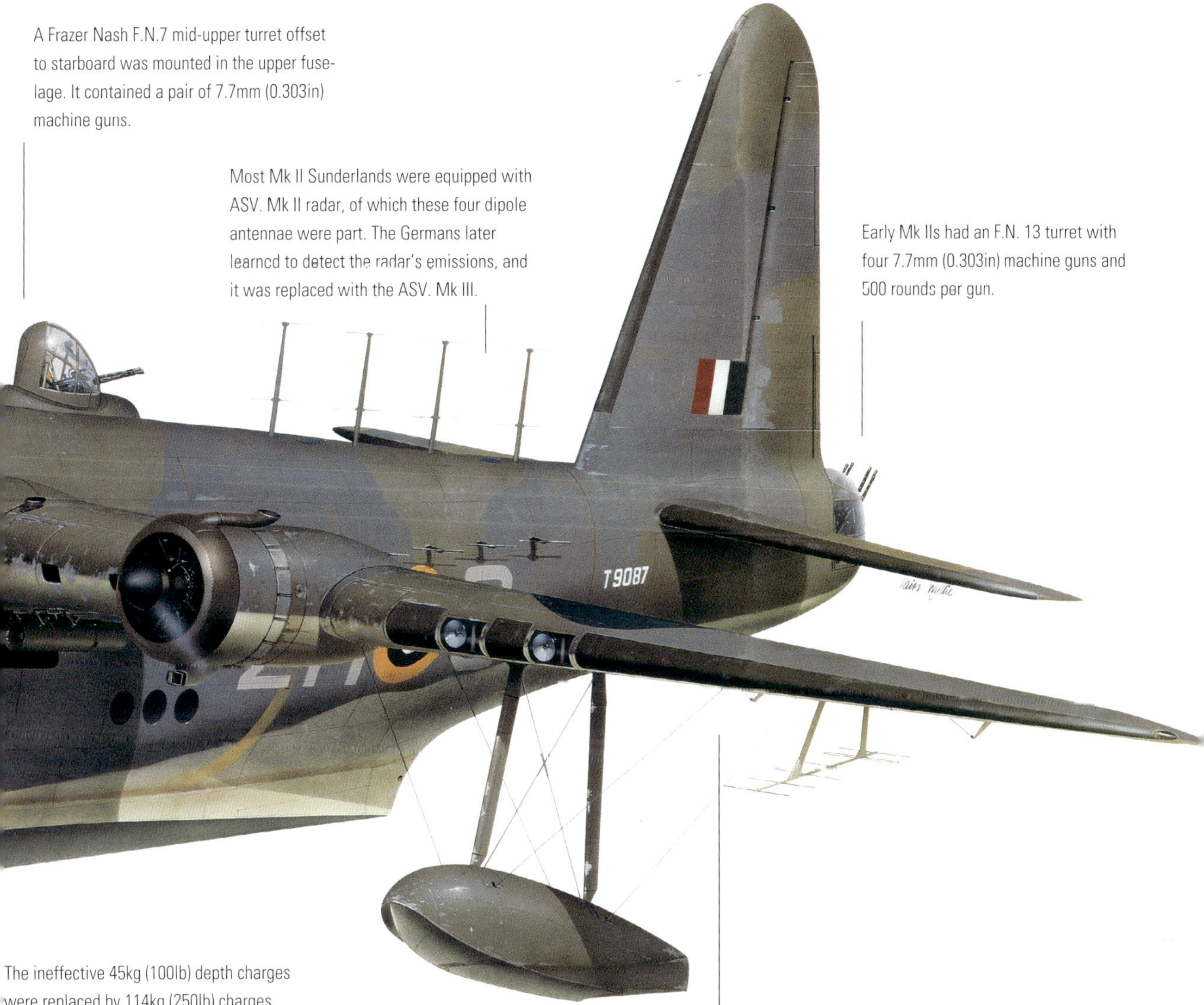

The ineffective 45kg (100lb) depth charges were replaced by 114kg (250lb) charges filled with Torpex explosive. Normally stored in a bomb room in the fuselage, they were electrically moved out onto the wing when in action.

This was one of 20 Sunderland IIs built by Blackburn. It was a member of No 201 Squadron, which flew from Lough Erne, Northern Ireland, from September 1941 until March 1944.

Above: Short Sunderland GR Mk V, the last of the line. The Mk V remained in first-line service with the RAF's Far East Flying Boat Wing until as late as 1959, at which time the last aircraft were withdrawn from No 205 Squadron at Singapore.

The design of the Short Sunderland, which eventually was to become one of the RAF's longest-serving operational aircraft, was based on that of the stately Short C Class 'Empire' flying boats, operated by Imperial Airways in the 1930s. When the Air Ministry issued Specification R.2/33, calling for a four-engined reconnaissance flying boat, the adaptation of the C Class design to meet the military requirement seemed a logical step to Short Brothers. The Air Ministry thought so too, and placed an order for 21 production aircraft of the S.25, as the military flying boat was designated, in March 1926, some 18 months before the prototype flew. The maiden flight of the prototype, K4774, took place on 16 October 1937, powered by four 708kW (950hp) Bristol Pegasus X radial engines. The first production Sunderland Mk Is, powered by Pegasus XXII engines and with a revised nose and tail armament, was delivered to No 230 Squadron in Singapore early in June 1938 and, by the outbreak of World War II in September 1939, three more squadrons: No 204 at Mount Batten, in Devon, No 210 at Pembroke Dock in Wales, and No 228, then in the process of returning to Pembroke Dock from Egypt.

The Sunderland was soon in the headlines; on 21 September 1939, two aircraft of Nos 204 and 228 Squadrons rescued the entire crew of the stricken freighter *Kensington Court*, which had been torpedoed by a U-boat.

Three more squadrons, Nos 95, 201 and 270, were equipped with the Sunderland Mk I, of which 90 were built before production switched to the Mk II. This was fitted with Pegasus XVIII engines with two-stage superchargers, a twin-gun dorsal turret, an improved rear turret and ASV Mk II radar. Production of the Sunderland Mk II reached 55 aircraft, these equipping Nos 119, 201, 202, 204, 228 and 230 Squadrons. The fitting of extra equipment meant that the Mk II had a much higher operating weight than the

Type: Long-range maritime patrol aircraft (Mk V)	
Crew:	10
Powerplant:	four 895kW (1200hp) Pratt & Whitney R-1830-90 Twin Wasp 14 cylinder air-cooled radial engines
Max speed:	349km/h (217mph) at 1525m (5000ft)
Time to height:	16 mins to 3660m (12,000ft)
Service ceiling:	5445m (17,864m)
Max range:	4796km (2980 miles)
Wing span:	34.36m (112ft 7in)
Wing area:	138.14m² (1487sq ft)
Length:	26m (85ft 3in)
Height:	10.52m (34ft 5in)
Weights:	16,738kg (36,900lb) empty; 27,216kg (60,000lb) max t/o
Armament:	two fixed forward-firing 7.7mm (0.303in) MG; two 7.7mm (0.303in) MG each in bow and dorsal turrets; four 7.7mm (0.303in) MG in tail turret; a war load of up to 2250kg (4960lb) of bombs, mines or depth charges on retractable racks in hull sides

Mk I, and a new planing hull bottom was designed, with a less pronounced forward step that gave better unstick characteristics. The hull was tested on a Mk II, which in effect became the prototype of the next variant, the Mk III, which was to be the major production model of the Sunderland. The first Short-built Sunderland Mk III flew on 15 December 1941 and the parent company eventually produced 286 Mk IIIs, a further 170 being built by Blackburn Aircraft. The latter company had already built 15 Mk Is and 5 Mk IIs.

One of the principal exponents of the Sunderland as an anti-submarine weapon was No 10 Squadron RAAF, which was based in Britain and which first experimented with a group of four 7.7mm (0.303in) machineguns mounted on either side of the aircraft's bow, bringing the total armament to 10 guns. The revised forward-firing armament meant that the Sunderland could lay down an effective fire on a surfaced U-boat as the aircraft made its run-in, and with 10 guns, the flying boat presented a dangerous target to enemy fighters, which learned to be wary of it an early stage of the war. The Germans nicknamed the Sunderland *Stachelschwein* (porcupine).

The Sunderland III equipped 11 RAF squadrons, including 1 Polish and 1 Free French, and was followed by the Sunderland IV, a larger and heavier development with 1268kW (1700hp) Bristol Hercules engines, eight 12.7mm (0.5in) machine guns and two 20mm (0.79in) cannon. In fact, only two prototypes and eight production aircraft were built and given the name Seaford, but after evaluation by Coastal and Transport Commands, the Sunderland IV/ Seaford was abandoned and the aircraft later converted for commercial use as the Short Solent. The last operational Sunderland, therefore, was the Mk V, 100 of which were built by Shorts and 50 by Blackburn. The MK V, powered by four 895kW (1200hp) Pratt & Whitney R-1830-90 Twin Wasps and carrying the ASV Mk VIc radar, made its appearance late in 1943 and continued to serve for many years after World War II, the last RAF Sunderland Vs retiring from No 205 Squadron at Changi, Singapore, in 1959. Nineteen Sunderland Mk Vs were exported to France's Aéronavale, retiring in 1960, and 16 to the RNZAF, where they served until 1966.

In the early stages of its operational career, the Sunderland, like other RAF maritime patrol aircraft, was armed with the standard 113kg (250lb) bomb, a weapon almost completely ineffective against U-boats. It was not until 1940 that the depth charge was acknowledged as the really effective anti-submarine weapon, and even then the early depth bombs, filled with Amatol, were notoriously unreliable and prone to disintegrate on hitting the surface of the sea. Matters improved with the introduction of modifications in 1941 and in particular with the use of a new explosive called Torpex, which was 30 per cent more effective than Amatol. The 113kg (250lb) charge was set to explode at a depth of 7–15m (25–50ft), and the weapons were dropped in sticks, usually of six, with 30m (100ft) between them, earlier spacings of 11–18m (36–60ft) having proved unsuccessful. Release height was very low at 15-23m (50–75ft).

By the end of World War II, Sunderland aircraft equipped as many as 28 RAF squadrons, both at home and overseas.

Below: Always a majestic sight, a Short Sunderland Mk I ploughs through the sea on its take-off run. The Sunderland prototype flew for the first time in October 1937 and four squadrons were equipped with the type at the outbreak of World War II.

Supermarine Spitfire

The Spitfire VC was powered by the Rolls-Royce Merlin 45 12 cylinder engine. The Mk V's airframe was especially strengthened to compensate for the increased weight of the engine and the greater power it generated.

The pilot sat under a blown sliding canopy with a partially glazed fairing to improve his rearward vision. A rear view mirror was also attached to the top of the cockpit frame. The pilot was protected by an armoured plate to his rear, and a bulletproof windscreen.

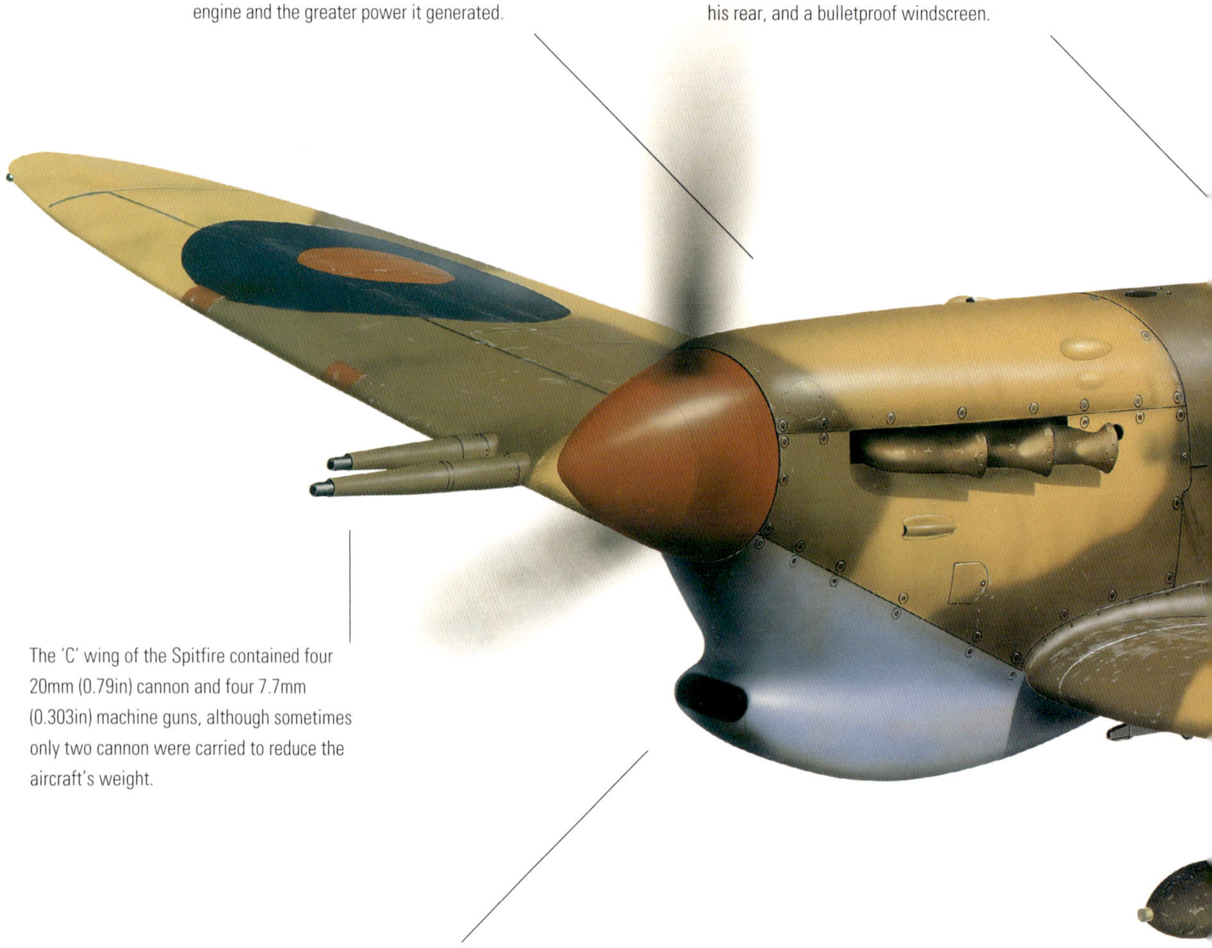

The 'C' wing of the Spitfire contained four 20mm (0.79in) cannon and four 7.7mm (0.303in) machine guns, although sometimes only two cannon were carried to reduce the aircraft's weight.

The Mk VC was fitted with a tropical filter when serving in the tropics or the desert. In this case it is a Vokes filter; an Aboukir filter was also available.

The Spitfire was an effective fighter-bomber, and had two hardpoints under its wings as well as a centreline pylon. The latter could carry a 227kg (500lb) bomb, while two 114kg (250lb) bombs could be carried under the wings of the Mk VC.

This Spitfire carries the markings of No 2 Squadron of the South African Air Force, tasked as a fighter-bomber unit in the North African desert in the fight against Rommel's *Afrika Korps*.

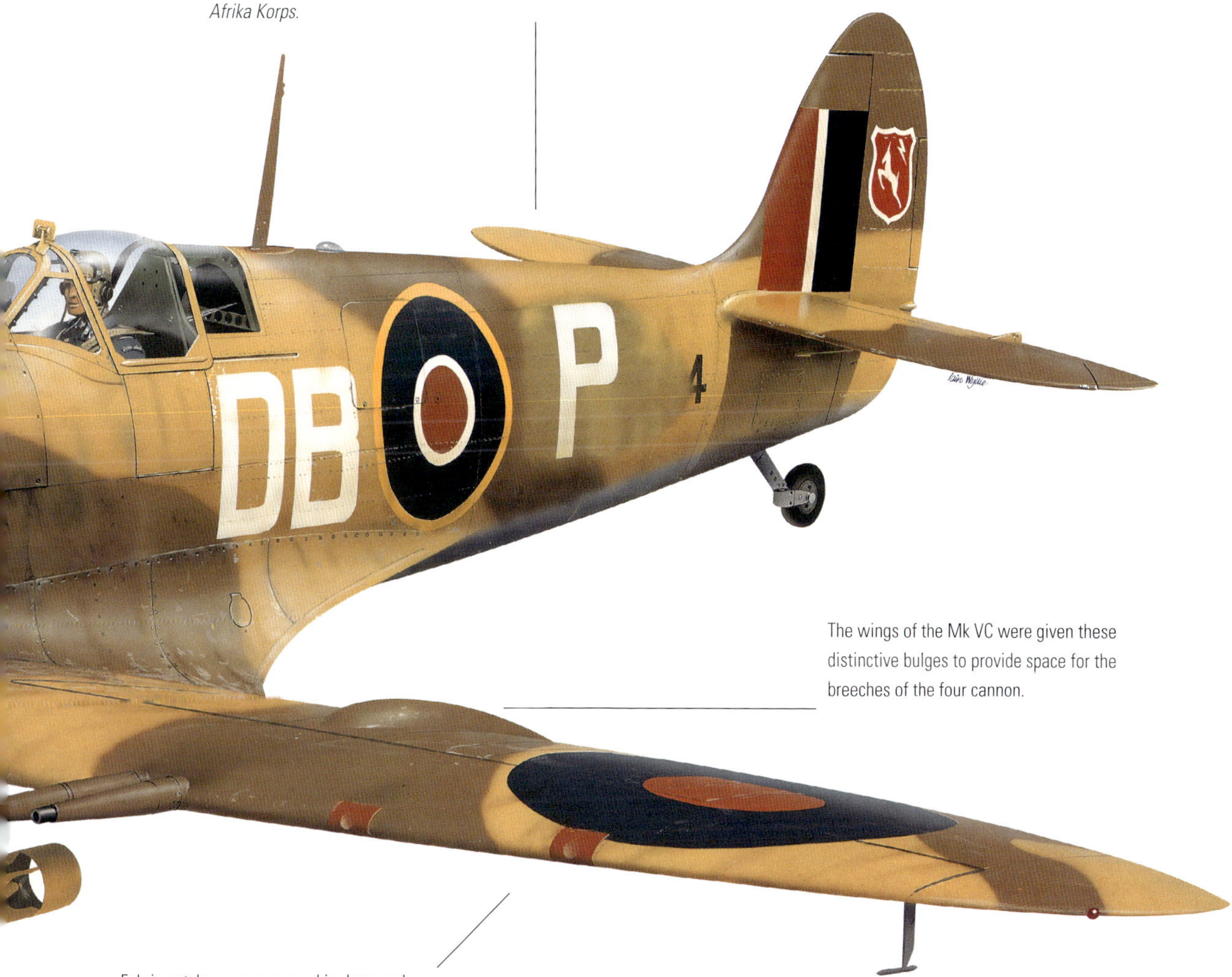

The wings of the Mk VC were given these distinctive bulges to provide space for the breeches of the four cannon.

Fabric patches were covered in dope and stuck over the muzzles of the machine guns in the wings to prevent foreign objects entering them before they were first fired by the pilot.

The legendary Supermarine Spitfire was designed by a team under the direction of Reginald Mitchell, and traced its ancestry to Supermarine's racing floatplanes developed for the Schneider Trophy contest. The design was so evidently superior to the original Air Ministry Specification to which it had been submitted, F.5/34, that a new one, F.37/34, was drafted to cover the production of a prototype. This aircraft, K5054, made its first flight on 5 March 1936 and, like the Hawker Hurricane, with which it was to share so much fame, was powered by a Rolls-Royce Merlin 'C' engine. A contract for the production of 310 Spitfires was issued by the Air Ministry in June 1936, at the same time as the Hurricane contract, and the first examples were delivered to No 19 Squadron at Duxford in August 1938. Eight other squadrons had been equipped with Spitfires by September 1939, and two Auxiliary Air Force units, Nos 603 and 609, were undergoing operational training. Production of the Spitfire Mk I, which was powered by a 768kW (1030hp) Merlin II or III engine, eventually reached 1566 aircraft. It was this variant that saw the most combat in the Battle of Britain, the Mk II with the 876kW (1175hp) Merlin XII engine being issued to the squadrons of Fighter Command in September 1940. Mk II production, including the Mk

Above: Spitfire Mk XIV of No 610 Squadron. An Auxiliary Air Force unit with a proud record, No 610 Squadron operated from bases all over north-west Europe, taking part in actions from December 1944 until the end of the war.

Left: The Spitfire Mk Vb had its wings clipped to improve performance at low altitude, but despite this, it was outclassed by the Focke-Wulf 190 and suffered badly in the early months of 1942. The later model, the Spitfire Mk IX, restored the balance.

IIB, which mounted two 20mm (0.79in) cannon and four 7.7mm (0.303in) machine guns in place of the standard eight, totalled 920 aircraft. During the battle, from 1 July to 31 October 1940, 361 of the 747 Spitfires delivered to Fighter Command were destroyed, not all in combat.

The Spitfire Mk III was an experimental 'one-off' aircraft; the Mk IV (229 built) was a photoreconnaissance version. It was actually produced after the next variant, the Mk V, which began to reach the squadrons in March 1941. Converted from Mk I and II airframes, the Mk V was to be the major Spitfire production version, with 6479 examples completed. The majority of Spitfire Vs were armed with two 20mm (0.79in) cannon and four machineguns, affording a greater chance of success against armour plating. The Mk V was powered by a Rolls-Royce Merlin 45 engine, developing 1055kW (1415hp) at 5800m (19,028ft) against the 858kW (1150hp) of the Merlin XII fitted in the Mk II. Nevertheless, the Mk V was essentially a compromise aircraft, rushed into service to meet an urgent Air Staff requirement for a fighter with a performance superior to that of the latest model of Messerschmitt. The debut of the Spitfire V came just in time, for in May 1941 the Luftwaffe fighter units began to receive the Messerschmitt Bf 109F, its service debut having been delayed through technical problems. On 11 May, a group of bomb-carrying Bf 109Fs attacked Lympne and Hawkinge, one being shot down by a Spitfire. The Spitfire V, however, failed to provide the overall superiority Fighter Command needed so badly. At high altitude, where many combats took place, it was found to be inferior to the Bf 109F on most counts, and several squadrons equipped with the Mk V took a severe mauling during that summer.

To counter the activities of high-flying German reconnaissance aircraft the Spitfire Mk VI was produced, with a long, tapered wing and a pressurized cockpit; the aircraft was assigned to one flight of the RAF's home defence squadrons. A Rolls-Royce Merlin 60 engine, a two-stage, two-speed, inter-cooled powerplant that was to take development of the Merlin to its ultimate, also with a pressurized cockpit, powered the Mk VII. Early in 1942, Air Staff envisaged production of both the Spitfire VII and, in much larger numbers, of the Spitfire VIII, which was basically an unpressurized version of the Mk VII intended for low-level air superiority operations. But the Mk VIII design needed a lot of refinement, including a general strengthening of the fuselage, which meant that production would be delayed for an unacceptably long

time, and Air Staff thoughts consequently turned to an interim aircraft: a Mk V Spitfire airframe combined with a Merlin 61 engine. The resulting combination was the Spitfire Mk IX, which for a stop-gap aircraft turned out to be a resounding success. Deliveries to the RAF began in June 1942 and 5665 were built, more than any other marks except the Mk V.

The Spitfire Mk X and XII were unarmed PR variants, while the Mk XII, powered by a 1294kW (1735hp) Rolls-Royce Griffon engine, was developed specifically to counter

Type: Fighter (Mk VB)	
Crew:	1
Powerplant:	one 1074kW (1440hp) Rolls-Royce Merlin 45/46/50 V-12 engine
Max speed:	602km/h (374mph) at 3960m (13,000ft)
Time to height:	7 mins 30 secs to 6095m (20,000ft)
Service ceiling:	11,280m (37,007ft)
Max range:	756km (470 miles)
Wing span:	11.23m (36ft 8in)
Wing area:	22.48m^2 (242sq ft)
Length:	9.11m (29ft 8in)
Height:	3.48m (11ft 4in)
Weights:	2313kg (5121lb) empty; 3078kg (6785lb) max t/o
Armament:	two 20mm (0.79in) cannon; four 7.7mm (0.303in) MG in the wings

the low-level attacks by Focke-Wulf 190s. It first went into service with No 41 Squadron in February 1943. The squadron shot down its first FW 190 on 27 April, while operating from Hawkinge. The second unit to re-equip with the Mk XII, No 91, destroyed five enemy fighter-bombers in a running battle over the Channel on 25 May 1943. Only 100 MK XII Spitfires were built, followed by the more numerous Mk XIV. The latter, based on a Mk VIII airframe, was the first Griffon-engined Spitfire variant to go into large-scale production, and the first examples were issued to No 322 (Netherlands) and No 610 Squadrons in March and April 1944. The next variant, the Mk XIV, was based on the Mk VIII, with an airframe strengthened to take a 1529kW (2050hp) Griffon 65 engine. The Spitfire XVI, which entered service in 1944, was a ground-attack version similar to the Mk IX, but with a Packard-built Merlin 266 engine. The Spitfire XVIII entered service at the end of World War II, and was a fighter-reconnaissance variant, as was the PR Mk XIX. The last Spitfire variants, the Mks 21, 22 and 24, produced until 1947, bore very little resemblance to the prototype Mk I of a decade earlier. Total Spitfire production was 20,351, plus 2334 examples of the naval version, the Seafire.

Left: A tropicalized Spitfire Mk Vc pictured on Sicily after the Allied invasion of July 1943. Spitfires of the Desert Air Force – which would retain its name during the Italian Campaign – were able to provide valuable support for the Eighth Army.

Vickers Wellington

The pilot and co-pilot sat side-by-side, the co-pilot sitting on a folding seat which allowed access to the nose section. Behind the flight deck were the wireless operator and navigator.

This Wellington wears the standard Bomber Command camouflage scheme, with dark earth/dark green upper surfaces, and matt black sides and undersurfaces.

The Mk III carried the Frazer Nash FN 5 turret containing two 7.7mm (0.303in) Browning machine guns. Behind and below the turret was the prone bomb-aiming position with downward-facing window.

In the top of the bomb bays under the centre of the fuselage were flotation bags which inflated if the aircraft ditched to give the crew time to escape.

The Wellington Mk I was equipped with the Pegasus radial, but the Mk III was powered by the Bristol Hercules XI 14-cylinder engine. The Mk II had been intended to use the Merlin, but this was cancelled due to its relative low priority.

The Wellington was equipped with single flexibly-mounted 7.7mm (0.303in) Browning machine guns in the waist positions. Forward of these was a rest bunk and a chemical toilet.

The rear turret was a Frazer Nash FN 20A equipped with four 7.7mm (0.303in) Brownings. The inital Wellington aircraft also had a ventral turret, but this was deleted from most production aircraft.

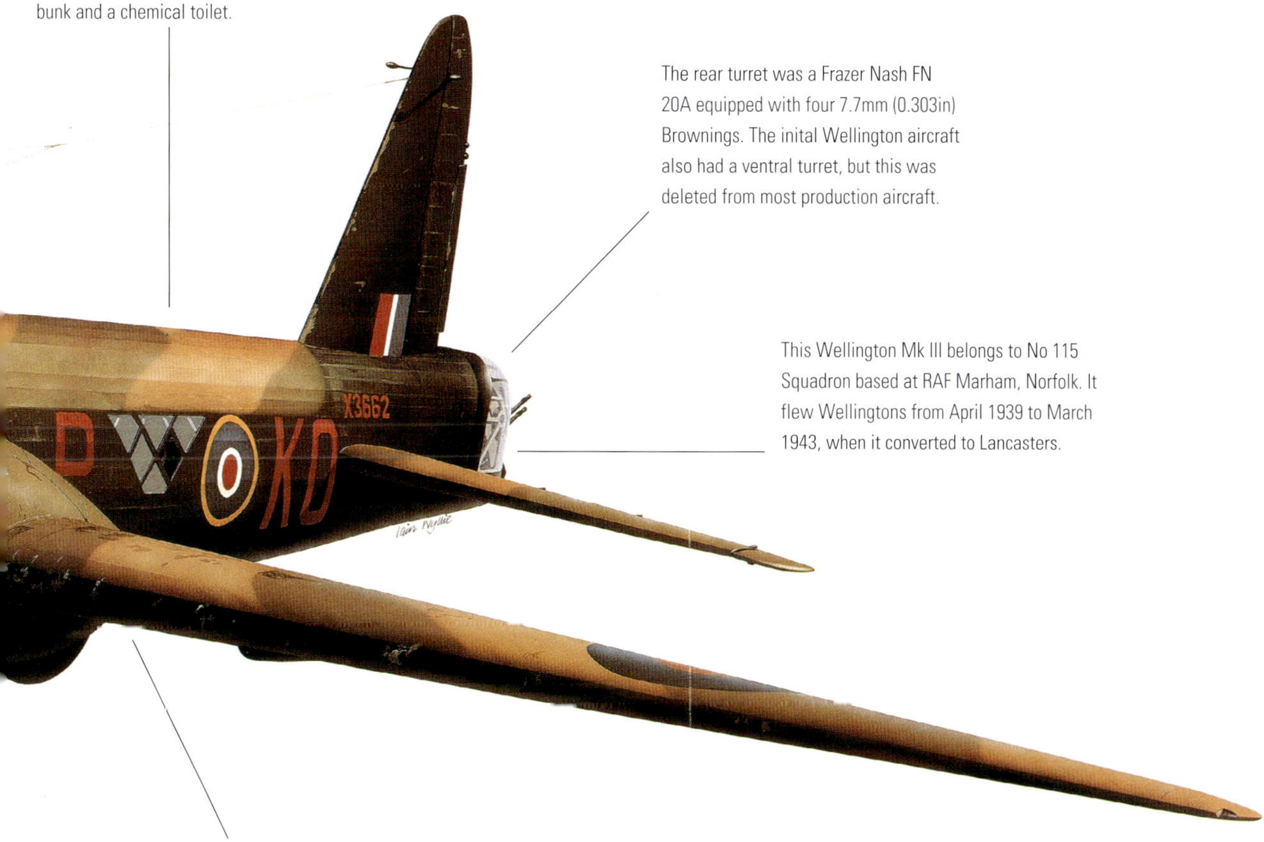

This Wellington Mk III belongs to No 115 Squadron based at RAF Marham, Norfolk. It flew Wellingtons from April 1939 to March 1943, when it converted to Lancasters.

The Wellington was built to a 'geodetic' design developed by Barnes Wallis, which gave the fuselage immense strength and allowed it to be covered only with fabric to reduce weight.

The Vickers Wellington was designed by Barnes Wallis, who was later to conceive the mines that destroyed the Ruhr Dams, to Specification B.9/32. Like its predecessor, the Vickers Wellesley, the aircraft featured geodetic construction, a 'basket weave' construction system producing a self-stabilizing framework in which loads in any direction were automatically equalized by forces in the intersecting set of frames, producing high strength for low weight. It was a system that enabled the Wellington to absorb a tremendous amount of battle damage, and still survive. In December 1933 Vickers was awarded a contract for the construction of a single prototype under the designation Type 271, this aircraft (K4049) flying on 15 June 1936. This aircraft was lost on 19 April 1937 when it broke up during an involuntary high-speed dive, the cause being determined as elevator imbalance. As a result, the production prototype Wellington Mk I and subsequent aircraft were fitted with a revised fin, rudder and elevator adapted from a parallel project, the Vickers B.1/35, which would enter service later as the Warwick. The fuselage also underwent considerable modification, so that production Wellingtons, ordered to Specification 29/36, bore little resemblance to the ill-fated prototype. The first Mk I, L4212, with two Pegasus XX engines, flew on 23 December 1937. The first Bomber Command squadron to re-arm, No 9, began receiving its aircraft in December 1938.

The Wellingtons in RAF service at the outbreak of World War II were the Pegasus-engined Mks I and IA, the latter having a very slight increase in wing span and length. A prototype of the Merlin-engined Mk II and the Mk III had Bristol Hercules engines, and it was this powerplant that would be generally adopted. The most numerous early model, however, was the Mk IC, which had Pegasus XVIII engines; differing little from the IA, the fuselage of the Wellington IC was slightly cut down behind the nose turret and re-shaped in order to allow the turret a greater traverse. The aircraft was also fitted with beam gun positions in place of the ventral gun turret, which caused too much drag, and self-sealing fuel tanks, adopted after two disastrous daylight raids in the Heligoland Bight area on 14 and 18 December 1939, when 17 out of a total force of 34 Wellingtons sent out were shot down by flak or fighters. In all, 2685 Wellington Mk 1C aircraft were built.

After the experience of December 1939, Bomber Command's Wellington force was switched to night-bombing only. In August 1940 Wellingtons took part in the first British air attack on Berlin, and on 1 April 1941 modified Wellington IIs of Nos 9 and 149 squadrons dropped two 1812kg (3995lb) bombs on Emden, with devastating results, marking the first operational use of this weapon. The Wellington made its appearance in the

Below: Armourers loading up a 1812kg (4000lb) bomb on to a Wellington. Known as 'cookies', these particular bombs produced a devastating blast effect on their targets. They were therefore deadly when directed against built-up areas.

Above: Vickers Wellington Mk X bearing the insignia of South-East Asia Command, with the red of the RAF roundel deleted because of possible confusion with Japanese markings and the white toned down to light blue for night operations.

Middle East in September 1940 and in the Far East early in 1942. By this time, the principal version in service with Bomber Command was the Mk III (1519 built), with two 1500hp Bristol Hercules engines replacing the much less reliable Pegasus, although four squadrons (Nos 142, 300, 301 and 305, the last three being Polish units) used the Mk IV, which was powered by American Pratt & Whitney Twin Wasps. The Wellington III entered service with the experienced No 9 Squadron on 22 June 1941, and was to be the backbone of Bomber Command's night offensive against Germany until such time as the Command's four-engined heavy bombers became available in numbers. On the night 30/31 May 1942, when 1042 aircraft set out for Cologne on Bomber Command's first 'thousand-bomber' raid, the raiding force included 599 Wellingtons.

Coastal Command also found its uses for the versatile Wellington. The first general reconnaissance version of the aircraft, which made its appearance in the spring of 1942, was the GR III, 271 being converted from standard Mk IC airframes. The aircraft were fitted with ASV Mk II radar and adapted to carry torpedoes. Use of the GR III torpedo bomber was mainly confined to the Mediterranean, where squadrons operating from the island of Malta preyed on the Axis convoys plying between Europe and North Africa. Fifty-eight more GR IIIs were equipped as anti-submarine aircraft, being fitted with a powerful Leigh Light searchlight to illuminate U-boats travelling on the surface, which they often did at night in transit to and from their Biscay bases. The ASW Wellingtons were used by Nos 172 and 179 Squadrons from Chivenor in Devon and Gibraltar.

The last bomber version of the Wellington was the Mk X, of which 3803 were built, accounting for more than 30 per cent of all Wellington production. Its career with Bomber Command was brief, but it was used in the Far East until the end of the war. Coastal Command's next version was the GR Mk XI, the first of four purpose-built variants; the GR XI and GR XIII were specifically intended for the torpedo-bomber role, while the GR XII and GR XIV were dedicated anti-submarine aircraft.

Other Wellingtons were converted as transports and trainers, and a special variant which was designated DWI was fitted with a large electro-magnetic ring to trigger off enemy magnetic mines. A pressurized high-altitude variant, called the Wellington Mk V, was flown in prototype form only.

Type: Medium bomber (Mk III)	
Crew:	6
Powerplant:	two 1119kW (1500hp) Bristol Hercules XI radial engines
Max speed:	411km/h (255mph) at 3810m (12,500ft)
Initial climb rate:	283m (928ft) per minute
Service ceiling:	5790m (18,996ft)
Max range:	2478km (1540 miles) with 2041kg (4500lb) bomb load
Wing span:	26.26m (86ft 2in)
Wing area:	78.04m² (840sq ft)
Length:	19.68m (64ft 6in)
Height:	5m (16ft 4in)
Weights:	8605kg (18,970lb) empty; 15,422kg (34,000lb) max t/o
Armament:	two 7.7mm (0.303in) MG in nose turret, four in tail turret and two in beam positions; up to 2041kg (4500lb) of bombs

Ilyushin Il-2M3

Many Soviet aircraft carried slogans. This aircraft carries two: 'For Leningrad', and 'Revenge for Khristenko!', the latter being a downed pilot. This aircraft flew on the Leningrad Front in the summer of 1944.

Early Il-2 aircraft were single-seaters, but these proved vulnerable to the Luftwaffe's fighters. A rear gunner was thus installed, armed with either a BS or Berezin UBT 12.7mm (0.5in) machine gun.

The large undercarriage fairings of the Il-2 left the undercarriage partially uncovered, which meant that forced landings didn't cause too much damage to the aircraft. In extreme circumstances, they could carry a passenger, as long as the undercarriage wasn't raised.

The Il-2M3 could carry a pair of 37mm (1.45in) cannon, but the usual armament was a pair of 23mm (0.9in) cannon outboard, with 7.62mm (0.3in) machine guns inboard.

The cockpit was surrounded by a one-piece armoured 'bathtub' which formed part of the aircraft's structure. The back of the bathtub was closed off with a sheet of armour plate, and the whole thing was inpenetrable to rounds smaller than 20mm (0.79in).

The powerplant of the Il-2M3 was the Mikulin AM-38F, a glycol-cooled V12 engine which used parts from a number of Western engines. The intake on the top of the fuselage was for cooling the radiator.

The circular piece of metal projecting from the spinner of the propeller is not a machine gun or cannon, but a Hucks starter dog used for firing the engine.

The Il-2 could carry up to eight of these RS-132 rockets which carried hollow-charge or 'Blockbuster' warheads. They were extremely effective against German tanks.

In the autumn of 1938 – a time of great international tension – the Soviet Air Force General Staff, influenced by the air-combat lessons of the Spanish Civil War, issued a requirement for a new close-support aircraft capable of destroying the latest tanks and armoured vehicles of the types then being mass-produced in Nazi Germany. Two designers, Sergei Ilyshin and Pavel Sukhoi, were ordered to proceed with the design of such an aircraft.

After an extensive evaluation of the proposals which had been submitted, the Ilyushin design was accepted, and materialized in the BSh-2 (or TsKB-55) prototype, which flew for the first time on 30 December 1939. BSh was an abbreviation of *Bronyirovanni Shturmovik*, or Armoured Assaulter, and it was as the Shturmovik that the definitive aircraft would be known throughout its operational career. Of mixed construction, the TsKB-55 was fitted with extensive armour protection for all vital components, and virtually the entire forward fuselage was built as an armoured shell weighing 700kg (1543lb), this area accommodating the engine, water and oil coolers, the fuel tanks and crew members.

Tests with the first two prototypes showed that the aircraft was underpowered and lacked longitudinal stability. Consequently, the third prototype, TsKB-57, the original 1007kW (1350hp) AM-35A engine was replaced by an AM-38 which, although having a lower altitude rating than the AM-35A, offered 1600hp for take-off and 1550hp at 2000m (6562ft). The problem of longitudinal stability was rectified using an enlarged horizontal tail surface and moving the aircraft's centre of gravity, and the second crewmember (radio operator/gunner) was eliminated to provide space for an extra fuel tank. Other changes included increasing the thickness of the rear armour plate from 7mm (0.27in) to 12mm (0.47in), and replacing two of the original armament of four 7.62mm (0.3in) ShKAS

Above: An Ilyushin Il-2m3 is shown wearing hastily applied winter camouflage. In February 1943, the Il-2 played a key role in the Soviet counter-offensive at Stalingrad, an operation which completed the encirclement of the German Sixth Army.

Below: A pair of Il-2s. The early model of the Stormovik had no rear gun position, and therefore suffered terrible losses when it encountered German fighters. It was some time before the matter was rectified and a rear gun position installed.

machineguns with a pair of 20mm (0.79in) ShVAK cannon. Provision was also made for eight 82mm (3.2in) RS-82 air-to-ground missiles on underwing rails as an alternative to a bomb load of 50–600kg (1100–1323lb). The TsKB-57 reached a maximum speed of 470mph (292mph) at sea level, and on successfully completing its State Acceptance Trials in March 1941, was ordered into full production as the Il-2, 249 being produced before the German invasion of June 1941. Most of these were used for training, and it was a small batch of pre-production aircraft, completed even before the TsKB-57 had completed its trials, that was the first to see combat.

The lack of a rear gun position proved to be a serious drawback, and losses were heavy. Following urgent requests from operational units, early in 1942, the decision was taken in principle to reinstate the rear gun position. More immediately, the firepower was increased by replacing the ShVAK cannon with 23mm (0.9in) VYa cannon of higher muzzle velocity, and the engine was boosted to reduce the take-off run from grass or dirt strips and improve combat manoeuvrability. These and other changes resulted in an increase in maximum take-off power to 1305kW (1750hp), the modified engine being designated AM-38F, and with a boosted engine and new armament, the modified single-seat Il-2M began to reach front-line units in the autumn of 1942, and was used in considerable numbers during the battle for Stalingrad that winter.

Further modifications were under way. The armoured forward section was extended rearwards to accommodate a rear gunner's cockpit. The new two-seater variant, the Il-2m3, entered service in August 1943, and thereafter played a prominent, and often decisive, part in the campaigns on the Eastern Front. By the winter of 1943–44, vast numbers of Il 2m3s were in service (some sources put the total as high as 12,000), equipping units of the Soviet Naval Air Arm as well as the Soviet Air Force. Naval Il-2s were used extensively for attacks on shipping in the Baltic and Black Sea, usually with bombs and rocket projectiles, but sometimes with torpedoes. During summer 1943, anti-tank grenades were added to the the Il-2's potential warload, as many as 200 of these small hollow-charge weapons being carried in launchers beneath the wings. If the aircraft came under attack, the launchers could be jettisoned and lowered to the ground by parachute to friendly forces.

Left: This well-publicized shot of a Stormovik shows the aircraft's armament to good advantage, as would have been used at the Battle of Kursk. The Il-2 was built in larger numbers than any other warplane throughout history; no fewer than 36,183 were produced.

It is for its part in the Battle of Kursk that the Il-2 is probably best remembered. Following a series of experiments, Il-2s were fitted with two long-barrelled anti-tank cannon, and these were used with devastating effect at Kursk on the latest German Tiger and Panther tanks. During 20 minutes of concentrated attacks on the 9th Panzer Division, Il-2 pilots claimed to have destroyed 70 tanks. During the course of the battle, the 3rd Panzer Division, with strength of 300 tanks and 180 men per infantry company, claimed to have been reduced to 30 tanks and 40 men per infantry company, largely as a result of Il-2 attacks.

The number of Il-2s built reached the staggering total of 36,183, more than any other type of aircraft in history. An improved version of the Il-2, the Il-10, flew for the first time in 1943 and deliveries to operational units began in the autumn of 1944. Both Il-2 and Il-10 saw action over Germany during the closing weeks of World War II, and in the post-war years, the Il-10 saw widespread service with Soviet Bloc air forces, with some seeing action during the Korean War.

Type: Assault aircraft (Il-2m3)	
Crew:	2
Powerplant:	one 1320kW (1770hp) Mikulin AM-38F liquid-cooled in-line
Max speed:	404km/h (251mph) at 760m (2493ft)
Time to height:	15 mins to 5000m (16,404ft)
Service ceiling:	6000m (19,685ft)
Max range:	800km (497 miles)
Wing span:	14.60m (47ft 9in)
Wing area:	38.54m^2 (414.8sq ft)
Length:	11.60m (38ft)
Height:	3.40m (11ft 1in)
Weights:	4525kg (9976lb) empty; 6360kg (14,021lb) max t/o
Armament:	(typical) wing-mounted armament of two 37mm (1.46in) and two 7.62mm (0.3in) guns; one 12.7mm (0.50in) MG in the rear cockpit; 200 PTAB hollow-charge anti-tank bombs, or eight RS-82 or RS-132 rocket projectiles

Lavochkin La-5

The La-5FN was powered by the Shvetsov M-82FN radial engine. It had two rows of seven cylinders each, with two-stage supercharging and direct fuel injection.

The La-5FN carried only two guns in its upper fuselage decking and synchronized to fire through the propeller disc. The guns were 20mm (0.79in) ShVAK cannon and had 200 rounds of ammunition each.

The annular intake around the front of the engine had louvres to control the amount of air entering the intake trunk which fed air into the engine housing.

The intake under the engine collected air for the engine oil cooler. The rear of the intake had a moveable flap to control the flow of air through the cooler.

The pilot's high position gave good all-round visibility apart from the frontal arc during taxiing, which was obscured by the long fuselage and supercharger. Compared to Western fighters, the pilot's gunsight was extremely primitive.

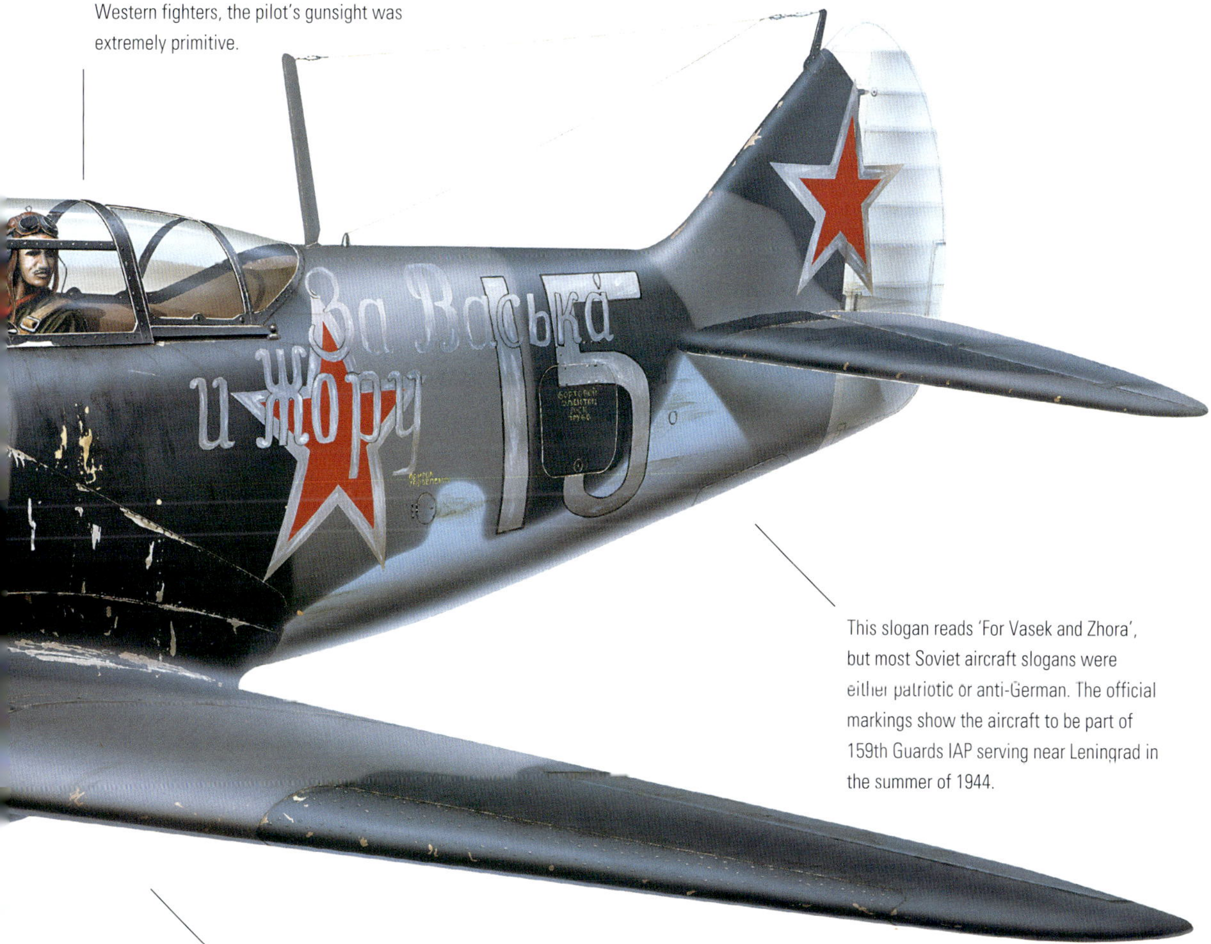

This slogan reads 'For Vasek and Zhora', but most Soviet aircraft slogans were either patriotic or anti-German. The official markings show the aircraft to be part of 159th Guards IAP serving near Leningrad in the summer of 1944.

The primary role of the La-5FN was as a low/medium-level fighter, but it was occasionally assigned ground-attack missions. For these the aircraft could carry up to six 82mm (3.23in) rockets, two 50kg (110lb) and two 25kg (55lb) bombs or a pair of 100kg (220lb) bombs on underwing pylons.

The Lavochkin La-5 was developed from the earlier LaGG-3 in response to a desperate requirement for the Soviet Air Force – which had suffered appalling casualties at the hands of the Luftwaffe in the second half of 1941 – for a modern fighter that could hold its own with the Messerschmitt 109. Semyon Lavochkin retained the basic LaGG-3 airframe, which was lightweight and made of a wooden construction and easy to assemble, and married it with a 992kW (1330hp) Shvetsov M-82F radial engine. Other modifications included a cut-down rear fuselage, providing much improved pilot visibility, and a heavier armament. The prototype La-5 completed its State Acceptance Trials in May 1942 and entered production two months later. The first combat formation to equip with the new fighter was the 287th Fighter Air Division, commanded by Colonel S.P. Danilin, which was assigned to the 8th Air Army on the Volga Front, in the defence of Stalingrad. The division went into action on 21 August 1942, and in the next month its pilots took part in 299 air combats and claimed the destruction of 97 enemy aircraft. By the end of the year, 1182 La-5s had been issued to front-line units, a remarkable achievement by any standard.

Early combats showed that the La-5 was a better all-round performer than the Messerschmitt 109G, although it rate of climb was inferior. Lavochkin, therefore, undertook some re-design work to reduce the fighter's weight, and fitted it with the 1126kW (1510hp) M-82FN direct-injection engine, which endowed the La-5 with better climbing characteristics and manoeuvrability than either the Bf 109G or the Focke-Wulf FW 190A-4. The modified aircraft, designated La-5FN, made its appearance at the front in March 1943, and soon began to make its presence felt in the hands of some very competent Soviet fighter pilots. Among them was Ivan Kozhedub, who made his combat début just before the Battle of Kursk in the summer of 1943, and who went on to score 62 kills while flying Lavochkin fighters, making him the top-scoring Allied air ace. In addition to Soviet Air Force units, the La-

Below: The Lavochkin La-5, flown by the Soviet air ace Ivan Kozhedub. With 62 victories, all gained between the summer of 1943 and the end of the war in Europe in 1945, Kozhedub was the leading Allied air ace, and was three times a Hero of the Soviet Union.

Above: This Lavochkin La-5FN has 31 kill stars on its fuselage, and was the mount of Vitali Ivanovich Popkov, one of the leading Soviet fighter pilots and a Hero of the Soviet Union. His eventual tally of kills was 41.

5FN also equipped the 1st Czech Fighter Regiment, whose pilots scored some notable successes.

The advent of the La-5FN, with its clear superiority over the German fighters that opposed it, enabled the Soviet Air Force to develop new tactics in readiness for the planned offensives of 1943. Soviet fighters now operated at full regiment strength, flying in stepped-up battle formation. Usually, they were employed in escorting assault and light bomber aircraft (Ilyushin Il-2s and Petlyakov Pe-2s) and the ratio of fighters to bombers on these missions depended on the number of bombers engaged. For example, 4 bombers would be escorted by 10 fighters, 16–24 bombers by 20 fighters. Offensive fighter sweeps usually involved one *Gruppa* (three or four pairs) patrolling within a defined sector, with a second *Gruppa* at readiness. In this way a fighter regiment with four *Gruppi* could maintain a constant patrol over the combat area. In addition, fighters operating in pairs frequently carried out ranger patrols (*svobodnaya okhota*). When escorting ground-attack aircraft, the fighter cover was split into two parts, the immediate escort and the assault group. The immediate escort remained constantly near the ground-attack aircraft and flew 90–300m (300–1000ft) higher. These fighters had the task of engaging any enemy fighters that managed to break through the forward assault group to present a direct threat to the ground-attack formation. They normally broke away over the target and circled out of range of the enemy anti-aircraft defences, ready to take up their original position for the withdrawal flight. Often, if no enemy fighters showed up, the immediate escort would

77

themselves dive down to strafe targets on the ground. La-5s sometimes operated as ground-attack aircraft, armed with four 8.2cm (3.23in) RS-82 air-to-ground rockets or two PTAB anti-tank mine dispensers. The fighters of the assault group flew 460-900m (1500-3000ft) higher than the immediate escort, and either directly above or 0.8km (0.5 miles) ahead of the assault formation. One pair was usually sent out in advance to scout for enemy fighters, while a second pair cruised at high altitude, up-sun of the assault formation, ready to dive out of the sun to surprise attacking enemy fighters. Over the target, the assault group usually went up to 3000m (9842ft), clear of the light flak, and patrolled the sky over a fixed area until they were required to cover the withdrawal of the assault aircraft.

The La-7 had a similar engine to the La-5 and differed in minor design detail. A two-seat trainer, the La-5UTI, was also produced, bringing total production of the La-5/La-7 series to 21,975 examples by the war's end. The last of the Lavochkin piston-engined fighter line were the La-9 and La-11. Design work on the La-9 began in 1944. It was slightly larger than the La-5/La-7, and had all-metal construction, a re-designed cockpit canopy, and square-cut wingtips. The La-11 had a slightly smaller wing area than the La-9 and carried a reduced armament.

Left: The La-5 was a superb fighter which could either match or surpass the fighter aircraft available to the Luftwaffe at the time, and it was rightly feared by German pilots. A number of Soviet aces flew the aircraft, testimony to its potentcy.

Type: Fighter (La-5FN)	
Crew:	1
Powerplant:	one 1215kW (1630hp) Ash-82FN radial engine
Max speed:	647km/h (402mph) at 5000m (16,404ft)
Time to height:	5 mins to 5000m (16,404ft)
Service ceiling:	11,000m (36,089ft)
Max range:	765km (475 miles)
Wing span:	9.80m (32ft 1in)
Wing area:	17.59m² (189.3sq ft)
Length:	8.67m (28ft 4in)
Height:	2.54m (8ft 3in)
Weights:	2605kg (5743lb) empty; 3402kg (7500lb) max t/o
Armament:	two nose-mounted 20mm (0.79in) ShVAK or 23mm (0.9in) NS cannon; provision for four 8.2cm (3.23in) RS-82 rockets or 150kg (331lb) of bombs or anti-tank mines

Polikarpov I-16

The whole canopy of the Type 5 slid forward on rails to allow entry and exit. The cockpit had only rudimentary instrumentation. A telescopic gunsight with simple crosshairs protruded through the windscreen.

The tail of this Type 5 is coloured with the markings of the Republican air force. The 'Popeye' emblem shows this aircraft belonged to the 4th *Ecuadrilla de Moscas* in 1937–38, during the Spanish Civil War.

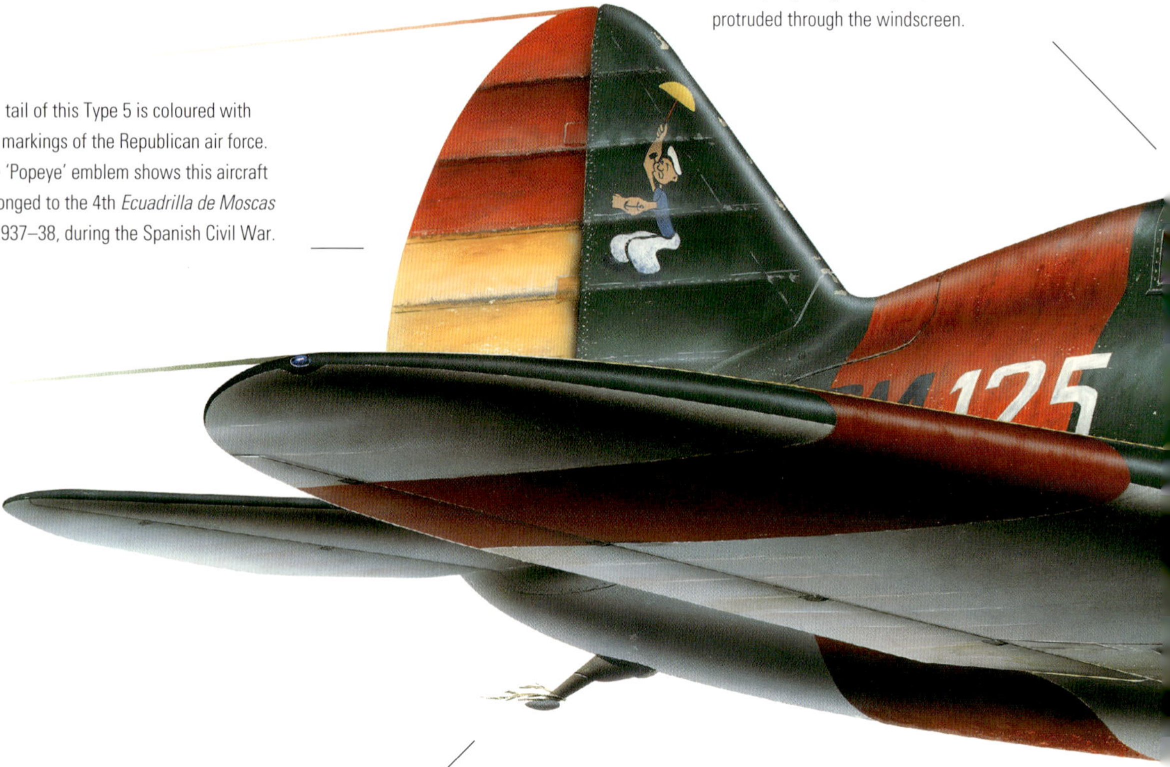

The Type 5 had a tailskid instead of a wheel, with a shock absorber in the rear fuselage.

The I-16 Type 5 was armed with two ShKAS 7.62mm (0.3in) machine guns in the wings. The guns were equipped with 900 rounds of ammunition each.

The I-16 Type 5 was powered by a Shvetsov M-25 9 cylinder radial engine, a Soviet version of the Wright Cyclone SR-1820-F-3.

The I-16 was the first Soviet fighter with retractable undercarriage. Unfortunately for the pilot, a handle had to be pumped no less than 100 times to retract it.

In common with many Soviet aircraft, the I-16 was fitted with a Hucks starter dog at the end of its propeller spinner, used for firing the engine.

On 31 December 1933, two months after the appearance of the I-15 biplane, a new Polikarpov fighter made its first flight. This was the I-16 or TsKB-12, a low-wing monoplane with a retractable undercarriage, two wing-mounted 7.62mm (0.3in) guns and a large 358kW (480hp) M-22 engine. As the first production monoplane in the world to feature a retractable undercarriage, the I-16 attracted great interest among foreign observers when several flights of five aircraft flew over Moscow's Red Square during the Air Parade of 1 May 1935. The I-16 was also the first Soviet fighter to incorporate armour plating around the pilot's cockpit. The first production versions, the I-16 Types 4, 5 and 10, were fitted with a 559kW (750hp) M-25B, increasing their top speed to around 466km/h (290mph). On these variants, wheels and flaps were wound down by hand, which required 44 turns of the crank handle and some mild gymnastics on the part of the pilot. It was soon apparent that the I-16 was an aircraft in which a novice pilot might prove lacking. Among other shortcomings, there was a serious problem of longitudinal instability, which was cured to some extent in subsequent variants. During the mid-1930s, the basic I-16 design was progressively modified to carry out a variety of different tasks. Among the variants produced was the TsKB-18, an assault version armed with four PV-1 synchronized machine guns, two wing-mounted machine guns and 100kg (220lb) of bombs. Armour plating in front, below and behind protected the pilot. In 1938 the I-16 Type 17 was tested, armed with two wing-mounted cannon. This version was produced in large numbers. Then, with the cooperation of the armament engineer B.G. Shpitalnii, Polikarpov produced the TsKB-12P, the first aircraft in the world to be armed with two synchronized cannon firing through the propeller arc. The last fighter version of the I-16 was the Type 24, fitted with a 746kW (1000hp) M-62R engine, which gave it a top speed of 523km/h (325mph). Altogether, 6555 I-16s were built before production ended in 1940.

The I-16 saw considerable action during its career, starting with the Spanish Civil War. The first machines to arrive in Spain went into battle on 15 November 1936, providing air cover for a Republican offensive against Nationalist forces advancing on Valdemoro, Sesena and Equivias. The I-16 – nicknamed *Mosca* (Fly) by the Republicans and *Rata* (Rat) by the Nationalists – proved markedly superior to the Heinkel He 51. It was also faster than its most numerous Nationalist opponent, the Fiat CR 32, although the Italian fighter was slightly more manoeuvrable and provided a better gun platform. Apart from that, the Nationalists' tactics were better; the Republicans tended to stick to large, tight, unwieldy formations that were easy to spot and hard to handle. Later in the campaign the Republican Air Arm was substantially reorganized, with many of the I-15 and I-16 units, which had hitherto been staffed exclusively by Russian personnel, now being turned over to the Spaniards. The first all-Spanish I-16 unit was *Grupo* 21, which began to exchange its Breguet XIXs for *Ratas* just in time to take part in the final stage of the Republican counter-attack at Jarama. The other I-16 squadron that featured prominently in the strafing attacks on the Nationalists during this battle was a Red Air Force unit based at Barajas.

Between 1937 and 1939 the I-16 also saw action during the Sino-Japanese conflict, and also over the disputed Khalkhin-Gol area on the Soviet-Manchurian border. The

Below: This Polikarpov I-16 carries the legend 'For Stalin!' The I-16 was the Soviet Union's first cantilever low-wing monoplane fighter with retractable landing gear. It saw its maiden flight in December 1933 and took part in the Spanish Civil War.

air battles over this region produced an interesting and novel incident. On 20 August 1939, five I-16s, led by Lt N.I. Zvonarev and armed with RS-82 air-to-ground rocket projectiles, fired their salvoes of these at a formation of Japanese aircraft and brought down two of them in what was the world's first aircraft-to-aircraft rocket engagement. I-16s also took part in the Russo-Finnish 'Winter War' of 1939–40, specializing mainly in low-level attacks on Finnish airfields by flights of three or four aircraft.

The I-16 still equipped the majority of the Red Air Force's first-line fighter units at the time of the German invasion in June 1941. However, out-performed and out-flown by their Luftwaffe opponents, the I-16 pilots often would resort to desperate measures. On at least five occasions during the first day of the air war in the east, Soviet I-16s deliberately rammed their adversaries. Three of the pilots involved were members of the 123rd Fighter Air Regiment. The only asset enjoyed by the I-16 during these desperate air combats was manoeuvrability; if an I-16 pilot found himself in a corner, he would throw his aircraft into a tight turn and head for his opponent at full throttle.

The I-16 continued to operate as a first-line combat aircraft on the Leningrad front and in the Crimea until 1942, when it began to be replaced by more modern types and was relegated to second-line training duties.

Above: The I-16 was a very tricky aircraft to handle, epecially in the longitudinal plane, as a result of its short fuselage. Retracting the undercarriage was a feat in itself, requiring the pilot to pump a handle 100 times. After 1942, it was relegated to training duties.

Type: Fighter	
Crew:	1
Powerplant:	one 820kW (1100hp) Shvetsov M-63 nine-cylinder radial
Max speed:	489km/h (304mph)
Time to height:	4 mins to 5000m (16,404ft)
Service ceiling:	9000m (29,527ft)
Max range:	700km (435 miles)
Wing span:	9.00m (29ft 5in)
Wing area:	14.54m² (156.5sq ft)
Length:	6.13m (20ft 1in)
Height:	2.57m (8ft 2in)
Weights:	1490kg (3285lb) empty; 2095kg (4619lb) max t/o
Armament:	two 7.62mm (0.3in) MG in upper part of forward fuselage and two 7.62mm (0.3in) MG or two 20mm (0.79in) cannon in wing; external bomb and rocket load of 500kg (1102lb)

Petlyakov Pe-2FT

The Pe-2 was flown by a crew of three, comprising the pilot, bomb aimer/navigator, and radio operator. The pilot had a typically spartan cockpit, but was protected by an armoured back and headrest.

The bomb aimer/navigator manned the rear-facing turret on the back of the cockpit. He fired a 12.7mm (0.5in) UBT gun. The turret had a weathervane on its rear to provide a counterbalance to the drag of the gun when the latter was not facing directly backwards.

The Pe-2 had a pair of 7.62mm (0.3in) guns mounted either side of its nose. Each gun was provided with 500 rounds of ammunition, and they were aimed by the pilot using a gunsight in the cockpit. Behind the guns was the bomb-aiming position in the glazed underside of the nose.

The Pe-2 could carry four 250kg (551lb) bombs in its bomb bay, two 100kg (220lb) bombs under its engine nacelles, and two further 100kg (220lb) bombs under each wing root.

The Pe-2 was equipped with slatted dive-brakes in its wings to slow its airspeed during a dive-bomb attack.

The markings show this aircraft to be from the 12th Guards Dive-bomber Air Regiment serving with the Baltic Fleet in 1944.

Most of the later Pe-2 aircraft were powered by the Klimov VK-105PF in-line engines driving a three-blade constant speed propeller.

The ventral gun was operated by the radio operator. He could aim the weapon by using either of the side windows or a special periscope provided. In this case the gun is a 12.7mm (0.5in) UB machine gun.

Above: The legend on the fuselage of this Pe-2 bomber reads 'Leningrad-Konigsberg'. The Pe-2 would play a key part in reducing the German strongholds in East Prussia, the Soviet advance into Poland, and the assault on Berlin.

The Petlyakov Pe-2 light bomber had its origin in the 1938 design of a high-altitude interceptor, the VI-100, which was to have been powered by two Klimov M-105R engines and fitted with a pressurized cockpit. Flight testing, which had begun in May 1939, was well advanced when the requirement was changed, transforming the VI-100 into a light high-altitude bomber carrying a crew of two (pilot and gunner). This was subsequently increased to three, the pilot and gunner being joined by a bombardier. The high-altitude bomber concept, however, was destined to be short-lived. No bomb-sight that would give the aircraft anything like the required degree of high-level bombing accuracy was even in development stage, and an analysis of air combat operations in the Spanish Civil War seemed to indicate that the way ahead lay with a high-speed horizontal and dive-bomber dedicated to tactical support. The VI-100 was consequently re-designated PB-100, the PB prefix denoting *Pikiruyushchii Bombardirovshchik* (dive-bomber). The TK-3 engine superchargers were deleted, as was the cabin pressurization, and the aircraft was fitted with wing dive brakes.

The PB-100 prototype flew for the first time in April 1940, and the test flight programme revealed a number of unpleasant shortcomings, including a tendency to enter a flat spin practically without warning if the aircraft stalled. Despite this, test pilots and Soviet AF personnel who flew the aircraft were pleased with its high performance, which was better than most Soviet fighters in production at the time. Dive-bombing accuracy was good, thanks to the very efficient dive brakes which limited diving speeds to 600km/h (373mph). The PB-100 was ordered into production, its designation being changed to Pe-2 in February 1941. By June that year, when the Germans invaded the USSR, the total number of Pe-2s delivered had risen to 462, but comparatively few of these saw action during the early days because of a shortage of trained crews. It was not until late August that the Pe-2 was committed to the battle in any numbers, making low-level attacks on German armoured columns. In these early actions the Pe-2's high speed and defensive armament proved their worth; in one action, when Pe-2s of the 39th Bomber Air Regiment were attacked by 10 Bf 109s, they shot down 3 of the German fighters and fought off the others.

Production of the Pe-2 was rapidly getting into its stride, a further 1405 aircraft being delivered to operational units in the second half of 1941. In January 1942 the Pe-2's designer, Vladimir M. Petlyakov, was killed while flying in a Pe-2 from Kazan, where most of the bombers were built, to a conference in Moscow. A.M. Izakson, who had been imprisoned with Petlaykov, took his place in 1937 on charges of passing technical information to the Germans. The two had still been under arrest when they were ordered to design the VI-100, which earned them their release.

Pe-2 operations received a setback in the spring of 1942, when the Messerschmitt Bf 109F appeared on the Russian Front. This aircraft was some 50km/h (30mph) faster than the Pe-2 at 3000m (9842ft), the Russian bomber's preferred altitude for horizontal bombing. The Pe-2s were forced to push up their bombing altitude to 5000-7000m (16,400-22,960ft), which presented problems to the 109Fs but at the same time reduced bombing accuracy. The solution was to improve the Pe-2's armament and armour, so that it could return to medium-level bombing operations with a chance of survival. Late in 1942 the Pe-2FT appeared, this variant having two 940kW (1260hp) Klimov M-105PF engines and a 12.7mm (0.50in) UBT machinegun in a dorsal turret, replacing the flexible ShKAS machinegun at the rear of the cockpit. The FT suffix denoted *Frontovoye Trebovanie* (Front Requirement). The increase in armour and armament, however, also meant an increase in weight and deterioration in performance, and losses began to climb when the Messerschmitt Bf 109G and the Focke-

Wulf FW 190 were deployed to the Eastern Front. Only when modern Soviet fighters like the Lavochkin La-5 became available for escort work in 1943 did the loss rate show a decline.

The leading Soviet Pe-2 dive-bombing exponent was twice Hero of the Soviet Union Colonel Ivan S. Polbin, who commanded the 150th Bomber Air Regiment in 1942 and, in 1943, the 1st Bomber Air Corps, which distinguished itself at the Battle of Kursk in July that year. In 1944 Polbin was given command of the élite 4th Bomber Air Corps, which he led in action during the Soviet advance into Poland. In the last year of the war, the Pe-2 played an important part in reducing German strongpoints ahead of the advancing Red Army, particularly in East Prussia, where many towns had been fortified. It was also used effectively against the Japanese in Manchuria in August 1945.

Numerous Pe-2 variants made their appearance during the aircraft's operational career. These included the P2-2M, a prototype with VK-105 engines and an enlarged bomb bay to carry a 500kg (1102lb) bomb; the Pe-2FZ, a variant of the Pe-2FT with better cabin facilities; the Pe-2I, which had a mid- instead of a low-wing configuration; the Pe-2RD, with an RD-1 auxiliary rocket engine in the tail (which exploded during trials in 1944); and the Pe-2UT dual-control trainer. A multi-purpose fighter version armed with cannon, machineguns and underwing rockets, designated Pe-3, was also produced. Total production of the Pe-2/3, all variants, was 11,427 aircraft.

Type: Light bomber	
Crew:	3
Powerplant:	two 940kW (1260hp) Klimov VK-105PF 12-cylinder V-type
Max speed:	580km/h (360mph)
Time to height:	9 mins 18 secs to 5000m (16,404ft)
Service ceiling:	8800m (28,871ft)
Max range:	1315km (817 miles) with a 1000kg (2205lb) bomb load
Wing span:	17.11m (56ft 1in)
Wing area:	40.50m² (436sq ft)
Length:	12.78m (41ft 9in)
Height:	3.42m (11ft 2in)
Weights:	5950kg (13,117lb) empty; 8520kg (18,783lb) max t/o
Armament:	two 7.62mm (0.3in) or one 7.62mm (0.3in) and one 12.7mm (0.50in) MG in nose; one 7.62mm (0.3in) MG in dorsal turret; one 7.62mm (0.3in) or 12.7mm (0.50in) MG in ventral position, aimed by a 1200 vision periscope; one 7.62mm (0.3in) or 12.7mm (0.50in) lateral-firing MG in window positions; bomb load of 1600kg (3527lb)

Below: Preparing a Pe-2 for a mission in the winter snows of 1944–45. The Pe-2 was produced in numerous variants to serve a multitude of roles, including nightfighter. The principal bomber version was the Pe-2FT, the Pe-2FZ was a variant of this, with better cabin facilities.

Tupolev Tu-2

The radio operator's position was also the rear dorsal gun position, equipped with a 12.7mm (0.5in) UBT machine gun.

The markings show this to be a Tupolev Tu-2S of the Soviet air force sometime in 1944. The aircraft wears a dark green upper camouflage with pale blue undersides.

The ventral gun position was armed with a 12.7mm (0.5in) UBT machine gun. Above it on both sides were three observation windows, which were replaced by a single large window on later models.

The Tu-2 was powered by a pair of Shvetsov M-82FN 14-cylinder two-row radials. The prominent intake on top of the cowling admitted air for the carburettor, while the intake below the engine was for the engine oil cooler.

The pilot and navigator sat back-to-back on the flight deck. The navigator was armed with a 12.7mm (0.5in) UBT machine gun. The prominent mast attached to the canopy contained a pitot tube, but also acted as an attachment for the radio aerial.

The navigator moved forward to the bomb-aiming compartment during the bomb run. The panes of the glazed lower section were optically flat.

Each wing root contained a forward-firing 20mm (0.79in) ShVAK cannon, aimed by a gunsight in the cockpit. The Tu-2 often took part in low-level strafing attacks.

The long bomb bay could carry a single 1000kg (2205lb) bomb or several smaller weapons. Additional large bombs were carried under the wing roots on racks, while smaller bombs could be carried on five racks each side outboard of the engine.

Above: First flown in prototype form in January 1941, the Tu-2 was one of the best high-speed bombers to see service during World War II. It is testament to its successes that more of these aircraft were in fact built after the conflict than during it.

In 1938, the design bureau led by Andrei N. Tupolev was assigned the task of devloping a light bomber that would have a performance equalling that of contemporary fighter aircraft while carrying a substantial internal bomb load. The aircraft must also have a good combat radius, and be suitable for dive bombing. The resulting project, known as Aircraft 103 for security reasons, was given the bureau designation ANT-58. An all-metal, mid-wing monoplane with a crew of three, it was fitted with two 1044kW (1400hp) Mikulin AM-37 V-12 in-line engines. The prototype flew for the first time on 29 January 1941 and subsequent flight testing showed that the aircraft had an outstanding performance. A second machine, Aircraft 103U (bureau designation ANT-59) flew on 18 May 1941, powered by the same AM-37 engines, but with some changes that included provision for a fourth crew member to man a new ventral gun position just forward of the tail, protecting an area which had hitherto been vulnerable.

Preparations were made for immediate series production, but at this point a crop of problems arose, not least of which was the AM-37 engine was in short supply. As a consequence, it was decided to replace the AM-37s with a pair of 992kW (1330hp) Shvetsov Ash-82 radial engines. These powered the third prototype, Aircraft 103V (ANT-60), which flew in December 1941 and carried the same crew and armament as the ANT-59. Limited production at last got under way at the beginning of 1942, the bomber now being designated Tu-2, but deliveries were slow because of the need to relocate many Soviet aircraft factories ahead of the rapid German advance into Russia. In some areas the design of the Tu-2 was too complex, so Tupolev was ordered to simplify the structure of the aircraft to make it more suitable for mass production. The hydraulic and electrical systems were simplified, internal equipment was revised, the structure was modified as ordered, and the overall result was a 20 per cent reduction in the number of man-hours required to build the Tu-2, accompanied by a marked improvement in serviceability.

The first three production aircraft were delivered to a service evaluation unit near Kalinin, completing their operational trials in September 1942. Pilots were enthusiastic about the bomber, their reports stressing its large bomb load and excellent combat radius, good defensive armament, its ability to fly on one engine, and the ease with which crews were able to convert to the new type.

Because of the earlier problems, however, series production of the Tu-2 did not start until 1943, and combat units did not begin to rearm with the bomber until the spring of 1944. The Tu-2 first saw action on a large scale in June 1944 on

Type: Light bomber (Tu-2S)	
Crew:	4
Powerplant:	two 1380kW (1850hp) Shvetsov Ash-82FN radial engines
Max speed:	547km/h (340mph) at 5400m (17,715ft)
Time to height:	9 mins 30 secs to 5000m (16,405ft)
Service ceiling:	9500m (31,170ft)
Max range:	2000km (1243 miles)
Wing span:	18.86m (61ft 10in)
Wing area:	48.80m^2 (525.3 sq ft)
Length:	13.80m (45ft 3in)
Height:	4.56m (14ft 11in)
Weights:	empty 8260kg (18,200lb); max t/o 12,800kg (28,219lb)
Armament:	two 20mm (0.79in) ShVAK cannon in wing roots, three 12.7mm (0.5in) UBT machine guns, plus a 3000kg (6614lb) bomb load

Above: The Tu-2 was much liked by its crews, and one veteran boasted that, with its bombs gone, it could match any fighter in a turn. It later saw action in the Korean War with the air force of the newly-formed People's Republic of China.

the Karelian (Finnish) front. In its primary bombing role, the Tu-2 carried out some extremely effective missions in the closing months of the war, particularly against fortified enemy towns such as Königsberg (now Kaliningrad) in East Prussia. The aircraft was also used extensively in the brief Soviet campaign against the Japanese Kwantung Army in Manchuria in August 1945.

Although total wartime production was only 1111 aircraft, the Tu-2 proved to be of immense value to the Soviet tactical bomber forces, and also saw service in a number of other roles. One of these was as a carrier for the GAZ-67B cross-country vehicle, which was widely used by Soviet paratroop units. The vehicle was carried partially recessed in the aircraft's bomb bay and dropped by parachute. In October 1944 a long-range variant, the Tu-2D (ANT-62), made its appearance; this had an increased span and a crew of five. A torpedo-bomber variant, the Tu-2T (ANT-62T), was tested between January and March 1945 and issued to units of the Soviet Naval Aviation. The Tu-2R, also designated Tu-6, carried a battery of cameras in the bomb bay and featured an extanded wing for high-altitude operations, a redesigned and lengthened nose section, an enlarged tail assembly, and modified engine nacelles. An experimental ground-attack version, the Tu-2Sh, was tested with various armament combinations; these included a 75mm (2.95in) gun mounted in a 'solid' nose, and a battery of 48 7.62mm (0.3in) sub-machine guns mounted in the bomb bay and directed to fire downwards on unprotected personnel.

After World War II, the Tu-2 proved to be an ideal test vehicle for various powerplants, including the first generation of Soviet jet engines. Production continued after 1945, some 3000 aircraft being delivered to various Soviet Bloc air forces. Chinese Tu-2s were encountered by UN fighter pilots during the Korean War, proving easy targets for jets such as the F-86 Sabre. On one occasion, on 30 November 1951, F-86 pilots of the 4th Fighter Interceptor Wing shot down eight out of a formation of 12 Tu-2s south of the Yalu River, together with three of their escorting La-9 fighters. The last Tu-2 model was the ANT-68, a high-altitude version that saw limited service as

Yakolev Yak-3

The standard machine gun armament on the Yak-3 was a pair of 12.7mm (0.5in) machine guns in the upper front fuselage. Some early production models only carried one machine gun on the port side.

The Yak-3 had a one-piece windscreen which replaced the four-piece version on the Yak-1, increasing visibility and decreasing weight and drag.

The Yak-3 carried a 20mm (0.79in) ShVAK cannon in its nose, firing through the propeller boss, with 120 rounds of ammunition. The Yak-3T carried a 37mm (1.45in) cannon in its nose, while the Yak-3K had a massive 45mm (1.77in) nose cannon.

The Yak-3 was intended to fly with the Klimov VK-107 engine, but due to the latter being delayed, the aircraft was powered by the VK-105PF-2. At the very end of the war VK-107-powered Yak-3s were built, with the designation Yak-3U.

The Yak-3, unlike the Yak-1, -7 and -9, had a large oil cooler intake mounted in the wingroot of its port wing rather than under its front fuselage. This acted as a recognition feature for Luftwaffe pilots.

Although the cockpit had good visibility, it had very little else. The gunsight was primitive, there were no instruments for blind flying, and there were no fuel gauges in the cockpit.

The radiator was mounted under the fuselage just behind the wing. Excess air was dumped through an ejector flap in the rear of the radiator fairing, which could be closed if not required.

The Yak-3 shown here was the personal mount of Major General G. N. Zakharov, the commander of 303rd Fighter Aviation Division. His personal marking is visible on the side of the aircraft, showing a knight killing a Göbbels-faced snake.

It was not until 1939 and 1940 that the prototypes of three Soviet fighters that could really be classed as modern made their appearance. The first was the LaGG-3, which took its name from the initials of the three engineers who conceived it: Lavochkin, Gorbunov and Gudkov. It was a remarkable little aircraft, built entirely of wood and bearing a strong resemblance to France's Dewoitine D 520. It was armed with one ShVAK 20mm (0.79in) cannon, two ShKAS 7.62mm (0.3in) machineguns and one 12.7mm (0.5in) BS (Beresin) machinegun. The LaGG-3 flew for the first time in March 1939. The second type, the MiG-1, which flew in March 1940, was the fruit of collaboration between the two aero-engineers Artem I. Mikoyan and Mikhail I. Gurievitch. An open-cockpit single-seater, it was not a particularly successful design, though over 2000 were built before it was replaced by the much-improved MiG-3. The third type, the Yak-1 *Krasavyets* (Beauty) made its first public appearance during an air display on 7 November 1940. It was Aleksandr S. Yakovlev's first fighter design, and it earned him the Order of Lenin, the gift of a Zis car and a prize of 100,000 roubles. The fighter was powered by a 746kW (1000hp) M-105PA engine and carried an armament of one 20mm (0.79in) ShVAK cannon, two

Below: The excellent Yak-3 was the last in a line of piston-engined fighters which had begun with the Yak-1 of 1940. The first Yak-3s reached the Eastern Front in the summer of 1943, and were in time to take part in the Battle of Kursk.

Above: The Yak-9, pictured here, was a phenomenal success. It was largely responsible for establishing Soviet air superiority from the summer of 1943 onwards, and during its career, it was also used as an effective ground-attack aircraft.

7.62mm (0.3in) ShKAS machineguns and sometimes six RS-82 rockets. The Yak-1 was of mixed construction, fabric and plywood covered; it was simple to build and service, and a delight to fly. Maximum speed was 500km/h (310mph). Series production of all three types was begun between 1940 and 1941.

Production of the Yak-1 was accelerated following the German invasion of Russia in June 1941, and in the second half of the year, 1019 aircraft were turned out. Production was disrupted in September 1941, when the Yakovlev factory was moved from Moscow to Kamensk, in the Urals, but the first Yak-1 was completed within three weeks of the relocation, and the monthly production of the Moscow works was exceeded after three months. In other re-located factories, however, particularly in Siberia, production of the Yak-1 was much slower, with a consequent reduction in deliveries to front-line units. So it was decided to convert a trainer variant of the Yak-1, the Yak-7V, into a single-seat fighter by covering the second cockpit with metal sheeting and arming the aircraft with one ShVAK cannon and two ShKAS machineguns. In this new guise the aircraft was designated Yak-7A; a robust aircraft, yet with a performance identical to that of the Yak-1, its development was to proceed through a line of variants with heavier armament and longer range, culminating in the Yak-9, a superb fighter aircraft that would do much to win air superiority over the eastern battlefront. The Yak-1's ongoing development, on the other hand, tended towards the pure interceptor. In 1942 it evolved into the Yak-1M, which had a smaller wing area, a revised rear fuselage and a three-piece sliding cockpit hood; it was also slightly faster than the Yak-1. Similar modifications to the Yak-7A led to the improved Yak-7B; a total of 6399 were built.

Further refinements to the Yak-1M were introduced before the aircraft entered quantity production in the spring of 1943, these including suppression of the radio mast (although it was re-introduced at a later date) and the transfer of the oil cooler intake from beneath the nose to the port wing root. Re-designated Yak-3, the production fighter's structure was similar to that of the Yak-1, in that the one-piece two-spar wing was entirely of wooden construction with plywood skinning, and the fuselage was of welded steel tube. The forward portion of this welded steel tube was covered by detachable metal panels, whereas the aft portion was covered by plywood and, finally, doped fabric.

The aircraft was powered by a 911kW (1222hp) VK-105PF engine; its armament comprised one 20mm (0.79in) ShVAK cannon with 120 rounds, which was designed to fire through the propeller shaft, as well as two 12.7mm (0.5in) Beresin BS machineguns in the forward fuselage decking.

Right: The predecessor of the Yak-3, the Yak-1 Krasavyets (Beauty). Here a number of Yak-1s are seen outside an assembly shop of one of the newly-built Soviet aircraft factories located outside the range of Hitler's bombers.

Type: Fighter	
Crew:	1
Powerplant:	one 911kW (1222hp) VK-105PF-2 or 1208kW (1620hp) VK-107 engine
Max speed:	658km/h (409mph) at 3500m (11,483ft)
Time to height:	4.1mins to 5000m (16,404ft)
Service ceiling:	10,800m (35,433ft)
Max range:	900km (559 miles)
Wing span:	9.2m (30ft 2in)
Wing area:	14.85m² (159.8sq ft)
Length:	8.55m (28ft)
Height:	3m (9ft 8in)
Weights:	2105kg (4641lb) empty; 2660kg (5864lb) max t/o
Armament:	one 20mm (0.79in) ShVAK cannon with 120 rounds firing through the propeller shaft; two 12.7mm (0.50in) Beresin BS MG in the forward fuselage decking

The first Yak-3s reached the front line during the early summer months of 1943, just in time to take part in the Battle of Kursk. However, it was not until the spring of 1944 that the fighter was available in really substantial numbers. The Yak-3 quickly proved itself in combat; it rarely operated above 3500m (11,483ft), below which it was markedly more manoeuvrable than either the FW 190A or Bf 109G; in fact, it was probably the most manoeuvrable

fighter aircraft to see service during World War II. As well as performing the role of interceptor, it was extensively employed in close support of the ground forces, and for the escort of Pe-2 and Il-2 assault aircraft, one formation of Yak-3s preceding the bombers and attacking German fighter airfields while another provided closer escort. At a relatively early stage in the production life of the Yak-3 the wooden wing spars were replaced by spars of light alloy, first introduced in the Yak-9, and the VK-105 engine was replaced by the more powerful 1208kW (1620hp) VK-107. During State Acceptance Trials with the new engine early in 1944, the aircraft reached a speed of 720km/h (447mph) at 5750m (18,865ft).

At 5000m (16,404ft) the Yak-3 was 95–110km/h (60–70mph) faster than the FW 190A-4 or the Me 109G-2. The Soviet Air Force received a total of 4848 Yak-3s.

Mitsubishi Zero

The A6M5c had a pair of guns in the upper fuselage deck, with the breeches accessible from the cockpit. One gun was a Type 3 13.2mm (0.52in) machine gun, while the other was a Type 97 7.7mm (0.303in).

The pilot had 360° vision from his all-glazed cockpit with sliding canopy. The reflector gunsight was slightly offset to the right.

The aircraft was powered by a Nakajima NK1F Sakae 21 radial engine. Unfortunately it was underpowered for the weight of the aircraft, and the A5M5c suffered against its Allied opponents as a result.

This large intake under the fuselage admitted air for the oil cooler, which was mounted behind the engine.

A 337 litre (47 Imp gal) drop tank was usually carried on the centreline stores station to extend the aircraft's range. For suicide missions this was often replaced by a single 250kg (551lb) bomb.

The standard wing gun for the aircraft was the Type 99 20mm (0.79in) cannon. However on the Model 52C a Type 3 heavy machine gun was added outboard of each cannon.

The pilot was protected from shots from the rear by armour plate. Behind him was a prominent aerial mast for the radio and a loop antenna for the direction-finding equipment under the canopy.

The markings show this A6M5c Model 52C to belong to the Imperial Japanese Navy. At the end of the fuselage was a sting-type arrester hook for carrier landings.

The Model 52C had racks under the wings added suitable for carrying eight 10kg (22lb) unguided rockets. Bombs could also be carried – usually two 60kg (132lb) weapons.

The Japanese Army Air Force's poor performance in the fighting against the Russians during the frontier wars of the 1930s, and the clear superiority of Russian equipment and tactics, led the Japanese High Command to consider the USSR as the principal potential enemy. Equipment planning was influenced by the requirement to be prepared for a renewed conflict on the Manchuria–Siberia border. New combat aircraft were developed to carry out tactical missions in cold weather, so that they were poorly suited to long over-water missions among the Pacific islands in the coming war of 1941–45. The Imperial Japanese Navy, on the other hand, bore the brunt of long-range operations against Chinese targets during the Sino-Japanese wars, the aircraft industry developing bombers for missions at extreme range and also a fighter capable of escorting them to the target and back. The result was one of the finest aircraft of all time, the Mitsubishi A6M *Reisen*. Designed by Jiro Horikoshi to specification 12-shi (1937), this superb fighter first flew on 1 April 1939, powered by a 582kW (780hp) Zuisei 13 radial engine. After 15 aircraft had been evaluated under combat conditions in China, the type was accepted for service with the Japanese Naval Air Force in July 1940, entering full production in November that year as the A6M2 Model 11. Sixty-four Model 11s were completed, these being fitted with the more powerful Sakae 12 engine, and were followed by the Model 21 with folding wingtips. This was the major production version at the time of the attack on Pearl Harbor in December 1941.

The A6M2 soon showed itself to be clearly superior to any fighter the Allies could put into the air in the early stages of the Pacific war. Armed with two 20mm (0.79in) Type 99 cannon and two 7.62mm (0.3in) Type 97 machineguns, it was highly manoeuvrable and structurally very strong, despite being lightweight. Instead of being built in several separate units, it was constructed in two pieces. The engine, cockpit and forward fuselage combined with the wings to form one rigid unit, the second unit comprising the rear fuselage and the tail. The two units were joined together by a ring of 80 bolts. Its main drawback was that it had no armour plating for the pilot and no self-sealing fuel tanks, which meant that it could not absorb as much battle damage as Allied fighters. One well-placed burst of gunfire was usually enough to make the aircraft disintegrate.

Right: The Mitsubishi Zero's phenomenally long range made it ideal for conducting combat missions over the vast expanse of the Pacific Ocean. However, although it was highly agile, it suffered from a lack of protection for both fuel tanks and pilot.

In 1942 the Americans allocated the code-name Zeke to the A6M, but as time went by the name 'Zero' came into general use. The Japanese word *reisen* meant 'Zero fighter', the aircraft having been adopted in the Japanese year 2600 (1940). During the first months of the Pacific War the Zeros carved out an impressive combat record. In the battle for Java, which ended on 8 March 1942, they destroyed 550 Allied aircraft, including large numbers of fighters such as the Brewster Buffalo, Curtiss-Wright CW

Right: The A6M Zero remains the most famous Japanese warplane of those engaged in combat World War II, and it was the first carrier-borne fighter anywhere in the world to achieve parity with its land-based contemporaries.

BII-144

21, Curtiss Hawk, Curtiss P-40 and Hawker Hurricane. Japanese losses were extremely light. In one big dogfight that took place over Soerabaya on 19 February 1942, 23 Zeros operating from Borneo took on a force of 50 Dutch and American P-36 and P-40 fighters and destroyed more than half of them for the loss of only three of their own number. These remarkable victories earned enormous prestige for the Japanese Navy pilots and tended to overshadow the achievements of their Army colleagues, who fought no less tenaciously, albeit with less spectacular success. Throughout the war, the demands of the Navy were to receive priority. Unlike the Army, the Navy followed the practice of concentrating its best pilots in élite units. One of these was based at Lae in New Guinea in April 1942, and was assigned the task of providing fighter cover for the Japanese drive on Port Moresby, the capture of which was an essential stepping-stone to the invasion of Australia. By the end of the month the Lae Fighter Wing included such redoubtable pilots as Saburo Sakai, with 22 victories, Hiroyoshi Nishizawa with 13, and Takatsuka with 9. On 17 May, in a gesture of supreme arrogance that symbolized their complete air supremacy, Sakai, Nishizawa and another pilot named Ota carried out a sequence of aerobatics over the Allied

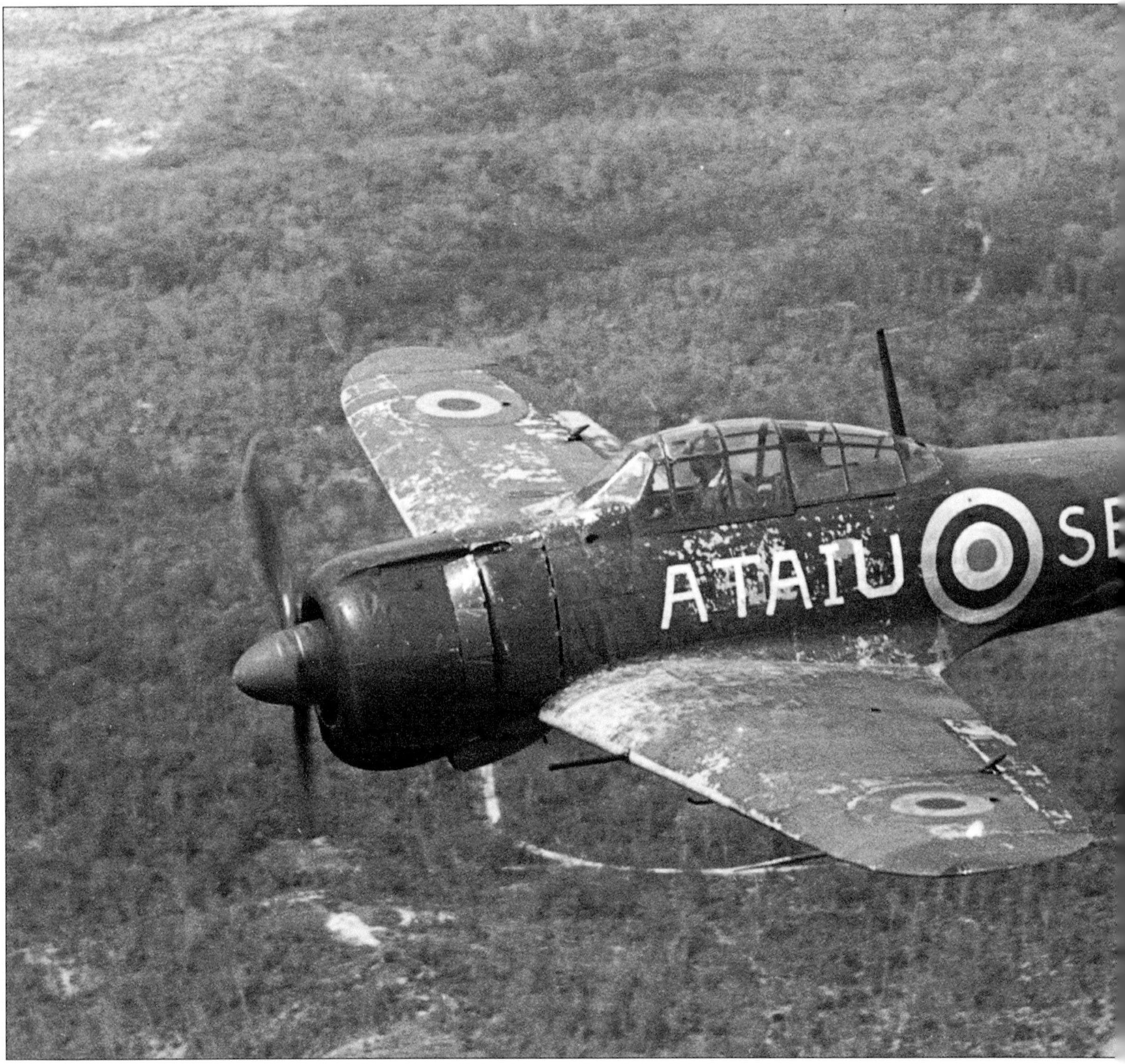

airfield at Port Moresby without being molested. Most of the pilots of the Lae Wing continued to fly the Zero throughout their combat careers. Nishizawa, before being shot down and killed on 26 October 1944, was credited with 94 victories; he destroyed 6 enemy aircraft on one day over Guadalcanal late in 1942. Another pilot, Kenze Okabe, shot down seven American aircraft on one day over Rabaul in August 1942. Saburo Sakai went on to end the war with 64 victories, making him the surviving Japanese top-scorer.

In 1942 Japanese Navy fighter units began to receive the A6M3 Model 32, with a supercharged 1300 Sakae 21 engine. This model had its folding wingtips removed to improved performance, but this impaired the fighter's manoeuvrability, and the full-span wing was restored in the A6M3 Model 22. By early 1943 it was becoming apparent that the A6M3 could no longer retain superiority over the latest Allied fighters, so the A6M5 Model 52 was developed, retaining the Sakae 21 engine but having a shorter-span wing (in essence, a Model 32 wing with rounded tips). Sub-types produced included the A6M5a Model 52A, with strengthened wings and increased ammunition, the A6M5b Model 52B with heavier armament and armour protection, and the A6M5c Model 52C, with more armour, two 20mm (0.9in) and three 13mm (0.5in) guns. The latter sub-type had a Sakae 31 engine with methanol injection, bulletproof fuel tanks and underwing rocket rails. The A6M7 Model 63 was a special Kamikaze version, of which 465 were built; hundreds more Zeros were also expended in suicide attacks. Other versions were the A6M8c Model 54C, with a 1500hp Mitsubishi Kinsei 62 engine and four wing guns, a twin-float seaplane, the A6M2-N, and the A6M2-K2 two-seat trainer. In all, 10,937 Zeros of all versions were built. The specification applies to A6M2.

Type: Carrier-borne and land-based fighter (A6M2)	
Crew:	1
Powerplant:	one 708kW (950hp) Nakajima NK1C Sakae 12 V14 cylinder
Max speed:	534km/h (332mph)
Time to height:	7 mins 27 secs to 6000m (19,685ft)
Service ceiling:	10,000m (32,808ft)
Max range:	3104km (1929 miles)
Wing span:	12m (39ft 4in)
Length:	9.06m (29ft 7in)
Height:	3.05m (10ft)
Weights:	1680kg (3704lb) empty; 2796kg (6164lb) max t/o
Armament:	two 20mm (0.79in) Type 99 (Oerlikon) fixed forward-firing cannon in wing leading edges; two fixed forward-firing 7.62mm (0.3in) MG in forward fuselage; external bomb load of 120kg (265lb)

Left: A captured Zero under test by the South-East Asia Command's Allied Tactical Air Intelligence Unit over Malaya at the end of the war. The Zero was kept in production past its effective limits due to the lack of an adequate Japanese successor.

Macchi MC 202 Folgore

Italian aircraft carried a white fuselage band for identification purposes. The Stormo badge was painted on top of it – in this case the 'cat and mice' badge of 51st Stormo.

The pilot was protected by an armoured backplate and headrest, and from Serie VII onwards, a bullet-proof windscreen. The canopy hinged to starboard. A reflector sight and ring-and-bead sight were provided for the pilot.

This Macchi carries the classic Italian desert camouflage pattern of 'sand and spinach', green disruptive patterns painted over the sand finish. It also carries the Fascist party symbol on its wing, a bundle of rods with an axe-head protuding from them.

From Serie VII onwards a pair of wing guns were added to give the fighter more punch. These were 7.7mm (0.303in) Breda-SAFAT machine guns with 500 rounds of ammunition each.

A pair of 12.7mm (0.5in) Breda-SAFAT machine guns were mounted in the upper fuselage firing through the propeller arc. The guns had 400 rounds of ammunition each.

The Macchi was powered by a R. A. 1000 R.C41-I° Monsoni, a Daimler Benz DB 601Aa licence-built for the aircraft by Alfa Romeo.

Cooling for the engine was provided primarily by a large radiator bath under the centre section. This had an ejector flap at its rear to help provide a good flow of air.

The air intake under the nose admitted air for the oil cooler which was mounted behind the engine. Small intakes on top of the cowling also gathered air to help cool the engine in flight.

Above: A Macchi MC 202 Folgore of the 155th Squadriglia, 5th Stormo Caccia Terrestre, which was operating with the Italian Co-Belligerent Air Force in 1944. Like many other Italian aircraft types, the MC 202 fought on both sides of the conflict.

Italian monoplane fighters were making their appearance by the late 1930s and were proving to have excellent aerodynamic design. They were, however, handicapped by the lack of a suitable powerplant. A case in point was the Macchi MC 200 *Saetta* (Lightning), designed in 1936 by Mario Castoldi, who had considerable experience in designing high-speed racing seaplanes. He drew heavily on this experience when designing the MC 200, but found that any attempt to produce the clean lines of his MC 72 record-breaking floatplane was frustrated by the need to use a bulky, drag-producing radial engine, instead of a high-powered, lowdrag, liquid-cooled engine such as those available to British and German designers. The 2088kW (2800hp) Fiat AS 6 24-cylinder Vee-type engine that had powered the MC 72 had been purpose-built, and was not suitable for series production. When the MC 200 flew for the first time on 24 December 1937, therefore, it was with an 634kW (850hp) Fiat A 74 RC 38 14-cylinder two-row radial, which endowed it with a less than inspiring performance. Although it was manoeuvrable, its low maximum speed and poor rate of climb made it ineffective as a bomber interceptor, and to compensate in part for the weight of the engine, armour protection had to be sacrificed.

Attempts to improve the performance of the MC 200 began in 1938, only weeks after the prototype had flown. There was still no available in-line engine, and the only powerplant remotely suitable for installation in a fighter aircraft was another radial, the 746kW (1000hp) Fiat A 76 RC 40. Castoldi decided to adapt the existing MC 200 airframe to take the A 76, the modified aircraft being designated MC 201. The development of the A 76 engine was set back by numerous teething troubles, and although the MC 201 airframe was test-flown with a standard A 74 engine, it never received its intended powerplant. Eventually the A 76 was abandoned, and the MC 201 with it.

Castoldi's much-needed breakthrough came in early 1940, when an example of the German Daimler-Benz DB 601A-1 liquid cooled in-line engine was delivered to Macchi's Varese factory. This was installed in a standard *Saetta* airframe and flown on 10 August 1940 at Carestiato. The subsequent flight tests produced excellent results, and the aircraft, designated MC 202 *Folgore* (Thunderbolt) was ordered into production fitted with the licence-built DB 601, the engine being produced by Alfa Romeo as the RA 1000 RC 411. Since the MC 202 used many of the

Type: Day fighter (MC 202 Serie VII)	
Crew:	1
Powerplant:	one 802kW (1075hp) Alfa Romeo RA 1000 RC 41-I 12-cylinder inverted Vee-type
Max speed:	600km/h (373mph) at 5600m (18,373ft)
Time to height:	4 mins 36 secs to 5000m (16,404ft)
Service ceiling:	11,500m (37,730ft)
Max range:	610km (379 miles)
Wing span:	10.58m (34ft 8in)
Wing area:	16.80m² (180.8sq ft)
Length:	8.85m (29ft)
Height:	3.50m (11ft 5in)
Weights:	2490kg (5489lb) empty; 2930kg (6459lb) max t/o
Armament:	two 12.7mm (0.5in) Breda-SAFAT MG in nose; two 7.7mm (0.303in) in wings; late production aircraft, two 20mm (0.79in) cannon in wings

Above: One of the MC 202's main drawbacks for the pilot was its poor visibility, as is evident in the photograph. Nevertheless, it was an excellent fighter aircraft, and in expert hands was a match for the RAF's Spitfires and Hurricanes over Malta.

same jigs and tools that had been used in the manufacture of the *Saetta*, no problems were experienced in switching production to the new type, which was soon being turned out in quantity by the Macchi works at Varese-Schiranna and Lonate Pozzolo, the Breda factory at Sesto S. Giovanni, and the SAI-Ambrosini plant at Passignano, all of which had been involved in the manufacture of the MC 200. Initially, the *Folgore* retained the same armament as the *Saetta* (two 12.7mm (0.5in) machine guns), but this was later augmented by two 7.7mm (0.303in) machine guns in the wings, and late production machines had a new wing in which the 7.7mm (0.303in) guns were replaced by two 20mm (0.79in) MG 151 cannon.

The MC 202 entered service with the 1st *Stormo* at Udine in the summer of 1941, moving to Sicily to take part in operations over Malta in November. Its stay was brief, however, as the 1st *Stormo* was deployed to North Africa later in the month to reinforce the Axis air forces in Libya. It eventually served with 45 squadriglie of the 1st, 2nd, 3rd, 4th, 51st, 52nd, 53rd and 54th *Stormi Bombardamento Veloce* (High Speed Bomber Groups)in North Africa, Italy, Sicily, the Aegean and South Russia. The MC 202 had a better performance in 1942 than its main opponents, the Hurricane and Kittyhawk, but its armament remained inferior until the introduction of the 20mm (0.79in) cannon at a very late stage.

The *Folgore* was, without doubt, the best fighter produced by the Italians during World War II. It remained in production until the Italian armistice of September 1943, although the rate of production was always influenced by the availability of aeroengines. Macchi built 392 MC 202s; other companies (mostly Breda) subsequently produced a further 1100. The ultimate wartime development of the Macchi MC 200 series of fighters was the MC 205V *Veltro* (Greyhound), which in essence was an MC 202 airframe converted to take the DB 605 engine. It also had larger wing panels. The *Veltro* flew for the first time on 19 April 1942 and the prototype carried an armament of two 12.7mm (0.5in) and two 7.7mm (0.303in) machine guns, but production *Veltros* had two wing-mounted Mauser MG 151 20mm (0.79in) cannon. *Veltro* production came to 262 aircraft, the first of which went into action in July 1943.

After the armistice, MC 202s and MC 205s equipped fighter squadrons of both the Italian Co-Belligerent Air Forces, fighting on the side of the Allies, and the National Republican Air Force, which continued to fight alongside the Germans. According to some P-51 Mustang pilots with the Italian-based Fifteenth Air Force, the Macchi 202 and 205 were the most formidable enemy fighters they had to contend with, as they were capable of out-turning the American fighter.

Savoia Marchietti SM 79

There were five crew on an SM 79. Two pilots sat side-by-side on the flight deck, with the radio operator and flight engineer behind them, and the bomb aimer in the rear. The pilot had a fixed forward-firing 12.7mm (0.5in) gun above the cockpit.

Defence of the rear upper hemisphere of the aircraft was the responsibility of either the flight engineer or radio operator, who used a 12.7mm (0.5in) gun on a flexible mount. The gun could be retracted and a panel put in place to cover the hole in the fuselage.

Early versions of the SM 79 were powered by only two engines, but most production versions for the Regia Aeronautica were three-engined. The aircraft shown here was powered by the Piaggio P.XI RC.40 radial.

The SM 79 was most successful as a torpedo-bomber, and it could carry one or two weapons under the fuselage, such as the 450mm (17.7in) one shown. Other options were five 250kg (551lb) bombs, or two 500kg (1102lb) bombs, or 12 100kg (220lb) bombs.

A 7.7mm (0.303in) waist gun was mounted on a lateral bar so that it could be fired out of either beam window.

This SM 79 has its *squadriglia* number on the rear fuselage, followed by the individual aircraft's number. This aircraft belonged to 283rd *Squadriglia* of the 130th *Gruppo Autonomo Aerosiluranti*, a specialist anti-shipping unit, based in Sicily in 1942.

A 12.7mm (0.5in) rear-facing Breda-SAFAT machine gun was mounted in the rear of the ventral gondola. It was covered by a hinged fairing when not in use.

The ventral gondola contained the bomb-aimer. He had a small wheel which allowed him to make minute corrections to the aircraft's course by adjusting the rudder. A camera could also be fitted for reconnaissance purposes.

Although the bomber force of the Regia Aeronautica did prove effective in the limited wars in which Italy was involved in the 1930s, it never equalled – either in the quality of the aircraft types it used, or in numbers – that of the allied air forces that opposed it during World War II. Typical examples of the bombers that formed the backbone of the Regia Aeronautica were the three-engined machines produced by Savoia-Marchetti, a firm with considerable experience in the field of commercial aircraft design. One such design was the SM 73, an 18-passenger airliner with a tapered cantilever low wing and a fixed undercarriage; the military version was the SM 81 *Pipistrello* (Bat) which, when it made its service debut in 1935, represented a considerable advance over the Regia Aeronautica's existing bomber types. Fast, well-armed and with a good range, it was used to good effect during the Italian campaign in Abyssinia, which began in October 1935, and from August 1936 it was also used operationally during the Spanish Civil War.

Although it shared the SM 81's three-engined configuration, the SM 79 was in fact a completely new design, the prototype of which was an eight-seater airliner that flew for the first time in October 1934. Built specifically to take part in the prestigious London–Melbourne air race, it had a high maximum speed, and in September 1935 it captured six world speed records over distances of 1000 and 2000km (621 and 1243 miles) with respective payloads of 500, 1000 and 2000kg (1100, 2200 and 4400lb). As a result of this performance, the Italian Air Force showed an interest in the type, and asked for a second prototype to be completed as a bomber version. This did not vary greatly from the airliner, the only difference being the addition of a ventral gondola and of a raised cockpit, which gave the aircraft its characteristic hunch-backed appearance. Production of the military SM 79 began in October 1936 and was to have an uninterrupted run until June 1943, by which time 1217 aircraft had been built.

The Regia Aeronautica lost no time in testing the SM 79 operationally in Spain, where the type was used with considerable success by the 8th and 111th *Stormi Bombardamento Veloce* (High Speed Bomber Groups). The initial production version, the SM 79-I, was powered by three 582kW (780hp) Alfa Romeo 126 radial engines and had a range of 1898km (1179 miles).

In 1937 an SM 79-I underwent trials with a 450mm (17.62in) torpedo, and later two, beneath the fuselage, and these indicated that the aircraft could easily carry two of these weapons if it were fitted with more powerful engines. In October 1939 production began of the SM 79-II, equipped with 746kW (1000hp) Piaggio P XI radial engines (apart from one batch with 768kW (1030hp) Fiat A 80 RC 41s) for the torpedo-bomber squadrons of the Regia Aeronautica, and it was in this role that the aircraft was to excel during World War II. When Italy entered that conflict in June 1940,

Below: Enthusiastic ground crews wave off an SM 79 as it departs from Sicily on a sortie to Malta in the summer of 1940. Italian bomber crews, flying in close formation, could often execute beautiful precision attacks from high altitudes.

Above: An SM 79 pictured in the markings of the Lebanese Air Force, which, long after the war, continued to use the type for transport and other general duties. The Sparviero (Sparrowhawk) was one of the best torpedo-bombers of World War II.

SM 79s of both variants accounted for well over half the Italian Air Force's total bomber strength. The type's first war operation of World War II was flown on 11 June, when 35 SM 79s of the 2nd, 11th and 41st *Stormi*, escorted by Macchi MC 200 fighters, attacked Hal Far airfield and the seaplane depot at Kalafrana on the island of Malta. The first Italian loss over Malta occurred on 22 June, when two Gloster Sea Gladiators shot down a lone SM 79 of the 34th *Stormo*, on a reconnaissance mission. From June 1940 onwards, SM 79s saw continual action in the air campaign against Malta and in North Africa, becoming renowned for their high-level precision bombing, while the torpedo-bomber version was active against British shipping in the Aegean during the German invasion of Crete and against naval forces and convoys in the central Mediterranean. Royal Navy warships sunk in SM 79 attacks included the destroyers HMS *Husky*, HMS *Jaguar*, HMS *Legion* and HMS *Southwall*, while the battleship HMS *Malaya* and the aircraft carrier HMS *Indomitable* were damaged. The majority of these ships were hit during Operation Pedestal in June 1942, when a convoy of 14 merchant ships under heavy escort sailed to relieve Malta. Despite the obvious value of the SM 79 to the Axis war effort in the Mediterranean, the aircraft (like most Italian types) suffered from poor servicing arrangements, with the result that only about half the total force was available for operations at any given time.

After the Italian surrender in September 1943, SM 79s continued to fly with the Co-Belligerent Air Force, while the pro-German *Aviazione della RSI* went on to employ several SM 79-IIIs. This was a cleaned-up version, without the ventral gondola and mounting a forward-firing 20mm (0.79in) cannon.

The SM 79B, first flown in 1936, was a twin-engined export model, the middle engine being replaced by an extensively glazed nose. Brazil took delivery of 3, Iraq 4, and Romania 48, each version with a different powerplant. The Romanian IAR factories also produced the SM 79B under licence, equipped with Junkers Jumo 211D in-line engines, and used the aircraft in both bomber and transport roles on the Eastern Front. Including the export models, total production of all SM 79 variants reached 1330 aircraft before output ceased in 1944. Post-World War II, small numbers of SM 79s would go on to serve as communications aircraft and target tugs with the Lebanese and Spanish Air Forces well into the 1950s.

Type: Bomber/torpedo-bomber	
Crew:	5
Powerplant:	three 740kW (1000hp) Piaggio P XI RC 40 radial engines
Max speed:	435km/h (270mph) at 3650m (11,975ft)
Time to height:	19 mins 45 secs to 5000m (16,404ft)
Service ceiling:	6500m (21,325ft)
Max range:	1900km (1181 miles) with a 1250kg (2756lb) bomb load
Wing span:	21.20m (69ft 5in)
Wing area:	61.7m² (664sq ft)
Length:	15.62m (51ft 2in)
Height:	4.40m (14ft 4in)
Weights:	7600kg (16,755lb) empty; 11,300kg(24,912lb) max t/o
Armament:	three 12.7mm (0.5in) Breda-SAFAT MG in two dorsal and one ventral positions; one 7.62mm (0.3in) Lewis gun on a sliding mount in the rear fuselage; two 450mm (17.62in) torpedoes or 1250kg (2756lb) of bombs

Morane-Saulnier MS 406 C1

A simple ring and bead gunsight was mounted outside the cockpit for the pilot to aim his guns. The pilot sat in a sliding glazed cockpit. His rear vision was somewhat limited by the fairing.

A 20mm (0.79in) cannon mounted in the engine and firing through the propeller hub gave the MS 406 some teeth.

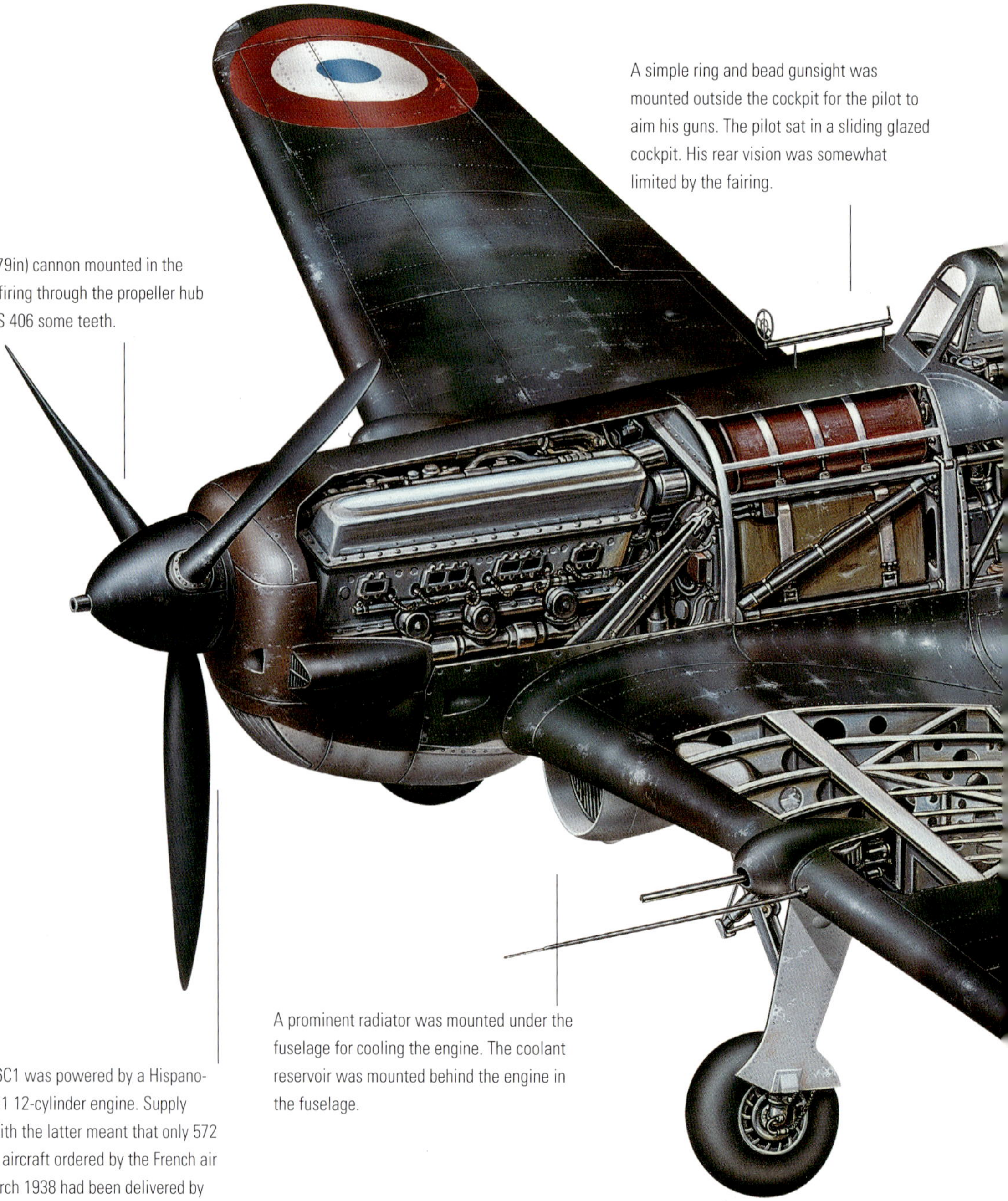

The MS 406C1 was powered by a Hispano-Suiza 12Y-31 12-cylinder engine. Supply problems with the latter meant that only 572 of the 1000 aircraft ordered by the French air force in March 1938 had been delivered by September 1939.

A prominent radiator was mounted under the fuselage for cooling the engine. The coolant reservoir was mounted behind the engine in the fuselage.

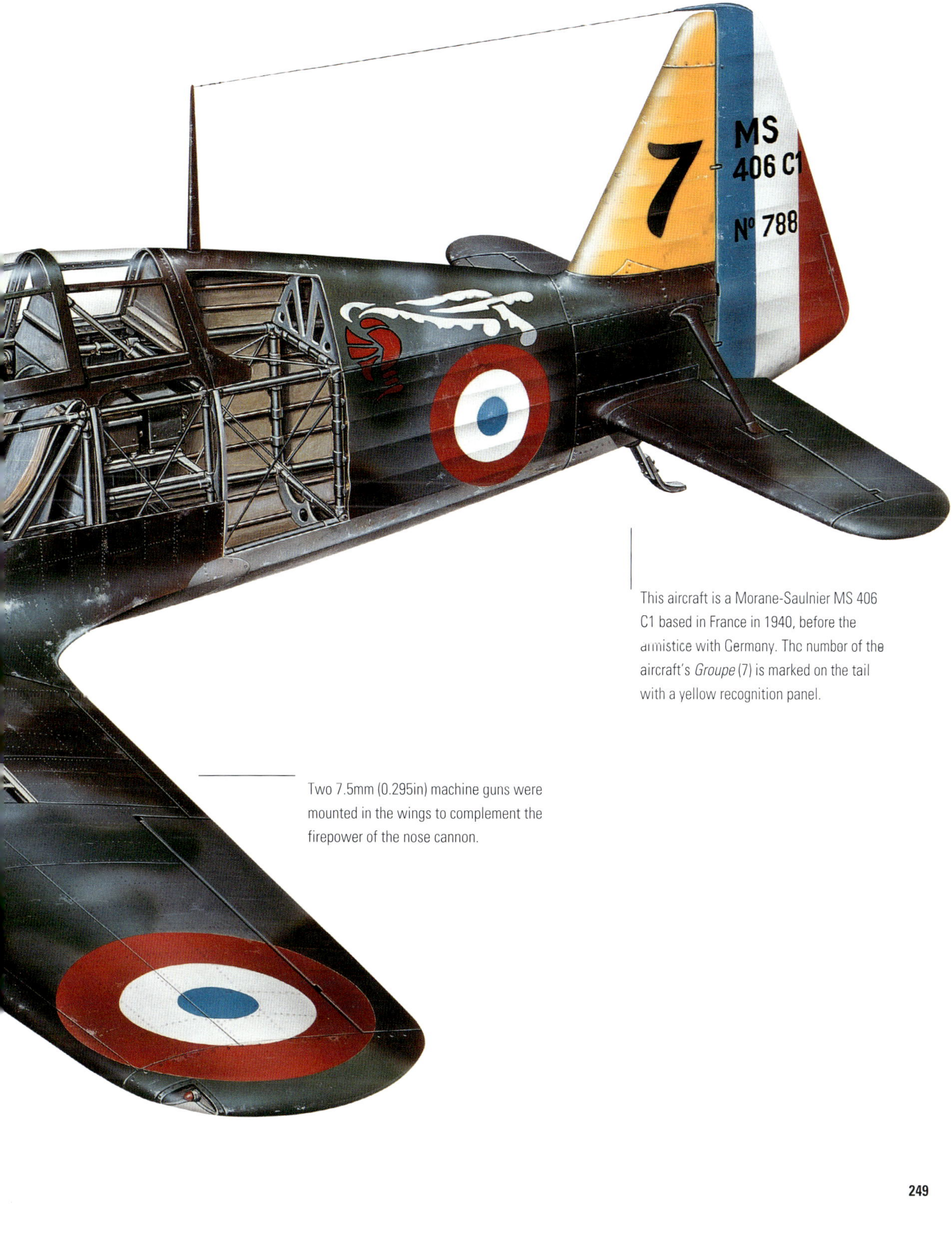

This aircraft is a Morane-Saulnier MS 406 C1 based in France in 1940, before the armistice with Germany. The number of the aircraft's *Groupe* (7) is marked on the tail with a yellow recognition panel.

Two 7.5mm (0.295in) machine guns were mounted in the wings to complement the firepower of the nose cannon.

Above: The MS 406 was numerically the most important French fighter in service at the outbreak of World War II, and although it was a rugged and manoeuvrable aircraft and could absorb a lot of battle damage, it was ultimately outclassed by the German Bf 109.

The Morane-Saulnier MS 406 was a straightforward development of the 1935 MS 405 (the first French fighter with a retractable undercarriage and enclosed cockpit), which flew for the first time at Villacoublay on 8 August 1935. Official trials of the MS 405 began at the CEMA (*Centre d'Essais de Matériel Aérien*) at the beginning of 1936. A second aircraft, the MS 405-02, joined the test programme in February 1937. This aircraft was destroyed on 29 July when its pilot passed out owing to the failure of his oxygen supply. All official trials had been completed by July 1937, the MS 405-01 emerging as the winner of the fighter design contest. The machine was returned to the manufacturer, who used it as a demonstration aircraft until it crashed on the approach to Villacoublay on 8 December 1937, with a Lithuanian pilot at the controls.

A pre-production batch of 15 machines had been ordered in August 1936, and it was the fourth aircraft of this batch, fitted with an 641kW (860hp) Hispano-Suiza 12-Ycrs engine driving a Chauviäre propeller, that became the prototype MS 406. Essentially similar to the MS 405, the MS 406 carried one 20mm (0.79in) Hispano Suiza cannon mounted between the engine cylinder banks, and two 7.5mm (0.30in) MAC 1934 M39 machineguns, one mounted in each wing above and slightly outboard of the undercarriage attachment points. The fuselage comprised four duralumin-tube longerons with rigidly braced bulkheads forward and wire-braced vertical and horizontal tube struts aft, the forward section being metal covered and the aft section fabric covered.

The rugged MS 406 was numerically the most important fighter in French service in September 1939, with 225 aircraft equipping the 2e, 3e, 6e and 7e *Escadres de Chasse* and a further 1000 on order. Each *Escadre* comprised three *Groupes de Chasse*, each with inventory strength of 25 machines; the actual number of Morane 406s in service at the outbreak of World War II was 275, but two *Groupes*, from the 6e and 7e *Escadres*, were based in North Africa. The number of MS 406s eventually built reached 1080. The aircraft was very manoeuvrable and could withstand a tremendous amount of battle damage, but it was outclassed by the Bf 109, and losses were heavy,

150 aircraft being lost in action and between 250 and 300 lost through other causes. The Morane's inferiority was underlined during the period of the 'Phoney War', when Allied and German fighters skirmished over the Maginot Line. In one particularly tragic incident, on the last day of March 1940, 11 Moranes of GC III/7 were patrolling the Morhange area between 6100m (20,013ft) and 8750m (28,707ft) in four separate, widely spaced flights when they were attacked by 20 Bf 109s. In less than five minutes, two of the Moranes were shot down in flames, a third crashed out of control, two more were written off after making forced landings, and a further two received such severe battle damage that, although they returned to base, they were classed as irreparable.

By the time production of the MS 406 began in May 1938 the type had become the subject of foreign orders. The Lithuanian Government ordered 12 aircraft, but these were never delivered; 30 were ordered by Finland, being delivered early in 1940, too late to take part in the Russo-Finnish winter war of 1939–40; they later saw combat against the Russians in 1941. A total of 45 were supplied to Turkey, and Poland ordered 160. Fifty of the latter aircraft were actually embarked for the Polish port of Gdynia in September 1939, but failed to reach their destination before Poland's collapse. Thirteen aircraft were shipped to China, but these were taken over by the French Colonial Administration when they reached the port of Haiphong, in Indo-China. Later, a number of captured MS 406s were handed over to Croatia. The MS 406 was also built under licence in Switzerland, where it received the designation D-3800. Several MS 406 developments were in progress at the time of France's surrender, these including the MS 420 with a completely retractable radiator, a nightfighter variant designated MS 440, and the MS 450, with a metal monocoque fuselage and a more powerful engine.

The only Vichy Air Force unit to be equipped with the MS 406 was GC I/7, based in the Levant, and in July 1941 they saw limited action against British forces during the campaign in Syria. The Morane fighter also equipped the 2e *Escadrille* of the Free French Air Force in North Africa before this unit converted to Hurricanes in 1941. Several MS 406s were still flying with the French Test Centre at Bretigny as late as 1947, these probably being the last aircraft of the type to be used by the Armée de l'Air.

Type: Fighter (MS 406 C1)	
Crew:	1
Powerplant:	one 641kW (860hp) Hispano-Suiza 12Y-31 12-cylinder V-type
Max speed:	490km/h (304mph)
Service ceiling:	9400m (30,840ft)
Max range:	1500km (932 miles)
Wing span:	10.62m (34ft 8in)
Wing area:	20.40m² (219.56sq ft)
Length:	8.17m (26ft 8in)
Height:	3.25m (10ft 6in)
Weights:	1872kg (4127lb) empty; 2722kg (6000lb) loaded
Armament:	one 20mm (0.79in) cannon or 7.5mm MG in an engine installation, and two 7.5mm MG in wing leading edges

Below: The MS 406 was a development of the MS 405C, an example of which is seen here in the markings of the Escadron d'Entrainement (Training Squadron) of the Vichy French Air Force. This unit was based at Toulouse in 1941.

Index

Page numbers in **bold** indicate captions

PICTURE CREDITS
Photographs supplied by: **TRH Pictures**
Artworks and photograph pg 227 supplied by **Aerospace Publishing**
Artwork page 64: **Wieslaw Baczkowski**

SHIPS AND SHIPYARDS OF IPSWICH 1700–1970

Above: This snow or brig from a painting of Ipswich by John Cleveley the Elder looks like a warship, to judge by her gun ports, hull decoration and masthead pennants.

Title page: Shipping in the Wet Dock, 1934. The steamer *Firecrest* is discharging grain for R. & W. Paul, while in the foreground one of Cranfield's barges is warped past by means of the dolly winch.

R&W. PAUL Ltd
R&W. PAUL
CRANFIELD BROS Ltd

SHIPS AND SHIPYARDS OF IPSWICH 1700 –1970

A contribution to the Maritime history of an ancient East Coast Port

HUGH MOFFAT

MALTHOUSE PRESS, SUFFOLK 2002

Published by Malthouse Press, Suffolk,
17 Reade Road,
Holbrook,
Suffolk, IP9 2QL

ISBN 0 9539680 0 6

British Library Cataloguing-in-Publication Data

A catalogue record for this book is available from the British Library.

Designed by Robert Malster
Typeset by John Walton
Printed in Great Britain by
The Five Castles Press, Ipswich

Contents

Preface

In his book *The Rise of the English Shipping Industry* Ralph Davis wrote, 'The next advance in the history of the merchant marine may well come from the writing of substantial histories of the ports. . .'. I hope that this book may be considered to be a contribution in this direction, because there is a great need for it. East Anglia is a region about which there is widespread ignorance and indifference.

With regard to Ipswich in particular, recent archaeology indicates that the town was a flourishing port in the 7th century, and if its apparent area of 50 hectares is any indication, it was one of the largest settlements in Britain and possibly in north west Europe.[1] The Danes and Normans dealt it bitter blows, but later the town prospered from the wool and cloth trades.

It became a leading shipbuilding centre until it declined in the 17th century. In the 18th century it briefly ventured into whaling, and its shipyards were among the very few in the country, outside the Thames, where East Indiamen were built. The port had a steam dredger by 1806: it was built in the town, and local yards constructed steamers and iron vessels in the early days.

Ipswich Wet Dock, completed in 1842, was the largest in England at that time. At the end of the era of sail Ipswich was one of the few ports in the country to receive shipments in big Cape Horn sailing ships. These of course were under foreign flags, but the locally owned barges were among the very last British vessels to carry cargo under sail alone.

One of the principal sources for this account has been the Customs House Register of Ipswich Ships, which I was first allowed to consult many years ago and later transcribed under the voluntary scheme organised by the National Maritime Museum. The books containing first registrations before 1898 are now in the Suffolk Record Office, Ipswich Branch (under reference IG 2/2), but the Librarian and Archivist of HM Customs and Excise kindly allowed me access to the Register Books for the later part of the period under review: these were at that time kept in the Customs House at Ipswich.

The Ipswich Customs House Register extends back only to 1824. Between then and the end of 1935, at which date my researches in the books concluded, some 795 vessels were registered at the port. These included some 95 yachts (although I may not have identified all the earlier ones correctly) and a handful of working craft belonging to Woodbridge and Aldeburgh. All these I have generally ignored, but some early data are taken from the Woodbridge Register (SROI ref: IG 2/4), which extends back to 1786.

Another important source I have used are the files of early local newspapers, mainly those of the *Ipswich Journal*. This paper was first published in 1720, although the files in the Suffolk Record Office are incomplete before 1739. My chapters on local shipping in the 18th century and the Ipswich whaling industry are based mainly on press reports and advertisements.

Early copies of *Lloyd's Register*, for details of the whaling ships, were consulted in the Library of the National Maritime Museum. Kind friends have loaned other editions to me at various times.

The chapters on the shipyards are also largely based on old newspapers, particularly the advertisements therein. Some account books from the Dock End Yard during the regime of William

This model of a brigantine of about 1870 is named *Annie*, of Sunderland, but has not been identified with an actual vessel. Some details of the hull are questionable, and the rigging and sails have been extensively repaired. *Author's collection*

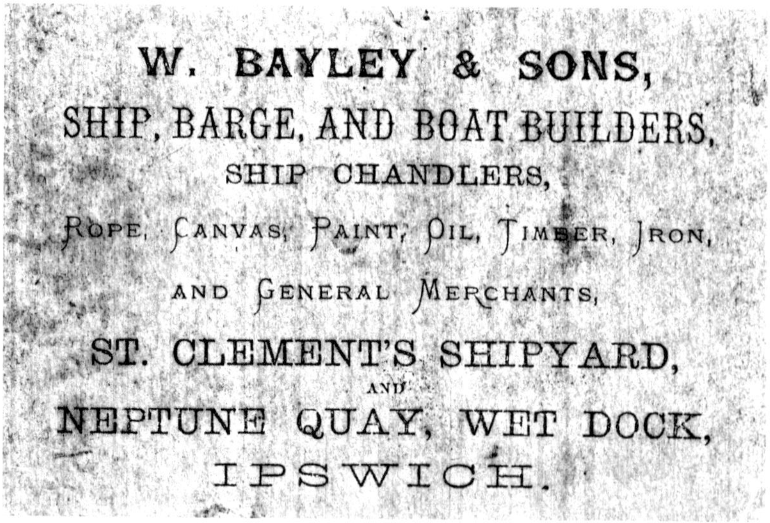
W. BAYLEY & SONS,
SHIP, BARGE, AND BOAT BUILDERS,
SHIP CHANDLERS,
ROPE, CANVAS, PAINT, OIL, TIMBER, IRON,
AND GENERAL MERCHANTS,
ST. CLEMENT'S SHIPYARD,
AND
NEPTUNE QUAY, WET DOCK,
IPSWICH.

Business card of W. Bayley & Sons, *c.*1850. The operations of this firm are described in chapter nine.

Colchester are now in the possession of Philip Hubert (the great-great-grandson of the yard foreman at that time), to whom I am much indebted.

Other primary source material is in the Suffolk Record Office at Ipswich:

Coal Meters' Accounts	(Ref: C9/27)
18th century Bills of Sale	(Ref: W3/2/1)
1728 Lease of shipyard to Edmund Goodea	(Ref: HD 6/1/1)
Court Books of the Manor of Wix Bishop	(Ref: HB 8/1)
Wills – proved before 1858	(Ref: IC/AA1)
– proved after 1858	(Ref: IC/AA2)
St. Clement's Parish Overseer's Rates, 1697–1766	(Ref: B98/G12)
Ditto, 1809–1830	(Ref: FB98/G5)
Ditto Churchwardens' Rates, 1727–1812	(Ref: FB98/E3)
Ditto Guardians' Rates, 1850–1902	(Ref: DC2/17)
St. Peter's Parish Overseers' Rates, *c.*1695–1709	(Ref: FB101/G9)
Ditto, 1760–1829	(Ref: FB101/G9)
Ditto Churchwardens' Rates, 1743–1763	(Ref: FB101/E1)
Ditto Guardians' Rates, 1843–1887	(Ref: DC2/17)
St. Mary Stoke Overseers' Rates, 1746–1835	(Ref: FBA92/G1)
Ditto Guardians' Rates, 1836–1837	(Ref: DC2/17)
Records of the Ipswich Dock Commission and the preceding River Improvement Commissioners	(Ref: EL1)

Secondary sources consulted in the Record Office at Ipswich include extracts from the records of Ipswich Corporation by V.B.

Redstone and copies of local Land Tax assessments 1702–1711, the latter under Ref: K30/2/2.

Concerning secondary sources, no historian of the town can completely ignore G.R. Clarke's *The History & Description of the Town and Borough of Ipswich*, published in 1830, or John Wodderspoon's *Memorials of the Ancient Town of Ipswich*, which appeared 20 years later. Both are now valuable mainly for what their authors knew or heard first hand. Clarke's book contains the story, from a now-forgotten publication, of Woolward's wherry being struck by lightning, and it was his remark about Sir Thomas Slade's gravestone in St. Clement's churchyard which sent me to see the burial register in the church many years ago. These parish registers, with many others, are now available on microfiche in the Suffolk Record Office.

Many details of ships built in Ipswich for the Royal Navy are taken from David Lyon's monumental work *The Sailing Navy List 1688–1860* (London, 1993). Some background information on the northern whaling trade is taken from *The Arctic Whalers* by Basil Lubbock (Glasgow, 1937). My remarks on salt water in marine boilers are taken from *The Marine Steam Engine* by Sennett and

Sloops lying at the Common Quay, seen in John Cleveley's *Prospect of Old Ipswich*, painted in 1753. *Ipswich Borough Council Museums and Galleries*.

Oram, a work long used for training engineer officers in the navy. My copy is of the 1917 edition and I was surprised to find such material still in it at that date. Other secondary sources are mentioned in the Notes.

As I have tried to show that there is more to the port of Ipswich than sailing barges I have not devoted much space to these craft, which have been – and are being – more fully researched by others. Some details of the last to be owned in the port are taken from *Sailing Barges* by Frank G.G. Carr (Lavenham, 1989) and *A Cross in the Topsail* by Roger Finch (Ipswich, 1979).

My mother's family, the Hamblins, have been Freemen of Ipswich since 1621 and my relationship to those mentioned is derived from genealogical work commissioned by my father long before I was born. In recent years the rules for admission have been broadened, so that I am now a Freeman and so is my daughter.

My thanks are due to the staffs of the Suffolk County Record Office at Ipswich, the Borough Museums and Galleries, the Public Libraries at Ipswich, Woodbridge and Lowestoft, the National Maritime Museum at Greenwich and the Public Record Office at Kew. I am also indebted to Mrs. Cynthia Brown of Woodbridge for calling my attention to the article on Betsey Thompson's steamer trip in the *Journal* of the Carmarthen Historical Society; to

Barges, some apparently under repair, and other vessels in the Wet Dock towards the end of the 19th century. *Richard Smith.*

Trade card of W.B. Horn. In 1855 William Bell Horn was not just a sailmaker and ship chandler but also the licensee of the *Ram* in Key Street and a fishmonger.
Dr. John Blatchly

Geoffrey Best, the former Registrar of Shipping at Ipswich; to Brian Pinner, formerly of Pauls & White Ltd; to Norman Scarfe, my near neighbour, for reading the typescript and his helpful comments on it; and to Frank Tanner of Tunbridge Wells for information about the Bayleys, from whom his wife is descended.

Publication of this book has been aided by a generous grant from the Ann Ashard Webb Bequest, for which I am most grateful.

Lastly, but by no means least, I would like to thank my old friends John Barnard, John Blatchly, Bob Malster and Richard Smith, all of whom have helped in many ways. I alone am responsible for any mistakes.

The illustrations are individually acknowledged, and those which are unmarked are from my own collection. Some of the latter are from paintings and old photographs, given or lent to me to copy many years ago by friends who sadly are now dead. I do not know the present whereabouts of the originals and I can only apologise for any annoyance caused to the present owners.

To the memory of my brother Jim (1918–1958). He was the first in modern times to realise that the designer of Nelson's *Victory* had been buried in Ipswich, and that the painting shown on page 84 depicts the Orwell and not the Medway. He also made the model illustrated on page 5.

Ipswich Ships 1700 –1824 1

It is difficult to give a detailed picture of the town's ships before the advent of universal registration in 1786, and even then the earliest registrations for the port of Ipswich are no longer in existence.

In 1702, as war clouds gathered, the Admiralty sought details from the Customs authorities of the numbers of ships and seamen belonging to the various ports of England and Wales, and these lists survive.[1] Lighters and fishing craft, and the men employed in them, were excluded. In terms of total tonnage, Ipswich, with 11,170 tons, came third in the national league table – after London and Bristol – and was marginally ahead of Newcastle, which had 11,000 tons. Fifth and sixth came Yarmouth and Liverpool, with 9,914 tons and 8,619 tons respectively. In the number of its ships, however, Ipswich trailed far behind, with only 39 vessels, which put it in 24th place; in the number of its seamen it came eleventh, with 576.

The figures show that the average size of an Ipswich ship was 286 tons, far and away the highest figure in the country. The 560 ships of London averaged only 151 tons each; they would have included those engaged in the East India Company's trade, which were usually of over 500 tons, and many small coasters. The 165 vessels belonging to Bristol had a mean tonnage of only 105, whereas Newcastle's 63 ships averaged 174 tons apiece – the highest figure after Ipswich – and most of those were probably in the coal trade. No other port could show an average tonnage above 100. Yarmouth, with an extensive coastal trade to London, owned 143 vessels – the third largest number after London and Bristol – but they averaged only 69 tons apiece.

The large average size of the Ipswich vessels confirms Defoe's statement in his *Tour Through the Whole Island of Great Britain* that in the 17th century the town had been the greatest town in England for large colliers employed between Newcastle and London; but by the time he wrote it, in about 1724, Ipswich had lost its pre-eminence to Yarmouth.

From 1702 to 1704, 13,272 chaldrons of coal were shipped out of Newcastle in 211 Yarmouth vessels (not, of course, in 211

Opposite: Shipping in the Wet Dock, *c*.1860, seen in a photograph by pioneer photographer Richard Dykes Alexander. The vessels appear to be a Dutch galliot and the snow *Fanny* of Ipswich, built at Gainsborough on the Trent in 1827 and hulked in 1875.
Suffolk Record Office

different vessels); London followed with 11,230 chaldrons in 168 ships; then came Whitby, with 6,385 chaldrons in 98 ships, and Ipswich was fourth, with 5,774 chaldrons in 40 vessels.[2] The average lading of the Ipswich ships was 144 chaldrons*, more than double the figure for the other three ports.

Defoe did not use the word *cat*† when describing the Ipswich vessels, but G.R. Clarke in his 1830 *History of Ipswich* wrote of 'those huge colliers called Ipswich cats', adding that he could remember seeing one or two. One such vessel was the *Humphry*, advertised for sale at Lloyd's Coffee House in London in 1743: she was described as 'an Ipswich-built Catt, Burthen 300 Tons, more or less, which carries about 20 Keels of Coals'.[3] Defoe said that there were then scarce 40 sail of good colliers that belonged to the whole town. Many would have come to their home port only to lay up and refit.

By 1730 Ipswich was importing about 10,000 chaldrons of coal each year, but barely a fifth of this quantity arrived in local vessels. In that year nine different Ipswich craft, with a combined lading of about 600 chaldrons, featured in the coal meters' accounts. Five had a capacity of 70 chaldrons or more, and were probably brigs, whilst the others would have been sloops. These nine would have had a combined burthen tonnage of perhaps about 700 – at a time when the town was said to have owned a total tonnage of 1,414 in the coasting trade. Clearly there had been a considerable decline since the time of which Defoe wrote.

A year or two later, one small vessel bringing in cargoes of about 33 chaldrons was the *Alp*, named no doubt after a local family of that name. 'There is just come to the Port of Ipswich, the *Alp* Sloop, Captain Robert Hamblin, loaded with Scotch Bone to be sold at the Common Quay', said a newspaper advertisement.[4] She would have been of about 40 tons burthen, and Captain

*The chaldron was a unit of capacity. The Newcastle chaldron was based on the wagons used in the collieries, varying from about 17 cwt in Tudor times to 52½ cwt in the 18th century. The Newcastle chaldron was used by the coal meters in some east coast ports, e.g. Yarmouth, but the meters in Ipswich used the London chaldron, or 'King's Measure', which was latterly 36 bushels or about 28 cwt. The sale of coal by 'heaped measure' ended in 1835.

†A cat was a vessel with no head and a stern which was full on the waterline surmounted by a narrow range of windows. The keel was a type of barge used on the Tyne: at that time their capacity was fixed by law at 8 Newcastle chaldrons, i.e. 21 tons. The term was commonly used as a unit for defining the capacity of ships in the coal trade.

Hamblin was probably my six-times great uncle, mariner of Ipswich and Felixstowe, born in 1693.

By the middle years of the century, to judge by John Cleveley's 1753 Prospect of Ipswich, sloops were by far the most common type of vessel to be seen at the town's quays. In hull and rig they corresponded to Chapman's hoy,[5] but in Suffolk they were invariably called sloops. Most of them had 'pink' sterns, i.e. with the planking curving in to the sternpost, whilst the bulwarks were continued aft to enclose the head of the rudder. Only a few pink-sterned sloops survived to feature in the official Register of Ipswich Ships dating from 1824, of which the oldest and one of the largest was the *John and Jane* of 95 tons, built in the town in 1746 and broken up in 1832. The *Bee* of 45 tons, Ipswich-built in 1740, must have been one of the first to have a square stern, almost universally used later.[6]

Their mainsails were usually loose-footed and brailed up to the gaff; only the larger vessels seem to have had a boom. There was a foresail and a jib; nowadays they would be called cutters, but in the 18th century vessels were classified by hull shape rather than by rig – a cutter then was something built for speed. They were rigged with standing, or fixed, bowsprits but later the sliding bowsprit, easy to run in when in port, was adopted. This was the hallmark of

Collier cats of the 1770s inward bound to Harwich harbour, seen in a wash drawing by Francis Swaine. © *National Maritime Museum, London*

the smack rig. A new 'smack-built' vessel, measuring about 72 tons and advertised for sale at Ipswich in 1810,[7] undoubtedly had a sliding or running bowsprit; but in Suffolk most single-masted cargo carriers continued to be called sloops, even when fitted with sliding bowsprits, after about 1820. Craft described as smacks were usually small and employed in fishing or salvage work.

Most of these sloops were employed in the corn trade to London, whence they returned with general cargo. Some were in the coal trade, as we have seen, whilst others traversed the narrow seas to any port between the Baltic and Spain. They carried a crew of between three and seven. Some at least could sail without ballast, like the *Three Brothers* of 100 tons, built at Ipswich about 1765.[8] They were deep – a loaded draught of less than about seven feet being considered worthy of mention in sale particulars; and they were unweatherly – advertisements often appeared in the press describing in detail the ground gear which they had been obliged to slip when caught by adverse tides in rising winds. The big mainsails of the larger sloops must have been a bit of a handful, and several were re-rigged as brigs or, later, as schooners.

Some of the local trading vessels belonged entirely to one individual, but usually several owners, although rarely more than six, had a share. John Richman was a corn and coal merchant in the town and his shipping interests were advertised for sale when he became bankrupt in 1758. He owned the whole of one sloop, three-quarters of another, one half of another, a quarter of two others, an eighth of two more and a sixteenth of yet another. He also owned one sixteenth of a vessel termed a ship – the 150-ton *John and Grace* – two thirds of one brig and a sixteenth of another, besides an entire lighter and a 1/20 share in a 50-ton fishing vessel, which was probably based in Harwich. Two of the sloops, of different tonnages, were named *Amey and Mary*; this was not a unique instance and illustrates the difficulty of tracing individual vessels at the time.[9]

Before it was enacted that the property in a ship was to be divided into 64 shares, it seems that ownership was apportioned in any convenient way. In most cases binary division down to sixteenths or even smaller parts was used, but other fractions were often recorded. Apart from the 1/20 share of a fishing vessel referred to, 2/13 of another, the *Philip and Elizabeth* of Harwich, were advertised for sale in 1777.[10] At least two of the seven owners of the Woodbridge brigantine *Alert* each owned a seventh of her in 1816.[11] At Ipswich, lighters and other small craft were not infrequently divided into thirds and sixths; but the most unusual

A model of a pink-sterned trading sloop of the mid-18th century, made by one of the author's brothers.

apportionment must surely be in the ownership of the sloop *Constant Trader*, of which 1/10 and 1/16 were offered for sale in 1803. In 1816 her master, Francis Newson, purchased 2/10 and 1/16 for £350.[12] What other shares he then held is unknown, but by 1825 his interest in the vessel had been adjusted to 52/64 to comply with the law at that time.

One 18th-century shipowner has left quite a detailed account of his activities by his advertisements in the *Ipswich Journal*. This was Ralph Hare, who first appeared as a partner in a lime-burning business at the Ipswich wharf known as Nova Scotia in April, 1753; six months later he had two vessels and was offering weekly sailings to London from a quay in St. Clement's parish.[13] The limekiln closed early in the following year and Hare devoted himself entirely to his shipping; he skippered one of the vessels, the newly-built sloop *Mary*, and advertised 1/8 and 1/16 shares in her for sale to increase his working capital.[14] In August, 1762, he expected to take delivery of a new vessel, probably a replacement for the other.[15]

He reminded his customers that he was still in the London trade in 1767, when he announced that in response to 'repeated applications' he was about to start a monthly service to Hull and Gainsborough. If a sufficient quantity of wool was offered from Suffolk he would put a second vessel into the trade.[16] He was competing with 'The Old Ipswich and Hull Traders', John Forsett, Benjamin Cole and Turrell Lambly.[17] Cole had been in that trade for at least nine years, and in 1764 Lambly was master and owner of the 70-ton Ipswich-built sloop *Turrel and Sarah*, listed in *Lloyd's Register* as trading between Hull and Dunkirk. Hare's venture was obviously successful; in December, 1767, he had a new sloop, the *Bishop Blaze*, named after the patron saint of wool-combers, built at the St Peter's shipyard in Ipswich.[18] The Old Traders' partnership was dissolved at about the same time and Cole continued on his own; there was keen competition over freight charges, but by November, 1768, Hare seems to have monopolised the trade to the Humber, for a time at least.[19]

A lighter on the Orwell, a detail from the well-known print of Ipswich by the brothers Buck, 1741.

A few months later he acquired a wharf and warehouse at Colchester Hythe.[20] By the early 1770s the *Molly*, skippered by John Hare, the *Sage*, the *Joseph,* and the *Bishop Blaze,* Captain King Wiles, featured in the frequent advertisements about Ralph's Hull trade; there were regular announcements saying which vessel was about to sail or expected to arrive. His London trade continued and a small sloop, the *Commerce,* plied between the Orwell and the Colne; she was said to be about to be replaced with a larger vessel.[21]

The Seven Years War had little effect on the east coast but the American War of Independence, in which Britain found herself without allies, fighting the colonists and eventually France, Holland and Spain as well, was felt much more in our home waters. American privateers arrived in the North Sea about 1777, and Hare advertised that he was arming his Hull traders with 4-pounder 'great guns', i.e. on carriages.[22] Since all his vessels were sloops, both deck space and hands to serve the weapons must have been a problem; but it was a necessary precaution in view of the reports of coasters and fishing smacks being ransomed off the Suffolk and Norfolk coasts. Even a couple of the Harwich packets, hitherto regarded as neutrals, were captured.

However, the only loss which Hare suffered was due to the ordinary perils of the sea rather than the King's enemies. In October, 1780, the *Joseph*, Captain Thomas Hayward, ran aground off Yarmouth and sank in deep water. Hare published an account of his efforts to raise her, using slings passed beneath her hull and hove tight at low water, but she would not come free. Eventually the counter broke away and then the forward slings slipped, pulling up the bowsprit. His clients were asked to pay 5d. in the pound towards the cost of the attempt to recover their goods, while Hare replaced the vessel with the Ipswich-built sloop *Betty*, under Hayward as before.[23]

Ralph Hare was declared bankrupt in November, 1785. His property advertised for sale included several warehouses with their own quays in the parish of St Clement. Apart from his own house there were others occupied by mariners named John and Joseph Hare – presumably his sons. His vessels, which he apparently owned wholly, were the *Bishop Blaze* of 80 tons and the *Betty* of 75 tons, both in the Hull trade; his London traders were the *Molly,* 70 tons, the *Defiance* of 60 tons, the *Industry*, 50 tons, and the 40-ton *Grocer.*[24] John and Joseph Hare continued the Hull and Gainsborough trade with the same two vessels. Ralph informed his clients that 'a friend' was carrying on that trade; he even published a hopeful announcement about resuming his business to London, but then there was silence. He died in March, 1788, aged 66.[25]

John continued the business, skippering the *Bishop Blaze*. He seems to have last advertised in 1789, and died in October, 1802, at the age of 52, 'master of one of the trade hoys from this port'.[26]

When the newly-established *Suffolk Chronicle* began publishing shipping movements at Ipswich in 1801, the *Bishop Blaze*, Palmer, often featured arriving with coal from the north-east or sailing to Hull with wool. In 1816 a half share in 'the brig *Bishop Blaze*, of 79 tons burthen by register, Peter Palmer, master' was advertised for sale. I have not found any mention after 1819 of what may well have been Ralph Hare's former sloop.[27]

We can make a guess as to the fate of the *Betty*. In June, 1808, a sloop of that name, admeasuring 73 tons, was advertised for sale, 'as she now lies at Mr Godbold's wharf' and in October, 'the materials of the sloop *Betty* (broke up)' were offered. In the following March another sloop of the name, of 75 tons, was advertised, and in September, 1810, 'the materials of the sloop *Betty* (broken up)' featured in a timber sale at a riverside yard in the town.[28] This at least shows that there were two sloops of the same name and almost equal tonnage; surely one of them had been Hare's?

Few three-masted ships were owned in Ipswich during the 18th century after the great cats had gone. Due to the shoaling estuary of the Orwell any sizeable vessel had to bring up at Downham Bridge (a one-time ford, just below the present Orwell Bridge) and discharge her cargo into lighters. This was an expensive operation. The port was not in a thriving state and its trade did not require large shipments, apart from coal. Most local owners could not afford to invest in or operate large ships. One who did was John Trapnell, three times a bailiff of the town in the 1760s.[29] His ship the *British King*, of 300 tons and Ipswich-built in 1760, was listed in the earliest surviving *Lloyd's Register* in 1764 when she was in the London to Leghorn trade. The book also included the *Ipswich*, Captain Harrison, of 260 tons and built in the town in 1761. However, she had already foundered in the North Sea on 6th September, 1763, on passage between her listed ports, Stockholm and London, while laden with 390 tons of iron and 2,000 deals.[30]

Another large Ipswich ship was the *Elizabeth*, Captain Rayment or Raymer, which stranded on the Knock John sand in August, 1764, with a cargo of masts for the navy. 'It is feared the ship will be lost', said the *Ipswich Journal*. In the following January the hull of the 450-ton flyboat was advertised for sale as she lay beached at the mouth of the Colne, and a few months later she was being broken up at Brightlingsea.[31] She may have been one of the Dutch flyboat war prizes, which, according to Defoe in his *Tour*, gradually robbed the Ipswich shipbuilders of their market for large colliers.

By the middle of the century only a very few Ipswich brigs, perhaps no more than two or three, were employed in carrying coal to their home port. The coal meters' accounts mention only the masters' names and the only clue is the size of each shipment; all the larger consignments – over about 150 chaldrons – arrived in vessels owned in north east coast ports. When the property of Roger Beart, a merchant, was advertised for sale after his death in 1744, it included 'a Vessel call'd a Brig, of about 150 Tons' and five sloops, perhaps indicating that larger vessels were unusual for local shipowners.[32]

Only 22 Ipswich-built brigs appeared in the 1764 *Lloyd's Register*; others owned in the port may have been built elsewhere, but it is difficult to identify them from the sparse data. The *John and Jane* of 180 tons, Ipswich-built in 1763, was owned by Ralph Hare and in trade between London and Leghorn. The *Trotman*, of 100 tons, was built in the town in 1760 and in the Hamburg trade; she was owned by Richard Lockwood and named after a well known local family. Lockwood was three times a bailiff of the town between 1759 and 1765; earlier he owned vessels in the coal trade and imported 'Muggs, Juggs and Chamber-Pots', probably from Holland, in his 'large ship'.[33]

Probably the best-documented 18th-century ownership transactions to have survived relate to the brig *Prince of Orange,* owned by seven merchants and others in 1/16 shares. In 1768 Edward Lavender, master and mariner, exchanged the vessel, of which he owned four shares, with one Zachary Hope of Rotterdam for the snow *Industry* and 300 guineas. The *Industry* was of 120 tons when Hope had purchased her for £660 from two London owners in the previous year, and he had apparently rebuilt her, for after the exchange she was said to be of 140 tons and was valued at £720. Lavender immediately re-rigged her as a brig and changed her name to *Prince of Orange*. Later, William Christie, master and mariner, briefly owned 7/16 of her, and her skipper was named Christie when she stranded near Calais in 1778, on passage from Ipswich to Bristol. It was feared that she would be a total loss.[34]

One brig, the *Dunn*, built in 1783 at Fishlake in Yorkshire, survived to be registered in 1824. When she was first owned in

Ipswich is not known, but in 1799 she was in John Hare's Hull trade under a Captain Benjamin Scholding. After being owned for many years by a succession of Suffolk farmers, she was purchased by the Ipswich shipbuilders, Read & Page, in 1839 and lost near the Dogger Bank early in the following year.

Another brig which featured for several years in the arrivals and sailings at the port, early in the 19th century, was the picturesquely-named *Air Balloon*. Yet another was the *Resolution*, Captain W. Bayes. In 1803 she was in the corn trade to London, when she was blown over by a squall in Erith Reach, being salved to feature in the coal trade soon afterwards. In 1807 she was taken by a privateer whilst homeward-bound with fruit from St Michaels in the Azores – a surprising trade for a one-time collier.[35]

The first Ipswich schooner that I can trace was the *Two Brothers* of 76 tons, built in the town in 1795 and sold to Woodbridge owners five years later. She was re-rigged as a brigantine in 1801 and lost in 1804.[36] The number of schooners in the Ipswich Register increased rapidly; by 1830 there were 31, as against 22 brigs, brigantines and snows.

An Ipswich-built ketch, the *Three Brothers,* was advertised for sale in 1794.[37] She was said to 'shoot 660 quarters of corn under the hatches, or from 95 to 100 chaldrons of coals'. Perhaps she was new, or perhaps her ketch rig was, but unfortunately the inventory mentioned in the advertisement has not survived. This is an early mention of a mercantile ketch, and it is a pity that we do not know precisely how she was rigged.

Many of the vessels arriving at Ipswich had to lighter out their cargoes, due to the increasing shoals in the River Orwell, and as the 18th century progressed even sloops were obliged to be partially unloaded before they could proceed up to the town quays. Lightering was an essential part of the working of the port, and had been so since the 16th century. What were the lighters like? Pictorial evidence is scanty.

The *South West Prospect of Ipswich*, engraved and published by the brothers Buck in 1741, shows what may be a lighter; she has a conventional bow with a raking stem, a transom stern and sets a single squaresail on her mast. Similar craft appear in pictures of other places, and such a basic type of vessel may well have been used on the Ipswich River. In this case, however, the mast is stepped slightly abaft of amidships, and it inspires little confidence in me – like some of the topographical details in the picture, it was probably added in the artists' London studio. John Cleveley's painting of a launch on the Orwell, dated 1758, shows two large

Opposite above: Henry Davy's watercolour showing Ipswich from the Ostrich, an engraving of which was used as the frontispiece in G.R. Clarke's history of the town. *Ipswich Borough Council Museums and Galleries*

Opposite below: A view from the same spot in more recent times. The former tar works on the left marks the site of the Halifax shipyard, and the isolated small white boat with a mast is floating in what survived of the channel excavated for the launch of Jabez Bayley's East Indiamen. This foreshore now lies under the West Bank Terminal.

ships anchored at Downham Bridge and one of them has a lighter alongside. Cleveley, of course, was a reliable marine artist: his lighter here has a round bow and a transom stern, and she is rigged with a sprit-mainsail and a foresail, without any bowsprit.

In 1770 what were described as 'two Ipswich lighters', bound for London, collided off Harwich and one sank. She was loaded with 485 firkins of butter and 50 weigh of cheese – not a very large cargo, but these lighters were usually of about only 35 tons measurement. They were obviously capable of making coastal passages, and the matter-of-fact way in which the incident was reported in the *Ipswich Journal* suggests that it was not unusual for them to put to sea.[38]

Shares in a number of vessels were advertised for sale after their owner became insolvent in 1780, and the list included lighters named *Primrose*, *Daisy*, *Violet* and *Foxhunter*. The last-named was advertised again in 1796, when she was described as 'a Sloop or Lighter'.[39] She survived to be re-registered in 1826, when she was revealed to have been built at Ipswich in 1780, of 34 tons measurement. She was 40ft. 10in. long by 14ft. 9in. beam by 6ft. 10in. depth in hold. Sloop-rigged, she had a standing bowsprit and a lute stern; i.e. similar to a pink stern in a small vessel, but the part overhanging the sternpost was wider, and decked, the planking beneath it either curved in to the sternpost or terminating at a flat transom. A sloop named *Daisey* (*sic*) featured in the Ipswich Register in 1824; she was of 39 tons, built in the town in 1771 – probably the vessel which had been advertised in 1780. Her length was 40ft. 9½in., her beam 15ft. 4in. and her depth 6ft.; she also had a standing bowsprit, but a pink stern.

Both were beamier than the larger sloops, but for such small craft the most remarkable feature was the great depth, although when fully loaded they would probably have drawn less than 5ft. Had they had sprit-mainsails, the rig – by the 1820s – would have been termed 'barge', but almost certainly the sail would have been brailed up. The standing bowsprits are surprising, but they may not have been very long; perhaps there was only one hatchway and the mast was stepped well forward, in which case any bowsprit would have allowed the foresail to be larger, and so improved performance to windward. Little is known about these craft, but they obviously bore little resemblance to the swim-headed lighters of the London River, which in any case may not have been so common in the 18th century as some authorities would have us believe.

Sailing barges began to appear during the second half of the

18th century. The earliest reference that I have found to one on the Orwell was in 1773, when a barge carrying timber from Ipswich to Barnard & Turner's shipyard at Harwich was swamped by 'a Storm of Wind' in Lower Reach. Five large baulks of timber were lost, and finders were asked to contact the yard.[40] It is easy to imagine the lumpy sea knocked up by a southerly wind as the barge, coming down on the ebb, rounded Collimer Point at the head of the reach. She was probably loaded right down, with a large open hold – no side decks or coamings – so that 'the Sea broke into the Barge and sunk her'. No details of the barge were given; there was apparently no loss of life and presumably the vessel was later salved. Incidentally, Turner transported timber to his yard in interesting ways apart from that; in 1775 he advertised that 'Sundry Pieces' had been 'Lost at Sea, out of a Raft of Memel-Timber off Woodbridge Haven'[41] – we can only guess at what was happening.

A sketch of the lighter shown alongside a ship at Downham Bridge in Cleveley's painting *Launch of a Sixth Rate*.

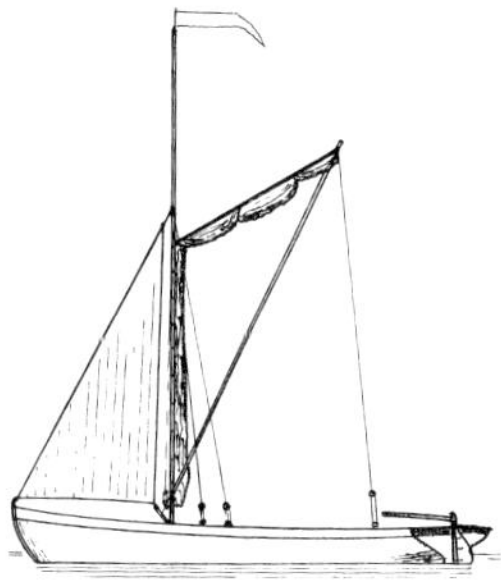

A London barge, the *Samuel* or *Sally,* bound for the Thames with timber from Harwich, capsized off the Essex coast in 1782. She was salved and brought back to the harbour the next day by a couple of local smacks, which also picked up the four men, two women and a boy who had been aboard.[42] Hervey Benham, in his *Once Upon a Tide,* showed that early barges, small as they were, usually carried a crew of at least three. These people had probably not all gone along for the novelty of the trip, but it may well have been further than usual.

During the 1790s the local newspapers carried the occasional advertisement of barges for sale in Essex – including a newly-built one at Mistley – but gave no hint of any such craft at Ipswich. However, a barge was built and registered at the port in 1793, the earliest that I have found. She was the *Richard and Thomas* of 35 62/94 tons; she measured 48ft. 10in. by 13ft. 2$\frac{1}{2}$in. beam and her depth in hold was 4ft. 10in. She was described as barge-rigged, with one mast and, oddly enough, a fixed bowsprit. Whether or not she was spritsail rigged is unknown; such indications as there are show that most early barges in Essex and Suffolk were boomsail rigged. She was re-registered in 1825, showing her to have been owned by two local merchants until 1830, when she was sold to a couple of mariners, one of whom was thereafter her skipper. Her work rarely seems to have taken her beyond Manningtree or Woodbridge. In 1847 she was sold to John Pattrick, the Dovercourt cement manufacturer, and her ultimate fate was to be broken up at an unknown date.

Probably the earliest pictorial record of a sailing barge on the

This sketch by the Ipswich artist George Frost (1745–1821) is the earliest known representation of a barge on the Orwell. It probably dates from about 1800.

Orwell is a pencil sketch by the local artist George Frost (1745–1821) of a spritsail-rigged stumpie at the Nova Scotia wharf in Ipswich. The barge's bow is hidden but the characteristic budget* stern, with massive rudder and tiller, is clearly shown; she has no mizzen. Another early representation appears in the well-known print of the East Indiaman *Orwell* on the Halifax yard in 1817. Here the sprittie barge has a topmast, but again no mizzen.

Newspaper advertisements provide a few details of some of the earliest Ipswich barges. In 1810 'The entire hull of the Barge *Friends,* John Hadgraft, late master, with her pumps, windlass and hatches' was on offer, together with 'the mast, gaff and boom, anchors, Spanish windlass. . .'.[43] She had been in the London trade under Captain Hadgraft since 1801 at least. In 1805 was advertised 'A Sloop-sail Barge, called the *Farmer's Increase* of Ipswich, 92 tons per register, 43 last of corn, with room boards compleat for 7 rooms' – a last of corn was 40 bushels, about 1.5 tons, and she was fitted with movable partitions so that consignments from different merchants could be separated.

We may conjecture that she was the identical barge which was for sale in London in 1798, when she was said to be 'British built, 95 tons per register, is well calculated for the corn and coasting

*A stumpie barge was one without a topmast. With a budget stern, the bottom slopes up as on a river punt and the rudder is hung on a fin; it survived on the latter-day Thames lighters.

trade, and is well known in the trade between Southend and London... Abraham Vanderwood, Master'. The skipper's name was probably Vandervord, a family well known later as barge owners at Southend. In 1817 a man was swept to his death off the barge's bowsprit as he took in the jib, and in 1823 her timbers were advertised for sale, she having been 'lately broken up at Mr. Catt's Yard, in St. Clements'.[44]

Another early Ipswich barge was the *Kent,* of 80 tons, which was advertised for sale in 1809. She had probably been built in the county after which she was named, and was said to be 'in constant employ with government dock yard timber', although she could also be used in the corn trade. Perhaps she was not fit for anything, for she was broken up about a year later, and her mast, yards, boom, gaff, leeboards, etc., were among the materials sold.[45]

Apart from the *Richard and Thomas,* the only other early barge which survived to appear in the Ipswich Register after 1824 was the *Hazard*. She had been built in London in 1780, of 55 82/94 tons, and was 58ft. 3in. long by 17ft. 1in. beam with a depth in hold of 5ft. 3in. She was boomsail rigged with one mast and a fixed bowsprit, later changed to a sliding one. For many years she had been skippered by one Edward Markham in the London corn trade. Rebuilt in 1831, being slightly lengthened and deepened, she was sold to Woodbridge three years later.

The arrival at Ipswich in 1807 of the *John and Henry*, from Aldeburgh with hay, was perhaps an early instance of stack work at

A somewhat crude depiction of a barge seen in a print of the East Indiaman *Orwell* on the Halifax yard. The artist was not very knowledgeable when portraying her sprit rig, but the small sprit-rigged boats, one lying under the Indiaman's stern and two others visible beyond the barge, are more accurately shown.

sea.[46] Frank Carr, in his *Sailing Barges*, mentioned an accident involving a stack barge at the old London Bridge in 1798, but we do not know where she had come from. A few freights of hay and straw were recorded leaving Ipswich for London in 1817 and 1818; the trade was never mentioned much in the press, which probably ignored traffic from the creeks and little wharves further down the Orwell.

For at least two centuries passengers were carried between Ipswich and Harwich in craft called wherries; the earliest reference that I know of was in 1624, when one was run down in the Orwell.[47] For most of the 18th century much of the business was in the hands of the Woollward, or Woollard, family. John Woollward's boat was struck by lightning in 1708, killing him and three others; according to a contemporary account,[48] two of these unfortunates were 'within the tilt', and a witness saw the flash strike the vessel's bowsprit. This wherry was obviously similar to a Gravesend tilt boat, used for passenger work on the Thames. Another John of the family advertised in 1734 that he had 'a very good new Wherry, with a handsome Stateroom with a Fire-Place',[49] but whether this meant anything more than a rudimentary stove in a cuddy with perhaps a solid deckhead, we shall never know.

The earliest pictorial records of what seem to be wherries on the Orwell are in the paintings of John Cleveley the Elder. These show vessels with two masts of equal height, each rigged with a loose-footed gaff sail or spritsail, and having a foresail set on a bowsprit. They seem to have tilts to shelter the passengers.

In July, 1788, fifteen convicts were put aboard a Woollward wherry to be taken to Portsmouth, doubtless *en route* to Botany Bay. 'As they passed along the streets they held out their hats to the spectators, many of whom gave them money', said the *Ipswich Journal*. We can only guess what it must have been like for those chained wretches, with their guards and the crew, in a craft only about 40ft. long. Upon arrival it was discovered that the skipper had neglected to obtain customs clearance when he left Ipswich, with the result that the wherry was detained until her papers arrived.[50]

The wherries seem to have been associated with certain inns in Ipswich and Harwich, which would have provided refreshments and shelter to passengers awaiting the uncertain arrival of the boats, or upon the termination of their journeys, which were, of course, dependent upon the vagaries of wind and tide. The roles of wherryman and innkeeper were closely intertwined. For example,

Thomas Smith advertised in 1807 that his new wherry would sail from the *Ram* Inn, by the Common Quay;[51] the publican there was one Joseph Elmy. About 10 years later Smith became the innkeeper himself, but he continued to skipper his boat, the *Generous Friends*. For a time he was in partnership with a former publican there, Joseph Bell, who took his turn with another boat, the *William*. The partnership was dissolved in 1819, when Smith continued on his own—'wherries daily from the *Ram* Inn, Common Quay, Ipswich, *Golden Lion* and *Queen's Head* Inns, Harwich'. Half shares in the two wherries were offered for sale. The *Generous Friends,* of 28 tons, had been built at Ipswich in 1807, and the *William*, of 13 tons, similarly in 1797.[52] Both later appeared in the Ipswich Register as wherry-rigged, presumably with loose-footed mainsails, with one mast, running bowsprits and square sterns. Both were carvel built, and the *William* in particular was beamy and shallow – 28ft. 1in. long, by 10ft. 10in. beam and only 4ft. 9in. deep below her deck. By 1825 Smith owned both

A passenger wherry on the left and a large sloop with a boom to her mainsail from John Cleveley's *Prospect of Old Ipswich*. *Ipswich Borough Council Museums and Galleries*

boats jointly with a Harwich publican; a few years later, when the new steamers were denting the trade, both were sold for fishing and stone dredging.

The other Ipswich inn from which wherries plied was the *Wherry*, further to the east along the quays, where modern leisure facilities still commemorate the name. In 1797 William South took over the inn, and 'the Wherry Passage Boat, (late Mr. John Woollward's, deceased)'. The boat was probably the *Prince of Wales,* a smack-rigged vessel built in 1791, which would explain how a boy was knocked overboard by the boom 'on Mr. South's wherry'. After a ten-year tenancy South disposed of the *Prince of Wales* and the *Lord Nelson,* another smack-rigged craft which had been built in 1804, but they continued to sail from the quay at the inn.[53] Edward Cook, variously described as a wherryman or an innkeeper, at the *Wherry* inn, was the last to work them as passage boats on the Orwell. Both were sold about 1835: the *Prince of Wales* was eventually condemned at Dover for smuggling, whilst the *Lord Nelson* was wrecked at Southwold in 1844.[54]

The advertised tariff of freight charges in the wherries had always included items like hogsheads, and from time to time, even before there was competition for passengers from the steamers, the sailing boats carried cargoes, usually of timber, up and down the river. The *William* even took a flock of sheep down to Harwich on one occasion. A voyage to Maldon with cheese is on record; and at other times the *Prince of Wales* took the odd freight of bricks to London, although the cargo could scarcely have consisted of more than four or five thousand.[55] It is clear, however, that the wherries had hatchways of a good size, and for coastal passages they probably had proper hatch covers. It is equally clear that the later craft differed considerably from the two-masted vessels of Cleveley's time; the Orwell wherry was never a precisely defined type of vessel.

The Ipswich Whale Fishery 2

Daniel Defoe visited Ipswich in about 1722, and wrote in his *Tour* concerning the Greenland whaling trade:

> But at this present time an occasion offers to speak in favour of this port, namely the Greenland fishery lately proposed to be carried on by the South Sea Company, on which account I may freely advance this, without any compliment to the town of Ipswich, no place in Britain is equally qualified like Ipswich, whether we respect the cheapness of building and fitting out their ships and shalloups, also furnishing victualling and providing them with all kind of stores, convenience for laying up the ships after the voyage, room for erecting their magazines, warehouses, rope-walks, cooperages, etc, on the easiest terms, and especially for the noisome cookery which attends the boiling of their blubber which may be on this river (as it ought to be) remote from any places of resort; then their nearness to the market for the oil when it is made and which above all ought to be the chief thing considered in that trade, the easiness of their putting out to sea when they begin their voyage, in which the same wind that carries them from the mouth of the haven is fair to the very seas of Greenland . . . Ipswich must have the preference of all the port towns of Britain for being the best centre of the Greenland trade . . . .

The Greenland whaling trade was highly speculative and many British merchants came to grief in it, in spite of a government bounty paid to encourage it. It became more profitable after the end of the American War of Independence, and the number of ships which set out towards the northern seas increased steadily year by year.

In 1784 Defoe's words were remembered when Ralph Hare, the Ipswich shipowner, advertised his intention to fit out a whaling ship if there were sufficient backers. He estimated that the ship and her gear would cost about £3,200 and he invited subscriptions for 1/8, 1/16 or 1/32 shares.[1] But a few months later he was declared bankrupt, and his scheme came to nothing.

Enterprise revived in 1786, when Emerson Cornwell, a local banker, and Captain Timothy Mangles, a Londoner who was then working the St. Peter's and Nova Scotia shipyards in the town, promoted a company for whaling. The company, or perhaps Mangles alone, purchased the *Ipswich,* a ship of 320 tons newly built at Yarmouth, and chartered the *Orwell* from Captain John

Hall, of Wapping. A third ship was said to be 'not nam'd, but provided'.[2] The *Orwell,* Captain Harrison, had been built at Whitby in 1754 and lengthened in 1779, increasing her tonnage to 380. Her original name had been *Centinel* and she had previously been in the Archangel trade. She carried a crew of about 50, and the *Ipswich,* under Captain Gardner, had a complement of 41. Mangles had both ships doubled, i.e. given an extra skin of planking to help withstand the pressure of the ice, should they be frozen in. There was a delay in the equipment of the third vessel, with the result that she was not ready for the 1787 season. All the ships were initially fitted out on the Thames, and the *Ipswich* and the *Orwell* sailed from there for the seas to the east of Greenland on 20th March, 1787. At the same time a try works, for rendering down the blubber, was under construction at the Nova Scotia yard in anticipation of their return.[3]

The *Orwell* arrived back at Downham Bridge on 30th July, but she was unable to reach Nova Scotia because of the shallowness of the river. She had caught seven fish (as whales were always known in the industry), which had provided 150 butts of blubber and about 4 cwt of whalebone. Whales were not brought back in their entirety: the blubber was cut from the body and put into barrels, and the whalebone – horny material with hairy edges that sieve the creature's food from the seawater – was cut from their mouths. The rest of the carcass was abandoned – it was a wasteful business. The *Orwell* reported that when she had spoken the *Ipswich,* in latitude 76 degrees North on 7th July, the latter had been 'clean', i.e. empty.[4]

The *Orwell* began to discharge her cargo, and 'the noisome cookery' commenced on 6th August. According to the *Ipswich Journal*, 'the inhabitants of this town were released from the apprehension of being very much incommoded by the nauseous smell that arises in the process of extracting the oil. The stench did not reach any part of the town, neither was it scarcely to be smelled within 100 yards of the place'. No doubt people in the 18th century, used to primitive methods of sanitation and waste disposal, were fairly tolerant of odours. The paper continued, 'The *Orwell* still remains at Downham-bridge, and lighters are employed in bringing up her cargo, which will all be boiled off in 14 days'.[5] The *Ipswich* arrived in the river on 24th August, still with no whales but with 1½ butts of blubber, obtained from 54 seals.[6]

The enterprise probably returned a reasonable profit, and nationally the industry was booming. A second company was promoted in Ipswich, under the leadership of Charles Crickitt,

A watercolour by George Frost of Nova Scotia Yard, the home base of the Ipswich whale fishery. This particular building was probably a granary. *Ipswich Borough Council Museums and Galleries*

another banker.[7] They purchased the *Simond*, a ship of 336 tons, which had been built at Newcastle in 1780, and chartered the *Charlotte* of 320 tons, built at Whitby in 1776 and owned by a man named Dowden. Both vessels were already in the whaling trade. According to *Lloyd's Register*, both were doubled in 1788 – presumably before they sailed to the Arctic in that year. Crickitt's ships always operated entirely from the Thames; the facilities there would undoubtedly have been better than on the Orwell.

In February, 1788, news arrived that a whale had been sighted in the Wallet, a channel off Clacton. Captain Harrison of the *Orwell* quickly made arrangements with James Woollard, owner of one of the wherries on the river, to take him out to hunt the animal, which would be trapped within the sandbanks and unable to 'sound', or dive deep, in the shallow water. Several men 'with proper implements' were taken along, but at first the whale was so wild that they could not get near it. At last Harrison himself managed to hurl a harpoon into the creature, but too near its tail to be really effective. The chase continued for a couple of days, but after Harrison had fallen overboard, and returned to Ipswich for a harpoon gun, contact was lost. The whale was later sighted off Dunwich and remained in the area for more than a fortnight, but no further attempt to catch it was made.[8]

At the end of February the *Ipswich* moved from her moorings at Nova Scotia to Downham Bridge to complete preparations for the new season's voyage. She later sailed for Davis Straits, while the *Orwell* left Harwich Harbour on 7th April bound for the Greenland seas as before.[9] Cornwell & Mangles' third ship was ready now, but the press did not record her departure, presumably from the Thames. She was the *Christopher,* Captain Dearon, a 350-ton ship built at Whitby in 1762 and carrying a crew of 38. Owned by a syndicate headed by Hall, she had previously been in the Jamaica trade and was doubled for her new work.

Crickitt & Co's ships also sailed from the Thames. The *Simond*, Captain Gordon, bound for Davis Straits, was reported sighted off Orfordness on 1st March, whilst her pilot left the *Charlotte*, Captain Watson, near the same place on the 24th, reporting her all well on her way to Greenland.[10]

The season was not successful. At the end of August the *Orwell* arrived back in Harwich Harbour with two fish, and a day or two later the *Christopher* followed her in from Greenland, also with two, described as 'small'. The *Ipswich* returned from Davis Straits on 4th September; she was again clean. According to Wodderspoon, the *Orwell* brought back 13 casks of blubber and 4 cwt of whalebone, while the *Christopher* had 17 casks of blubber and a similar weight of bone. Crickitt & Co fared no better; the *Charlotte* returned to the Thames with the produce of a single fish, found floating with no bone, and 108 seals, whilst the *Simond* also caught only one, with 11ft. of bone.[11]

In spite of the disappointing results a third voyage was undertaken in 1789. Crickitt and his associates, however, dispatched only the *Simond*. Early in May it was reported that the *Charlotte*, 'late in the Greenland trade', had been wrecked off Elsinore.[12] Cornwell & Mangles sent their three ships to Greenland: the *Ipswich* and *Orwell* sailed from the Ipswich river on 9th April and the *Christopher* followed four days later.[13] The *Simond* sailed from the Thames and it was reported that she had taken three fish in Davis Straits by 29th May. She later caught a fourth; all were said to be sizeable.[14]

On 27th July the *Orwell* arrived home with two fish. She reported that when she left the ice the *Ipswich* had caught one under disputable circumstances and the *Christopher* was clean – the local ships evidently kept in touch.[15] The *Ipswich* returned on

22nd August with her one fish, but for a time the mate refused to take the necessary oath regarding its capture, as required under the Bounty Acts, and was committed to the bridewell until he saw the error of his ways. Meanwhile bounty payments were withheld, and there was 'a considerable disturbance' among the crew as a result.[16] The *Christopher* arrived in mid-September with one fish, picked up dead at sea; it was described as sizeable and provided 'upwards of twelve tons' of blubber.[17] The *Orwell*'s catch yielded 27 tons, and that of the *Ipswich* 17.

The only record of the quantities of blubber brought back is that of Wodderspoon, and it is strange that he used different units for each year. According to him, it would appear that a whale yielded about 20 butts, whereas Lubbock cites figures at Whitby which indicate that the yield was nearly twice as much: the metrology of the 18th century often featured local variations. The

An old quay wall at Nova Scotia about 1970. These last remains of the old shipyard have now been obliterated by the construction of the West Bank Terminal.

casks referred to at Ipswich seem to have equalled about two butts.

The 1789 season was unprofitable and Cornwell & Mangles abandoned the venture. *Lloyd's Register* for 1792 lists the *Ipswich* engaged in the Jamaica trade out of London, but by 1798 she was back in the Davis Straits fishery and she continued in whaling – on and off – until 1823.[18] Re-rigged as a brig, owned in Plymouth and engaged in trade with North America, she disappeared from the *Register* after 1842. The *Orwell* briefly featured as engaged in general trade from London, but I have not been able to trace her after 1792. A cargo of mahogany from a vessel of the name, advertised for sale at Ipswich in 1790,[19] was probably not from her – the name was not unique. So large a ship would have been uneconomical in the silting estuary after which she was named, as Mangles must have found. The timber was probably shipped down from London, perhaps even direct from the tropics, in the sloop which certainly existed a few years later. The *Christopher* did not feature in *Lloyd's Register* after 1790; perhaps the names of both these ships were changed.

On the other hand, Crickitt & Co continued to send out the *Simond*. She was in the Davis Straits in 1790, and whilst still there was reported to have caught three fish, 'one of which is said to be the largest seen for some years'. In the following year she was there again but came home clean.[20] As far as I know, that was the end of Ipswich whaling, but the ship appeared in *Lloyd's Register* as owned by Crickitt and destined for the northern seas until 1795. Latterly she may have been employed in some other trade where the profits were more predictable – the *Charlotte* was described as 'belonging to this port', i.e. Ipswich, when she was lost.

It was not until March, 1793, that the try works, or rendering plant, at Nova Scotia was put up for sale. There was a pantiled timber building, 35ft. by 26ft., in which were five 'backs', or cooling vats, and another, 20ft. by 19ft., which contained the large coppers for boiling the blubber and clarifying the oil; the latter structure collapsed on the day before the sale.[21] In the following January, the boats, harpoons, lances, etc, from the *Ipswich* and the *Christopher* were advertised for sale at the yard: there were 18 boats, ranging in length from 20ft. to 25ft. A large warehouse, which had been erected as a store for the whaling, blew down in a gale a month later.[22]

G.R. Clarke said that some of the buildings were taken down in 1820 and others were still standing at the time he wrote. Of the whaling, he added, 'it is probable that another attempt would be more successful'.[23] But no one ever tried.

Ipswich Ships 1824–1860 3

The official Register of Ships for the Port of Ipswich, as for most British ports, goes back only to 1824, when a new form of registration was introduced.[1] Four years later an Act of Parliament[2] required all vessels recorded under the earlier scheme to be re-registered under the new one, so that we may assume that by 1830 all vessels belonging to the port appear in the Register.

In that year some 136 sailing craft, apart from obvious yachts, and two steamers were registered at Ipswich. Both the steamships, the *Ipswich* and the *Commerce*, were locally built, and 79 of the sailing vessels also came from the town's shipyards.

The largest of all was the snow *Hannah* of 146 tons, built by William Bayley in 1826, originally for Harwich owners. Most of the vessels measured less than 100 tons, as was the case at every British port. As to rig, 48 were sloops, mostly above 50 tons, with fixed bowsprits and employed in the carriage of bulk cargoes. Another similar vessel, the *Stevens* of 55 tons, built at Queenborough in 1810, was said to be hoy rigged, and, remarkably at that date, she had a pink stern.

Twenty four vessels were described as smacks, mostly of less than 50 tons, with running bowsprits. These were usually engaged in fishing, stone dredging or salvage work – several ended up being seized by the Customs authorities for smuggling – but by this time a few smacks were employed as cargo carriers, particularly in the cheese trade, where speed was more important than a large capacity.

Also, there were 31 schooners, 20 brigs (or square-rigged vessels with two masts), one brigantine and the snow *Hannah*. Four vessels were said to be barge-rigged and there were four yawls. In addition, there were two wherries: one, the *William*, was described as wherry-rigged, whereas the other, the *Generous Friends*, was by then said to be smack-rigged.

Under the 1824 Registration Act the property in a vessel was divided into 64 shares – as it still is – and for the first time the registrations showed how many shares each owner held. In 1830, Ipswich vessels were owned, wholly or in part, by some 239 individuals. As was usual in most ports, the largest occupational group was of mariners, 71 of them, together with five fishermen

A page from R.H. Dana's *The Seaman's Manual* (1846) illustrating the main sailing ship rigs. What Dana terms a hermaphrodite brig is referred to in the text of this book as a brigantine.

and a solitary lighterman: these were usually the masters of their vessels.

The next largest group, 47 in number, described themselves as merchants: these were mainly corn or coal merchants, for the coastal trade in these commodities made up most of the commerce of the port, and many dealt in both; others handled timber, iron or seeds. Thirty-nine owners were tradesmen such as bakers, bootmakers, butchers, grocers, innkeepers or tanners. The demarcation between this group and the merchants was somewhat blurred; a few may have been employees in their trades, but most of them owned their own businesses and can be found in *Pigot's Commercial Directory* for 1830. A further 32 owners were described as gentlemen; they belonged either to the professional classes – bankers, lawyers and the like – or they were of independent means, like Sir William Middleton of Shrubland Hall. Twenty-one of the owners were farmers or yeomen, mostly from villages within about a dozen miles of Ipswich, although one farmer was at Wakes Colne in Essex and a yeoman came from London.

Only 10 of the owners were in shipbuilding or ancillary trades, but these included William Bayley, who became the most important owner in the port over the next 20 years or so. Another 10 were women. Some were widows, like Elizabeth Howard who owned 8/64 of the sloop *Howard*, whilst others, described as spinsters, often with the same surnames as co-owners, were probably the daughters or sisters of those men. Only three of the 239 owners called themselves shipowners; they were probably retired members of other groups and none of them owned as many shares as those similarly styled in the town a few decades later.

In 1830, forty Ipswich vessels had only one owner each; these included 14 mariners, together with the five fishermen and the lighterman noted earlier. The latter was one James Osborn and his lighter, the *Success*, measured just less than 10 tons. She had originally been an open boat of unknown age, previously registered at Blakeney and Cley in 1826. Her rig was given as sloop but in 1831 she was re-registered as a smack. Nine years later her registry was cancelled without explanation; 15 tons was the minimum for which it was compulsory, but many small craft were registered.

The largest vessel belonging to one person was the delightfully-named sloop *Friends of Eliza* of 101 tons, built at Ipswich in 1792 and owned by a mariner named Edward Caston. After his death she was re-rigged as a schooner by his widow Rhoda, and in 1842 she passed to another Caston, a schoolmaster of Wivenhoe, and then to the Colchester registry.

Another vessel entirely owned by one person was the 45-ton sloop *James and Ann*, which had been built at 'Camphire[3] in Zealand about the year 1731', according to the Register. In 1830 she was the oldest vessel belonging to the port, where she had been owned since at least 1822. She belonged to John Hare the Elder, mariner, and was skippered by his son of the same name. Rigged with a striking mizzen, she was employed in the corn and coal trades, and in 1831 she was rebuilt, being lengthened to measure 64 tons and re-rigged as a ketch. In 1833 she was sold, advertised as 'that well-known, fast-sailing and fortunate Schooner',[4] to be purchased by John Cobbold, one of the leading owners in the port. She continued trading until 8th January, 1854, when she was wrecked at the mouth of the Tyne – not, as might be thought, outward bound with coal that could stand a bit of wetting in a leaky hull, but inwards with grain. All on board were saved.[5]

The number of owners of each ship bore little relation to either its size or its age; most Ipswich vessels had from two to four owners. The sloop *Friends*, built in 1823, was one of the few with as many as 12, whilst a number of other vessels in the London trade had five or more. Five people owned the brig *Enterprize*, built in the town in 1794 and one of the older vessels then on the Register. Thirty-two shares were held by a seed merchant, Frederick Seekamp, and the remainder by her master, a shipowner in the town, a widow in Dereham, Norfolk, and a London gentleman – both the latter seem to have had family connections in Ipswich. Conversely, although most of the vessels that were entirely owned by one person were small, they included the brig *Dunn*, built in 1783 and owned in 1830 by Robert Smith, shipowner. At the other end of the time scale, the schooner *Kate*, built at Woodbridge in 1824, was entirely owned by John Cobbold throughout her short life; she was wrecked off north Wales in 1833.[6] Apart from the mariners with a large stake in one vessel, most owners usually had shares in several.

The most important Ipswich shipowner in the first half of the 19th century was William Bayley (1791–1857), a shipbuilder who had moved his business from Woodbridge to Ipswich in 1826. While he was in Woodbridge he did not involve himself in shipowning, but soon after the move he invested in 1/8 of the sloop *Mary*, one of the first craft he built in his new yard; half the shares in her belonged to her master, Benjamin Baker. In 1830 she was lengthened by 10 feet – doubtless in his yard – and re-rigged as a schooner. The investment proved profitable and Bayley, with his building yard prospering, gradually began to acquire shares in other vessels, by no means all of them built by himself. Nor were they new, but he had doubtless repaired many of them before, and would have known what they were like in their bones and how much their previous owners were prepared to spend on them.

It was three years before Bayley invested in any other bottom, when he bought the whole of the little schooner *Susan*, of 49 tons, which had been built by his kinsman Jabez in 1824. William immediately disposed of half of her and a little later her skipper became a part owner, Bayley being able to advance him £87 by mortgage. Soon he was similarly advancing money to the owners of many small craft new from his slipways, or lengthened in his yard: he obviously had the capital to allow his customers to pay in instalments.

During the 1830s Bayley acquired shares in 17 vessels and a further six entirely, although he retained sole ownership of only two: the *Kate*, a small cutter which he later sold, and the *Union*, an elderly brig which he eventually broke up. Most of his vessels were in the coasting and short sea trades. His co-owners were a group of diverse people, including in some cases the masters of the vessels, but it is noticeable that in many cases they were members of the Christie family, whose interests included clothing, pawnbroking and the coal trade; the Sheppards who were in the corn trade, and John Cobbold.

It was not until 1834 that Bayley next invested in a vessel newly built by him, when he took a quarter share in the schooner *Enchantress* in partnership with some of the Christies and a London insurance broker. She was coppered for warmer seas and departed to Liverpool to load her first freight. Bayley was beginning to look further afield in his ship-owning enterprise and in 1836 he launched the schooner *Matilda* (named after one of his daughters) for himself and Cobbold; a few years later she was lost on her return passage from Lisbon. In 1838 he built the 157-ton brig *Courier* mostly for himself. For nearly seven years 16 of the shares in her were held by one William Bantoft, a legal clerk, until Bayley bought him out. He lengthened the ship by 12 feet and re-rigged her as a barque, with a tonnage of 184 – quite a big ship by local standards. She was wrecked in 1850, on passage from Cardiff to Galati in Romania, with railway iron.[7]

Other vessels partly owned by Bayley and built in his yard included the brig *William Bayley* of 1840. He owned 40 shares, the remainder being held by five other people, including his son, also named William. Her registration shows a very rare transaction: the sale of $2\frac{1}{2}$ shares by Bayley to one of the other owners, and back again a few years later. Shortly after his death in 1857 news arrived home that the vessel, loaded with South African wool for London, had caught fire after leaving Algoa Bay and had been beached further along the coast. It was reported that the wool might be saved, but the ship was not.[8]

Another was the schooner *John Cobbold*, built in 1847. In spite of her name, Bayley owned 40 of her 64 shares while her eponymous owner had only 16, although his family acquired full ownership after Bayley's death. On her maiden voyage she carried a prefabricated church out to the Holy Land for a missionary society, before loading a return freight of Egyptian corn.[9] Her skipper's account book, which I once saw many years ago, showed that she sailed to Mauritius for sugar and round Cape Horn to Iquique for hides. In those days a master would often be out of touch with the owners for many months and had to conduct all the ship's business himself. One item of expenditure was for 'Hire of horses for warping up to the bridge at Gloucester', and the next for 'Repairs to Bridge'. Alas, I do not know the present whereabouts of this rare record, if it still exists, and I did not study it as fully as I should have done.

Of all the vessels which Bayley built, he retained only two entirely, right from the beginning: the 156-ton brig *Agile*, for the Mediterranean trade in 1841, and the little 43-ton coasting schooner *Teaser* in 1845. Curiously, the latter was not first registered until three years later. She measured 57.6ft. in length by 13.9ft. beam by 7.2ft. depth in hold, and when she was wrecked at Plymouth in 1867 her crew numbered no more than three, according to the mate's statement closing her registration. She may have been an early schooner barge, built on speculation and for which Bayley could find no buyer. He owned no other barges.

Among his many older vessels was the 199-ton brig *Cambria*, built at Swansea in 1816, which he purchased in 1837 to be divided with several of his closest associates. Within a few weeks she was wrecked in the Baltic. A journalist, reporting the loss, commented, 'It was this vessel that took the crew from the *Kent*, East Indiaman, when in flames'.[10] In fact, rather more than the crew; in 1825 the *Kent*, outward bound with five companies of troops included in her passengers, caught fire during a gale in the Bay of Biscay. The situation was desperate when the *Cambria*, with a crew of 11 and carrying mining machinery and 36 Cornish miners and engineers to Vera Cruz in Mexico, hove in sight. She rescued 547 of the 629 souls in the Indiaman and at once put back to Falmouth, where she met with a great reception; medals were struck for her crew. It

The barque *John Cobbold* rendering assistance to the Sunderland barque *Derwent* in an Atlantic storm in March, 1874.
Mr. P.W. Hope-Cobbold

remains one of the classic rescues of all time. What it was like during the passage home, with nearly 600 people in a storm-tossed vessel only 84ft. long, we can only try to imagine.

Bayley himself wrote of his shipowning business in March, 1850: 'More or less, I have a proprietorship in 32 vessels and am managing owner of 29 of them; and not only in the coasting, but in the foreign trade as well'.[11] Some were then in the Mediterranean, and one had just arrived in London from Buenos Ayres. Between 1826 and the time of his death, Bayley had owned, 'more or less', some 68 vessels. He had disposed of many of them and some had been lost, but only 21 had been built in his own yard, mostly for foreign trade. At the end he had an interest in 33 vessels and was the sole owner of 12 of them.

The Cobbolds, still well known in Suffolk, were one of the leading families in Ipswich in 1830. Although the name is now mainly associated with brewing, the Cobbold brewery was then but one of several in the town, albeit probably the oldest. The family was also involved in the malting, wine, corn and coal trades, beside banking. They were considerable landowners; they featured in many aspects of local life, and they owned ships.

In 1830 they were represented by three generations, all named John. The eldest (1746–1835) had had shipping interests earlier, but he seems not to feature in the surviving Register of Ipswich Ships (unless the registrar inadvertently omitted 'the Elder', whereas he usually specified 'the Younger'). He is remembered today as the one-time employer of a servant girl named Margaret Catchpole.

John the Younger (1774–1860) was then the head of the family businesses: he was also involved in early schemes to bring railways to Suffolk and was one of the original directors of the Eastern Counties Railway Company when it was incorporated in 1836. The youngest John (1797–1882) was always known as John Chevallier Cobbold. He had trained as a lawyer but was also engaged in the family commercial and banking interests. He too was prominent in early railway promotions and was Chairman of the Eastern Union Railway (the first to come to Ipswich) until it became part of the Great Eastern Railway: he was an M.P. for Ipswich for many years and was later High Steward of the Borough. After 1860 he disposed of most of his father's shipping interests, but he continued to acquire some vessels and some of his younger brothers were also involved in shipping.

In 1830 John Cobbold the Younger owned eight vessels jointly with Henry Aldrich, another local corn and coal merchant. They were the snow *Hannah*; the schooners *Agnes*, *Betsey*, *Emma*, *John*

Built as a brig in 1811, Cobbold's *Orwell* was lengthened at least three times during her life and was rigged as a barque between 1849 and 1867. *Miss M.M. Raymer*

and Henry and *Mary*, and the sloops *Amy* and *Jane*. The oldest of these was the *Emma*, built only 10 years before but owned by them since at least 1824. The *John and Henry* was probably the nearly completed vessel advertised for sale by Jabez Bayley in 1823[12] – certainly her name suggests that they had owned her since she was new. In 1827 the pair each purchased 16 shares in an older brig, the *Orwell*, built in 1811. With others, Cobbold had partly owned the schooners *Harriet* and *Emily* since they were built in 1825 and 1827 respectively; in addition the schooner *Kate* was wholly owned by a John Cobbold, who may have been his father, as noted before. All this suggests that the Cobbold fleet was just being established, but it quickly grew.

During the 1830s John Cobbold purchased shares in 10 more vessels. These included the Sunderland-built barque *Faithful*, of 246 tons – the largest vessel belonging to the port at that time (1834) – and by 1847 he owned the whole of her. This vessel achieved fame in 1860, when she stood by the disabled American ship *Alice*, of Bath in Maine, for four days in the Channel, rescuing her crew one by one as the seas allowed and landing them at Cowes; Captain Thomas Allen received an award from President Lincoln for that.[13] The veteran of Cobbold's fleet was the little sloop *Endeavour*, of which he acquired 16 shares in 1834. She had been built at Faversham in 1783 and had carried supplies to the fleet at the Nore during the long wars. By 1847 Cobbold owned her entirely and in 1860 it was reported in the press that her then master, John Thorne, was aged 79 and had been at sea for 67 years, 17 of them in the Royal Navy.[14]

In 1838 Cobbold purchased a half share in the spritsail barge *Three Friends*, built on the Thames in 1830 and the first sprittie known to have been registered at Ipswich. His co-owner was William Colchester, now best remembered as a barge builder but then he was a timber and slate merchant. Cobbold sold out to him after a few years and owned no more barges until the *Cliff*, new in 1858.

Cobbold began by buying several new, and almost new, vessels jointly with Henry Aldrich and then acquiring the latter's share. Throughout his life he tended to purchase part-ownership and gradually increase his holding over several years until he was the sole owner. In all, he had an interest in some 49 vessels; and at the end of his life he owned 13 wholly and nine partly.

One of Cobbold's associates in shipping was James Cuckow, one of the few described only as shipowner in the Register: he first appeared as owner of a small smack, the *Friends Goodwill*, in

1830. Three years later he was a mariner living in the village of Shotley, sole owner of the brig *Arno*, the schooner *Dispatch* and the small barge or lighter *Brisk*, of which he was skipper. He seems to have moved back to Ipswich after a time and he became the principal owner, with 40 shares, of the 112-ton coasting schooner *Competitor*, newly built in 1840; his co-owners were John Cobbold and William Mulley, the local agent for Lloyds. In 1843 he purchased the schooner *Panther* from Yarmouth and Cobbold became joint owner with him; the vessel was later re-built as a barque and sheathed with yellow metal for ocean voyages.

White's *Suffolk* (1844) did not mention Cuckow, but later directories listed him as a master mariner, sailmaker and ship chandler. According to the Register he took his ships to sea from time to time, among them the 346-ton barque *Majestic*, one of the largest vessels belonging to the port.

At different times Cuckow owned 24 vessels entirely and had shares in a further 20, but he had disposed of them all by 1871. His chandlery and sail loft were taken over by his son Walter, a master mariner, at about the same time.

The shipbuilder William Read was also an important owner in the mid-19th century. He began with the smack *Prosperous* in 1830 and in the course of the next few years he acquired shares in another smack, three schooners and a brig, but he retained few of his vessels for long. After 1838 almost all his vessels were owned jointly with his partner Enos Page. These included the cutter *Vivid*; the schooners *Ranger* and *Rover*, both in the Mediterranean trade, and the barque *Hope* in the Canadian timber trade; all these were built by them and soon mortgaged to provide working capital, before being sold after a few years. Another barque they built and owned, the *Hero*, was lost after a few months on passage from London to Liverpool in 1840.[15]

They also owned the Canadian-built brig *Collina* which foundered off the Texel in 1841. Three years later her master, William Simpson, and Read were tried at the Central Criminal Court on a charge of barratry, i.e. fraudulently losing the ship in order to claim the insurance. Although Simpson admitted boring holes in the vessel's bottom, he insisted that he did so on Read's orders. Read was, however, acquitted after many influential acquaintances had testified to his character, while Simpson was sentenced to transportation for life. The case aroused considerable public interest, but soon afterwards justice was seen to be done when Simpson received a royal pardon.[16]

When the partnership was dissolved in 1844 most of the jointly owned vessels were immediately sold. Read later owned two steamers, *Caledonia* and *Endeavour*, used as tugs on the Orwell, and a number of other vessels, including the brigantine *Dazzler*, sheathed for warm seas, which he sold to Melbourne owners after a few years. All had been disposed of by the time of his death in 1869, apart from the boomsail barge *Endeavour*, built in his yard, and an elderly partly clinker-built schooner, the *Children's Adventure*. Read was a pioneer builder of iron vessels, both for himself and for other local owners.

A remarkable group of four iron schooners came on to the Ipswich Register from London in 1848. These were the *Admiral Codrington* (159 tons), *Admiral Hood* (155 tons), *Admiral Jervis* (154 tons) and *Admiral York* (151 tons); all were built at Walker-on-Tyne in 1846, apparently by a builder named Coutts. They were all owned jointly by Frederick Ransome, who owned coke ovens at Griffin Wharf in Ipswich and later achieved some transient fame as the inventor of a patent artificial stone, and one George Parsons, a member of the local gentry. For about 18 months all four vessels were engaged in the coal trade from the north-east until they were

Shipping at Ipswich in the early 19th century, before the building of the dock, seen in an illustration from Dugdale's *England & Wales Delineated*.

sold to a London barrister in the summer of 1849. Only the *Admiral Hood* seems to have been listed in *Lloyd's Register* and as late as 1857 she was still listed as belonging to Ipswich and belonging to Ransome. Perhaps they had a sister ship: the *Admiral Duncan* of London was wrecked near Boulogne in November, 1846, with the loss of Captain Archer, formerly of Ipswich, and three of his crew.[17] A Captain George Archer was later the skipper of the *Admiral Hood*.

Although the popular view seems to be that 19th-century shipping in east coast ports consisted mainly of sailing barges, this was not the case at Ipswich. In 1860 only 32 barges were registered at the port, as against 138 round-bottomed vessels such as barques, brigs, schooners and sloops: the 10 smacks were mainly employed in septaria dredging for cement, and in fishing. Pictures of the time show few barges, and not until about 1880 did their numbers equal those of round-bottomed craft.

The leading barge owner in the port in the earlier part of the century was William Colchester, a timber and slate merchant when we first hear of him about 1836, with premises in the parish of St. Clement and also at Woodbridge. In 1838 he purchased the barge *Three Friends* jointly with John Cobbold and then began to buy entire vessels. Then he started to build his own barges, beginning with the *Raven* in 1841, and continuing with a series named with Latin ordinal numbers. In all, there were eight of these but he did not build the *Quartus*. He ran his own yard for over 35 years.

In the 1840s he diversified into stone dredging and the manufacture of Roman cement, in partnership with John Watts of Harwich, and producing 'artificial manure' from coprolites. His fleet was at its greatest strength at the beginning of 1860, when he owned 14 barges, 13 wholly and seven from his own yard. He also owned a couple of schooners – the *Ann* entirely and the *Rose* jointly with Watts – a couple of billyboy sloops and a trio of other sloops. His billyboys have their claims to fame: the *Director* was the first vessel to lock into Ipswich Wet Dock in 1842, and the *Monarch*, built at Woodbridge in 1839, was probably the most southerly-built example of her kind.[18] By 1882 Colchester had disposed of all his vessels and seven years later he retired to Cambridgeshire, but his fertilizer business continued under his name until about 1913.

Many of the businessmen of Ipswich had taken a big step forward in 1837, when an Act was obtained to create a wet dock. A channel, still called the New Cut, was excavated to bypass two reaches of the Orwell where most of the quays were located. This section was then dammed off at each end and an entrance lock constructed to give access from the New Cut. At the time of its completion, Ipswich Wet Dock was the largest enclosed dock in the country.

Among the many small coasters owned in the port at that time was the schooner *Lady Leighton*, and she has a peculiar claim to fame. She had just arrived with 120 tons of coal at about 4.00 a.m. on 30th July, 1850, when her master was directed to take her into the dock close astern of a partially ballasted Norwegian barque, the *Oscar*. Unfortunately the two vessels became jammed together in the lock chamber; the outer gates could not be closed – and then the tide began to fall.[19] The *Lady Leighton* was nipped and began to leak. Desperate efforts were made to unload her cargo as both

Scrubbing away under the vessel's hull to clean and tar it before the tide returns, the men hardly register in this photograph by Robert Burrows owing to the lengthy exposure. Is the figure seated on the boat in the foreground a supervisor or merely a spectator? *Suffolk Record Office*.

vessels settled on the floor of the lock chamber, and about 25% of the coal was removed before the rising water of the next tide prevented further access to her hold, but despite continuous pumping she failed to float.

At high water that afternoon the inner gates were opened and the *Oscar* was taken into the dock. Then, as soon as the schooner's deck was exposed again, men resumed pumping and getting out her coal. There were no easily-portable powered pumps available in those days, and such small manually-operated cranes as the port possessed were not located at the lock: the pumps were the vessel's own, and the coal had to be hoisted up in baskets, all by hand.

Still the *Lady Leighton* would not float, but the task of hoisting out her coal continued until the flood tide again sealed off her hold for a few hours. The work was resumed the next morning. Meanwhile, a large number of empty barrels had been brought from Cobbold's brewery, and when it was decided that sufficient coal had been removed, these were packed into the schooner's hold. Fortunately her deck and deck beams stood the strain, and so she was floated out into the New Cut, having sealed off the dock for over 36 hours.

The sequel was scarcely less remarkable. The owners of both vessels claimed damages from the Dock Commission, who sought counsel's advice. They were told they could not be held liable, although some Commissioners wondered why the schooner had been directed into the lock by their harbourmaster when some barges were also waiting. They learned, too, that when the lock men called upon the schooner's crew to throw them a warp to check her way, the rope had parted.

I do not know how the claim from the owners of the *Oscar* was handled. The Commission appointed surveyors to examine the barque and thereafter nothing was recorded. But the *Lady Leighton* was a local vessel, owned by her skipper, William Matt, and a cooper with the same surname. It was ascertained unofficially that the pair had abandoned the idea of legal action; the damage to their vessel was assessed at £220, less £50 for betterment. The Commissioners felt considerable sympathy for them, but they were advised that they had no power to make *ex-gratia* payments from their funds. After much discussion they had a 'whip round' at their next meeting, which raised about £75, and launched a public appeal, to compensate 'these individuals who are well known to be industrious and deserving characters', which raised somewhat more. The *Lady Leighton* was repaired, sold and continued in trade for another 22 years.[20]

The First Steamers 4

The first steam vessel to sail upon the Ipswich River was the *Orwell*, which briefly operated a service for passengers between Ipswich and Harwich. The impending arrival of a steamer was first reported in September, 1813. In the following June it was announced that the steam packet *Orwell* would commence running in about a fortnight's time from Mr Seekamp's Quay, between the Common and the Wherry Quays. No steamer appeared, and after a couple of months it was announced, 'this delay has arisen from a deficiency in the power of the steam engine … another engine is preparing with all possible expedition, and is so far advanced, as to give every reason to expect that in three weeks the *Orwell* will start'.[1]

The vessel had been built in Yarmouth by a shipwright named James Lepingwell in 1813 but her intended engine, from the works of a long-forgotten firm, Aggs & Curr of Norwich, was a failure, and another had to be shipped down from London. The steamer eventually arrived at Ipswich on 8th August, 1815, having made the passage up from Harwich in about 2½ hours.[2] The service was operated for a couple of months until it was suspended for the winter,[3] but it was never resumed. I do not know who ran the steamer. Perhaps the service did not pay; passengers may have been apprehensive of new-fangled steamboats.

A steam packet, the *Swift*, began to operate from the Thames to Harwich in 1821, but nothing more was heard of steamboats on the Orwell until 1824, when the Ipswich Steam Navigation Company was promoted to provide twice-weekly sailings for passengers and goods between Ipswich and London. The initiators were Henry Ridley, a local merchant, and William Cubitt, the noted civil engineer, who acted as secretary.[4] The company was founded on 1st January, 1825: the capital was £20,000 in £100 shares, and within a short time contracts were placed with George Bayley, of the St. Peter's shipyard in the town, for the building of two wooden ships, and with John Penn of Greenwich for their engines – Penn had constructed Cubitt's first treadmill for him. The two vessels must have been among the very first to be powered by this famous firm, later known as John Penn & Sons, which built the machinery for many well-known ships, including HMS *Warrior*, Britain's first armoured battleship, in 1860, and HMS *Thunderer*, the last big ship to be built on the Thames, in 1911.[5]

The first vessel, the *Ipswich*, was launched on 12th September, 1825, and taken to the Thames for her machinery to be installed. The second, the *Suffolk*, went down the ways a couple of months later. The *Ipswich* returned in the following March and towed her sister to Greenwich.[6] Both vessels were of about 75 tons register, with a fore and aft schooner rig. Few details of their machinery have survived, but they seem to have had twin-cylinder engines of 40 nominal horsepower: at that date they would certainly have been of the side lever type, like inverted beam engines, with the beams low down in the hull. The boiler pressure would have been only about 4 lb. per sq. in.

After a trial sea trip, when the speed was said to be 'nine miles an hour', the *Ipswich* made her first scheduled sailing on 14th April, 1826, departing from Seekamp's Wharf at 5 a.m. on what was expected to be an 11-hour passage to Cox & Hammond's Quay near London Bridge. She carried about 20 passengers, with some cargo, and her master was my first cousin four times removed, a local coasting skipper named Benjamin Garway Hamblin (*c*1789–1849).[7] Incidentally, cousin Benjamin was also the Dock Commission's first dredging contractor when the New Cut was made in 1840. Tenders were based on the use of the Commission's own dredger, as no other was available, but the barges to carry away the spoil were supplied by David Thornbory, the main contractor for the Dock. Not surprisingly, this led to disputes and the work was taken away from Benjamin. At the risk of being accused of bias, I think it would have been better if the dredger had been hired out direct to Thornbory.

After a week the steamer was advertised as sailing from Ipswich every Tuesday at 6 a.m. and from London at the same time every Friday, calling at Harwich each way. Fares were ten shillings (50p) in the 'Chief Cabin' and six shillings (30p) in the fore cabin, which compared very favourably with stagecoach travel, where the fares were £1 inside and eight shillings (40p) outside for journeys of comparable distance. As the service became better known, there were sometimes 60 or more passengers being carried each time. The *Suffolk* entered service in September, and Captain Hamblin transferred to her. For a brief period there were two weekly sailings each way, until at the end of October the service was suspended for the winter, 'as is the general practice of Steam Vessels'.[8]

The bankers Samuel and Henry Alexander, who were shareholders in the Steam Navigation Company, then started a regular service with six sailing craft to carry on the goods traffic to London. Each of the vessels was only partly owned by them, but a corporate identity was given by the name 'Ipswich & Suffolk Trade Vessels'.

In April, 1827, only the *Suffolk* returned to service, for passengers only, while the associated sailing craft – soon numbering 12 – offered regular sailings three times a week from the Salt Office Quay adjacent to Seekamp's Wharf. The steamer fares were increased to 12 shillings (60p) and eight shillings (40p) for the two classes, and sailings were on Mondays and Thursdays to London, returning on Tuesdays and Saturdays. Season tickets were available at three guineas (quickly raised to four), but in which class was not made clear. Again the service was suspended in October.

The associated sailing vessels changed their name to 'Suffolk & Norfolk Traders', with the company offering wagons to convey goods to and from Norwich in seven hours, claiming that these would be a better proposition for Norfolk merchants than the new navigation to Lowestoft. It is hard to avoid the impression that the 'Traders' were dissociating themselves from the I.S.N. company when they announced that they were going to have their own

Built at Yarmouth, the *Orwell* of 1813 was the first steamer on the Orwell. A more finished print or drawing of this vessel also survives, but this watercolour suggests that at one time she had no paddle boxes. ©. *National Maritime Museum, London*

The steamer *Ipswich* of 1825 seen in a drawing by the Rev. Richard Cobbold. The building on the left is the Ipswich gasworks.

steamer to tow their vessels – now numbering 14 – up and down the Orwell.

This steamer was the *Commerce*, of 35 tons register, newly built by Jabez Bayley and fitted with a 22 N.H.P. engine by R. & W. Hawthorn of Newcastle. She entered service in the spring of 1828, when the Suffolk & Norfolk vessels sailed from Ipswich and London on Tuesdays, Thursdays and Saturdays. The role of the *Commerce*, skippered by Captain Hamblin, was to tow the London-bound coaster up until she met the other sailing down, when the tow would be transferred and the steamer returned to Ipswich. The *Commerce* was also fitted to accommodate passengers, and on Thursdays she was scheduled to 'proceed direct to London', whence she returned on the Saturday. Whether on these days she towed a sailing vessel part of the way is not clear – the wind and tides may have been factors – but the passenger fares were only eight and six shillings respectively for the two classes. Meat was conveyed in 'ventilated frames on deck'.[9]

By this time there was no competition from the other steamers. The *Suffolk* and *Ipswich* did not re-appear for the 1828 season; in March they had been offered for sale in London. They were advertised as stoutly built, with the spaces between their oak frames filled up with fir; they were copper fastened up to the wales, and their decks were also laid with copper nails. Each was fitted with 'two steam engines (by Penn of Greenwich), each engine of Twenty-horse Power'. Only the *Suffolk* was fit for sea.[10] No buyers came forward. A year later the two ships were 'peremptorily sold by auction' in Ipswich, and they both fetched only £1,800, 'about a seventh part of their original cost', according to G.R. Clarke. The *Suffolk* was sold to Thomas Shields of Newcastle, for trade between there, Hull and King's Lynn, and in September, 1830, she was wrecked at the mouth of the Tyne, happily without loss of life.[11]

The *Ipswich* was bought by her builders, George Bayley and his partner, John Ridley. She seems to have been completely rebuilt, with her beam increased to reduce her draught. The ship was advertised to resume service in June, 1830, but at the eleventh hour the proposed sailings to London were cancelled, 'the Boilers having been found not sufficiently large for the increased power of the Engines. The Proprietors have ordered New Boilers to be completed as soon as possible. The Vessel may be had for a day's excursion, by giving two days notice, until the present boilers are removed'. This offer can hardly have reassured intending trippers, but a sea trip was advertised for the 15th June.[12]

Meanwhile, the passenger service to London operated by the *Commerce* seems to have been short-lived and she was mainly employed as a tug on the Orwell.[13] Benjamin Hamblin went back into sail early in 1830. At about the same time the Suffolk & Norfolk Traders were reconstituted into a joint stock company headed by the bankers Samuel and Dykes Alexander, reducing its interest in the *Commerce* to 12/64. As banking partners, the Alexanders held a further 8/64, and about a dozen local merchants or shipowners took the remainder, none owning more than six shares; very few Ipswich vessels were so diversely owned.

For a time in 1834 the *Commerce* operated a service between Aldeburgh and Ipswich, calling at Harwich so that passengers could change to the *Ipswich* for London.[14] The tides in the Ore estuary must have made the connections very difficult, and the service did not last long.

One night in November, 1835, the *Commerce* caught fire at her berth in the dock near the gas works in Ipswich, and had to be scuttled to extinguish the flames. It was reported that the clearance between 'the furnace' and her wooden ceiling was only a couple of inches, and it was feared that she was beyond repair. She was bought by two of her shareholders, F.F. Seekamp and Captain Enos

Page (the father of a block and mast maker whom we shall meet later), but her steaming days were over; within a short time she was sold to a merchant at Bristol and re-registered there as a sailing vessel. At the time of her loss at sea in 1868 she was registered at Cardiff and owned at Padstow in Cornwall.[15]

The *Ipswich* had returned to service in April, 1831, with weekly sailings to London: these were soon increased to twice weekly, interspersed with occasional excursions to Aldeburgh or Walton-on-the-Naze. All services were suspended during the winter. Her nominal master was Captain Page, but George Bayley, her builder, had closed his yard that spring and was having difficulty in finding suitable work, so Page deputed the post to him. No doubt Page was unaccustomed to the new technology but he remained on hand to give 'efficient help' with navigation; Bayley was no seaman, but there were no Masters' Certificates at that time.[16] At the end of the 1831 season Captain Charles Wing took over, and, according to the Register, the ship was sold to a syndicate which included the Alexanders and F.F. Seekamp, who had all been among the trustees of the Steam Navigation Company. I suspect they had had an interest in her for as long as her builders had.

In May, 1832, according to the *Ipswich Journal*, 'The passengers by the *Ipswich* steamer experienced a disappointment on Tuesday last, after having pursued their voyage with great dispatch until off Walton-in-the-Naze (*sic*), when it was discovered the engineer had neglected to turn one of the cocks of the pumps supplying the boiler with water, and for want of which the boiler became too much heated; it was found desirable to extinguish the fires, and instead of proceeding on their voyage to return to Harwich. The damage, which was not considerable, will be speedily repaired, and the proprietors trust no future delay to the steamer's regular proceeding will occur'. The *Suffolk Chronicle* added the information, 'The application of cold water to the hot boiler occasioned some damage, but of so trifling a nature, that the vessel sailed yesterday morning as usual'.[17]

There was more to boiler feed water in those early days than might be apparent to the modern eye. Until the advent of the compound engine in the 1860s salt water was almost universally used in marine boilers; the pressures, and hence the temperatures, were so low that the salt caused little trouble unless its concentration was allowed to become excessive. Boiler corrosion was more likely to be caused by the fatty acids in the tallow then used for lubrication. Seawater contains about 3% by weight of various dissolved salts; most of it is common salt (sodium chloride), but among the others it also contains a small quantity of gypsum (calcium sulphate). It was this which could cause great trouble, for if its concentration is raised by evaporation it is soon deposited as an insoluble scale, even at atmospheric pressure.

Marine engines in those early days were used with jet condensers, the steam being exhausted into a closed chamber where it was condensed by direct contact and mixing with sprays of seawater. Air, and the water, were constantly pumped from the chamber, as any appreciable back-pressure would have had a serious effect on the power of the engine. The water was taken to the hot-well, but as it contained more than the condensate from the boiler, any excess of the warm and brackish liquid was discharged into the sea. At the same time, the density of the water in the boiler had to be watched closely to ensure that the concentration of dissolved solids did not approach 9%, at which level the gypsum scale would begin to be formed. At regular intervals, therefore, some of the water in the boiler had to be blown out to the sea and replaced by less salty water from the hot-well: this procedure was known as 'brining', and it represented an enormous loss of heat. When working pressures were raised above 35 lb. per sq. in. the temperature caused the immediate formation of gypsum scale and salt water feed had to be abandoned: it was quite impracticable with compound engines.

After the mishap the *Ipswich* continued in service, but when she resumed her sailings in the spring of 1833 she was said to have been 'fitted up with Boilers upon a new principal'.[18]

A young girl, Betsey Thompson, travelling up to London in 1834 wrote a brief account in her diary of her voyage in the steamer. It was low tide when she embarked, and she watched the vessel 'coming close to the Quay' so that passengers could be ferried to her in a boat. There were 60 to 80 passengers, including half a dozen convicts on their way to the hulks off Woolwich. The sea was calm, but the passage took longer than usual due to contrary winds and the need to bring up to disembark the prisoners, who were taken off in a boat which came out to meet them. By the time the steamer passed Greenwich it was dark, so 'a lanthern was now hoisted to the mast head, and by the aid of that light our Captain soon guided us safely amongst the numerous shipping'.[19]

In September that year, when the *Ipswich* discontinued her sailings as usual, a concern known as 'The Old Company' of London announced their intention to continue a twice-weekly service throughout the winter with their steamers *Fame* and

Eclipse.[20] The latter vessel continued in the summer of 1835, sailing on different days from the *Ipswich*, and fares in both ships were reduced to seven and five shillings for the two classes respectively. In the following year the *Ipswich* seems to have been on her own again; she was lengthened by about six feet and her engine 'improved' in time for the 1837 season.

At the end of that summer the General Steam Navigation Company of London advertised that their steamer *Brocklebank* would begin twice-weekly sailings, just as the owners of the *Ipswich* – now calling themselves 'The Ipswich Steam Packet Company' – were announcing the usual suspension of their service for the winter, 'it being considered that the danger in going up and down the Thames in the dark and foggy weather will create too much risk'. However, passengers were evidently not deterred, and it was reported in November that the *Brocklebank* was carrying from 50 to 60 travellers on every voyage. In December the sailings were reduced to once a week in each direction, with another steamer, the *Albion*, which sailed from the wharf that still bears her name, on the north side of the Wet Dock.[21]

The steamer *Orwell*, built of iron on the Thames in 1839 for the Ipswich Steam Navigation Company, leaving Ipswich.

When the *Ipswich* returned to service in the spring of 1838 there was keen – even hostile – competition. The G.S.N. Company's advertisements extolled the *Albion* as 'a splendid modern built Steamer, which possesses the most recent improvements in naval architecture and steam-boat machinery; she is propelled by fine Engines of 100 Horse Power, while the only other Steam-boat at this Port is the *Ipswich*, a small vessel that was unable to perform the passage during the winter months, being only provided with Engines of 40-Horse Power'. They mentioned one occasion when the steamers sailed for London at the same time, and the *Ipswich* 'displayed a disposition to compete with the speed of the *Albion*, but the result, as might have been anticipated, was that the voyage of the *Ipswich* was suddenly arrested near Harwich, by some of the machinery giving way, and the *Albion* took her passengers on board'.[22] This was not denied, but an advertisement appeared in the form of a letter, signed 'A Lover of Truth', enquiring 'whether the *Albion* Steam vessel, now on the Ipswich Station, is not the same *Albion* that was built some twenty years ago, and is considered to be one of the oldest steam vessels on the Thames, and was employed as a common tug or tow boat 14 or 15 years since; if so, which I understand is a fact, I think the public are most shamefully imposed upon by her being represented as "a splendid modern-built Steamer".'[23] In fact, she had been built in 1823.

This cooled the war of words, but feelings continued to run high. There was a court case concerning a fight between rival boatmen, waiting to embark passengers at a hard – probably Redgate Hard below the present Orwell Bridge. The case was dismissed, but it 'excited great interest'. An excursion in the *Albion* on a Sunday caused 'much dissatisfaction among certain religious classes of the town'.[24] In spite of this, steamship travel was undoubtedly popular: the number of people travelling to and from the metropolis rose from 6,843 in 1836 to 8,762 in 1837, and was set to rise higher in 1838.[25]

The *Ipswich* was certainly elderly and under-powered, and a meeting was called in the Town Hall on 3rd October, 1838, at which it was decided to form a new Ipswich Steam Navigation Company, with a capital of £10,000 to provide and operate a new steamer; she was to be built of iron. Three months later the capital was over-subscribed, so it was increased by a further £5,000 so that a second, smaller steamer could be provided to act as a tender for the first.[26]

The contract for the first ship, the *Orwell*, had already been placed with Ditchburn & Mare of Blackwall, and the smaller *River*

Queen was soon ordered from the same yard. The company chartered the *Ipswich* until the new ships were ready, and began building a new wharf adjacent to Stoke Bridge.

The *Orwell* duly arrived in the Ipswich River on 15th August, 1839, amid scenes of great festivity – she was even saluted by two cannons on the Albion Wharf. Her engines were of 80 horsepower, from the Blackwall firm of Miller & Ravenhill, and were said to work 'with scarcely any vibration'. She entered service four days later, sailing twice a week to London, sometimes with over 200 passengers. The *River Queen* began operating a service to Harwich in the middle of September.[27]

The I.S.N. Company announced its intention to increase its capital by a further £10,000 to provide an additional iron steamer, to be built by Read & Page, the Ipswich shipbuilders. After two meetings to consider the proposal it was apparently decided that only if the new ship was as satisfactory as the *Orwell* would the company buy it, for £9,000.[28]

Read & Page immediately began building their ship, the *Orion*, but they had difficulty in recruiting and retaining labour to work with the new material. Even the boilers were constructed in their yard, whilst the engines came from the little-known London firm of Lloyd & Easter. After further delay caused by a fire in the shipyard the *Orion* was launched on 27th October, 1840, and taken to London to receive her engines. According to one account, the machinery was brought to Ipswich in sections, but this seems unlikely and the ship certainly spent some time in the Thames during the following months.[29]

The *Orwell* remained in service throughout the winter, and the *Orion* took her place for a time in the ensuing spring while she had a refit. Read & Page's offer of their ship to the I.S.N. Company for £9,000 seems to have been quite informal, as a prospectus was issued at that time to form a 'London & Ipswich Commercial Steam Navigation Company' with capital of £12,000 to purchase the *Orion*, which had been offered for 10,000 guineas. She began a twice-weekly service soon afterwards, operated by her builders in partnership with John Lloyd and Henry Easter.[30] The *Albion* was withdrawn at the end of the year. The *Ipswich* was sold to owners in London and Jamaica, for service across the Atlantic, but disappeared from *Lloyd's Register* after 1844. I do not know her fate.

The *Orwell* and the *Orion* operated a regular service between Ipswich and London for several years, sailing on different days and with one or the other being withdrawn in the winter. The *Orion* used Seekamp's Wharf, which was to be inside the new Wet Dock, and consequently she had for a time to negotiate the tide race through the incomplete lock, but apparently without mishap. She was sold to Fleetwood owners in 1845.

In 1846 the Eastern Union Railway opened from Ipswich to Colchester, which was already the terminus of the Eastern Counties Railway from London. The lines were extended to Bury St Edmunds a few months later and to Hadleigh in 1847. People could now travel as never before to take a trip down the Orwell to Harwich, or further afield. By 1852 the E.U.R. itself was operating three steamers, the *Atalanta*, *Cardinal Wolsey* and *Prince*, but by that time the company's lines had reached Norwich and it thereby incurred bitter enmity from the E.C.R., which controlled the whole of the slightly longer route from London to the Norfolk city by way of Cambridge and was determined to preserve its traffic. Trains on the Cambridge line were speeded up, while only poor connections were arranged for E.U.R. trains at Colchester. In 1852 the E.U.R. began to offer steamer travel between Ipswich and London to bypass the E.C.R. altogether. At first the I.S.N. Company's vessel *Orwell* was used but the railway company soon acquired three steamers of its own: *Pearl, Orion* (returning to the Ipswich River after a few years) and *Prince Albert*. These, and the river steamers, were officially owned by Peter Bruff, the E.U.R. engineer and manager, as the company itself had no statutory powers to operate ships. The I.S.N. Company went into liquidation in 1853 and its two ships, *Orwell* and *River Queen*, were purchased by Alfred Cobbold, a younger brother of J.C. Cobbold, the E.U.R. chairman, and added to the railway fleet.

It was a brave effort, but the E.U.R. was unable to compete and was compelled to lease its system to the E.C.R., which operated its trains and ships in return for a fixed share of the total receipts, as from 1st January, 1854. In 1862 the two companies, with others, were amalgamated to form the Great Eastern Railway.

Following the takeover of the Eastern Union by the E.C.R., Edward Dorling, the goods manager at Ipswich, was promoted to the post of superintendent of the entire former E.U.R. section, but in April, 1857, he refused a transfer to Stratford – at a lower salary – and was dismissed.[31] Less than four months later he started running steamers from Ipswich to Walton-on-the-Naze, calling at Harwich, in competition with his former employers. For this he chartered a steamer, the *Alma*, of 48 tons, built in 1856, from the Medway and operated her from the Flint Wharf Stairs, on the opposite side of the New Cut from that where the railway vessels sailed.[32] The enterprise was an immediate success. Dorling's fares were about the same as those on the railway steamers, but he was a well-known and popular figure in the town, where many people resented the fate of the E.U.R – a local company – at the hands of the E.C.R.

At the end of October Dorling purchased a steamer of his own, the *Queen of the Isles*, from Chatham to continue the service throughout the winter to Harwich only.[33] In June, 1858, Dorling advertised that the *Alma* would sail to Harwich three times a day on weekdays and once on Sundays. The chartered vessel was returned to her owners at an unknown time, but Dorling's vessels were always referred to as *Alma* in his advertisements, even though their names were never changed in the Register. The *Ipswich Journal* reported the arrival of 'Mr Dorling's new paddle steamer *Alma No 2*' in July, 1858. She was in fact the *Lady Elizabeth* from Southampton, built by Day, Summers & Co. of that port in 1856; she was fitted with oscillating engines, and a bow rudder to help her move astern out of the New Cut.[34]

Dorling, determined to provide the best possible service, arranged for boatmen to come out from Pin Mill and Levington Creek when required to land or embark passengers, as his steamers shuttled five times daily in each direction. On one occasion the funeral of an Ipswich policeman was to take place at Chelmondiston. 'The entire force', according to the *Ipswich Journal*, accompanied the coffin to Bourne Bridge, where they embarked in boats and were taken out to board a passing *Alma* steamer. They were taken off at Pin Mill and proceeded up to the church for the funeral, afterwards returning to Ipswich in the same way. The coffin travelled by land.[35]

The four E.U.R. river steamers continued to ply on the Orwell for a few years after the takeover. The *River Queen* was withdrawn from service in 1857 and laid up at Ipswich: her engine was taken out for use in Farrow & Grimwood's Roman cement works on the dockside after they were destroyed by fire in 1861, and the hull was broken up in the following year.[36] The *Cardinal Wolsey* was sold away to Middlesbrough in 1863, while the *Atalanta* and the *Prince* continued in service until 1864, when they were reported to be 'quite used up' and scrapped.[37]

Meanwhile the *Orwell* and the *Orion* sailed between Ipswich and London in the summer for a couple of years or so. The E.C.R. sold the *Prince Albert* in 1855, and two years later they disposed of the *Pearl* and the *Orwell* to a ship breaker at Rotherhithe.[38] The latter was soon re-sold, and after a refit she returned to Ipswich to

Opposite: A photograph by Richard Dykes Alexander, chairman of the Ipswich Dock Commission, showing a steamer in the New Cut about 1860. It is difficult to identify the vessel, but she could be Dorling's *Alma No 2*. Note the rudimentary bridge and steering wheel right aft. *Suffolk Record Office*

operate for a time to Thames Haven, where passengers were landed to take the London, Tilbury & Southend Railway to Fenchurch Street. In 1859 the ship was reported to have been sold to owners in Hull. She was then chartered by Giuseppe Garibaldi, seized by his supporters at Genoa in 1860, re-taken by the Royal Navy and laid up at Malta, after which she was said to have been chartered by the Bey of Tripoli. In 1864 she was reported to be under repair at Plymouth, having sprung a leak shortly after sailing from there to Nassau.[39] I do not know her ultimate fate. The G.E.R. sold the *Orion* in 1863: she is said to have been taken up as a blockade-

runner in the American Civil War and to have been captured on her first voyage.[40]

Before the *Orwell* began sailing to Thames Haven, Captain Samuel Rackham, who had been her master almost continuously since 1842, re-appeared on the Ipswich run in command of London-owned steamers, first the *Telegraph* and then the *Sons of the Thames*. In 1859 he was in the *Father Thames*, belonging to the Waterman's Steam Packet Company, which registered the ship at Ipswich. She sailed from Dorling's Alma Wharf, as it was called, and was soon joined by the Woolwich Steam Packet Company's ship *Metis*, also registered at Ipswich.[41] Dorling acted as local agent for both companies; and in 1862 both ships were replaced by two brand-new ones, *Queen of the Thames* and *Queen of the Orwell*, owned by the Waterman's and Woolwich companies respectively, on the London run. These, too, were registered at Ipswich.[42]

Dorling sold both his steamers to the Waterman's Company in 1863. So ended the last locally-owned passenger steamship business, although the ships continued to be known in the locality as 'the *Alma* steamers' until their river service ceased in 1867.

The *Queens* continued to sail between the Orwell and the Thames. The Woolwich Company, having taken over several concerns, absorbed the Waterman's Company in 1870 to gain a monopoly of the services on the Thames, which at that time were by no means confined to the leisure sector. However, there was growing competition from omnibuses and the railways, and five years later the company was reorganised as the London Steamboat Company. In 1884 it became the River Thames Steamboat Company. Continuing competition led to the gradual curtailment of the more distant services, and the *Queens* were withdrawn about 1885.[43]

The river services operated by the G.E.R. after 1864, and the later coastal paddle steamers, are outside the scope of this account.

Ipswich Ships after 1860 5

The year 1860 probably marked the zenith of shipping enterprise in Ipswich. William Bayley had died three years earlier, and although the bulk of his fleet was still in the hands of his two sons and others, as executors, they were beginning to dispose of the ships as required by his will.

The schooner *Frederick William* was sold to Padstow in 1859; others went to Yarmouth, the *Page* was lost at sea and Bayley's 40 shares in the *John Cobbold* were transferred to her eponymous owner. Bayley's will required all his shipping interests to be sold within five years of his death, to any purchaser and in any way that might seem best; but in most cases they were re-purchased, sometimes within a few days, by his sons.

John Cobbold, the other great Ipswich ship owner of the time, died early in 1860. Most of his vessels, wholly or partly owned, were sold within the next few years and his son, J.C. Cobbold, retained only five beyond the end of the decade and built but one for himself, the brig *Adela*. Named after his daughter-in-law, she traded all round the world.

By 1870 some 162 sailing vessels, apart from yachts, and 11 steamers were registered at the port: 66 of the former had been built in the town's yards. The largest of all was the barque *Zelia* of 257 tons, built apparently on speculation at Barnstaple in 1862 and bought soon afterwards by Edward Packard, the Suffolk fertilizer manufacturer. She was for him an isolated venture, but he kept her in deep-water trade for nearly 20 years before selling her to an owner in Colombia.

The next two largest vessels were also barques, the *Faithful* and the *John Cobbold*: the latter had been lengthened and re-rigged in 1856. J.C. Cobbold inherited both from his father, and both were trading to the Mediterranean.

There was a solitary barquentine, the *Orwell*, locally built as a brig in 1811 (unfortunately the name of her builder is unknown), trading to Spain in 1870. She had been wholly owned by the Cobbolds from 1840 until she was sold to a Waterford owner in 1888, but she remained on the Ipswich register until she was wrecked at Waterford nine years later. She had been lengthened in 1835, again in 1849 when she was re-rigged as a barque, and yet again in 1867 when altered to a barquentine. This rig was in fact unknown to the registrar, who recorded her as a brigantine with three masts. The *Zelia* and the *Faithful* were similarly re-registered in the 1870s, and the usage is known elsewhere.[1]

The most numerous type of vessel was the schooner: there were 65 of them, 23 of which had been built in the town. Most were in the coasting and home water trades, but about half a dozen were sailing further afield. The oldest of all was the *Draper*, built at Woodbridge as a sloop in 1798 and owned there for the first part of her life.[2] Transferred to Ipswich in 1831, she was re-rigged as a diminutive schooner a couple of years later, and she was subsequently lengthened no fewer than four times before being sold to Faversham in 1875. She was still afloat 15 years after that.

Other round-bottomed vessels registered at the port included 20 brigantines, 11 brigs, two snows, three ketches, two dandies and about a dozen smacks. The brigantines *Constance*, *Dauntless* and *I.O.U.*, all only a few years old, were trading in deep water but most of the others were in the home and coastal trades. The ketches were the *Golden Fleece* – unusually for Ipswich, a trawler built for a Lowestoft owner and at that date owned in Grimsby – and two

Shipping in the Wet Dock about 1860. The vessel on the left is probably the coaster *Providence*, built at Huddersfield as a billyboy sloop in 1826 and re-rigged as seen here by William Colchester in 1852.

elderly craft which began life as smacks. The dandies *Eagle* and *May Flower* were both fine-lined vessels owned by the May family and employed in their cheese trade from the Netherlands.

The smacks were mainly engaged in the fishing and stone-dredging industries and were mostly owned in Pin Mill, in the parish of Chelmondiston: an exception, named *Orwell*, was used by the local river pilots. The oldest among them was the *Syren*, built in 1819 as a yacht – at Cowes, no less – and once owned by the Rev. George Naylor, a one-time vicar of Bramford and one of the first yachtsmen in the district. However, she had probably been a working craft since 1837.

By 1870 sailing barges were becoming common on the east coast and 37 were registered at Ipswich. Some of the 10 craft described as barge rigged were doubtless boomsail rigged, as were William Colchester's *Tertius* and *Septimus*, then rigged as sloops. Three were rigged as ketches: the *Alpha*, the *Earnest* and the *Kate*. All the others were spritsail rigged and all bona fide Thames barges except the *Providence*, an old billyboy, and the *Two Brothers*, built at Hamburg many years before, which had been re-rigged when Colchester had acquired them. Doyenne of all was the sprittie *Benjamin and Ann*, built at Pangbourne, far up the Thames, in 1791. Of the 37, twenty came from Ipswich yards and almost all the others from long-forgotten small yards on the Thames, or at Newbury on the Kennet and Avon canal.

The steamers in 1870 included 10 paddlers, eight of which were passenger vessels owned by the Waterman's and the Woolwich companies, which amalgamated before the end of the year: there was one tug and the last was the old *Atalanta*, laid up and appropriated by three creditors of the struggling G.E.R., although worth little more than scrap.

There was a solitary screw steamer, the first belonging to the port, the *Speedwell*, owned by one Henry Ward. She plied to and from Hull, taking grain there and returning with coal and other goods. She had been built on the Tyne in 1862 and had spent most of her life owned in Hull before Ward invested in her in 1868. But alas, her life was short. One stormy day in 1872 she sailed towards the Humber but never arrived. A week or so later an Aldeburgh smacksman who knew her well reported that he had sighted her off the north Norfolk coast flying distress signals, but she had gone down before he could reach her and there were no survivors.[3]

In 1870 the 162 Ipswich-registered sailing vessels were owned by 158 individuals, and 70 of those vessels were owned entirely by one person: since 1830 there had been a marked decline in the number of people owning ships or shares in them. As earlier, the largest group was of mariners: 59 of them were now termed 'master mariners', and the other three called themselves only 'mariners', although this trio all owned their own smacks.

Twenty-one of the master mariners were the sole owners of their vessels, and one of them, Walter Cuckow, owned two, the schooners *Competitor* and *Larch of the Morrell*, although in the registration of the latter he called himself a shipowner. (I have tried to place owners in one category only.) The others included the delightfully named Philander Garrod of the brigantine *Hedley*, one of the several Canadian-built craft at the port: she was cut down to a ketch a few years later. There was also Captain Israel Rands (Did R.L. Stevenson hear of him when writing *Treasure Island*?). His schooner *Swift* had been built for the Royal Navy at Woolwich Dockyard in 1817, but she did not come to Ipswich until Rands bought her in 1864; six years later she was lost off Heligoland.

The next largest group was of merchants of various kinds. There were 25 in all, most of them in the coal, corn or timber trades. One coal merchant, Frank Christie, was the sole owner of three vessels, the brigantines *I.O.U.* and *Star of the Sea* and the schooner *John and Margaret*. Charles Andrews, a corn merchant, was the sole owner of three barges, and six other merchants each owned a vessel entirely.

In 1870, 22 of the owners called themselves shipowners. Some were former master mariners or ex-members of other professions; others had by then passed the management of their businesses to their sons. Others yet again perhaps felt that shipping was not their principal occupation, like Ebenezer Goddard, who was the manager and engineer of the local gas company. J.C. Cobbold, who owned six vessels entirely, was another. He was at that time the head of his family, but he was mainly involved in banking and politics, whilst the corn, coal and brewing parts of the family empire were run by his eldest son, John Patteson Cobbold, who called himself a merchant in the registration of the *Constance*, of which he owned 56 shares.

Nine other individuals who may be included among the ship-owners described themselves as gentlemen, but whether they really qualified according to the standards of the time must remain an open question. One was George Deward, a member of an Ipswich family which had gone to sea for decades: he owned the whole of the schooner *Burfield Brothers* in 1870.

Other categories of people with shipping interests at that time are difficult to define, but it is probably true to say that 15 were traders or artisans of some kind and nine were members of a profession. The former included three publicans, a couple of iron-founders, a butcher, a baker and a tailor; while the professionals comprised three accountants, two shipbrokers, an auctioneer, a banker, a clerk and a schoolmaster. The banker reminds us of J.C. Cobbold and highlights the nebulous boundaries of classification. None of these professionals owned a vessel entirely, but three of the traders did: one of the publicans was William Curtis, of the *Shiplaunch* inn, soon to become a barge builder nearby while retaining his licence.

Another nine were involved in shipbuilding or allied trades. These included William Colchester, who usually described himself in the register as a merchant or shipowner, although he is best remembered today as a barge builder. Others were the brothers William and James R. Bayley, Ebenezer Robertson, and John and Alfred Lambert, all of whom had their own yards, then or soon afterwards. There were also James Hubert, who managed Colchester's yard, William Read Robertson, ship joiner, and Frederick Beaumont, a sailmaker. Of all these, Colchester was the sole owner in 1870 of seven barges – only three from his own yard

The brigantine *William Parker*, seen here lying in Ipswich Dock in front of the Custom House, was built at Wells in Norfolk in 1840. She was owned in Ipswich from 1857 until she was sold to Lowestoft in 1892, to be broken up the following year. *Suffolk Record Office*

– James Bayley and Hubert had two vessels each, and the Robertsons one apiece: the others were only part owners.

There was a solitary pilot, Charles Hadgraft, and lastly six widows. The latter seem mostly to have been the executors of their husbands' estates, and they included Mrs. Elizabeth Paul who, with her co-executors, owned one of the larger Ipswich fleets which was later, under the name of R. and W. Paul, to be the last large group of vessels owned in the port.

One class of owner which had died out after 1830 was that of farmer (see Chapter 3). After more than 20 years of prosperity – the so-called 'high farming period' – their capital was more likely to be invested in their farms and farm machinery.

By 1870 few vessels were owned by three or more individuals, and the owners were usually members of the same family or partners in business. Ipswich was by then a considerable manufacturing centre, but the principals were not shipowners. The Ransomes, for example, had rarely invested in their own ships, either to import the coal or iron they needed or to carry the agricultural machinery they produced to an increasingly worldwide market. An exception to this was in the late 1870s, when the partners in the engineering firms of Ransomes, Sims & Head, Ransomes & Rapier and E.R. & F. Turner all briefly owned a few shares in a small coasting screw steamer, the *Eider*, but it was an isolated venture. Their products could most economically be exported in large vessels from the London docks, to which they were carried by rail. The operation of such ships was a specialised business, beyond the scope of Ipswich capital.

Coasters and the railway shared the traffic in moderate quantities of imported commodities down from London, but the increasing imports of cheap grain from America and Russia arrived direct in larger ships which, since the repeal of the Navigation Acts, were sometimes under foreign flags. The first United States vessel to arrive at Ipswich with cargo was the 400-ton barque *Pamelia Flood* with wheat from New York in 1860:[4] she was expected to berth in the Wet Dock, but others were often too large for this. They would lie in Harwich Harbour or Butterman's Bay (not a bay, but a broad, deep reach of the Orwell below Pin Mill) and discharge their cargoes into barges for shipment up to the mills and maltings around the dock.

The shallow upper reaches of the river were not the only obstacles. Another hindrance was the entrance lock to the dock which was located some distance up the New Cut. Vessels had to be towed or warped up the cut and then turn to enter the lock, which was actually built more squarely to the cut than when shown on the earliest plans as a proposal. Even small coasters ran aground from time to time when making the turn, but not until 1881 was a new and larger lock made through the lower dam, in line with the natural channel of the river.

During the 1860s the elder Bayley's two sons, William and James Rogers (the latter was usually known by both his Christian names), emerged as the leading shipowners in the port. Both had been co-owners with their father, and usually with each other, of several coasters, and at least one vessel in the Mediterranean trade: she was the schooner *Queen*, built in the family yard in 1838. Most were sold off when the father's interests were disposed of. The *Queen* went to Yarmouth, probably for the salted herring trade; but after a few years she was back in Ipswich under new owners, and finished her days lumping coal down the east coast. She was lost by collision off Scarborough in 1888.

When the brothers had re-acquired those vessels which they wanted they found themselves owning jointly about a dozen coasters and most of the shares in three others, in company with the respective skippers. They continued the family business as shipbuilders, trading as William Bayley & Sons and building some vessels for themselves, such as the boomsail barges *Alpha* and *Earnest* and the remarkable flat-bottomed schooner *Problem*, with three keels. Her maiden voyage was to the Tyne, to load locomotives for Riga;[5] that was not her only voyage to the Baltic, and she later made several to Lisbon.

They owned at least two schooners in the fruit trade, the *James R. Bayley* and the *Nonpareil* (the latter built by Read). Another, the west country-built *Cassandra*, they lengthened and re-rigged in 1863 to make her the first three-masted schooner in the port and, at 206 tons, the largest. She seems to have been employed in the coal trade before she was wrecked off Felixstowe in 1872.

Earlier in that year the brothers had decided to go their separate ways and their ships were shared out. Of those which had belonged to their father, William took the schooners *Orwell* and *Alert*, while James became sole owner of the *Compass, Draper, Harriet, London Packet* and *Mary Ann*. The *Zabina* seems to have uniquely continued in their joint ownership until she was broken up in 1877. William also received the schooners *Mute*, *Nonpareil* (he later learned that she had been wrecked off the Azores only the previous day!), *Problem* and *Thought*, together with the ketches *Earnest* and *Ranger*. James took over the *Alpha, Cassandra* and *James R. Bayley*. Earlier, they had jointly owned 11 other vessels, but these had all been lost or sold before 1872: they included the 399-ton barque *Reserve*, probably the largest vessel to be registered at Ipswich during the century.

After the separation James continued as a shipowner. In addition to the vessels mentioned, he had owned the schooner *Emily* and the brig *Triumph* since the 1860s, both built by his father many years before. The *Emily*, which had been part of the Cobbold fleet before he purchased her, was wrecked in 1879. The *Triumph*, the last of all his ships, was sold to Seaham, in County Durham, in 1883.

William continued his trade as a shipbuilder and his fleet of vessels gradually declined in number. When he died in 1892 he owned only a couple of barges, *Inflexible* and *Intrepid*, both built in his yard; and an elderly brigantine, the *Arno,* which went to Cranfields, the millers, as a lighter. His son, yet another William, died only eight days after his father. He had worked in the family yard, and when it closed he carried on as a ship chandler. He owned the ketch barge *Alert* and the spritties *Albatross* and *Lady of the Wave*.

Over the last thirty years of the 19th century there was a steady decline in the numbers of schooners, brigs and brigantines. In the 1870s 32 Ipswich-registered vessels of these types were lost, mostly in the North Sea, on which they plied in the coasting and home waters trades.

The brigantine *Dauntless*, lost near Montevideo in 1877, was one of the few still employed in deep waters; and it had been only 14 years since she was built in the town. The coasters were usually older, like James Bayley's schooner *Harriet*, originally built as a sloop at Gillingham in 1801. In February, 1875, she was battling across the Thames Estuary with a cargo of scrap iron from Portland to Goole when she stranded in a blinding snowstorm. As her elderly hull began to break up, her part owner, Captain Joseph Hudson, and his crew of three took to their boat and managed to reach the Maplin lighthouse. Here they were sheltered until the weather moderated a couple of days later, when they resumed their boat journey to Southend.[6] Twenty others were sold away to other ports and nine more were hulked or broken up.

A further 15 were lost during the 1880s, including Cobbold's barquentine *Faithful*, wrecked off the mouth of the Tyne in 1881. A one-time smart little Mediterranean trader, the schooner *Visitor*, which had latterly been supplying the Ipswich gasworks, sailed into oblivion out of Seaham in November, 1888. Another east coast casualty was the schooner *Silver Cloud*, never heard of again after she left her home port for Scotland in February, 1881; one of the

Built as a sloop at Gillingham in 1801, the *Harriet* was registered at Ipswich by 1811, if not earlier. She was lengthened and rebuilt as a schooner by William Bayley in 1839, and was eventually wrecked in the Thames Estuary in 1875.

last deep draught vessels to be built in the town, she was only a couple of years old at the time of her loss. She was owned by George Morton, a local hatter. The very last round-bottomed sailing vessel to be built for a local owner was the fore-and-aft rigged schooner *Ariel*, launched in 1881, and she too lasted only a few years before being wrecked off the Northumberland coast in 1887.

Among the last Ipswich schooners to sail on deep waters was the *Snowdrop,* lost in a storm at Smoky Run on the Labrador coast in 1885. There were fears for the *Lily*, which was believed to be there also at the time, but she later arrived safely at Lisbon with her stockfish.[7]

Eleven other round-bottomed craft were sold away to other ports in the 1880s. The *Zelia* and the *John Cobbold* went to foreigners, in Colombia and Portugal respectively, and the *Fern* was sold to Adelaide. Cobbold's *Adela* was owned in Swansea for a few years before being transferred to London and re-registered there in 1890, while the barquentine *Orwell* was sold to Ireland, as

Ketch aground off the Cliff, a photograph of 1858 by Robert Burrows. *Suffolk Record Office*

we have seen. Several vessels sold to owners in other ports continued to feature in the Ipswich register, since the original requirement that a ship should be registered at her home port was by then relaxed. Conversely, some vessels purchased by Ipswich owners remained registered elsewhere.

The decline continued, and by the beginning of the 20th century only four were left. The brigantine *Anna Sarah* went missing after she left Lymington bound for Bristol in January, 1901. The schooner *Amy*, built by William Bayley way back in 1827, and owned by John Cobbold for many years, was wrecked near Yarmouth in October, 1902, and the schooner *Jessie* was hulked about 1904, but neither of these had been owned in Ipswich since the 1870s. The last round-bottomed sailing trader owned in Ipswich, the *Rose*, stranded off Felixstowe on 30th March, 1901, and the Harwich steam lifeboat *City of Glasgow* saved her crew of four. It was her first voyage since her owner, Captain William Scarf, had ceased to be her skipper.

The most important local shipowners of the last quarter of the 19th century, and indeed thereafter, were undoubtedly the Paul family. The business was established by Robert Paul (1806–1864), of whom we first hear in Ipswich as a saddler on St. Margaret's Plain: by the early 1840s he was the wharfinger of the United Shipping Company at Wherry Quay.[8]

This concern, unlike the Suffolk & Norfolk Company, did not own any vessels but was a partnership of merchants which provided quayside facilities and chartered coasters, from themselves and others, which sailed regularly with agricultural produce to Wool Quay on the Pool of London and returned with general cargo. The company had been formed in 1840 by the amalgamation of two much older syndicates, the Old Established Traders and the Crown & Sceptre Traders, and by 1853 Paul seems to have assumed overall control.[9] At that time he purchased the billyboy sloop *Sarah*, which had previously been chartered by the company, and the barge *Julia Wood*, and a few months later he acquired the iron barge *Gipping* and a second billyboy, the *John & Thomas*.

The company name was soon discarded and Robert Paul traded under his own name as a corn merchant and shipper. His business prospered, and by 1855 he was listed among the maltsters of the town.[10] At the time of his death he also owned the barges *Albert, Ann, Princess Royal* and *William*, all built at or near Newbury in Berkshire.

Robert Paul's sons, Robert (1845–1909) and William (1850–1928), were only in their teens when their father died and they did not immediately take over the business, which remained in the hands of trustees as Robert Paul & Co.[11] Under their father's will, either or both of them, having reached the age of 24 and satisfying certain conditions within the next two years or so, could inherit the ships and other capital assets of the business. It was therefore not until January, 1876, that Robert Paul's surviving vessels were registered as owned by his sons, although they were doubtless managing the business by that time: the *Sarah* had been lost in 1865, the *Gipping* sold in 1868 and the *John & Thomas* had been a lighter since 1871.

However, the business was expanding and new vessels were required. As early as April, 1868, Robert had purchased the almost-new barge *Andromeda*, but after only a couple of weeks she was transferred to the trustees, no doubt to protect her from possible creditors until her young owner had more experience in the world of business. The first vessel which Robert and William owned jointly was the barge *Champion* which they bought in 1871: they retained her, and she was followed by the *Mabel*, new from William Colchester's yard in 1875. The ketch barge *Ida*, named after William's wife, was built by William Bayley in 1881, while the sprittie *Emily*, named after Mrs. Robert Paul, was launched from the same yard in the following year.

With these vessels the Paul brothers carried on their coastal trade in corn, coal and salt – the *Ida* was built expressly for the coal trade – combined with regular sailings with general cargoes up and down from London. Direct grain imports from overseas were unloaded in Harwich Harbour or Butterman's Bay into barges and shipped to other local ports or brought up to the dock. Sometimes the Pauls shared a shipload with other Ipswich merchants, but by the end of the 1870s they were handling whole cargoes themselves.[12]

To compete more effectively with the railway in the London trade the brothers invested in their first steamer in 1886: this was the *Swift*, new from her builders at Wallsend-on-Tyne. She was evidently a success, and within the next few years the Pauls purchased three more steamships, the *Speedwell* and *Endeavour*, former Yarmouth fish carriers and trawlers, and the *Colchester*, which had been in the 'hoy' or regular trade between London and the port of her name.[13] These were less successful: the trawlers had unnecessarily powerful engines, and the *Colchester* was probably found to be too small. All were disposed of after a few years, and the *Endeavour* was not even re-registered at Ipswich.

Robert and William then decided to have new ships built to their requirements and in 1891 they took delivery of a replacement *Speedwell*, followed at yearly intervals by the *Swallow* and the *Seagull*. The first two were sold after about a dozen years, and another trio ordered: a new *Swift* in 1904, and a second *Swallow* and the *Tern* in 1905. All six ships came from the Paisley yard of John Fullerton & Co. Steel steamships had a shorter economic life than wooden sailing vessels, but for many years Pauls adopted a policy of purchasing new barges too. After the *Emily* was acquired they bought seven spritties in the remaining years of the century, six of which came straight from their builders: the *Gipping* and *Orwell* (1889), *Colne* (1890), *Stour* (1891), *Waveney* (1892) and the second *Ida* in 1895. The seventh was the *Albatross*, 24 years old when Pauls bought her in 1893, soon after the firm had become a limited company, R. & W. Paul Ltd.

Pauls, however, had quite a large fleet which did not go to sea – hulks and lighters moored in the dock in which they stored grain; others were used to ferry it up the river. One elderly hulk, the *Mary A. McKay*, was fitted with a steam-driven elevator to lift grain from vessels' holds and discharge it into barges or lighters lying alongside.

They also owned tugs, not only to tow these lighters but also to assist with berthing the ships which brought the grain. Their first tugs were the *Harwich* and the *Robert Owen*, both paddle vessels bought from Vaux, the Harwich shipbuilder. The former had been used from time to time for salvage and rescue work in the Thames Estuary, a practice which the brothers continued. Their first screw tug was the *Little England*, which they purchased in 1889, replacing her two years later with the *Garnet*. The larger paddle tug *Merrimac* was acquired in 1890, and she was long remembered in the locality because she was used for summer pleasure trips. The company's last two tugs, like their steam coasters at the time, were built for them by Fullertons: the *Spray* in 1897 and the *Foam* in 1904. They were sold in 1906 and 1912 respectively, at about the same time as many of the lighters.

R. & W. Paul even had their own shipyard when they took over the Dock End Yard in 1901. Here they built six barges for themselves, beginning with the *Marjorie* in 1902 and ending with the *Jock* in 1908. The two newest at the time, *Hilda* and *Ena*, were renamed *Gravelines I* and *Gravelines II* respectively in 1906 and chartered to a French owner until 1912.[14] Upon their return the

Shipping in Ipswich Dock in 1890 photographed by Charles Emeny. The large vessel on the left has perhaps brought a cargo of barley from the Black Sea, and the brig lying with its head to the quay in the middle of the picture is possibly unloading timber from the Baltic. *Robert Malster*

latter was renamed *Bijou*, but her sister kept her French name for the rest of her life: in the meantime the company had acquired a new *Hilda* and a new *Ena*.

During the First World War the steamer *Seagull* was mined in the English Channel and a little later, taking advantage of the high price commanded by ships of all kinds, Pauls sold the *Swallow* and the *Swift* to a pair of shipowners in Grimsby. To the same purchasers went four barges, including the veteran *Albatross*, and also the *Mary A. McKay* with its steam elevator. In 1916 the company had the coasting steamer *Oxbird* built at Yarmouth by Crabtree & Co.

After the war the hoy trade to London had all but disappeared, but Pauls' ships were kept busy by the company's branches at Hull, Kings Lynn, Yarmouth and elsewhere. New steamers were acquired: the *Crossbill*, also new from Crabtrees in 1920, the *Oarsman* and *Coniscrag*, the latter being the company's first ship with triple expansion engines. In 1929 Pauls added the *Glynconwy* to their fleet, renaming her *Goldcrest*; and their last and largest ship was the *Firecrest*, built for them by John Lewis & Sons of Aberdeen in the same year. The *Oarsman* was lost in 1932, whilst crossing from Rotterdam in storm conditions, and the *Coniscrag* and *Goldcrest* were sold in the following couple of years.

Raising the gear on Pauls' barge *Anglia* at Dock End Yard.

A few new barges were added to Pauls' fleet in later years, notably the two large steel vessels *Aidie* and *Barbara Jean*, both built by Aldous of Brightlingsea in 1924. Both were lost at Dunkirk in 1940, together with the *Doris*, but the company's *Ena* and *Tollesbury*, which also took part in the evacuation of the British Expeditionary Force, returned safely.

Small steamers with their disproportionately large crews were by now becoming increasingly uneconomic, so the *Crossbill* was sold in 1944, followed by the aging *Oxbird* in 1946. The *Firecrest* was the last to go, sold to Irvings of Sunderland in 1952; she was by then the port's last steam trading vessel. Similarly, a number of the company's sailing barges were fitted with diesel engines in the post-war years, but all except one had been disposed of by the mid 1970s. Many of the company's outstations had by then been closed, and the all-conquering lorry was making inroads into the coastal trade. Ironically, the engineless spritsail barge, with her low overheads, was still basically economic but had become an anachronism in a business world of tight time schedules. There was difficulty, too, in finding young men as mates, willing to have their working hours determined by the winds and tides rather than by the clock. Pauls' last barge to carry cargo under sail alone was the *Anglia*, which was also the last they acquired, in 1940. Although Ipswich-built in 1898, she was never registered at the port of her birth, and in 1961 she was sold for conversion to a yacht.

From first to last, the Pauls, and the company they founded, owned 44 barges, two billyboys, 16 steam coasters, two steam tenders, seven tugs and about 30 hulks and lighters.

Apart from R. & W. Paul, the fertilizer manufacturers Edward Packard & Co. also operated sailing barges and steam coasters in the latter part of the 19th century, but in smaller numbers. The company was founded by Edward Packard (1819–1899), who was one of the pioneers of superphosphate fertilizers in this country. After obscure beginnings in the Suffolk village of Snape, he established a plant on the dockside at Ipswich in 1851. The principal raw material was coprolite, dug from various local sites and brought in by barge.[15]

The first barge owned by Packard was the *Fossil*, built at Blackfriars in London in 1853 and purchased four years later. He probably renamed her, as it seems too much of a coincidence that her original name should so accurately describe the basis of his product. It is equally strange that the registration of the *Fossil* should describe Packard as a barge builder of Blackwall: this probably refers to the vendor, erroneously entered by the registrar.

Primary sources are not always strictly accurate. He was not her sole owner, since her skipper, William Bell of Harwich, owned eight shares, and he later moved to Ipswich to become ship's husband of the firm's barges. The *Fossil* was followed by the *Ammonite* (1859), *Dewdrop* (1867) and *Nautilus* (1870), all newly built and all partly owned by Bell.

Packard's business grew. He made his own sulphuric acid and within a few years he was having to import most of his raw materials. Very soon his dockside premises, by the aptly-named Coprolite Street, were too small; also the Corporation disapproved of his malodorous processes in a densely populated area. In 1854 the manufactory was relocated to Bramford, a few miles up the canalised River Gipping, although the dockside premises were retained for storage purposes, whence the fertilizers were shipped away in coasters. The movement of raw materials and finished products between Ipswich and Bramford was mainly by rail, but by the mid 1860s the railway company was in financial difficulties and its services were in a deplorable state.

One of Packard's steam barges on the River Gipping in the early 20th century.

Packard decided to transfer all his traffic to the river navigation and invested in a steam barge. Remarkably, this vessel was designed by his son, Edward junior, who was also in the business: he seems to have had a feel for ships, as he was, later at least, a keen yachtsman. The barge was built of iron at Hull and arrived in Ipswich in June, 1868, towed by the steamer *Speedwell*: she was fitted with twin screws, the engines for which were reported to be coming from the Ipswich firm of E.R. & F. Turner.[16] All this was most unusual at that time. Steam barges on inland waters were generally regarded as uneconomic because of the space occupied by the machinery; speed was in any case limited to protect the banks, although the twin screws may have been intended to reduce the wash.

Later, Packards were said to have owned several steam barges on the Gipping, but few details are recorded. According to those who remembered them, the first was named *Orwell*, and most of them had black funnels. They had non-condensing engines, since most of their passages were in fresh water, and they were known, presumably after 1906, as 'Packard's dreadnoughts'.

Two of these steam barges were registered: the *Stour* (1905) and the *Trent River* (1916), both from the Ipswich yard of Orvis. The latter is known to have had a white funnel with a black top, and the *Stour* probably had one too, to match the company's coasting steamers. Both were wooden vessels fitted with small tandem compound engines, and both were probably employed from time to time in towing lighters up and down the estuary to Butterman's Bay. The *Stour* was reduced to a lighter about 1931, while the *Trent River*, which, as far as I can ascertain, was the last cargo carrier to be built in Ipswich, must have put to sea to go to her last recorded owner, a contractor at Haddiscoe in Norfolk, in 1938. She was broken up, probably during the Second World War.

Like R. & W. Paul, Packards also owned steam coasters, carrying partly their own goods and partly general cargo, usually between Ipswich, Hull and Newcastle. They were all registered as owned by Packard's sons, Edward junior and Henry, who took over the management when their father retired and converted the firm into a limited company about 1895.

The coasters operated as the Ipswich Steam Shipping Company. The first was the *Dartmoor*, of 154 nett registered tons, compound engined, which came new from her builders, Edwards & Symes of Cubitt Town, in 1882. In the following year the brothers bought the *Sedgemoor* from Cardiff owners; of 112 nett tons, she had been built by Schlesinger, Davis & Co. of Wallsend in 1872 and was fitted with only a simple expansion engine. Packard's third steamer was the *Exmoor*, purchased from Glasgow in 1885. She had been built at Preston in 1883 as the *Briton,* of 234 nett tons, and the Packard brothers soon renamed her to fit in with the names of their other ships. In 1889 they went back to Schlesingers to take delivery of another new vessel, the *Ringmoor* of 134 nett tons, which was propelled by a triple-expansion engine.

The coasting steamers of the Packard brothers were dogged by ill luck, however, for within a few years three of these vessels had been lost. Early in May, 1888, the *Exmoor* foundered in heavy weather in the North Sea, whilst on passage from Ipswich to Libau with superphosphate:[17] superstitious people may have recalled the old belief that it is unlucky to change a ship's name. Then, in October, 1890, the *Dartmoor* was lost by collision in fog off Filey in Yorkshire, on her way to Newcastle with flour and burnt ore.[18] Less than a year later, in August, 1891, the *Sedgemoor* sprang a leak in a gale whilst on passage from Goole to Ghent with coal. With her boiler fires extinguished several hours previously and the crew pumping by hand, the doomed vessel was sighted by the steamer *Hecla* of Hartlepool, but she was unable to take the *Sedgemoor* in tow as she was short of bunker coal and had no suitable hawser. Captain Turner gallantly refused her offer to take his people off, but about five hours later he was obliged to order his ship to be abandoned. The crew were picked up by a French fishing vessel after a further three hours and landed at Ostend.[19] Happily there was no loss of life in any of these events.

Shortly before this last disaster Packards had purchased the *Onyx*, of 179 nett registered tons: she had been built at Dumbarton in 1883, and perhaps significantly she was not given a *Moor* name. Their next acquisition was the *Winifred* of 149 nett tons in 1894, new from Rennoldsons of South Shields. The *Ringmoor* was disposed of to London owners in 1896, and the *Onyx* was sold to Swansea in 1903 and was replaced by the *Woodland* of 108 nett tons, newly built at Grangemouth. The *Winifred* and the *Woodland* continued trading to the Humber and the north east coast.

In 1911 the Ipswich Steam Shipping Company was converted into a limited liability one, and its last vessel was the *Shotton*, of 110 nett tons and built at Selby in 1909, which was purchased in 1913 to replace the *Woodland* when she was sold to Cardiff. The last pair was disposed of during the First World War. Incidentally, the company had no connection with the later Ipswich Steamship Company, which was owned by the Horlock family at Mistley.

The barge *Dewdrop* had been run down in the Swin in 1889.

The spritsail barge *Flower of Essex* in the Lower Hope, *c.*1938. Built by Peck in 1890, she was owned by Cranfield Bros. from 1927 to 1947.

The brothers bought out Bell at the time the firm became a limited company, and disposed of their other barges after the First World War. The last to go was the *Ammonite*, broken up in 1934.

Space does not permit a mention of every Ipswich vessel but the story of one, the *Paradox*, is unusual. She had been built as a yacht, a lugger with auxiliary steam power, at Eastbourne in 1889 – presumably on the beach like the local fishing boats, although she was considerably larger. She was 70ft. long, of 61 gross tons and she was fitted with a vertical tandem compound engine, not much more powerful than those in Packard's river barges. Later she became an auxiliary ketch-rigged coaster out of Southampton, and on at least one occasion she brought moulding sand to Ipswich and left with fertilizer. By 1909 her skipper, Captain Walter Jackson, was also her owner and he moved her to Ipswich, his native town.

Jackson then promoted a company, Arctic Enterprises Ltd, to recover seal produce left on Baffin Island by a former employer of his who, he said, had authorised him to recover it and dispose of it on a commission basis. Trade with the Eskimos was also intended. As a young man, Jackson had had considerable experience of the

Cranfield's barge *Spinaway C* taking part in the Blackwater barge match in 1962, with several laid-up tankers in the background. *Robert Malster*

Arctic, both in whaling and trading, but a traumatic enforced over-wintering with scant supplies seems to have affected his judgement and he was later blamed for the company's misfortunes.

He vested the *Paradox* in the company in return for a third of the shares: another third was taken up by a Captain Skellern of Cardiff, who was to command the ship, with Jackson as ice master and supercargo. The other subscribers were two Ipswich business-men, a London solicitor and various members of the crew.

The ship sailed from Dundee on 23rd June, 1909, but about five weeks later she was trapped by ice and damaged at the entrance to the Hudson Strait, between Baffin Island and Labrador. After several days they were sighted by the Hudson's Bay Company's ship *Pelican*, which took off the crew and towed the *Paradox* to Churchill, at the southern end of Hudson's Bay, where she later sank at her moorings after the crew had left.

Two years later Arctic Enterprises sued the Hudson's Bay Company for converting the *Paradox* and her cargo to their own use; but judgement was given for the defendants, who counter-claimed for salvage. Jackson's Arctic enterprise was a disaster.[20]

As we have seen, some of R. & W. Paul's barges survived in trade until the second half of the 20th century, a distinction shared by another Ipswich company, Cranfield Brothers Ltd, the millers. The vessels of both were always smart and well maintained so that, with other craft from away, the port was generally considered to be the best place to see barges in the closing years of sail. Cranfields was not established until 1884 and they did not own any barges until shortly before the First World War. In the 1930s they had 14, but only six were registered at Ipswich, viz: *Felix*, *Flower of Essex*, *Kimberley*, *May*, *Petrel* and *Spinaway C*. Most of the others had originally been built for Harwich owners, and they remained registered there: latterly it was very rare for barges to be re-registered at another port. Their work was mainly bringing wheat down from London, interspersed with spells of lightering from grain ships in the Orwell, or the dock, up to the company's mill at the dock head.

By 1960 Cranfield's fleet was reduced to three pure sailormen, as sailing barges without auxiliary power were colloquially termed: *May*, *Spinaway C* and *Venture*. The *May* was named after my father's cousin who was born in 1891, shortly before the barge was launched from Cann's yard at Harwich. Her father, Captain John Hooker of Ipswich, owned half the shares in the barge, sharing ownership with members of the well-known Haste family until the vessel was sold to Cranfields in 1912. *Venture* was the last Ipswich-

The barque *Abraham Rydberg* in Ipswich Dock in 1939. The third, and best, of the very first photographs taken by the author with a borrowed Box Brownie.

owned vessel to trade under sail, in June, 1960, and Cranfield's remaining motor barges were all sold within the next ten years or so.

Apart from owning the last Ipswich cargo carrier under sail, Cranfield's other claim to fame in the story of the port was that the company was instrumental in bringing the last of the big square-rigged ships into the Orwell, with wheat from Australia. By that time, these were not even British vessels: most were owned by Captain Gustav Erikson and were registered at Mariehamn in the Aland Islands. The first was the *Melbourne* in 1931, followed by the *C.B. Pedersen* and the *Winterhude* in 1932. Five others followed in the next four years, but the *Herzogin Cecilie*, having received her orders at Falmouth, was wrecked near Bolt Head, Devon, in 1936 and never arrived in Ipswich. The very last was the four-masted barque *Abraham Rydberg* in 1939, and I am pleased to recollect that the very first photographs I ever took were of her in the Wet Dock.[21]

Almost all the vessels registered at Ipswich in later years have been yachts: these have generally been disregarded in this account, but two should be mentioned.

Edward Keble Chatterton was a prolific writer on ships and the sea, and three of his books were about his cruises in his $5\frac{1}{2}$-ton yawl *Charmina*, which had been built at Cantley, Norfolk, in 1923. Her original name was *Charmian*, but Keble Chatterton renamed her when he bought her in 1928. He made at least one passage to the Mediterranean in her, and kept her until 1944, only about a year before he died.

The most famous, and certainly the largest, Ipswich yacht was undoubtedly Alan Villiers' *Joseph Conrad*, in which he sailed round the world as recounted in his book, *The Cruise of the Conrad*. She was a full-rigged ship, built at Copenhagen in 1882 as the schoolship *Georg Stage* for a private trust from which Villiers bought her in 1934. His intention, in his own words, was to man her with youngsters who would profit from the experience of sailing her, but she could not be registered as a schoolship as he had no formal qualifications to command her. To his great disgust, he had to register her as a yacht.

He sailed her from Ipswich, via New York, Rio de Janeiro, Cape Town and Australia back to New York where, with his funds exhausted, he was obliged to sell her in 1936. Probably the last-ever full-rigged ship registered at a U.K. port to round Cape Horn, the *Joseph Conrad* is now preserved at Mystic Seaport in Connecticut, U.S.A.

Shipbuilding 6

In the early 17th century the shipbuilding industry in England was centred on the Thames and the ports of East Anglia. Ipswich was then a major shipbuilding centre, but unfortunately we know little of its yards at that time. It was not until the 18th century that sufficient records were created, and have survived, to enable a reasonably complete picture to be put together: land tax returns, lease agreements, parish rate books, registers of ships, reliable maps and pictures and, not least, newspapers.

Daniel Defoe has described how, before the 17th-century wars against the Dutch, Ipswich was the leading port in England where ships in the east coast coal trade were built and owned, but he did not tell us how many yards there were. Unfortunately for Suffolk, large numbers of Dutch war prizes flooded the market and the demand for new ships declined. It has been suggested that when the market revived the builders in Suffolk were too conservative and unenterprising to build the larger ships which owners, with their experience of the Dutch vessels, were finding more economical; and the trade passed to the shipyards of Whitby, Scarborough, and the rivers of the north east.

The old St. Clement's shipyards, showing the *Biddeford* in Barnard's yard and a sizeable vessel in frame on Goodea's yard, from John Cleveley's *Prospect of Old Ipswich*. Note that both these ships are being built with their bows towards the water. The L-shaped building behind the right-hand vessel moored to the quay features in Pennington's map and other early plans. *Ipswich Borough Council Museums and Galleries.*

It is probable that the estuaries of Suffolk, with their shallow, tortuous channels and their shifting bars, were the real reason for the decline. Even so, Ipswich remained an important shipbuilding centre. An indication of the nation's most productive building ports is provided by an analysis of *Lloyd's Register* for 1776.[1] Of the home-built total of 561,563 tons, 41,435 tons had been built in yards described only as 'British', or in some cases as a 'King's Yard'. Many vessels, of course, would not have been included at all, but the *Register* gives an interesting comparison between those shipbuilding centres which were identified.

In England, the 12 leading centres with more than 10,000 tons of shipping to their credit were as follows:

	Total tonnage	No. of vessels	Average tonnage
'River' (Thames), including Blackwall, Deptford and London	92,661	299	310
Whitby	77,355	253	306
Hull	39,630	202	196
Liverpool	36,465	245	149
Scarborough	26,410	105	252
Yarmouth	22,275	184	121
Bristol	21,595	114	189
Newcastle	18,136	82	221
Ipswich	13,075	81	161
Whitehaven	12,380	76	163
Sunderland	12,265	63	195
Stockton	11,230	61	184

In Scotland the leading centre was Leith, with 98 vessels totalling 9,750 tons: the Clyde, represented by Glasgow and Greenock, was credited with only 2,260 tons. From Wales the total tonnage was 13,740, but in most cases the ports where the 188 vessels had been built were not specified.

Lloyd's Register showed that most of the vessels from the Thames-side yards and from Whitby were ship-rigged, and a large part of the tonnage from the other centres was in brigs and snows. The lower average tonnage in Yarmouth and Ipswich was because more sloops were built there than almost anywhere else, apart from Emsworth in Hampshire; much of the foreign trade of East Anglia was to the shallow harbours of the Netherlands, and East Anglian yards specialised in such craft. On the other hand, 26 full-rigged ships were listed as built at Ipswich, as against 19 at Yarmouth, 20 at Newcastle, 11 at Whitehaven, 13 at Sunderland and 15 at

Stockton. The Orwell builders supplied owners in other ports, but they often had difficulty in launching their ships and floating them away.

Later at least, they were certainly not unenterprising. Two Ipswich builders managed to enter the exclusive circle of those who built for the prestigious trade of the Honourable East India Company, although precisely how they contrived to do so is a mystery. Others built steamers and were among the pioneers in constructing vessels of iron.

We have few details of how they ran their businesses. One early 19th-century builder, the younger George Bayley, has left some autobiographical notes covering the earlier part of his life, which have been used as the basis for an excellent article in *The Mariner's Mirror*.[2] Certainly many earlier builders became insolvent. To build or repair wooden ships it was essential to hold large stocks of timber, as well seasoned as possible: this

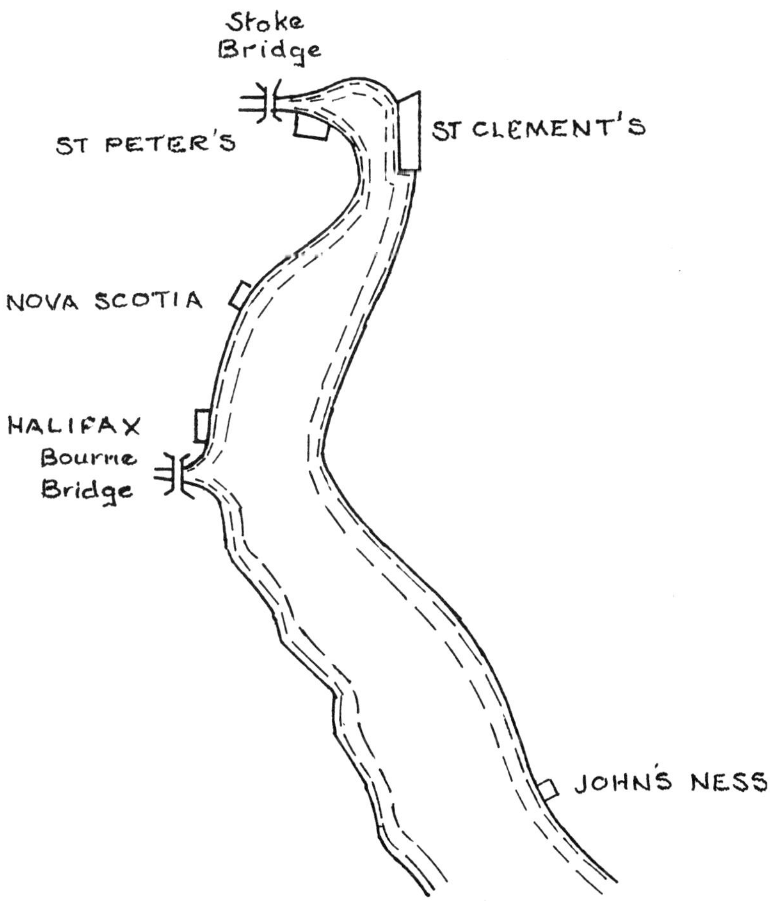

The 18th-century shipyards, including the downriver site at John's Ness.

represented a considerable investment, even though builders often received a payment of 20% or so of the contract sum as soon as an order was placed. The alternative left the builder at the mercy of an uncertain and highly competitive market in this vital raw material.

On the other hand, others, such as the William Bayleys, father and son, survived for years with the cost of many vessels which they built or reconstructed advanced on mortgage to their customers. The registration of ships provided the means for recording the debts on the vessels, and increased prosperity in the 19th century enabled the builders to provide the capital.

In Ipswich the principal shipyards were in three parishes. Firstly there was a group in St. Clement's, between Duke Street and the left bank of the Orwell, which moved to the vicinity of the Cliff when the Wet Dock was built. A second group was in St. Peter's parish, on the right bank of the river just below Stoke Bridge, whilst the Nova Scotia and the Halifax yards were in the parish of St. Mary Stoke. Occasionally a vessel was built at John's Ness (also sometimes known as King John's Ness), lower down the river, and at least two barges were launched from a timber yard above Stoke Bridge, but there is no evidence that either site was in continuous use as a shipyard.

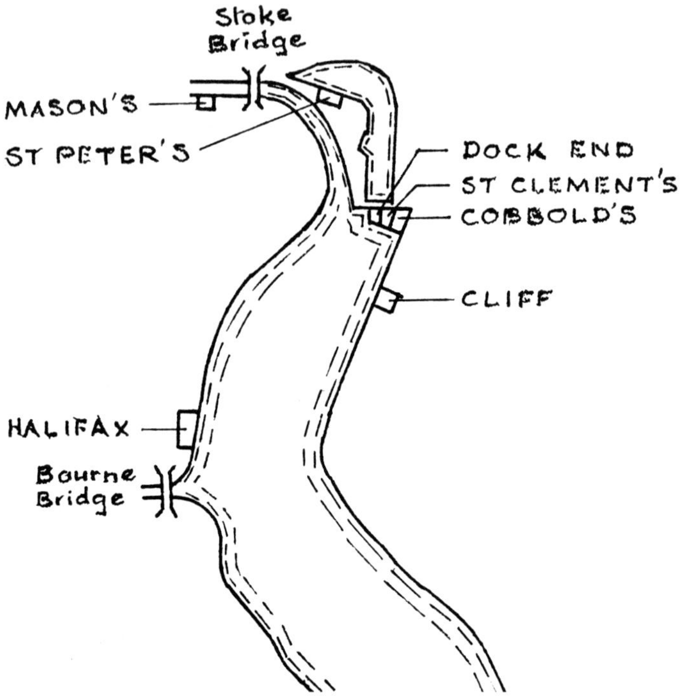

The 19th-century shipyards after the opening of the Wet Dock in 1842.

The Old St. Clement's yards 7

For several hundred years the principal shipbuilding area in the port was undoubtedly in the parish of St. Clement, just at the eastern end of the town wharves where the river turned sharply to the south and the channel was close inshore. It was probably also the oldest site of the industry: the earliest vessel known to have been built at Ipswich was a galley for Edward I in 1295, of which one of the builders was a certain Philip Harneys who had a shipyard at Ding Quay in St. Clement's parish.[1]

Three shipyards next to each other are shown on Pennington's map of Ipswich of 1778, and yards of roughly the same shapes and areas are depicted on Ogilby's of 1674. Land adjoining the northern side of the group was certainly a shipyard later, and later still two more were established on land reclaimed to the south. These yards may conveniently be referred to as Numbers 1 to 6, beginning at the northern end: all of them lay well within the limits of the present Wet Dock.

Careful superimposition of an 1836 plan of the proposed dock upon a modern 1/2500 scale Ordnance Sheet shows that the northern boundary of yard No. 2 coincides with the building line on the northern side of the present Coprolite Street, and that the stone-built wall of the River Commissioners' ballast wharf of 1810, which was to the south of all the shipyards, survived projecting from the brick quay wall of the dock, in front of Ransomes' old Orwell Works, until it disappeared under the present Orwell Quay in 1968.

A plan drawn by John Bransby, a well-known local surveyor, in 1811 indicates that yards Nos. 1 and 2 were copyhold land of the Manor of Wix Bishop.[2] A surviving indenture of 1728 relates to the lease for 21 years of two shipyards in the parish by Edmund Goody, shipwright, from Arthur Barnardiston of Brightwell Hall, a member of an old Suffolk family, who was also Lord of the Manor of Wix Bishop.[3] The shipwright, incidentally, signed himself as 'Goodea', but others usually misspelt his name. The leased property comprised an empty tenement, an anchorsmith's and a smith's shop – both occupied – and a cottage then occupied by one William Wright. 'And also two Keys and Keyyards thereunto

A plan of the old St. Clement's shipyards c.1830, based on a modern dyeline print in the author's collection from an 1836 tracing by John Bransby. Not all the yards were extant at the same time: No. 5 and the area to the south were reclaimed in the years after 1808, by which time No.1 was no longer used as a shipyard.

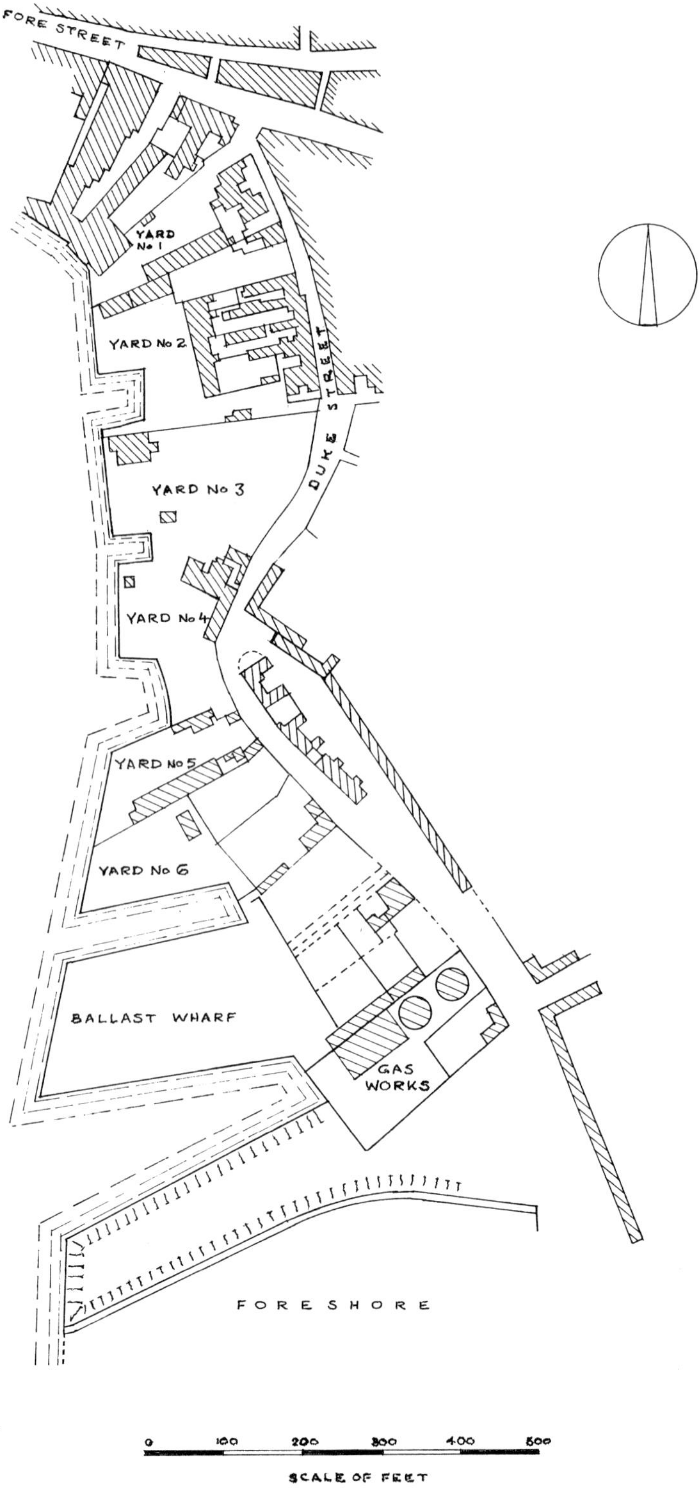

belonging with one Dock lying between. And also all that Yard Key and Dock late in the possession of Mary Barnard Widow and now in the occupacion of the said Edmund Goody, all which premisses are abutted upon the Chanell flowing from bone Bridge towards the Common Key of Ipswich aforesaid on the part of the West and upon the Highway leading from the Cock Corner to the Southernmost part of the said premisses on the part of the East and on a yard Bond of the Manor of Wix Bishop belonging to Isaac Sutton in the present occupacion of John Clemens on the part of the North…'. (Bourne Bridge, on the opposite side of the river, was here referred to as 'bone' Bridge.)

In the churchwardens' rates for the parish for 1727 the lands included 'Mrs Wright's Shipyard', valued at £6 per annum, and Goodea's shipyard at £2; in the following year there appeared only Goodea's yard at £8. It is clear that Goodea, the occupier of the yard referred to in these pages as No. 4, had taken over No. 3.

Mary Barnard was the widow of John Barnard, a shipwright whose will survives. It was made on Christmas Day, 1716, and in it Barnard left all his property to his wife Mary, including 'all that my lands and yard commonly called the Dock Yard together with the Wharfe, Launch, Dock, Key…which I lately purchased of Thomasin Bloomfield and Mary Hubbert'. Barnard was buried in the parish churchyard on 3rd January, 1716/17.

Mrs. Wright's shipyard had been mentioned in the parish poor rate assessments for some 20 years previously. In 1709 her shipyard was occupied by John Barnard, Walter Clements (or Clemens) and John Birchett, but in 1707 Barnard had been the only occupier mentioned; at other times none was listed, but the yard was never described as empty. During this period the Land Tax assessments show Mrs. Wright as owning land in the parish with an estimated annual value totalling £12, occupied by Richard Cole and others; this must have included the shipyard.

Earlier, in 1702, it was a Mr. Wright who owned the land, as he had in 1689,[4] with Cole always mentioned as a tenant. Richard Cole was a fairly affluent shipwright, owning agricultural land in the Suffolk villages of Offton and Willisham, but when he made his will in 1710 he had no transferable tenure in a shipyard. He died in 1712. For many years 'William Wright, shipwright' lived somewhere in the parish of St. Clement: he may have been the man who lived near the yard in 1728, but he did not own it. Both Wrights and Coles had built large ships in the town in Elizabethan and early Stuart times,[5] but whether either family did so in this No.3 yard at a later period I do not know.

John Barnard was first assessed for rates in St. Clement's parish in 1704, for a modest shilling. For a couple of years he was then assessed for 'Mr. Hubbard's Yard', valued at £10 per annum, in addition to a dwelling; then he was in Mrs. Wright's shipyard. By 1710 he owned his own dockyard, valued at £2 per annum: this must have been the No. 4 yard, purchased from Hubbard's estate, since Mrs. Wright owned, and continued to own, the adjacent No. 3.

This Hubbard was William Hubbard, who is known to have been working in St. Clement's parish in 1689, occupying a house and yard owned by one John Luscoe and valued at £3 per annum; probably yard No. 4.[6] By 1702 he owned land and yards valued at £26 per annum in the hamlet of Wix Bishop (an ancient name by which the whole of this riverside area was sometimes known), as well as property elsewhere in the parish, on the 'South Side' (of Fore Street, in St. Clement's parish?). He was also taxed on 'Vendible Stock' valued at £50, and his poor rate assessment was on the highest scale in the parish: he was obviously one of the wealthiest inhabitants.

We know something of his work, for in 1695 he built the small fifth-rate *Milford* for the Navy Board, and a bill of sale has recently come to light that records the name of a 300-ton merchantman, the *Prosperous Mary*, 'built by Mr. J. Wm. Hubbert att Ipswich' at about the same date. The other ship which he built for the navy was the *Greyhound*, a larger fifth-rate, in 1703. She was too large to be floated at St. Clement's and was therefore built at John's Ness, about three miles further downstream.[7] There is evidence to suggest that Hubbard's wife was handling the business before the *Greyhound* was completed:[8] William himself was buried on 31st October, 1704.

After John Barnard's death his business, too, may well have been carried on by his widow, Mary, which would explain how their son John, born about 1705, was later said to have supplied men and materials from his shipyard to help build a Dissenters' chapel in the town.[9] We know that she had left the yard by 1728, when Goodea was in occupation.

Goodea may have been Barnard's foreman, helping the widow to run the business: the younger John Barnard was apprenticed to him in 1723.[10] 'Edmund Goodey, Shipwright' can be traced back to 1718 in the rating assessments, and there were others of the name in the trade earlier. He was never able to raise the capital to buy a yard of his own, but in 1728 he expanded his business into the adjoining yard No. 3, as we have seen, and continued until his death in 1756. The name of at least one vessel that he built is known: the 70-ton sloop *William and Mary*, 'lately built by me', which he sold, unrigged, to William Cole, a Colchester merchant, for £305 in 1741. Goodea was married twice, in 1726 and 1739, but when he drew up his will in 1754 the only relatives mentioned were his sisters, a nephew and a niece.[11]

The lease agreement shows that the copyhold yard on the northern side (No. 2) was owned by Isaac Sutton and occupied by John Clemens in 1728. Both names were listed among those of former Ipswich shipbuilders in a song sheet and pamphlet published to commemorate the launch of the *Orwell* East Indiaman in 1817.[12] Sutton's father, Isaac senior, had certainly been among the more prosperous townsmen of his day. When he died in 1722 he left land in the Suffolk villages of Coddenham and Creeting St. Mary to his wife Thomasine, and several properties in the parish of St. Clement to his son Isaac: these included the house in Wix Bishop Hamlet in which he lived, with his shipyards adjoining, 'one of which shipyards I purchased of Richard Horner, all which shipyards are now in the occupacon of John Clemens my son in law'. The use of the plural may indicate that he owned yard No. 1 as well as No. 2, but I have not been able to identify No. 1 separately before 1788. On the other hand, it may just indicate that No. 2 had been sub-divided earlier, as Ogilby's map suggests.

At the beginning of the century Clemens was assessed for rates at only a low figure, but in 1707 he occupied a 'house and yard' charged at the same figure as Sutton, whose assessment fell at the same time. Perhaps this was when he took over yard No. 2 from his father-in-law: he had married Sarah Sutton in 1695.[13] Clemens died in 1729 and the No. 2 yard was briefly occupied by one Cornelius Goldsbury, but for what purpose is now unknown. In 1730 he was followed by John Darley, who was described as a shipbuilder when he died four years later: Isaac Sutton was one of his executors, and he had three sons, one of whom later built ships at Woodbridge.

We know little of the activities of these men. The shipbuilding industry in East Anglia had declined sharply since the time of Charles II, but even if there was little demand for new ships there was always work available in repairing and refitting the coasters which brought in coal or took away the local agricultural produce.

In 1734 John Barnard the younger established in the No. 2 yard what was to become the best-known and most successful shipbuilding business in the town during the 18th century. He had first appeared in the rating assessments in 'The Hamblitt' (of Wix Bishop) in 1728, when his name replaced that of 'Widow Barnard'; perhaps he took over as householder from his mother when he married. Mary Barnard died in March, 1734. He purchased the copyhold of the yard from Sutton's executors in 1738 and subsequently enlarged it by buying small pieces of adjoining manorial land.

An intriguing item, copied from a London newspaper, appeared in the *Ipswich Journal* on 29th September, 1739:

> Yesterday a Boat of about three Tons Burthen, of a new Device, built by Mr Barnard, according to the Direction of Col. Fuller, was hoisted by Slings off a Wharf near the *Falcon* in the Presence of the Right Hon. The Lords of the Admiralty, the Commissioners of the Navy and many other Gentlemen curious and skill'd in the Art of Navigation. She is built in so particular a Manner that she cannot sink, tho' full of Water, but will clear herself. But there not being Depth of Water enough, she stuck upon a Pile, and stove a Hole in her Bottom; whereby the whole Design was defeated.

It is tempting to believe that this boat – which must surely have been the world's first lifeboat, ante-dating the designs of Lukin, Greathead and Would have by some 50 years – was built by John Barnard, perhaps in Ipswich. If so, it may have brought him to the notice of the authorities, for within a few weeks Barnard received

This painting by John Cleveley the Elder is dated 1758 and entitled *Launch of a Sixth Rate on the Orwell*. It shows the *Biddeford* being towed to Harwich and, beyond, the *Hampshire* on the ways at John's Ness. The unrigged ship at anchor in the foreground is the bomb ketch *Granado*; the relative lengths of her channels shows that she is to be ketch rigged, and the *Granado* was the only vessel of her kind at this time to have a full stern with windows. It is probable that this painting and perhaps Cleveley's other one of Ipswich were commissioned by John Barnard. © *National Maritime Museum, London*

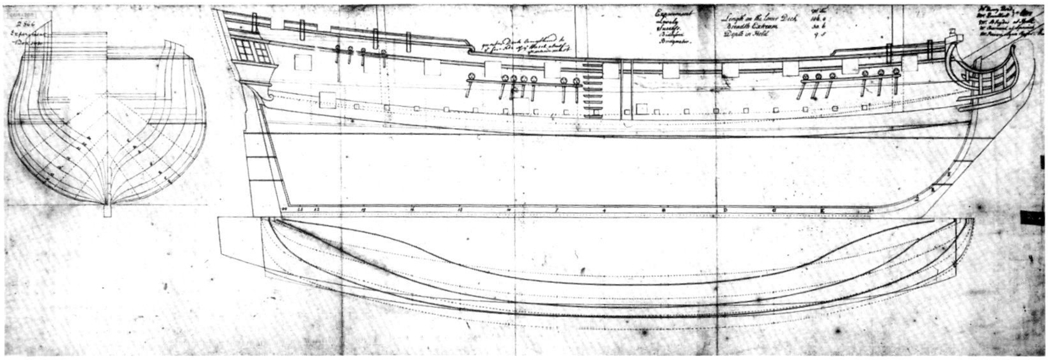

The draught of HMS *Experiment* (1740). The *Biddeford* was a sister ship, and the drawing is endorsed to the effect that a copy has been, or will be, sent to 'Mr. Barnard at Ipswich'. © *National Maritime Museum, London*

an order to build a 24-gun ship for the Royal Navy, part of an expansion programme necessitated by the imminence of war with Spain.

This ship was the *Biddeford*, launched from yard No. 2 on 15th June, 1740, and towed down the Orwell to be rigged at the former navy yard at Harwich.[14] She was a sixth-rate of 433 tons, built according to the Establishment, or specification, proposed in 1733. John Cleveley's *Prospect of Ipswich* shows the ship on the ways and in the same picture, in the artistic manner of the time, also being towed away down the river. Although painted in 1753, by which date the design of such ships had long been altered, the ship in the painting corresponds almost exactly with the draught of the *Biddeford*, which still survives in the National Maritime Museum at Greenwich.

In April, 1740, Barnard secured an order to build a larger warship, the fourth-rate *Hampshire* of 50 guns. She was too large to float away from his St. Clement's yard so, as Hubbard had done with the *Greyhound*, he built her at John's Ness, where the channel turned sharply across the river so that a vessel could be launched into the length of Back Again Reach. Measuring 854 tons, the *Hampshire* was launched on 13th November, 1741, and towed to Harwich to be rigged.[15]

Barnard also built a bomb vessel for the navy, the *Granado*, launching her on 22nd June, 1742: as she was quite a small vessel, of 267 tons, she was probably built at the St. Clement's yard. She, like the others, was towed to Harwich to be rigged.[16] In an age when many British warships succumbed to the ordinary perils of the sea, and most of the others were broken up when they became obsolete or too rotten for further service, the *Granado* was refitted for the merchant service after she was sold out of the navy in 1763. Renamed *Prince Frederick*, she was engaged in the West India trade.[17]

A portrait of Sir Thomas Slade by an unknown artist. Slade was Master Shipwright at Deptford when he was appointed joint Surveyor of the Navy in 1755. During a most successful career, he was largely responsible for introducing 74-gun ships and the classic frigate. © *National Maritime Museum, London*

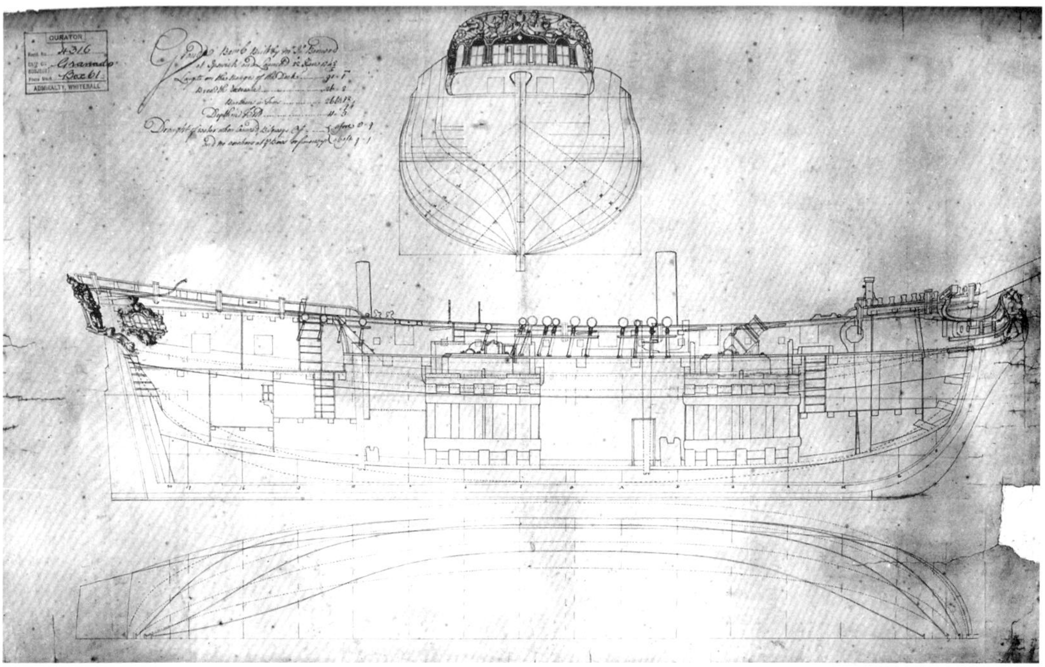

The draught of HMS *Granado*. Although the designer of the *Granado* is unknown, the drawing shows several features of the ship in considerable detail, e.g. her decoration and the mounting of her mortars. © *National Maritime Museum, London*

After building the *Granado*, Barnard leased the Harwich navy yard from the Crown and built many ships there, entering into partnership with John Turner of Ipswich in about 1755.[18] He continued to reside in the parish of St. Clement, and when he established his own business in 1734 he moved to a larger house near the shipyard, adding a warehouse, two timberhills (for storage), an orchard, a couple of stables and even a coach-house as the years passed. Pennington's map of the town shows the extent of his grounds by 1778. His shipyard nearby seems to have been used mainly as a timber yard and for the sale of left overs from the contracts at Harwich but, in peace time at least, he built some vessels there, such as the buss *Harcourt* for the Society of the Free British Fishery at Southwold in 1752,[19] and doubtless some of the ships listed as Ipswich-built in this period.

The memorial to Sir Thomas Slade in St. Clement's churchyard, Ipswich. Slade married Hannah Moore of Ipswich at Nacton Church in 1747. She died in 1763 and was buried with her parents at St. Clement's, being described in the burial register and on the surviving tombstone as 'wife of Thomas Slade, Surveyor of His Majesty's Navy'. Slade himself, by then Sir Thomas, died at Bath on 24th February, 1771, and was buried at St. Clement's, Ipswich, on 2nd March.

The overseer supervising Barnard's work on his early contracts for the Navy Board was a shipwright from the royal dockyards named Thomas Slade.[20] In 1747 he married an Ipswich woman, Hannah Moore, at Nacton.[21] By 1755 Slade had risen to the post of Master Shipwright at Deptford, when he was appointed one of the two joint Surveyors of the Navy. He revolutionised naval shipbuilding policy, and designed many famous ships, including H.M.S. *Victory*. In 1771, as Sir Thomas, he died at Bath[22] and was brought to Ipswich to be buried in St. Clement's churchyard with his wife, who had died nearly eight years earlier. The 'handsome stone' to his memory, which G.R. Clarke noted in 1830, had disappeared fifty years later, but in recent years the Borough Council, in connection with a landscaping scheme for the churchyard, has erected a new memorial to commemorate this man, who must surely be the most distinguished to lie in Ipswich.

In 1767 John Barnard opened a public swimming bath in his shipyard, the first such amenity in the town.[23] Precisely what it was like is not recorded, but a bath was still in existence there fifty years later, underneath the mould-loft which was some little distance from the quayside.

Edmund Goodea died in June, 1756, leaving the leasehold of his shipyards (Nos. 2 and 3) to his friend and partner, John Prentice (the younger). Prentice was building ' a large ship' in 1759, when berths for two or three apprentices to sail in her were advertised, and in 1761 he launched a 300-ton West Indiaman, the *Friendship*.[24] A year later he was declared bankrupt, a fate which befell many shipbuilders, and his yards were taken over by Richard Hales.

Hales is a mysterious figure. He described himself as a

shipwright when he drew up his will in 1773, but he was probably at one time a prosperous sea captain, owning at least part of his ship. Possibly he bought up Prentice's business when it failed and employed the insolvent builder to run it. The yard was usually described in the local press as 'Mr. Hales' shipyard', but occasionally as belonging to 'Captain Hales'; perhaps he was the Captain Hales of the Ipswich brig *Unity*, built in the town in 1747 and employed for many years in trade to the Baltic.[25] He owned a substantial house with stables in St Clement's Fore Street, but his will contained no mention of a shipyard.

In 1771, at a time when the *Ipswich Journal* rarely contained news of the launch of a merchant ship – and then only the larger ones – it reported:

> Last Tuesday was launched from Mr Hales' Ship-yard, a fine Sloop named the Heart of Oak, Benj. Garway, Master, to be one of the London Traders from the Common Key in this Town to Dice Key at London.

She is the only vessel known to have been built under Hales' regime and interestingly, in view of the publicity given to her launch, she survived to feature in the Ipswich Register over fifty years later. Re-registered at Beaumaris in 1843, she eventually foundered in the Menai Strait in 1863.[26]

Prentice was able to pay an interim dividend to his creditors in 1765, and he seems to have made an arrangement with them shortly afterwards, for he resumed business on his own account and trained apprentices in his trade. He reappeared in the rating assessments in 1769, occupying property valued at £6 per annum in 'Duck Street' (as Duke Street was often written; earlier, it had been described as 'From the Cock Corner to Seagers'). In the following year the annual valuation of Hales' shipyard fell from £25 to £17. In 1773 there was advertised for sale 'At the Dwelling House of Mr. John Prentice, Ship Builder, in St Clement's Ship-Yard… All the Household Furniture, Brewing Utensils, etc. Likewise the Stock in Trade…'.[27] (No doubt the brewing equipment was not unconnected with the shipyard.) He moved to a house in Fore Street, where 'Late Tyrell Lambly now John Prentice' was assessed on an annual valuation of £5.

A month later 'John Blomfield, Shipwright' advertised that he had 'taken the Ship-Yard (with the Stock in Trade) late in the Occupation of Mr. John Prentice'. He added a note that he had worked with Prentice as an apprentice and journeyman for 13 years. We may note that he had 'taken' the yard and not purchased it; the builders in the yards Nos. 3 and 4 were tenants only. Bloomfield also advertised the sale of his stock in trade in 1778, but unfortunately we know nothing of what he did in the interim.[28]

It is probable that Prentice and Bloomfield worked in yard No. 4, since No. 3 always seems to have had a higher annual valuation, as it appears that Hales' yard did. There, in 1774, 'John Turner, Shipwright' advertised that he had established his business, 'having taken the Yard at Ipswich (with the Stock in Trade) late belonging to Messrs. Hales and Fowler'.[29] John Fowler, a local corn and coal merchant, seems to have been only a sleeping partner in the shipbuilding business. Richard Hales died in 1777.

It is difficult to say with certainty who this John Turner was, since men of the name had lived in St. Clement's parish for many years, shipwrights among them. One, who died in 1737, mentioned his grandson John, the son of Christopher, in his will, while another, whose will was proved in 1769, left property to his sons, John and Samuel: both these testators owned several tenements in the parish. However, the phrase 'at Ipswich', with no further detail, suggests that he came from outside the town. Perhaps he was John Turner the younger from Harwich, who succeeded his father in partnership with John Barnard there, from 1765 until March, 1776, and was declared bankrupt four months later.[30] Whoever he was, his tenure of the yard in St. Clement's parish was short lived, and the only references to it are contained in advertisements for timber sales. By September, 1775, his entire stock, including timber, pitch, oakum and tools, was up for sale, and the yard was soon described as 'late in the Occupation of Mr. Turner'.[31]

John Barnard, the owner of yard No. 2, was declared bankrupt early in 1781.[32] For many years his activities had been centred on the Navy Yard at Harwich, where he was then building the *Irresistible*, a third rate of 74 guns. She was evidently completed by his assignees, one of whom was his son William, a shipbuilder of Deptford. John had obviously been a very wealthy man. Besides owning two shipyards in Ipswich, he also owned farms at Grundisburgh, Otley and Swilland in Suffolk, and two near Clacton, in Essex. He was the Lord of two Suffolk manors, Debach and Swilland.[33] His two shipyards, Nova Scotia and St. Clement's, included premises let to ancillary tradesmen, and both were soon purchased for continued use. His fine house on the east side of Duke Street, however, found no buyer and it, or a large part of it, was demolished in 1788: the materials offered for sale included a turret clock.[34] Barnard himself apparently went to live with his son in Deptford, where he died on 5th October, 1784, aged 79.[35] (He was not buried in St. Clement's churchyard; G.R. Clarke, writing in 1830 that he was, confused him with his father.)

After Barnard's insolvency, his No. 2 yard was taken over by one Jonathan Godbold, with a caulker named Robert Denny as his partner. Soon Godbold was on his own: he bought the copyhold in 1785 and continued his business for about 20 years. We know of some vessels which he built: the *Liberty*, of 200 tons, for Southampton owners in 1793; the *Princess of Wirtemberg* (*sic*) for Saunders of Harwich in 1797; the *Friends*, a 270-ton West Indiaman for London owners in 1800, and another, the *Dorothy Forster*, in 1801.[36] The *Friends* was bought by the navy in 1804 and for the next six years was H.M. sloop *Eugenie* of 16 guns.

On the side, he continued to run the swimming bath. By 1785 it catered for both ladies and gentlemen, and in 1792 the gentlemen's bath was 'fitted up with stone', suggesting that both sexes could then bathe simultaneously but not, of course, in the same water.[37]

Godbold put the shipyard on the market in 1806: it was advertised as 'Copyhold Premises…comprising a dock 61 feet wide, 103 feet of quay…115 feet in breadth…a coal warehouse 40 feet by 20, with 2 corn chambers, a mould loft 112 feet long, with a bath and warehouses under the same. A good dwelling house …also 15 tenements…The whole extend 164 feet along the River Orwell, 226 feet next the street and 261 feet in depth…'.[38] These dimensions enable the yard to be identified on scale maps until it disappeared. But no sale took place and Godbold still owned most of the premises when he died in 1830.

The yard was briefly occupied (1817–1818) by one William Cordingley, although Godbold continued to be assessed for rates on the swimming bath. Little is known of Cordingley. He had lived in St. Clement's parish since at least 1801, but his activities as a shipbuilder seem to have been mainly in St. Peter's, and will be dealt with in the next chapter.

After Turner's departure the No.3 and 4 yards were taken over by Benjamin Raymond. Bloomfield probably became his sub-tenant, since both were assessed for rates at a constant figure until some time after Bloomfield's business closed in 1778. Raymond had lived in the parish for many years and undoubtedly worked as a shipwright in some of the businesses we have noted. Again, we know little of his work: like many others at that time, when the launch of a humble sloop or brig was not newsworthy, he probably built some and was kept busy with repairs. In 1784, he handed

A brigantine lying at the Ballast Quay inside the Dock, seen in a photograph taken by Robert Burrows in 1858. *Suffolk Record Office*.

over to his son, also named Benjamin, describing himself as 'ship-builder at the Lower Ship Yard, St. Clement's Parish'.[39] The rating assessments and the Bransby map of 1811, already mentioned, confirm that Raymond occupied both the No. 3 and 4 yards. Pennington's map of 1778 shows no boundary between the two, and it seems that from 1728 until the whole area was redeveloped when the Wet Dock was built they were only rarely separately held.

When the River Commissioners were appointed in 1805 to improve the navigability of the Orwell they soon took steps to acquire a ballast wharf. The coarser material raised from the bed of the river was a saleable commodity: ballast was essential for ships sailing with no cargo, and the revenue from its sale was an important part of the Commissioners' income. For the storage of this ballast they took over the lease in August, 1805, of 'the Wharf, Warehouses and Shipyard in the parish of St. Clement now occupied by the widow Prentice'. Bransby's map shows that the ballast wharf abutted against the northern side of Godbold's shipyard.

Mrs. Sarah Prentice's late husband was Edmund, a one-time

shipbuilder in Woodbridge. His father William had been master and part owner of the brig *Unity*, in which he imported timber from Norway and the Baltic, as Richard Hales may have done before him. He usually landed and sold this timber in 'St. Clement's Shipyard', sometimes in 'the lower yard' or in 'Mr. Raymond's shipyard', but in 1788 the *Unity's* cargoes began to be sold in 'William Prentice's Timber and Deal Yard in St. Clement's Parish', a yard which may have been in the family for about 30 years. William died in 1789 and his widow Mary carried on the business, perhaps with help from her son, until her death in the following year. Edmund then took over, and the yard – which we must now refer to as No. 1 – was described as a timber yard in the rating assessments until 1800, when he resumed shipbuilding. In 1801 he launched the *Peace and Plenty*, of 200 tons, for the Baltic trade, followed in the next year by the collier brig *Newcastle*, both for local owners. He died in 1804, to be buried in St. Clement's churchyard like almost every other builder I have mentioned, but his widow Sarah carried on the business to launch the 370-ton *Friendship* for London owners in March, 1805.[40] These are the only vessels known to have been built in the No.1 yard.

In the meantime, the younger Benjamin Raymond carried on his business. In 1786 he advertised the hull of a newly built 70-ton vessel for sale, and another of 94 tons in 1789: these were obviously built on speculation.[41] By 1796 he had evidently acquired some reputation, when he built the *Boyton*, a 300-ton vessel for the transport service. This was a government agency which hired ships for the army's operations overseas: originally the Navy Board administered the service, but a separate Transport Board was set up in 1794. By 1809 its ships accounted for over 10% of all British merchant tonnage, and it appears that ships were specially built to be hired, as in the case of the East India Company. For the first time, the launch of the *Boyton* provides us with a glimpse of an incident at such an event: a swivel gun, fired as a salute, burst aboard a coaster lying at a nearby wharf. It was now wartime, and even the smallest craft was at risk from enemy privateers. The man who fired the gun was fatally injured, but nobody else in the small group standing round was seriously hurt. One bystander was knocked to the ground and found that a fragment had flattened the watch in his fob. 'The deceased was cautioned against overloading the swivel, and two persons observing him loading it, and finding him resolved upon firing it off, got into the cabin of a vessel to avoid the consequences they thought would ensue', said the *Ipswich Journal*.[42]

Jabez Bayley is shown looking at a draught of the East Indiaman *Orwell* in this drawing by George Rowe. *Suffolk Record Office.*

Thereafter there seems to be no further record of any vessel built by Raymond, apart from a 275-ton West Indiaman (of which I do not know the name) in 1800 and the coasting sloop *Fame* in 1811.[43] Towards the end of 1817 the yard was described in the parish rate books as 'Late Benjamin Raymond – a shipyard – empty'.

The shipbuilding industry in the town was now dominated by Jabez Bayley, who was launching a steady stream of vessels, both naval and mercantile, from his two yards on the opposite side of the river (see Chapter Eight). Following the launch of the East Indiaman *Orwell*, Bayley tried to monopolise all Ipswich shipbuilding. In the spring of 1818 he leased Godbold's yard from its ageing owner, and Raymond's yard from John Cobbold. He over-reached himself: the St. Clement's yards were in need of considerable investment, and within a few months he found himself unable to pay his creditors, and they appointed assignees. However, both his other yards were busy and he continued to attract orders.

At about this time, a 300-ton American emigrant ship, the *Marmion*, ran aground on the Shipwash Sand whilst on passage from Hamburg towards New Orleans and was brought into Harwich for repairs. Bayley secured the order, and the ship was brought up the Orwell: the work was apparently carried out at St. Clement's, for the people held a thanksgiving service in the parish church before resuming their voyage to the New World.[44] This ship seems to have been the first United States vessel to visit the town.

George Bayley, Jabez' nephew, who briefly managed the yard for his uncle, recorded that in 1819 he built at St. Clement's the schooner *Union* for local owners, and another vessel, the *Independence*, besides carrying out a considerable amount of repair work on Harwich cod smacks, but it was all not nearly enough to cover the outlay in restoration of the yards.[45]

The assignees soon closed down Godbold's old yard and managed Bayley's business for three years until his debts were paid, but then he carried on, convinced that his fortunes would improve. He reopened the No. 2 yard and built several vessels in the parish, including the *Thomas and Alfred* of 290 tons, for London owners and intended for the West India trade.[46] But he was in a parlous financial state, and was declared bankrupt in January, 1825. Probably with financial help from his foreman, William Read, he managed to launch his last vessel, the *Childe Harold*, 'a fine Indiaman, upwards of 400 tons burthen', in the following month: she may have been for the service of the East India Company, as she was certainly in the India trade by 1843, after the H.E.I.C. had lost its monopoly.[47]

All Bayley's property was put up for sale. The yard which I call No. 2 was advertised as having a dock with slipways where two 400-ton ships could be built at the same time. There was a quay 45ft. long (the northern part of the yard had been sold to Benjamin Batley Catt, a timber merchant, in 1815). The first-floor mould loft and joiners' shop was in a building 111ft. long, with various stores, including a copper-house (for sheathing) and a sub-let blockmaker's shop on the ground floor, where the bath had been. Raymond's former yards had a long range of quays, two slipways and various buildings. In addition, 'The following have been erected in this yard by Mr. Jabez Bayley, viz. a counting house (which is constructed that it may be removed) and a privy adjoining; a shed for winns; a crane on the quay, with cogged wheels and cranks, a long deal house, 2 long double saw pits, with double roofs, 1 double saw pit, with single roof, a boiling kiln, with leaded sides and coppered bottom ... a steam kiln ... a boat steam kiln ... a crane on the boat loft, an extensive smith's shop ... a flag staff ... and a shed, with pitch furnace ...'. Raymond's former yards were held under a lease from 'Mr. Cobbold', of which 14 years were unexpired.[48]

However, after little more than a year Bayley was able to resume business in a modest way at the No. 2 yard by entering into an arrangement with Read. According to the rating assessments, the yard was held by Bayley's assignees until 1827, when he was again assessed himself. It is said that when he was discharged from bankruptcy – apparently at that time – Read insisted upon being taken into partnership. Read was young enough to be Bayley's son, and he may have taken advantage of his employer's plight. In 1826 the brig *Shannon* was registered as built by both men, but a couple of months later the schooner *Fortitude* was entered as built by Bayley alone.

Perhaps Bayley was solely responsible for the tenancy of the yard and its upkeep – only his name appears in the assessments – and perhaps Read reserved the right to dissociate himself from certain contracts, as he wished. Several vessels were attributed to the partnership, but in 1828 Bayley was recorded as the sole builder of the steamer *Commerce*. More remarkably, there was no mention of Read when Bayley secured the contract to build a steam dredger at Lowestoft for the navigation company there: he followed it with the construction of lock gates and a patent slip.[49]

The dredger was launched in December, 1828, and, probably because she was built mainly of teak, she survived for many years. Latterly owned by the G.E.R. and named *Excavator*, or *Dredger No. 1* (I was once told by someone who remembered her that she was unofficially known as 'The Thing'), she eventually succumbed to a German shell during the naval bombardment of Lowestoft in April, 1916.

Back in Ipswich, Godbold died in October, 1830, aged 85, and his yard (No. 2) was put up for sale. Bayley and Read moved across the river to the St. Peter's Yard by Stoke Bridge.[50]

We must now go back in time to 1808. In that year, the River Commissioners purchased from Ipswich Corporation about $3^1/_2$ acres of mud flats, lying to the south of all the shipyards, upon which to spread the material that they were raising from the river bed. The tipping was initially arranged to reclaim two areas of land, leaving a space between them to be dredged out to form a dock. About an acre of this reclaimed land adjoined the yard referred to as No. 4, whilst the remainder, on the other side of the proposed dock, was built up from 1810 onwards to form a new ballast wharf; the old one, at Mrs. Prentice's former shipyard, was by then too small.

By 1819 the acre of new land was ready for industrial development, and about half of it, adjacent to the No. 4 yard, was leased for the erection of a limekiln. The other half was let to

The dredger built by Jabez Bayley in 1828 for the Norwich and Lowestoft Navigation Company, seen in the Haddiscoe New Cut with the Haddiscoe lift bridge and the *Queen's Head* in the background. Note pedimented entry port and sash window.

Benjamin Raymond, and it was called a shipyard in the rating assessments, so we will call it No. 6. Jabez Bayley was at that time in No. 4, 'late Raymond'. I have found no evidence of Benjamin using the yard: in 1822 a lighter named *Brisk* was built by Thomas Raymond, probably his brother of that name, and she may have been constructed here. Benjamin Raymond later took a lease of the other half in 1827. A small plan illustrating the leasehold shows that the former limekiln yard contained two cottages, a fair-sized malting and a covered saw pit with an adjoining 'shop'. It was also a shipyard, which we will refer to as No. 5.[51]

As Jabez Bayley's business failed in 1825, William Read advertised that he had taken premises 'adjoining Mr. Raymond's in St. Clement's' as a shipwright and boatbuilder, which must have been in yard No. 5.[52] Here he probably built the sloop *Ruby* in that year and a few other small craft until 1830, when the yard was noted in the rating assessments as empty.

The younger Benjamin Raymond died in October, 1830 (just a fortnight before Godbold), and two years later his leasehold of both yards was advertised for sale.[53] They were said to be occupied by William Cordingley, but he had lately died and for several years the business had been in the hands of his son John, who from time to time advertised sales of imported timber at his yard 'near the Ballast Wharf' or 'near the Gas Works'. Here in yard No. 6, or perhaps next door by arrangement with Read, he built at least a couple of smacks in the late 1820s and the barge *Maria*, named after his young daughter, in 1832.

John Cordingley's name survives in another context, for he published a book of poetry which prompted G.R. Clarke, when writing his *History*, to include him in a 'biographical catalogue' of people prominent in the story of the town, where he may be found listed with figures like Gainsborough, Nelson and Wolsey. Unfortunately all that Clarke said of the poet was that he was a native of the town, claiming 'but a very limited commercial education' to excuse his verse, which Clarke thought had 'a great deal of merit'.[54]

Not long after Raymond's death the lease of yard No. 5 was taken over by a mast and block maker named Enos Page (the younger), and that of No. 6 by my relative Benjamin Hamblin, although Cordingley seems to have continued to occupy both. By 1837 No. 5 had been taken for the first part of Ransomes' Orwell Works and when Hamblin put No. 6 up for sale in December, 1841, it was occupied by a timber merchant named William Colchester.[55] Colchester later became a considerable shipowner and barge builder; the first barge he built seems to have been the *Raven* in 1841. She was probably built in this No. 6 yard, but unfortunately she was too small and commonplace for her launch to be reported in the local press. The yard, and the adjoining ballast wharf, had been redeveloped as part of the Orwell Works by 1849.

After Godbold's death in 1830 his yard (No. 2) came into the possession of mortgagees, and seems to have been little used for a time after Bayley and Read moved out. It was advertised to let, with immediate possession, in 1832. John Cordingley occasionally broke up an old ship, or sold imported softwoods, either here or in No. 1, which B.B. Catt had taken over when the River Commissioners vacated their original ballast wharf in 1820.

After Jabez Bayley's death in 1834, Read entered into a partnership with the younger Enos Page and, as soon as his former business had been wound up, they moved to the St. Peter's yard. Their stock left behind in St. Clement's was sold in August, 1835, at 'Mr. Catt's Ship Yard', which may have been where they worked, although Page had leased the No. 5 yard only that February: unfortunately no rate books of the time survive.[56] Catt ran a timber business, among other activities, and the No. 2 yard

A print of Raymond's Lower Shipyard, St. Clement's, in 1801 shortly before reclamation of the shallows in the foreground. *Ipswich Borough Council Museums and Galleries.*

was often called his shipyard, although he never built any ships. He used his premises here as a bonded yard for imported timber, at that time subject to duty. He rented out space in a large four-storey building: the ground floor contained the kyanising tank of the Anti Dry Rot Company, there was warehouse space on the two floors above and the sailmaking loft of William Bell Horn on the top floor.[57]

Shipbuilding on this part of the waterfront, after at least five centuries, was by now drawing to a close, but it was not to peter out without a final burst of activity. When Jabez Bayley's business failed in 1825, William Bayley, who had been building ships at Woodbridge since 1819, had taken the lease of the yards 3 and 4. He was a distant relative of Jabez, and it was probably his grandfather who built boats at the Nova Scotia yard, on the other side of the Orwell, some 60 years earlier (see Chapter 8), before returning to Burnham in Essex, where William had been born. He moved into Benjamin Raymond's old yards early in 1826.

The first vessel which he is known to have built in Ipswich was the brig or snow *Hannah*, launched in that July for Harwich owners.[58] Among the craft he built in 1827 were the schooner *Flora* of 115 tons, for the port of London, and 'a fine yacht' for a member of the Royal Yacht Club (later the Royal Yacht Squadron).[59] By 1830 Bayley's yard was equipped with a patent slip, the invention of a Leith shipwright named Morton, on which a ship could be floated on to a multi-wheeled platform which could then be hauled up rails into the yard for work below her waterline.[60]

In about 1836 the business suddenly expanded. The local papers reported the launches of five vessels for other ports from his yard in that year and when the last, the 70-ton sloop *Damsel*, went down the ways on 24th November she was said to have been the fifth vessel built for Maldon at the yard within a few months – none of the others had been mentioned. The *Suffolk Chronicle* added 'There are now two large vessels nearly ready for launching by Mr. Bayley.' In May, 1837, the paper reported the launching of two vessels in the previous week and said that five were then under construction, 'beside several others under repair'. Such production was not possible without the use of more slipways than yards Nos. 3 and 4 contained, according to a contemporary drawing: Bayley was now building in yard No. 2 as well. His business continued to thrive: in July, 1838, when the schooner *Monarch* of London was launched for the Dutch butter trade, it was reported that Bayley had built nine vessels in the past year, with four then under construction and others under repair. Among the many fruit schooners which he built was the *Azorian* of London in 1839: she was reported to have been built in about two months.[61]

The Wet Dock was now under construction, and Bayley built a new dredger for the Dock Commission in 1839.[62] By 1840 the new quays being built out in front of the old ones along the northern side of the dock reached the slipways in the No. 2 yard, and there the work stopped for a while.[63] A new yard was being prepared for Bayley just outside the southern end of the dock, but it was not yet ready.

He must have regretted this when, on 22nd July, there was a serious fire in Catt's timber yard next door: it started in the four-storey building. Horn's sail loft was consumed, but his nine employees escaped. Bayley's mould loft, with the stores underneath where the swimming bath had been, was destroyed, together with about a dozen adjacent cottages. The wind, initially from the WSW, veered to the north but as it was not very strong Bayley's yard suffered little further damage, although for a time two brigs on the adjoining slips were thought to be in danger: one was able to be launched. Happily there was no loss of life.[64]

But the end was approaching. On 22nd April, 1841, Bayley launched 'a fine brig of 190 tons', the *Agile*, sheathed with yellow metal for warm waters, and two days later the last vessel to be built in the old yards, the fruit schooner *Doctor*, of 136 tons, for a Captain Stone of London, went down the ways. The launch was witnessed by a large crowd.[65] It was the end of an era. Bayley had already moved to the new St. Clement's shipyard.

However, one more vessel was built on this part of the Ipswich waterfront. In February, 1851, Ransomes & May constructed a small iron screw passenger steamer, the *Chevalier*, and 'launched' her from their Orwell Works: they also built her 20 NHP engine. The vessel was built to the order of a syndicate which included George Tomline of Orwell Park (the founder of Felixstowe Dock and its railway) and was originally intended for river service between Ipswich and Harwich, but by the time of her launch she was reported to be for sale. Although the venture was undertaken to 'encourage the building of iron steamers in this port', there may have been problems in getting such a vessel, 80ft. long, into the water and the experiment was not repeated.[66] Further details of the *Chevalier* and her career are unknown to me.

Yards on the Right Bank 8

There were three main sites where ships were built on the southern and western side of the Orwell within the borough boundary, the oldest of these being in the parish of St. Peter, not far below Stoke Bridge. Ogilby's 1674 map of Ipswich shows the site occupied by 'the King's Cooperidge', presumably where casks were made for naval stores. By 1702 one Joseph Clarke was assessed for land tax on 'a house and shipyard in Mabson's occupation', valued at £7 per annum. Arthur Mabson was briefly mentioned in the parish rate books after 1698, but he had disappeared by 1703 and the property he occupied is unknown.

In 1732 the headboroughs reported to the Corporation that 'John Barnard hath enclosed the old dock in St. Peter's, Ipswich, being the common soil'.[1] This may have been the shipbuilder we have already met in St. Clement's: the dock in question was on the western side of the shipyard where Great Whip Street ran down to the water's edge. It was possible for wagons to ford the river here at low tide, and carters were directed to do so when Stoke Bridge was under repair.[2]

Few rate books for the parish survive between 1709 and 1743. In 1747 some properties were listed in specific locations, e.g. 'From the Bell Corner to the Shipyard', but the yard itself did not appear among the assessments until 1751, when 'John Dymocks' was recorded as the occupier, and the Corporation granted the use of the dock to John Dymock the younger for an annual rent of ten shillings. We know nothing of Dymock's activities until 1760, when the Corporation threatened to evict him, 'unless he agrees not to build, lengthen or repair any vessel in the dock so as to obstruct the passage through the dock across the river to the opposite dock'.[3]

Later, the Corporation advertised an 11-year lease of 'the Dock or Slip-Way' to run from October, 1766; this may have been granted to Dymock, but he died early in the following year. The shipyard was taken over by a man named Pearl Betts: in 1770 he, or his family, opened a yard at Mistley, where they later built frigates for the navy.[4] The rating valuation of the St. Peter's yard remained at £7 per annum as before, but now the slipway was separately assessed on an annual valuation of £2; it was occupied

Opposite: The St. Peter's shipyard, with the church of St. Mary Stoke and the two windmills on Stoke Hill on the skyline above it. *Ipswich Borough Council Museums and Galleries.*

by a local merchant named Thomas Alderton, although after a short time he appears to have made no use of it.

Betts built several vessels at St. Peter's, including a 300-ton ship for the Jamaica trade in 1773, another, the *Mary and Ann*, in 1777 and a brig of 140 tons, the *Ark*, for the Oporto trade, wryly named after her master, Noah Squires, in 1778. It must have been difficult to float away the larger vessels, particularly as contemporary pictures indicate that the slipways were square to the channel. The largest ship that he built seems to have been the 400-ton West Indiaman *Springfield*, launched on the top of the tide at 3 a.m. one Sunday in April 1776.[5] By 1778 Betts was living nearby in a house with a large garden, but the debts were mounting and in the following year his business was in the hands of assignees.[6]

The next occupier was Captain Timothy Mangles, whom we have already met in connection with the Greenland whale fishery. In April, 1783, a 350-ton West Indiaman, the *St. James' Planter*, was launched from 'Capt. Mangles' ship-yard at Stoke' and, as the rate books indicate that he did not move into the Nova Scotia yard until the autumn, this ship must have been built in the St. Peter's yard.[7] Although the yard was indeed in the parish of St. Peter, Ipswichians have always referred to the area beyond Stoke Bridge as 'over Stoke'. Mangles seems to have had no experience as a shipwright; he may have been one of the assignees of Betts, 'late of Ipswich', overseeing the business on behalf of the creditors, who received a final dividend in 1785.[8]

The Nova Scotia yard was about three-quarters of a mile further down the river, although less by road, at a point where the channel again ran close to the western bank. It was in the parish of St. Mary Stoke: today the site, far behind the line of the present quay, is covered by the West Bank Terminal.

The yard seems to have been established early in the 18th century, according to a deed enrolled with the Corporation in 1713 which recorded the sale of a messuage and shipyard, with dock and marshlands, by Roger Mather of Ipswich, maltster, and Martha his wife, to John Blichenden of Ipswich, shipwright, and one William Potter of Colchester. The premises were said to have been late in the occupation of George Campion, Daniel Driver and John Bunn, and to have been purchased by Bunn from Edward Bartleby in 1707.[9] Blichenden probably built ships there, but whether any of the others mentioned did, I do not know.

Few rate books of the period survive until 1746, and there is no mention of a shipyard. In 1719 a Mr. Bardoe was recorded as occupying premises 'late Blichenden's', and one John Berdoe (*sic*) advertised in 1730 that the limekiln in the parish was then in operation: in 1746 this kiln was run by Abraham Goldsmith, followed by Robert Pooley.[10] The picture becomes clearer after 1749, when the shipbuilder John Barnard bought the property from John Goslin of Colchester, a glover by trade. It consisted of a messuage with stables, etc, and 'all that parcell of land thereunto belonging which was formerly a shipyard and whereon lately stood a lime kiln in all about 6 acres in the parish of St. Mary Stoke late in the tenure of Robert Pooley'.[11] Barnard made little immediate use of the property himself: he named it Nova Scotia, but why he did so is unknown.

The house was let. Barnard himself was briefly assessed for a limekiln, but it was soon let to others: he occupied 'granaries and wharf' in 1751, but then they were noted as 'empty' in the rating assessments. A boatbuilder named Richard Montravers became a tenant somewhere in the yard.[12] Barnard was again occupying the granaries in 1757 and, three years later, 'granaries etc' with the same annual valuation. There was an occasional sale of imported timber and coal was landed there, but the rate books gave no indication of what was happening.

St. Peter's Shipyard in 1801 showing a three-masted ship under construction, with her bows towards the water. *Ipswich Borough Council Museums and Galleries.*

The Nova Scotia yard burst into activity in July, 1762, when Barnard's son William, in partnership with one William Dudman, began to build a 702-ton East Indiaman, the *Speaker*. How these two, just starting up in business on their own account, managed to secure such a prestigious order is unknown. William Dudman (1719–1772) had been apprenticed in Portsmouth Dockyard and then worked in the dockyards at Plymouth and Woolwich before becoming an overseer at Deptford. William Barnard (1735–1795) may have served an apprenticeship at Deptford, and so got to know Dudman.

The *Speaker* was launched on 31st January, 1763. 'Being put off too hastily, some time before high water, she stopped before she was quite got off her ways but the next day was got safe afloat with little trouble and is now going down the river to Harwich to be rigged', reported the *Ipswich Journal*.[13] Within the next two years, Dudman and Barnard launched six more sizeable ships from Nova Scotia: three 300-ton West Indiamen, the *Dawes, Dunniker* and *Susanna*; another of 250 tons, the *Best in Christendom*; a 230-ton ship, the *Tuscany*, for the Leghorn trade, and the *Africa*, for the Guinea trade, which was claimed to be the first British merchant ship to be sheathed with copper.[14] As some of these launchings were only two months apart, the yard must have had at least two slipways of requisite length, besides others for the smaller vessels said to have been built at the same time.

Dudman and Barnard did not remain long in Ipswich. In February, 1764, John Barnard advertised a lease of the yard to begin at Michaelmas, with a partial clearance in May to allow the new tenant to bring in timber.[15] Dudman vacated his house near Stoke Bridge at the end of the year, and William left his a few months later. They had already taken a lease of a yard at Grove Street, Deptford, in partnership with Henry Adams of Buckler's Hard in Hampshire. The business prospered, although Adams never honoured his promise that he would live nearby. In 1779 William Barnard opened a second yard, lower down the Thames near Deptford Creek, and after the dissolution of the partnership with Adams in 1792 (Dudman being already dead) he continued there, developing one of the most important yards on the river. After his death his family continued to build large ships into the 19th century.[16]

Activity declined at the Nova Scotia yard: John Barnard used it for timber sales and perhaps ship breaking, but there is no evidence that he made much use of it for several years. Montravers' boatbuilding shop was taken over by William and John Bayley in

Although previously thought to show the Halifax shipyard, this watercolour is more likely to represent the Nova Scotia yard, where the 400-ton West Indiaman *Mary Ann* was launched on 25th July, 1786. 'The stern and quarter galleries were handsomely decorated with a beautiful group of figures, which does the greatest credit to Mr. Wm. Wollaston, carver of this town', said the *Ipswich Journal*. *Ipswich Borough Council Museums and Galleries.*

1764: it is unfortunate that the relationship between this pair is at present unknown, for each was the progenitor of an important branch of the family which was to become the best-remembered in Ipswich shipbuilding.

John was born in Rotherhithe about 1731, and was apprenticed there as a shipwright and boatbuilder. His wife Elizabeth was the daughter of a wealthy silk merchant and sacrificed a considerable inheritance to marry against her family's wishes. John worked in a Rotherhithe yard until business declined when, with 'a relative', William, he moved to Burnham-on-Crouch in Essex. Finding that there was insufficient work available in that isolated village to support them both, they moved on again, to Ipswich .[17]

Most of what we know about John comes from George Bayley, who was naturally more interested in his grandfather than in William, but there can be no doubt that at first the latter was the senior partner. The property which they occupied was assessed for rates in William's name alone. Their first advertisement in the local press, in 1765, announced:

> By William Bayley, from London, at Nova Scotia Yard, near Ipswich, are built, Sailing-boats, Carvell or Clenchwork; Long-boats, Carvell or Clenchwork; Pinnaces, Yawls, Cutters, Skiffs, Greenland Shallops and Pond Boats of all Sorts.

A little later both partners advertised a newly-built well smack for sale, in addition to general boat building work.[18]

At about this time, a certain Stephen Teague arrived in St. Mary Stoke parish. We do not know when he began to build ships, as John Barnard was always assessed for the rates on the Nova Scotia yard, but there in 1769 he launched a West Indiaman, the *Marquis of Rockingham*. Teague was declared bankrupt in the following year and all his stock in trade was advertised for sale. The yard reverted to timber sales, sometimes of leftovers brought up from Barnard's yard in Harwich.[19]

Down the river there, Barnard was having trouble with his associate, the younger John Turner, who had succeeded his father in the partnership. When the Navy Board placed an order for a 16-gun sloop in 1775, Barnard obtained permission to build her at Nova Scotia rather than at Harwich: she was duly launched, as H.M.S. *Cormorant*, in May, 1776. By this time the partnership with Turner had been dissolved, and Barnard built two other ship-rigged sloops at Nova Scotia, the *Zebra* in 1777 and the *Savage* in the following year. In 1779, the sixth-rate *Champion*, of 519 tons and 24 guns, was the last warship built by Barnard on the Orwell, and as she was larger she was built at John's Ness, according to G.R. Clarke. As soon as she was afloat, a Harwich packet, the *Prince of Orange*, was laid down at Nova Scotia.[20]

Barnard was declared bankrupt in 1781. Nova Scotia was put up for sale with his other property, and was described as:

> A Freehold Estate...consisting of a spacious ship-yard, in which ships of war, East and West Indiamen have been built, with convenient saw pits, wharfs, coal and corn warehouses, storehouses, mould loft, boat-builder's and smith's shops, boiling kiln, a public house, and about three acres of meadow land adjoining, well fenced in, and may be entered upon at Lady-day next, when a fire-ship (now building for His Majesty's service) is to be launched.

Enquiries were to be addressed to Emerson Cornwell, banker, or Peter Clarke, both of Ipswich, or William Barnard, shipbuilder of Deptford. In March, 1782, it was purchased by Timothy Mangles, described as 'of Leytonstone in the County of Essex', and the premises were said to have been 'now or late in the several occupations of the said John Barnard, Stephen Teague, Robert Sporle, and John Baily' (*sic*): Sporle occupied the house, which had become the public house.[21]

The fireship was the *Spitfire*, of 424 tons and 12 guns, and she was duly launched on 19th March, having been built by Teague, who also launched a sister ship, the *Megaera*, from the yard in the following year.[22] Again, we do not know when Teague resumed building: Barnard had continued to be assessed for rates on the shipyard until he became insolvent, and thereafter it was Teague. However, there is evidence to suggest that Teague, after his failure in 1770, became involved in farming in a small way and by 1777 he was conducting auction sales of timber round the district. A few months after the launch of the *Megaera*, Teague moved out and the yard was advertised to be let.[23]

Meanwhile, William Bayley had taken over a piece of marshland near his boatbuilding shop and by the end of 1781 his premises were described as 'part of Nova Scotia shipyard'. At some time he returned to Burnham. He was probably still in Ipswich in 1777, when he was first assessed for rates on a house near the parish church, but he was not mentioned in the conveyance of Nova Scotia to Mangles, although his name alone continued to appear in the assessments.

John Bayley carried on with his work and, coming to the notice of the Navy Board, he supplied boats for the *Spitfire* and other warships.[24] In March, 1785, he died after a riding accident and the name of his widow immediately replaced William's in the rating assessments. Elizabeth Bayley advertised that she would carry on the business with her sons and 'proper assistants'.[25] She had four sons then living: the eldest, John, signed on as a carpenter in a warship and died in the West Indies, although he seems to have been briefly involved in the family business before he went; the second son, George (1765–1807) was soon acting as her manager, and his two younger brothers, Philip and Jabez, were duly apprenticed to him. Philip remained a working shipwright all his life: he was, as his nephew George put it, 'not overstocked with brains'. On the other hand, the youngest son, Jabez (1771–1834), became a very successful builder, securing many orders for naval vessels and managing to enter the exclusive circle of those who built East Indiamen. His nephew said that he had 'a fondness for distinction and was susceptible to flattery', and summed him up as 'one of those good natured impulsive men on whom one cannot rely with confidence'.[26] Nevertheless, he became probably the most famous of all Ipswich shipbuilders.

Early in 1787 the rate books showed that Mrs. Bayley's 'part of Nova Scotia shipyard' was empty, no doubt in readiness for the whaling enterprise. When it started, Timothy Mangles built at least three more ships for the West India trade: the *Augustus* in 1788 and the *Lord Sheffield* in the following year, both probably at St. Peter's; then, after he had abandoned whaling, he launched the *Ferdinand* in 1791 at Nova Scotia, whence it was easier to float large vessels away. A week later all the stock there was up for sale, 'the present owner having declined shipbuilding'.[27]

The Nova Scotia yard was briefly occupied by James Betts, but his business was soon in the hands of assignees: he was declared bankrupt, although he was later able to resume work in his family's other yard at Mistley.[28] In 1793 Mangles sold the Nova Scotia property to a merchant named Benjamin King, and in 1795 he died at Leytonstone.[29] After the demise of the whale fishery there is evidence to suggest that the Bayleys used part of Nova Scotia until the end of the century, but to all intents and purposes its shipbuilding days were over.[30]

Mrs. Bayley's business seems to have moved to the St. Peter's yard, where it was described in 1790 as 'Mr. Bailey's Boat-Building Yard, near Stoke Bridge', indicating that George had by then taken over the management. Deals and leftovers of oak were advertised for sale at 'Stoke Shipyard' or 'the Wharf late Stoke Shipyard', while Mangles continued to be assessed for rates on what was called a shipyard, but it is difficult to say what was going on there. In 1793 'Mrs. Bailey, Widow', with Mangles and others, was assessed for rates on the place, but three years later George, having married, was the only one mentioned. It was said that at first he allowed his mother ten shillings and sixpence a week, which was more than the profits of the business, but he prospered and by about 1798 he was able to purchase the freehold of the yard, 'containing about $1^1/_4$ acres of land, with an extensive quay nearly 300 feet long, together with a large brick and timber building, or mould loft, counting-house, etc... sheds, boiling kiln, etc...'.[31]

Orders flowed in. In 1799 a ship of 450 tons, the *Caroline*, was launched: 'Her cradle was upon a new construction', reported the *Ipswich Journal*. She undoubtedly had to be launched bows first, as contemporary illustrations indicate, so that her fuller lines forward would float her up in the shallow water near Stoke Bridge. For some time, too, men had been deepening the river at the end of the slipway. A schooner, the *Eastman*, for the Hudson's Bay trade, and another 'fine new ship' were built in the following year.[32]

At about this time George took his young brother Jabez into partnership, and in 1802 they launched the largest vessel ever built so high up the river. This was the *Sir William Bensley*, of about 550 tons, for the East India Company's 'country trade', i.e. in eastern waters. She was to have been launched one Saturday, when about 10,000 people were estimated to have turned up to watch, but the tide was not high enough. Many stayed over the weekend, but the Bayleys, having strong religious views, probably deliberately postponed the launch until the Monday, when a strong northerly wind had had time to provide a good high tide. The ship was rigged down by John's Ness, and later sailed on her maiden voyage to London with a freight of bricks.[33]

It may be that George's health was beginning to fail, for on 2nd May, 1803, he left the business to Jabez, although he later began buying timber: 'Letters to be directed to his compting house, Stoke ship-yard'. He died in April, 1807, aged 41.[34] Jabez now appeared to be on his own, but the yard and all the capital belonged to his sister-in-law and he was only her manager until 1810, when he was able to put his own capital into the yard.[35]

In 1783 a sale of imported timber was advertised at 'Halifax Ship Yard, near Nova Scotia'. The advertisement stated that 'Dinner will be available for the buyers at the New York Coffee House, formerly known by the name of the Ostrich'*, but that name lasted only a few years. The Halifax yard, destined to become perhaps the most famous of all the Ipswich yards, was about half a mile below Nova Scotia, from which it most likely derived its name by association. Teague probably started it when he left Nova Scotia in 1782 but it was not until December, 1785, after several more timber sales, that his name was mentioned there, in connection with the sale of a nearly completed sloop of 80 tons.[36] The yard seems at first to have been used only for building the occasional coaster, ship breaking and timber sales, first appearing in the rating assessments in 1792, valued at a modest £8 per annum when the yearly valuation of the Nova Scotia yard was £40.

Three years later Teague's stock in trade was advertised for

*As I completed this chapter, I discovered to my horror that the pub's new owners had changed its ancient name, *Ostrich*, to *Oyster Reach*, presumably a reference to a supposed origin of the name. Far too many things are changed today for no good reason.

sale and he announced that he had 'declined business on account of ill health'. However, he continued to be assessed for rates on the yard until his death in 1803; the business may have been carried on by his son, also named Stephen, who died at Calcutta in November, 1820, 'many years an eminent shipbuilder there', but I have found no mention of him at Ipswich.[37]

In December, 1797, Teague launched the sloop *Cruizer*, of 384 tons and 18 guns, for the navy. She was with Nelson at Copenhagen and was the name-ship of a class of no fewer than 111 vessels built over the next 31 years, nine of them being built by Jabez Bayley.[38]

Bayley began the long series of small warships which he built when he launched the gunboat, or gun brig, *Daring* at the St. Peter's yard in October, 1804.[39] Over the next ten years he built 36 vessels for the navy, probably more than any other private builder outside the Thames, but not of course the largest total tonnage.

Details of the vessels built by Jabez Bayley for the government are given in Appendix 2. G.R. Clarke in 1830 listed them as 18 brigs and sloops, two corvettes, one transport, one advice boat, two sailing lighters and 11 gunboats.[40] Some can readily be identified: the two *Cyrus* class sloops, being flush decked, were later classified as corvettes, whilst the *Daring* and the *Hearty* were sometimes classed as gunboats.

Three of Bayley's warships have their place in history. H.M.S. *Peacock* was taken by the American sloop *Hornet* off the Guiana coast in 1812; her gunnery was poor, and she was so severely damaged that she suddenly sank after striking her colours. Her captain, Lieut. Peake, was killed and Captain Lawrence of the *Hornet* was later to die of wounds when his ship, the *Chesapeake*, was taken by H.M.S. *Shannon* in 1813. Incidentally, Captain Philip Broke of the *Shannon* came from the Suffolk village of Nacton, where his birthplace still overlooks the Orwell. A fine rigged model of the *Shannon*, which an old sailor I used to know remembered seeing there as a boy, is now in the Rogers Collection at the U.S. Naval Academy at Annapolis, Maryland.

H.M.S. *Favourite* carried a British envoy with a copy of the Treaty of Ghent, signed on Christmas Eve, 1814, to New York to inform President Madison that the war between the United States and Britain was over. Unfortunately her voyage took seven weeks due to adverse gales, and although Congress quickly ratified the treaty the fighting needlessly went on for a couple of months or so.

From 1822 H.M.S. *Leven,* under Captain William Owen R.N. and accompanied by H.M.S. *Barracouta*, surveyed the east coast of Africa from the Cape of Good Hope to the Red Sea. Ordered home

A portrait of Captain Richard Hall Gower, designer of some most interesting and unusual vessels. *Over Stoke History Group*.

in 1825, Owen carried out an outline survey of the west coast from the Cape to the Congo. So many of the people in the two ships died of disease in the three-year period that it was said it was as if the charts had been drawn in blood.[41] The *Barracouta*, incidentally, was not the one built by Bayley.

As orders for both warships and merchantmen flowed in, Bayley soon found the St. Peter's yard with its shallow water quite inadequate, and in 1805 he expanded his activities to the Halifax yard, which had been empty since Teague's death. Early in March, 1806, the local press reported that the keel of a sloop of war had been laid down there: it was H.M.S. *Favourite*.[42]

During the ensuing period of over two and a half years Bayley built 10 vessels for the navy, but in which of his yards seems not to have been recorded in most cases. The exception was the advice boat *Transit*, launched at Halifax in 1809. She was designed by

Richard Hall Gower (1767–1833), a former officer in the East India Company's service with an inventive mind. The son of an Essex clergyman, Gower received part of his education at Ipswich School, and after serving at sea for nearly 20 years he came ashore to devote himself to his inventions. He is best remembered for his remarkable narrow-beamed four-masted vessel *Transit*, built at Itchenor near Chichester in 1800. She was rigged as a barquentine, and although she consistently outsailed a naval sloop there was little official interest in her. The *Transit* built at Ipswich was even narrower and received a similar rig, but the navy immediately shortened her by about 20 feet, to Gower's fury, and she spent most of her life as a tender for pressed men. In 1816 Gower came to live at Nova Scotia in Ipswich, buying the property two years later.[43]

According to G.R. Clarke, from the time Jabez Bayley commenced business until August, 1817, the total output of his yards totalled 5,873 tons. For the merchant service, he built six ships, ten brigs, nine sloops, ten smacks and cutters, three schooners and three packets.[44] Some can be identified. In particular, the six ships were launched as follows: the *Harleston* of 579 tons, from Halifax in January, 1811; the *Grace* of 250 tons from St. Peter's in March, 1811; the *Mary* of 360 tons from Halifax in May, 1811; a ship of unknown name and about 300 tons in September, 1814, and the *Orwell* of 300 tons in April, 1815, both from 'Mr. Bayley's ship-yard in this town', followed by the

The East Indiaman *Orwell*, built by Jabez Bayley and launched 28th August, 1817, on the Halifax yard. She was at that time the largest vessel built in Ipswich.

This rough sketch of the *Orwell* at sea bears the unknown artist's caption 'Ship *Orwell* from China laden with 24,000 Chests of Tea beside St. Helena stores'. It may well be the only representation of this ship after her completion, and was purchased by the author for a few coppers from among a job lot at a London gallery in the 1950s.

Georgiana of 256 tons from St. Peter's in July, 1816.[45] The *Harleston* was built for the East India Company's country trade, and the other five were West Indiamen. The *Mary*, re-rigged as a barque, was in the Australian trade when she was wrecked in the Bass Strait in 1845. One of the schooners was for the Hudson's Bay Company, and one of the packets was the *Lord Castlereagh* for the Harwich station.[46]

In 1816 Bayley secured an order to build what was then the largest vessel ever built in the town, when he contracted with Captain Matthew Isacke of Greenwich to build an East Indiaman of the largest type at a price of £22 10s. per ton for the hull complete. This was about the ruling price from the Thames-side yards, but Isacke was said to have been impressed by Bayley's work on his naval contracts. The keel was laid at Halifax in May that year and the ship was built almost entirely of Suffolk oak which, although it was considered to be very green at the time, was found to be only partially decayed when the ship was broken up in 1840. This gave rise to the theory that Suffolk oak was immune to dry rot, but Bayley's attention to ventilation was probably responsible to a large extent.[47] Apart from when the ship was being painted, the public was allowed to visit the yard and, with interest thus fostered, a crowd estimated at nearly 20,000 watched the launch on 28th August, 1817, when the ship was named *Orwell* by Mrs. Isacke.[48] To launch so large a ship – she measured 1,337 tons – Bayley had been obliged to excavate a cut from the end of the slipway to the channel of the river. Even so, the *Orwell* briefly grounded, but as the tide was not quite full she soon floated off and was taken under jury rig to deeper water at Downham Reach, where the builder's responsibility for her ceased.[49]

The sketch on page 113 bears the caption 'Ship *Orwell* from China laden with 24,000 Chests of Tea beside St. Helena stores'. The number of chests of tea, large as it might seem, would have been correct. The hull tallies well with contemporary prints of the ship being built, but by that date the fore and main topsails would have had four rows of reef points. At some later date the drawing

R.H. Gower's *Ipswich* lifeboat, as shown in a plate in his book *Original observations regarding the inability of ships to perform their duty with promptitude and safety, with suggestions for their improvement, as practised on board the* Transit, *an experimental vessel, invented, built, and commanded by the author*. The book was his last, and appeared shortly before his death in 1833. *Suffolk Record Office*.

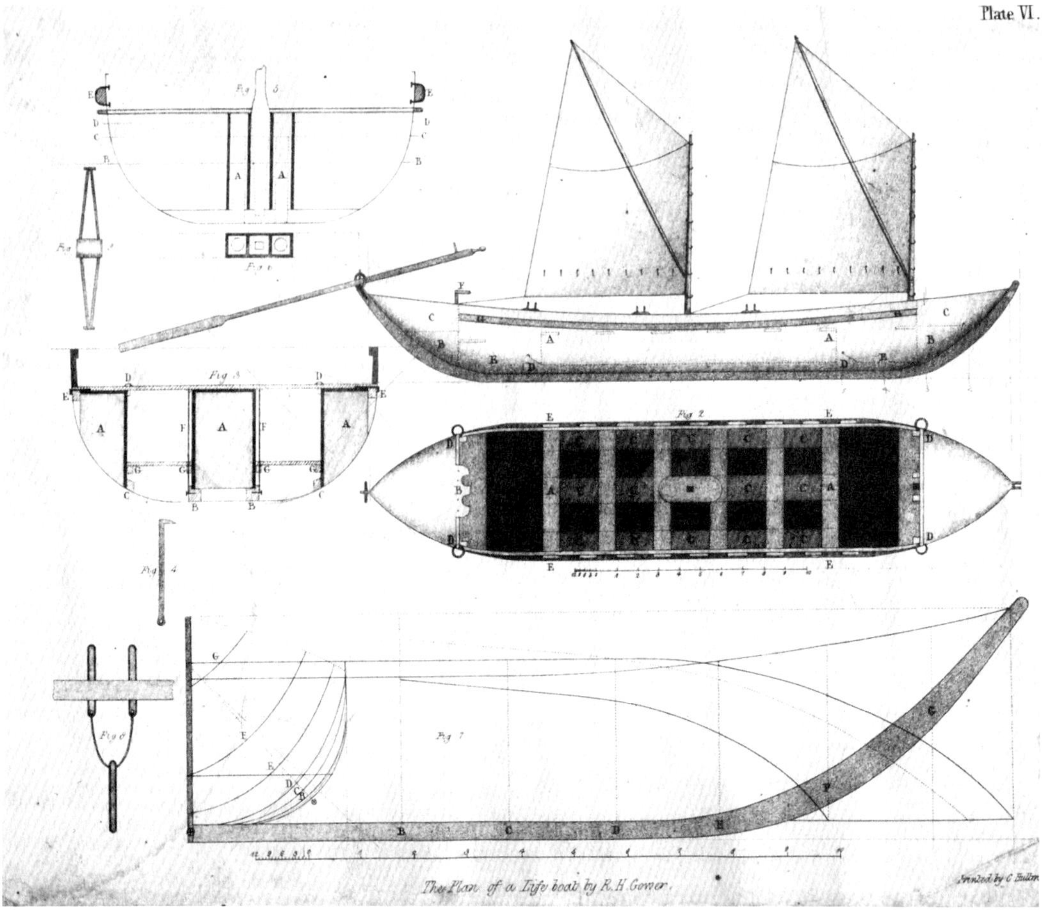

has been reinforced in blue ink, but it appears to be of contemporary origin and could possibly have been drawn by a passenger on board this or some other ship.

Jabez Bayley's prestige was now at its peak with the building of this important ship, and orders flowed in. He built a series of West Indiamen: the *Underwood* of 318 tons was launched from the St. Peter's yard in September, 1818, followed by the *Abberton*, 428 tons, and the *Celerity* of 450 tons, both from the Halifax yard. In August, 1819, the *David Lyon* of 450 tons went down the ways from St. Peter's, and in the following month a third *Transit*, designed by Richard Gower, was launched at Halifax. This last was a three-masted version of her sisters, built as a yacht for the Hon. George Vernon, son of the Archbishop of York. She was fully rigged when she went down the slipway and 'immediately after she was launched, her sails were hoisted and she proceeded down the river, in most gallant trim'.[50]

But Bayley had over-reached himself. As we have seen, he had unwisely tried to monopolise shipbuilding in the town by taking over two of the St. Clement's yards, and his affairs were in the hands of his creditors. The dredging of the channel to launch the *Orwell* had absorbed his profit from building her, but now he had the channel and he was convinced that other large contracts would restore his fortunes.

He secured an order from Captain Henry Templar of Limehouse to build two more large East Indiamen, and they were laid down in the Halifax yard early in 1820. No doubt at the insistence of Bayley's assignees, Templar was to provide the materials, whilst the builder was only responsible for labour, at £4 10s. per registered ton, and the use of his premises for 10 shillings per ton. When the ships were in frame, Templar sold his contract with the East India Company to Scott, Fairlie and Hare of London, who were well-known owners of Indiamen, but this did not affect his contract with Bayley.[51]

The first of the ships, the *David Scott*, was launched on 13th September, 1821. A strong wind blew her aground on one side of Bayley's channel and, although a steam tug was standing by to tow the ship to the Thames, there was a delay in getting her up to the scene. The tide was on the turn before the towropes could be passed; they broke, and the Indiaman remained fast until the next tide. The *William Fairlie* was launched without incident on the 27th September. These two ships, measuring 1,348 tons apiece, were the largest ever to be built on the Orwell. Their construction proved profitable for Bayley, and he was able to pay off his creditors.[52]

Among other craft built by Jabez Bayley at this time was a lifeboat, financed by an appeal organised in the town and to be stationed at Landguard Fort, on the Suffolk side of Harwich Harbour. Designed by Richard Gower, the boat was quite unlike any other lifeboat: she was of very light construction, 30ft. long by 6ft. beam, and she was rigged with spritsails on two short masts. She pulled only six oars, and was designed for a crew of seven. For added buoyancy she had cork-filled casings fore and aft and air tanks under the thwarts. She was built at the St. Peter's yard, christened *The Ipswich Life Boat* and launched on 4th April, 1821, 'from off the wharf into the river, a considerable descent', with a crew on board to simulate a service launching. She was immediately put through her paces for the benefit of the large crowd of spectators; the coxswain on that occasion being my relative, Benjamin Hamblin.[53]

Unfortunately the boat had only a short and unsuccessful life. Local pride required her to be stationed in Suffolk, but at Landguard Fort there were only soldiers to help launch her; the boatmen to man her would have to come across from Harwich, where there was already another lifeboat, provided by an Essex organisation. As far as is known, the *Ipswich* was launched only once in service – to assist a brig ashore on the Platters, a sandbank just outside the harbour entrance, and on that occasion she was manned by coastguards. When the Suffolk Shipwreck Association was founded in 1824 it voted £35 to put the boat in repair: she was refitted by Jabez Bayley and her beam was increased to 8ft. 6in., which sounds as though the design had not proved satisfactory. A year later the Association investigated the suitability of the station and decided that it was 'of no use whatever', whilst the boat was dismissed as 'totally inefficient'. She was sold and by March, 1827, was advertised for sale in Ipswich as a yacht, probably the first of the many lifeboats to be so converted.[54]

Meanwhile, George Bayley's son, also named George and whom we have already met, was apprenticed to Jabez in 1812, at the age of 14. He was an apt pupil and keen to learn. Jabez had promised him that he would take him into partnership, if he wished, when he was of age. He was surprised therefore when, in 1821, Jabez insisted that he should start up in business on his own account in the St. Peter's yard: after all, it was the young man's personal property, which he had inherited from his parents. But Jabez was at that time struggling financially: the Halifax yard was scheduled to close when the two East Indiamen were launched, and it seems likely that he wished to see his nephew standing on his own feet, even if perhaps as a competitor, before any crash. So it was that George set up his own business at the end of September, 1821, with capital of £1,500, while Jabez continued only in Raymond's old yard in St. Clement's. In January, 1825, Jabez was declared bankrupt.[55]

His property was advertised for sale. The Halifax yard, covering nearly six acres, was held under a lease from 'the late Mr. Ashmore' which would expire on Christmas Day, 1826 (apparently a 21-year lease); it contained many buildings, including covered saw pits, all erected during Bayley's tenure. He had also leased from the Corporation about $6^1/_2$ acres of adjoining mud flats, through which he had dredged the cut to launch the *Orwell*. Altogether he had spent nearly £4,000 on the premises. There were his yards in the parish of St. Clement, as we have seen. He owned standing trees as far away as Groton, Ixworth and Colchester. Among his other possessions were 'valuable draughts' (alas, where are they now?) and copies of the well-known books on naval architecture by Stalkartt and Steel. His shipping interests comprised only 8/64 shares each in the schooners *Elizabeth* and *Sincerity*, built at Ipswich in 1816 and 1818 respectively, probably by himself: both were listed in *Lloyd's Register*. There was also the whole of the little schooner *Susan*, employed in the coasting trade.[56]

Bayley had undoubtedly put Ipswich on the map and had brought considerable economic benefit to the town. There was widespread sympathy for him and, remarkably, a public appeal was launched to reinstate him in business. Captain Isacke and Messrs. Scott, Fairlie and Hare, for whom he had built the East Indiamen, were among the subscribers, and as a result Bayley was able to resume business in a modest way on the other side of the river.[57]

However, Jabez Bayley had never quite monopolised ship-building in the town. There was another yard in the parish of St. Peter – that of William Cordingley. Its precise extent is unknown, but it lay to the east of the Bayley yard, on marshland where the Fulcher family had a timber yard.

When he was reporting on proposed improvements to the river, the Newcastle engineer, William Chapman, recommended an earlier version of the New Cut across 'Mr. Fulcher's Ooze'. In 1804 it was to extend from 'Mr. Bayley's shipyard to Cliff Reach'. Two years later he was saying that if the fall in the river at low water 'between Mr. Cordingley's yard and the upper end of Mr. Fulcher's cut through the Ooze' was sufficient, the flow from the Gipping could be diverted down that cut so as to facilitate the work

This drawing by Jacob Dedham shows the St. Peter's shipyard as seen from the *Wherry Inn* on the other side of the river. The site of William Cordingley's shipyard can be seen further to the left on the far riverbank. *Ipswich Borough Council Museums and Galleries.*

of the men deepening the channel by the town quays. Fulcher had evidently made a cut to improve the access to his wharf.[58]

Cordingley's yard did not appear in the St. Peter's rating assessments until 1809, but he was evidently well established by 1805, when he secured an order to build a steam dredger for the newly appointed River Commissioners. They obviously had faith in his ability to build the hull so that the machinery being manufactured by Boulton and Watt in Birmingham would fit; she would need to be stoutly built, too. Cordingley also built the barges to attend the dredger.[59]

In 1811 Robert Fulcher purchased the hull of the *Ville de Lyons*, a captured French ship of 400 tons, to use as a dry dock, but a few months later he was breaking her up and selling her timbers.[60] He advertised the premises for sale in 1812, and the yard was described at that time as having 'a new-built quay with a slip-way for landing and laying timber, being 300 feet in front of the River Orwell'. There was a crane capable of lifting 6 tons and a three-storied coal warehouse, 100ft. long by 25ft. wide: it is all shown on Jacob Dedham's watercolour of Stoke as seen from the *Wherry* inn. There was also 'a piece of land or ooze lying contiguous to the wharf and timber yard, nearly enclosed with a bank, and used for laying and floating timber': this, deepened and altered, undoubtedly later became the pond for Tovell's roman cement mill and survived as the Branch Dock until the 1920s. In 1813 William Cordingley advertised that he had 'engaged the Timber Yard, Wharf and Crane, formerly belonging to Mr. Robert Fulcher, near Mr. Bayley's Ship Yard', and at the same time the annual valuation of his property in the rating assessments rose from £10 for 'a shipyard' to £14 for 'land, etc'.[61]

Little is recorded of Cordingley's business: he was completely overshadowed by Jabez Bayley so far as the newspapers were concerned. He rarely even advertised any sales of timber leftovers, those sure indicators of shipbuilding activity. After the dredger and her attendant barges, nothing seems to be recorded as built by Cordingley until he advertised a new 92-ton brig, ready for launching, in 1816.

With local building dominated by Bayley, Cordingley was obliged to concentrate on the lower end of the market – ship breaking and repairs – but as Bayley declined he began to secure orders for a few coasters. These included the schooner *Deft* in 1823, the sloop *Lady Middleton* and the schooner *Mary* in 1825 (the latter for Cobbold and Aldrich) and the schooner *Glory* in 1827. In June, 1828, Cordingley announced that he was declining business, but vessels continued to be registered as built by him, e.g. *Susan and Ann* (1831) and *Mary Jane* (1833), even though he died in March 1832 'after a long affliction', aged 71. It is probable that the Stoke yard closed about 1830 and the business, nominally headed by William but managed by his son John, moved across the river, as we have seen. Only John, in St. Clement's parish, featured in Pigot's *Commercial Directory* in 1830.[62]

George Bayley's venture into business on his own account in 1821 was not entirely successful. After a year of poor results he consulted John Ridley, an uncle on his mother's side of the family who was a prosperous local wine merchant, and was agreeably surprised when Ridley, having examined the books of the business, offered to enter into partnership with him, trading as George Bayley & Company. George had secured orders for three 500-ton vessels, but then he succumbed to typhoid fever and was gravely ill for several months, so that Ridley was obliged to purchase the release of the firm from the contracts at a total cost of £1,100. Their fortunes revived in 1824 when they built a 200-ton smack, the *Sir William Wallace*, for the passenger service between Leith and London, together with a few small craft for local owners and a schooner for the English Copper Company of London.

This schooner, the *Gower,* was designed by Richard Gower, and seems to have been the last vessel built to his plans. Her masts were stepped in tabernacles so that they could be lowered to enable the vessel to pass under London Bridge to the company's wharf. She was said to be somewhat tender on her trials, but she was still trading in 1884, registered at St. Ives, where she was owned by the Hodge family for many years. Latterly, Gower lived in Ipswich. An umbrella-like sea anchor which he had designed was tested off Harwich only about a fortnight before his death on 1st July, 1833, and he lies buried in the churchyard of St. Mary Stoke, where his grave may still be seen.[63]

In the meantime, George Bayley was designing vessels for his relative, William, who was then building in Woodbridge. He built the steamers *Ipswich* and *Suffolk*, together with four schooners for London owners and a second 200-ton smack, the *Earl of Wemyss*, for the Old Shipping Company of Leith. When the last of the schooners, the *Orwell* of 111 tons, went down the ways in July, 1826, she was reported to be the eighth new vessel built by the firm in twelve months.[64]

At the same time the firm invested in the first patent slip in the locality: it was capable of carrying three vessels side by side. A year later an advertisement described them as being also 'Chain Cable Manufacturers and Agents for Yetts' Patent Apparatus for the security of Ships' Windlasses'. William Yetts was an ironfounder at Great Yarmouth, and his apparatus was doubtless some type of pawl. They built a couple of sailing barges in 1827, the *Ipswich Trader* and the *Suffolk Trader*.[65]

Then, for the next few years there was little indication of any activity in the yard. At least one small smack, the *Industry*, was built for the stone dredging trade, but there were no advertised sales of even old ship timbers. Soon George was barely solvent and decided to give up business. He sold most of his assets to pay off his debts and the partnership with the Ridleys – John Ridley had by this time been joined by his son William – was dissolved on 25th March, 1831. However, he retained his ownership of the St. Peter's yard and it was leased to his uncle, Jabez, who moved in with his partner William Read, having vacated Godbold's former yard in St. Clement's.[66]

One of the first vessels they built at the St. Peter's yard was the barge *Merchant* for the Suffolk and Norfolk Shipping Company; measuring nearly 97 tons, she was the largest barge thus far built in Ipswich, and she seems to have been boomsail rigged. In 1832 the partners built the 304-ton barque *Orwell* on speculation; due to a

A brig in the New Cut, photographed by Robert Burrows in 1858. The cast-iron Stoke Bridge constructed by William Cubitt in 1818 can just be discerned in the right background. *Suffolk Record Office*.

hitch in the arrangements for checking her at her launch she ran across the river and collided with a warehouse on the opposite side, causing some damage. Bayley and Read also lengthened the Sunderland snow *Faithful* for John Cobbold and his associates, and among other craft they built were the schooners *Allihies* and *Law Ogilby* for the ports of Swansea and London respectively.[67]

Jabez Bayley died in September, 1834, and the scheming William Read tried to defraud his widow Susan of her share in the partnership capital. Although George Bayley, when an apprentice, had disliked her, considering her to be 'of an avaricious and grasping disposition', he was able to protect her interests now by accepting only her as the tenant of the yard. Read moved back to St. Clement's parish to work with the blockmaker Enos Page. After Jabez' affairs had been properly settled, it was Susan Bayley who announced that the St. Peter's yard had been let to Read & Page.[68]

The firm of Read & Page became notable among Ipswich shipbuilders, although the first vessel that they are known to have built, a 10-ton smack, the *Providence*, was too small to require registration: she may have been launched from one of the St. Clement's yards. In April, 1836, a sale of leftover timber 'arising from the building of several large ships' was advertised to take place at their St. Peter's yard. One of these was the 116-ton schooner *Guineaman*, for London owners, and another was the brig *Euphemia*, of 158 tons, for Greenock owners and intended for the Newfoundland stockfish trade. Like William Bayley, Read & Page were soon building vessels for owners in all parts of the country, for this was a time of increasing trade.[69] On one day in December, 1837, the partners launched the fruit schooner *Water Lily* for William May of Ipswich and the coaster *Wrestler* for Manningtree, followed a few weeks later by the 361-ton barque *Hope* for the Canadian lumber trade: the yard had at least three slipways.[70]

However, the construction of the Wet Dock was now about to involve the excavation of the New Cut, and it would pass right through the St. Peter's yard. The newly formed Dock Commission purchased the yard from George Bayley, and Read & Page, as tenants, were given notice to quit by the end of September, 1838. In May they moved to the Halifax yard.[71]

This yard had not been used for shipbuilding since Jabez Bayley had launched his East Indiamen, apart from one brief period when Edward Phillips built small craft there. In October, 1836, Phillips' stock had been advertised for sale there: he had a 10-ton smack nearly ready to launch, and another of 28 tons in the early stages of framing. He had probably become insolvent. Nothing else seems to be known of either Phillips or the craft he built.[72]

The first vessel to be launched by Read & Page from Halifax was apparently the schooner *Kate & Jane* for the port of Ipswich, followed by another for Manningtree on the same day in August, 1838.[73] In the following January the schooner *Osprey*, for the Swansea copper trade, went down the ways; like the *Gower*, her masts were stepped in tabernacles so that she could berth above London Bridge if required. By September the Halifax yard was equipped with a patent slip – perhaps brought from the St. Peter's yard. Among other vessels built by the firm in 1839 were the 200-ton brig *Chamois,* for London and coppered for the Brazilian trade, and the 205-ton barque *Hero* for the partners themselves; she was lost a few months later.[74]

In October, 1839, William Read visited Liverpool, travelling to London in the steamer *Orwell* and thence by rail. He was probably one of the first Ipswich people to travel in a train, and he wrote about his journey in the *Suffolk Chronicle*.[75] He did not say why he went, but it may well have been to consult John Laird or others on

Merseyside about iron shipbuilding, for as we have seen, it was shortly afterwards that Read & Page made their offer to build an iron steamer for the Ipswich Steam Navigation Company.

However, the *Orion*, as she was to be called, was not the first iron vessel to float upon the Orwell. In May, 1840, the *Ipswich Journal* reported:

> On Thursday the 30th ult ... several amateur mechanics, accompanied by the proprietors, made an experimental trip down the river Orwell, in the *Vulcan* iron yacht. This yacht is of a new construction; it answers every expectation, as it was sailed at a rapid rate with only a square sail, and with but little wind. The yacht was built by W. Teager, under the direction of Messrs. Teager and Singleton, juniors.

It is unfortunate that we do not know more of this vessel. Among the Singleton family in the town at that time were two described as 'Ironmongers and Braziers', while the Teagers were whitesmiths and gas fitters. These were people who worked with metal, but I suspect the newspaper was mistaken, and the *Vulcan* was actually built by Read, perhaps with help from these metal workers in cutting and handling the plates. By that time the Halifax yard contained 'a new building recently erected for manufacturing the iron work of the new steamer' when it was damaged by fire.[76]

In spite of very wet weather a large crowd turned up on 27th October to see the steamer launched. Her construction had not been uneventful: according to the *Suffolk Chronicle*:

> The *Orion* was laid on the stocks in the month of March last, and would have been launched much earlier had the men employed upon the iron part of the vessel been more disposed to hard work. Some of them, strangers to the town and neighbourhood were, in consequence of not giving satisfaction, discharged, and others left of their own accord. The difficulty of finding artisans suited to this part of the work, in this locality, caused delay...[77]

The building of the ship was a remarkable achievement for Read & Page, but due perhaps to these labour difficulties it did not lead to much new business.

They followed her by building an iron sailing barge, appropriately named *Ironsides*, which was first registered as owned by them on 29th October, 1841. She was not quite the first 'ironpot' barge (that honour must go to the *Frederic*, built at Blackwall in 1840) but she had an interesting history. She often carried beer direct from Stowmarket to London; with a length of 51.2ft. and a beam of 13.4ft. she could negotiate the locks on the river Gipping which were 60ft. long and 14ft. wide. After a few weeks in this trade she lost her first skipper, William Baker, who was crushed against Creeting Bridge, near Needham Market, when he slipped over the side whilst working the barge through. A month later his son, the mate, was lost overboard from the same barge in the Swin, tragically illustrating the range of her passages. At first she was described in the Register as clench-built, with a round stern and no bowsprit. She was sold in May, 1843, by which time she had been lengthened by 20ft. and her depth increased by 18in.: she then had a square stern and a lifting bowsprit. She was also described as carvel-built, suggesting that she had been sheathed with wood, as the *Frederic* was. In this guise she won the earliest known barge race, at Harwich in 1844. With a length to beam ratio of over five – which is very high for a barge – and a jib on her bowsprit she must have required careful handling, particularly as a contemporary engraving shows her with a topsail set above her sprit mainsail.[78] In 1852 she was re-registered at Harwich and in 1865 in London, where she was finally hulked in 1885.

Read & Page built a second iron barge, the *Gipping*, in 1842. She was marginally larger than her predecessor, but she too could just fit into the Gipping locks. Her first owner was John Stevens, a Stowmarket brewer, who may have ordered her construction. Unlike the *Ironsides*, she was described as carvel-built from the outset, so she was probably sheathed with wood: she also had a square stern and a running bowsprit. In 1854 she was sold to

A contemporary print showing the earliest recorded barge race, at Harwich Regatta in 1844. Presumably the *Ironsides* is the leading barge.

HARWICH REGATTA.—SIXTH CLASS SPRITSAIL BARGES.

Robert Paul, and when re-registered was said to be clench-built: at that date the Register contained the specific note: 'Her Framework and Planking is Wood and Iron'. She then had a round stern. A few years after Paul's death in 1864 his executors sold her to one Hugh Abbott of Ipswich, when she was said to be clench-built on iron frames – and spritsail rigged, as she may always have been. She was lost off Orfordness in 1870.

According to a history of Stowmarket written in 1844 'An artesian well has been formed by Messrs Stevens & Co (brewers) . . .for soft water for their ale and beer, that are sent in large quantities to London in iron boats of 45 tons by the canal and thence by sea without shifting their cargoes'. Whether there were others I do not know, but many wooden barges at that time were capable of negotiating the Gipping locks. Incidentally, the earliest instance of a sea-going vessel on the Stowmarket Navigation was in 1810, when the Yarmouth fishing lugger *Independence* arrived at Ipswich with a catch of some 4,000 mackerel. Finding the market glutted, her skipper 'hoisted his colours' and proceeded up the Gipping to Needham and Stowmarket, where he readily disposed of his fish.[79]

The next iron vessel to be built at the Halifax yard was the cutter-rigged yacht *Enigma*, of 25 tons, in 1843. She was originally registered as owned by both partners, but it seems to have been Read who was the sailing enthusiast. In June that year she won the Grand Challenge Gold Cup of the Royal Thames Yacht Club, when two of the other four competing yachts were apparently also of iron. She also won her race in the Eastern Coast Regatta at Harwich in 1844 (at which the first barge race was held) when she was reported to be owned by a Mr. Wilkinson of London. His purchase was not recorded in the Ipswich Register, but the vessel was transferred to London in 1847.[80]

William Read and Enos Page dissolved their partnership in 1844, and advertised their lease of the Halifax yard and all the stock for sale. No purchaser of the lease came forward, and after a time Read decided to continue the business on his own. In September, 1845, he launched a pair of 64-ton smacks for Samuel Hewett of Barking.[81]

In 1846 Read built what seems to have been his last iron vessel, the sloop *Vulcan*; two years later he lengthened her by 10ft. and re-rigged her as a ketch. He seems to have found little demand for iron ships and retained ownership of her too, until he sold her in 1858 to a trio of gentlemen who were all prominent in local affairs. She was listed in *Lloyd's Register*, but I do not know what she was used for; and her British registry was closed in 1859, when she was

Built by Jabez Bayley in 1826, the schooner *Fortitude* was Ipswich owned throughout her life and was eventually wrecked near Reawick in the Shetlands in 1868.

arrested for debt at Rotterdam and sold by court order: the purchaser was a Dutch national.

Her registry in 1858 gave her under deck and gross tonnage as 79.93, and her registered dimensions were 68.7ft. long, 17.3ft. beam and 7.9ft. depth in hold. From these figures may be calculated her 'coefficient of under deck tonnage' to obtain an indication of the fineness of her lines.[82] The under deck tonnage of a vessel is derived from the volume of the hull below the main or only deck, counting each hundred cubic feet as one ton. The product of the registered dimensions gives the volume of a cuboid of roughly the size into which the hull would fit, and the coefficient is obtained by dividing this block volume into the hull volume. The *Vulcan* must have been flat bottomed and of extremely bluff shape, for her coefficient was as high as 0.85: for barges and billy boys, not the most fine-lined of craft, it ranges from about 0.6 to something over 0.7.

The launches of these iron vessels were not mentioned in the local press, but enough was reported of Read's other work to indicate what he was doing. While he was building the two smacks for Hewett, Lord Alfred Paget, who was said to have owned more yachts than anyone else in the 19th century, visited the yard to order a similar vessel for himself, for 'pleasure fishing'. This, the *Albacore*, was launched in 1846: she went down the ways fully rigged, but ran aground and fell over, so that her topmast knocked a man into the water – it sounds as though she mounted the side of Jabez Bayley's cut. In the same year Read launched the *Teazer*, a pilot schooner of 71 tons for Liverpool.

In the following year the yacht *Proserpine*, a schooner of 120 tons, was built for the Hon. George Byron (the son of the poet's cousin, and himself destined to succeed to the title later) and taken into the wet dock to be fitted out. Two 180-ton schooners, *Shark* and *Snake*, for London owners, followed; it was reported that their design was aimed at sailing qualities rather than capacity and that no less a figure than Sir William Symonds, the Surveyor of the Navy, had visited the Halifax yard to see them. An officer from the Customs and Excise also came, following reports about the *Teazer*, but no orders for either warships or revenue cutters resulted, as far as I know.[83]

Read was arguably the most innovative of all the Ipswich builders. The skipper of his tug *Caledonia*, one Charles Hadgraft (a member of a well-known local seafaring family), was preparing to go to Harwich to repair a vessel's boiler on one occasion when he was injured by a steam sawing engine in the Halifax yard. Apart from this chance reference to mechanization in the yard, another press report stated that a small fire among shavings was smothered using plates recently removed from the bottom of the steamer *River Queen*. It is evident that Read continued to repair iron vessels after he had ceased to build them.[84]

When the barge *Mary* was built at the Halifax yard in 1848 Read provided her with wire rigging, which was a remarkable innovation in so small a vessel at that time. As with his iron craft, he retained ownership for a time. By the time he sold her in 1853 she was ketch rigged: she was certainly one of the very first ketch barges, but as she was lost in that year she has been but little remembered.[85]

Early in 1850 Read disposed of his business to Thomas Harvey & Son of Wivenhoe, a firm which had been operating on the Colne since 1832 and was well known for building fast vessels of all kinds. Their first launch in Ipswich seems to have been that of the *Avalon*, a 39-ton cutter-rigged yacht built for a Mr. Goodson of the Royal Thames Yacht Club. The only Ipswich-registered sailing vessel which they built at Halifax was the 62-ton schooner *Foam* in 1851: she was recorded as jointly owned by Thomas Harvey and Thomas Harvey Junior, 'shipbuilders and co-partners trading as Thomas Harvey & Son'. Thomas junior, born in 1833, was the younger brother of John, who later succeeded their father as head of the business in Wivenhoe, while young Thomas seems to have spent his time in Ipswich.[86]

In 1852 the wooden paddle steamer *Prince* was launched from the Halifax yard and towed to London to receive her engines. She was built for the Eastern Union Railway's service between Ipswich and Harwich and, remarkably for a wooden vessel, was reported to be fitted with watertight bulkheads. What was said to be the finest vessel built in the town for 20 years went down the ways at Halifax on the last day of June, 1855, when the 404-ton barque *Inkermann* was launched for trade to the Far East: she foundered in Chinese waters in 1859.[87]

In 1855 Thomas Harvey contracted to build four mortar vessels for the navy. The war with Russia (it was only the Crimean War from the army's point of view) was then in progress, and following the successful bombardment of fortifications at Sveaborg, near Helsinki, using small craft carrying mortars, the Admiralty ordered a further series of 34 such vessels from private yards. They were tubby round-sterned craft, 75ft. long with a beam of $23^{1}/_{2}$ft., measuring about 168 tons. They were given a cutter or dandy rig, and they were armed with a single heavy mortar amidships, on a massive mounting constructed of 12in. x 12in. timbers. This, and the need for rapid production, precluded steam power, but it was of little consequence as they were intended to be towed into position

Although briefly registered in London at one time, the schooner *Rapid* was also Ipswich owned throughout her life until being wrecked at the mouth of the Somme in 1866.

and to discharge their missiles at anchor, while the high angle of elevation of the mortars allowed them to operate beyond the range of conventional low-trajectory artillery. They were intended to form part of a large task force to attack Cronstadt and St. Petersburg in the summer of 1856, but in the event the war was over by the spring and most of these vessels became anchored watch vessels for the coastguard. They formed the last large class of sailing vessels to be built for the Royal Navy. Of Harvey's quartet, MV 45 and MV 46 were built at the Halifax yard in Ipswich and Nos. 47 and 48 at Wivenhoe. No. 45 was launched in March, 1856, to be towed away by the naval tug H.M.S. *Monkey*, and No. 46 a month later, to be fitted out at Woolwich.[88]

Harvey's tenure of Halifax was marked by disputes with their apprentices. In January, 1856, twenty-one lads appeared before the magistrates charged with 'insubordination in the service of their masters'. It was stated that on that morning they had refused to work because they were bound for seven years, and they had learned that Harveys had just taken on three or four other apprentices for only four years. The chairman of the bench told them that their masters could not submit to such 'tyranny', and eight of the lads were sentenced to 10 days imprisonment and the others were formally reprimanded.

A year later there was another stoppage, when 17 apprentices downed tools because their starting time had been brought forward

Halifax shipyard in 1858, when it was being operated by Thomas Harvey & Son. The figure on the second vessel from the left is Thomas Harvey junior, and the next vessel, with a mast stepped, is the fruit schooner *Nonpareil* of Ipswich, built in this yard in 1848. *Suffolk Record Office*.

to 5 a.m. and the customary half-hour break at 11 a.m. had been abolished. Young Thomas Harvey was in court to give evidence, but the magistrates noted that there was nothing in the indentures about working hours and they declined to take any action. In 1860 there was another case, when three apprentices were charged with absenting themselves without good reason.[89]

To take these matters to court appears excessive today. In the case of the four-year apprentices, it sounds as though Harveys had recruited extra cheap labour, perhaps to complete their mortar vessel contract on time. It might be that young Thomas Harvey handled the grievances tactlessly, determined to uphold his authority.

The end came a few years later, when Thomas senior wished to retire. Perhaps the Halifax yard had been losing money, or possibly the two sons did not get on with each other; but on the first day of 1864 the partnership between Thomas and his two sons was dissolved 'by mutual consent' and the Halifax yard closed for good. John continued to run the yard at Wivenhoe until he disposed of it in 1881 and emigrated to the United States, to practise as a naval architect specialising in yachts.[90] I do not know what happened to his younger brother, whose son, a retired architect, was living in Ipswich when I met him in the 1960s.

Loading a barge on the Orwell foreshore, *c.*1858. In this photograph by Robert Burrows the barge is lying on Cobbold's yard, just to the east of Bayley's St. Clement's yard. *Suffolk Record Office*

Yards round the Dock 9

By the 1820s the shipyards in the parish of St. Clement had been extended over the foreshore to the south, as described in Chapter Seven. At the southern end was the ballast wharf, and beyond it lay a wide area of mud flats which extended inland to the the line of the modern Cliff Road, which was then a rope walk. This adjoining land, protected by a bank, belonged to John Cobbold.

In 1829 Cobbold purchased the foreshore, down to his brewery and maltings at the Cliff, from the Corporation.[1] It was a far-sighted move. When the construction of the Wet Dock was proposed a few years later about half the area he had acquired would be inside the dock and thus ripe for reclamation and industrial development. As it turned out, the new Dock Commission would even require somewhere to dump the spoil raised from the bed of the river, and so would reclaim the mud flats for him. However, the first reclamation was on the foreshore nearer the Cliff, outside the dock.

William Bayley's shipyards on the old 'Carpenters' Row', also owned by Cobbold, would soon be inside the dock, and were doubtless being eyed by the Ransome brothers, eager to extend their agricultural implement works. It was arranged that Bayley should move to a yard to be established on the newly reclaimed land: he probably wished to have his business on tidal water, to facilitate the beaching of vessels for repair. The new site was ready by about the end of 1840, and the Dock Commission paid Bayley £1,100 to move.[2]

The business had been known as William Bayley & Company since about 1838, which was about the time when William Bayley junior had become a partner. The principals may also have included Charles Crowe, who was described as a shipbuilder in the Shipping Register and who owned shares in one or two of Bayley's ships from about 1845 until he died in 1854. By 1855, when James, the younger son, had entered the partnership, the firm was named William Bayley & Sons.

The first vessel to be built in the new yard was probably the cutter *Eagle* for the Dutch cheese trade of John May, a local merchant. November, 1841, saw the launch of the schooner *Invincible* for the port of Swansea; and in the following April the schooner *Laura Ann* for Burnham in Essex was reported to be the sixtieth vessel which the firm had built in the past ten years. Among other vessels launched at that time were the 250-ton barque *Ipswich* for a Jersey owner and two of 300 tons, the *British Tar* and the *Mary Montague*, for the same London owners. All were sheathed for deep-water voyages.[3]

The buildings in the yard were, of course, all new, and the workshops were laid out in accordance with the latest ideas. There was a steam engine from the local firm of Bond, Turner & Hurwood for driving a sawmill, making treenails and hauling ships up on the patent slip. Soon Bayley himself was living on site in a spacious house, which incidentally survived until after the Second World War as a lodging house. When the *Mary Montague* was launched in 1849 a journalist reported that the yard covered an area of four acres. So it did in total, but the Bayleys were not the only occupiers.

At the end nearest to the brewery John Cobbold had a small yard where timber could be landed and his vessels beached for repairs. Here he may have built his barge *Cliff* in 1858, but not until 1862 was it described in the rating assessments as a shipyard, when the *Adela*, 'a beautiful clipper brig which has lately been built in Mr. Cobbold's yard near the Cliff' was launched on 29th May. The launch was intended to be part of the festivities when a lifeboat named *Ipswich*, paid for by an appeal in the town, was brought from her builders in Limehouse to be christened, formally handed over to the R.N.L.I. and launched into the Orwell for the gratification of the townspeople. Unfortunately the *Adela* remained fast on the ways and was not put afloat until a day or two later.[4]

The Cobbold fleet was greatly reduced after the death of John Cobbold in 1860 and the family did not operate their yard for long: five years later it became part of the Bayley premises. It was only small and, although it contained a workshop, it is difficult to believe that it had all the facilities for building an ocean-going vessel; some of the work for the *Adela* was probably done next door.

At the other end of the complex was William Colchester's yard, part of which lay between the Bayleys' yard and the tree-lined roadway running along the lower dam forming the dock. It was later called the Dock End Yard, although that name did not appear until the end of the century. Exactly when the yard was established is unknown. Colchester was still occupying his timber yard on the old 'Carpenter's Row' at the end of 1841, and it is possible that the first two barges he is known to have built – *Raven* and *Primus* –

were constructed there. White's 1844 *Directory of Suffolk* did not mention William Colchester even as a boatbuilder: he was listed only as a timber and slate merchant in College Street, where contemporary drawings indicate there was no room for a slipway.[5] The following advertisement appeared in the *Ipswich Journal* dated 26th January, 1850:

> SHIPYARD, IPSWICH. W. Colchester will be glad to Repair Vessels, Boats and Barges of every description at his Shipyard, St. Clements, at the very Lowest Charge, for Work and Materials. A large Assortment of Excellent Blocks to be Sold very Cheap.
>
> Blockmaker's, and Sailmaker's, and Smith's Work at the Lowest Price.
>
> Also, a Large Assortment of Red and White Wood Deals and Timber, to be Sold very Cheap.

Perhaps this was when the yard opened, in which case the barges which Colchester had launched earlier, *Quintus* and her predecessors, were probably built on slips rented from the Bayleys. It is significant that the *Quartus* (1846) was built in London, but we shall never know why. So far as is known, nothing larger than a

The ceremonial launching of the lifeboat *Ipswich* from the Promenade in 1862, seen in a contemporary engraving. The *Adela* on John Cobbold's yard is barely visible in the background on the extreme right. *Robert Malster.*

A view from Stoke Hill in 1887 showing the site of the short-lived yard on which the barges *Grace* and *Augusta* were built in 1874. *Robert Malster*

barge was ever built in Colchester's yard, but as the launches of these humble craft were not usually reported in the local press it is difficult to identify those which were built there. Apart from the *Quartus,* Colchester built all his barges, which were named with Latin ordinal numbers; the last was the *Octavius* in 1863.

The earliest that I know of which was built for another owner was the spritsail-rigged *Express* of 1854, owned initially by three local men and a Westminster brewer; she was sold to Yarmouth owners in 1858 and re-registered there in 1865. The *Express* was also the first Ipswich sprittie to be initially registered as having two masts: with earlier craft, the registrars ignored the small mizzens stepped on the rudders. The Pauls had the *Mabel* built by Colchester in 1875, and later they bought the *Albatross*, which had been built in the yard in 1869. Colchester also built the ketch barge *Fearless* in 1876, the dandy-rigged *Davenport* in 1877 – she was partly owned by her first skipper, Captain John Hooker, my great uncle – and the *Mary Offer*, for Harwich, in 1880.

During this time George Mason & Co, a local firm of timber and cement merchants, decided to have their own barges. Remarkably, they built the first two themselves in 1874, the *Grace* and the *Augusta*, launching them from a yard of theirs in Burrell

A schooner on the grid near Colchester's shipyard, a photograph taken by Robert Burrows in 1858. The old Cliff Brewery can be seen behind. *Suffolk Record Office*.

Street (now Burrell Road) at the foot of Stoke Hill, not far from the railway tunnel. This short-lived shipyard was the highest up the river.[6] It was above Stoke Bridge, where the river is narrow and, as the site slopes steeply to the water, the barges must have been launched sideways. The experiment was not repeated. Mason's next barge, the *Kingfisher*, was built by William Colchester, who seems to have serviced their entire fleet.

Having many other business interests, Colchester did not run his shipyard himself. Indeed, by 1847 he lived at Little Oakley, near Harwich, and by 1860 he had moved to Grundisburgh Hall, near Woodbridge, where he resided for several years before moving back to Ipswich. A foreman named James Hubert managed the yard: he was a shipowner himself, owning at different times barges wholly and shares in others. In the Register he described himself as a shipbuilder or a bargebuilder. Fortunately, and I believe uniquely for an Ipswich shipyard, many of its records survive.

These include several disbursement books from the 1870s. Every week Hubert paid the rent for the yard, which was £1 18s. (£1.90), the workers' wages and various other outgoings. At its busiest, the yard employed 18 hands. Six of these, including

Hubert himself, received 4s. 6d. (22½p) per day, three were paid four shillings but one, identified only as J. Benstead, with no explanation, received five shillings per day. One of these was no doubt the sailmaker – the yard employed its own – and another the blacksmith. Two other men were paid 3s. 6d. each day and another 2s. 4d. The remainder were probably boys: two were paid something over a shilling each day and were probably apprentices, while the other three received only 8d.

However, under some system which defies explanation over a century later, the men were often paid for seven or more days each week. Usually, but not invariably, these enhanced payments were in the summer months, reflecting longer daylight hours. Not everybody received quite the same wage in the same week, and a man would often have an hour added to or deducted from, say, a 7½ day week. Hubert himself usually, but not always, received the highest pay, and occasionally the daily rate of pay for him and some of the others rose to five shillings for odd days. Night work, rarely mentioned, was worth only a few coppers more than in daytime. There was no consistency, and the scheme seems to have applied to all but the lowest-paid boys.

Other men, described as sawyers (the only trade mentioned), were paid a few pounds at irregular intervals: these were self-employed, or came from a local timber yard. One entry was for 'Mr Taylor's man 325ft. sawing' which cost 16s. 3d.; a William Taylor was among the town's timber merchants. Some sawing was said to be by steam.

The weekly outgoings, totalling over £20 in the summer, sometimes included travelling expenses to London, or some other port, or perhaps to villages in the district, when Hubert went to buy timber. He paid for carting trees from these villages, or rail freight charges for spars or pitch pine from further afield, but not usually for the timber itself. Chain, rope, wire rope, canvas, hair and nails also came by rail, together with larger items like anchors, stoves and windlasses, but Hubert seems to have paid only for the carriage. Men from the yard probably felled standing trees, and perhaps they also acted as bottom sawyers in the sawpits.

Among the sundry payments, there were purchases from time to time of a hundredweight or so of grease at 4d. per pound. This would have been for lubricating the ways when a vessel was to be launched: on one occasion Hubert bought 187 lb. of butter at the same price. Another unusual item was the expenditure of 2d. for 'Gunpowder for Furnace': perhaps this was for clearing soot from the flue, and significantly it seems not to have been repeated.

Hubert's outgoings were often offset by cash receipts, such as 'Mr. Ashby. Barge *Peace* Topmast £1 9s. 0d.' or 'Policeman. Repairing Perambulator 6d.'.

Other books recorded the cost of the various jobs carried out. Most were not remarkable in themselves, but considered together it is apparent that in the 1870s the yard maintained Paul's barges, and also those of George Mason as has been noted. Labour was always booked at five shillings per day and sawing at the same figure for cutting 100 feet. One job was for making a new 'caboose' for Colchester's own barge *Tertius*, at a cost of £2 7s. 6d.: this was a portable galley to be lashed in position on deck, not only to save space but to facilitate its jettison in the event of fire. The *Tertius*, less than 70ft. long and sloop-rigged, seems small to be so equipped – even the little 18th-century sloops had a stove below deck.

William Colchester gave up the shipyard in 1884 or 1885, and James Hubert seems to have retired. Thereafter he called himself a shipowner in the Register; he died in 1892.

We must now go back to 1850, when it was feared that the British shipping industry was about to go into recession following

The schooner *Mute* on St. Clement's Shipyard. This vessel, built at Fareham, Hampshire, in 1853, was owned by the Bayleys from 1867 until she was lost in 1893.

the repeal of the Navigation Acts. These, of which the principal was the Act of 1651, laid down that British exports were to be carried only in British ships, and the only foreign vessels permitted to bring imports were those flying the flags of the countries where the goods had been produced. The Acts were repealed as from 1st January, 1850, on which day it was reported that most of the vessels lying windbound in Harwich Harbour wore their colours at half-mast.[7] Shipowners feared that foreign ships would enter the east coast coal trade, but in the event the threat did not materialise. The British merchant navy was far and away the largest in the world, and other nations simply did not possess the tonnage to enter this traditional British trade. In general, however, British shipowners were obliged to look to their ships and their methods.

William Bayley at the St. Clement's shipyard noticed the effect almost at once. In March, 1850, he wrote to the *Ipswich Journal* saying that in the previous 10 years he had built, on average, four vessels a year, ranging from 60 to 400 tons apiece, and had often had to decline orders; but at that time, he was building nothing under contract and was receiving few enquiries. In that year, he seems to have built only two vessels – both clipper schooners. One was the *Ipswich Lass*, which he retained until he was able to sell her to a London owner early in the following year; the other, the *Acis*, launched in July, was to the order of another London owner, and Bayley was considered to have done well.[8]

The vessels shown in this photograph of St. Clement's Yard in 1862 bear some resemblance to those shown in a photograph and the print on page 133 of the launch of the lifeboat *Ipswich* in that year. The brig on the extreme right is in Cobbold's yard next door and must be the *Adela*. The workshop with its chimneystack almost concealed by the mainmast of the schooner on the left survived into the second half of the 20th century.

The recession in British shipyards was also caused by the high cost of home-built ships compared to those from Canada: in 1840 just over a third of the tonnage which was newly registered in Great Britain had been built there. Ipswich owners may have been more cautious than the national average over investing in softwood-built vessels, but in almost every year between 1837 and 1866 they bought one or two of these ships. However, there were none after 1849 until 1854, when five arrived, together with a 214-ton brig, the *Unrestricted*, newly built by Durand Freres at Granville in France. The discovery of gold in California and Australia had boosted international trade. We may note in passing that even in Suffolk a rumour swept through Hadleigh in July, 1852, that gold had been discovered at Friar's Hill, just outside the town, sparking off a mass exodus of people eager to make their fortunes.[9]

The business of William Bayley & Sons picked up, but the heady days of the previous two decades had gone for ever. Early in 1852 the firm launched a 250-ton barque that they had laid down on speculation, but she was sold before completion: christened *Arethusa*, she was towed to London to embark emigrants for South Africa.[10] Bayley's last vessel for himself was the brig *Susan Bayley*, launched in 1853. Her first voyage was to Genoa with railway chairs from Ransomes, and she once sailed from Plymouth to Beirut in 18 days. After Bayley's death in 1857 she was sold to London owners, and by 1884 she was under the flag of Argentina.[11]

The schooner *Alarm* was built in 1855 for a couple of local master mariners for the fruit and Mediterranean trades, and she survived as a coaster into the 20th century. A fortnight after she went down the ways, Bayley's career reached its peak when the ship *Siam* was launched with difficulty down her slip at the St. Clement's yard. She was of 743 tons, and intended for trade to the Far East. She was the largest ship to be built in the town since Jabez Bayley's East Indiamen and was soon taken up as a transport to the Crimea, registered at Newcastle.[12]

Meanwhile, in about 1852 William Read had opened a new yard inside the dock,[13] although it did not appear in the rating assessments until 1857. It was on or near the site of Cordingley's former premises, adjacent to the cement works opposite the Customs House: it was later called the St. Peter's yard. After Read had disposed of his business at the Halifax yard he had withdrawn altogether from shipbuilding work; he owned a couple of steam tugs, *Caledonia* and *Endeavour*, and several sailing craft.

His new yard was not ideally sited. It had no patent slip and, as the water in the dock was tideless, he could only repair vessels below the waterline by the ancient process of careening. This involved emptying the hull of all ballast and stores, and sending down all spars above the lower masts, to the tops of which stout tackles were rigged to heave the vessel down on to her side. With a large ship, it might be necessary to brace the masts with struts and preventers and put internal shores in the hull. It was a laborious procedure, and if anything should then shift or carry away it could be very dangerous. Nevertheless Read's people once hove down a 400-ton barque so that her keel was three feet out of the water.[14]

At first Read seems to have built only a few small smacks, but in 1859 he launched the fruit schooner *Maid o' the Mist* for a West Country owner, followed by one or two such vessels each year. Two of his best remembered schooners were launched in 1862: the *G.C. Love*, for trade in the Far East, and the *Bob Tail Nag*, both for London owners. On one occasion the *G.C. Love* suffered an unusual mishap in the East China Sea when a swordfish pierced her bottom planking. The *Bob Tail Nag* was later owned in Brisbane and is said to have been employed in 'blackbirding', or kidnapping men for labourers, among the Pacific islands.[15]

Over the next few years a succession of round-bottomed vessels was launched into the placid waters of the Wet Dock. For local owners, these were the brigantines *Dauntless* and *Mary Campbell* and the three-masted schooners *Emblyn* and *Fern*. For other ports they included the schooners *Audax, Eliza Reed, Devonia* and *Fruit Girl*, the barquentine *Minnie* and the brig *Woodbine*. Of course, Read also built smaller craft such as the *Alpha*, a pilot cutter for Southwold, and undoubtedly some barges; for example, he was the first owner of the sprittie *Active*, built in 1862, and the boomsail-rigged *Endeavour* of 1865. Unfortunately the official Register at that time often did not name a vessel's builder and, as sprities were not listed in *Lloyd's Register*, there is often no record of who built them.

Soon after the launch of the *Fruit Girl* in February, 1866, Read retired and the St. Peter's yard was taken over by his foreman, Ebenezer Robertson, who was also his great-nephew.[16]

One of Robertson's first moves was to install a patent slip, particularly important in this yard on tideless water. Under his direction St. Peter's became arguably the most productive yard in the port at that time, with the construction of from five to seven vessels each year, ranging up to 300 tons. The employees numbered up to 98 men and boys.[17]

Among the earliest launched was the barquentine (or three-masted brigantine) *Uncle Ned* in 1867 for Daniels Brothers of Whitstable. At first she traded on deep water but then, cut down to a brigantine and eventually as a schooner, she sailed in the coasting trade. Latterly owned in the Irish port of Arklow, she was not broken up until the Second World War, being the last Ipswich-built round-bottomed trading vessel to survive.[18] By no means all of Robertson's output can be identified, but 1870 saw the launches of the brigantine *Elizabeth Morton*, soon re-rigged as a schooner, and the dandy *May Flower*, both for Ipswich owners; followed in 1872 by the barquentine *William* for deep water trade from Yarmouth, the schooner-rigged barge *Lothair* for Watts of Harwich, and probably the composite-built spritsail barge *Lucretia* for a local owner.[19]

The yard shown in this photograph of about 1860 by Richard Dykes Alexander, the chairman of the Dock Commission, is probably William Read's St. Peter's Yard inside the dock.
Suffolk Record Office

A watercolour by an unknown artist of William Read's St. Peter's Yard in its earliest days.

In 1874 Robertson launched what was probably his most remarkable vessel when he secured the order to build a twin-screw iron steamer, the *Trafik*, for the Swedish port of Skelleftea in the Gulf of Bothnia. She was only a small craft, 66ft. long overall, for carrying passengers and light cargo between the mainland and offshore islands, but she seems to have been a rare instance of a vessel built in Ipswich for a foreign owner. Shortly after her launch the *Trafik* was reported to have been purchased by another company and to be destined for Gothenburg, to work as a tug and passenger vessel on the rivers there – presumably on the Gotha Canal. She carried a fore-and-aft rig. Her two 20 hp twin-cylinder condensing engines and her Scotch boiler came from William Mason's *Eagle Iron Works* on the dockside at Ipswich, which were by no means the largest engineering works in the town.[20]

Many of the later craft from the St. Peter's Yard were barges, notably the schooner-rigged *Alice Watts* and *Lucy Richmond*, both launched for Essex owners in 1875.[21] Robertson built several for himself, together with the fore-and-aft schooner *Ariel* in 1881: she was the last round-bottomed trading vessel to be built in the port for a local owner. Other craft included fishing smacks and several yachts, such as the composite-built dandy *Atalanta* for the younger Edward Packard. Another was the schooner *Blanche* of 62 tons in 1868: she was later acquired by Sir James Ferguson, the Governor of New Zealand.

In 1884 Robertson took over the old Lime Kiln Yard at Woodbridge to develop the yacht-building side of his business, which his son and then his grandson carried on for many years. He gave up the St. Peter's Yard in 1886 and by 1902 he was living in Rochester, working as a marine surveyor. He died in 1913.[22]

After the death of the elder William Bayley in 1857 his sons, William and James Rogers, carried on the family business. In his will their father left his leasehold in the St. Clement's Yard to them jointly, so long as they continued in partnership, but he seems to have thought that this might not continue, for he directed that if the partnership should be dissolved the remainder of the lease should pass to William.[23] As we have seen, the split came in 1872.

For a few years the brothers carried on building small deep-sea vessels: e.g. the schooners *Lily* (1858), *Snowdrop* (1859) and *Blue Bell* (1861) for local owners; and *Forest Fairy* (1859) and *Orange Blossom* (1860) for the port of Falmouth.[24] Their father had built

A photograph taken in 1858 by Robert Burrows showing a brig up on the patent slip in St. Clement's Yard. Note the clutter of timber typical of a small shipyard at that time. *Suffolk Record Office*.

up a reputation for his ships beyond his home town but the sons were comparatively unknown; after 1861 they seem to have built very few vessels to order, although pictorial evidence suggests that their yard was kept busy with repairs. They built several shallow draught coasters, but whether expressly for themselves or upon speculation with no purchaser coming forward is unclear. The ketch barge *Earnest* and the schooner *Surprise* were both sold after a time, but on the other hand the boomsail barge *Alpha* and the schooner *Problem*, with her three keels, remained in their ownership until they were lost.

The last vessels they built for themselves were the fruiters *James R. Bayley* (1863) and *Thought* (1864), but right at the end of their partnership they launched the barquentine *Elizabeth Stevens* for Welsh owners. Whether or not they built any spritsail barges, apart from the *Lady of the Wave* in 1862 for the port of Woodbridge, I do not know.

The brigantine *Clementine* on the ways at St. Clement's Yard in 1885. She was the last round-bottomed sailing craft to be built in Ipswich.

The brothers certainly had no lack of capital for their business. Whenever other Ipswich builders of the time constructed a vessel for themselves they usually mortgaged her at once, often to their banks to secure overdrafts, but the Bayleys never did.

Once he was on his own, it was not long before William resumed building for other owners, but whether this was due to a definite change in policy or merely the state of the market it is impossible to say. Certainly in 1873 a schooner barge, the *Parkend*, was launched for Sully of Bridgwater and in the following year the fruit schooner *Enchantress* went down the ways for Edwin Pope of Falmouth, for whom the Bayleys had built the *Forest Fairy* and *Orange Blossom* over a decade before.

Local owners, however, were turning increasingly to barges. The larger craft, rigged as schooners or ketches, were well able to trade to continental ports and were better suited to the shallow havens of east coast England. Even so, it was not until 1878 that Bayley built any more of them: *Azariah* and *Onward*, the latter remaining in his ownership for about a year. In 1879 he launched the sprittie *Invincible* and kept her for a couple of years: she may have been the first of her rig built at St. Clement's since 1862, but other builders in the town now specialised in these craft.

Bayley still traded as William Bayley & Sons: he had a son, yet another William, who ran the chandlery side of the business. Since the late 1860s the firm had advertised iron ship repairing among the services on offer, but few iron vessels visited the port and there was probably little demand for work of that kind. Bayley & Sons seem never to have ventured into building ships of iron or composite construction, or any steamships.

In his later years Bayley's output consisted mainly of barges, mostly ketch rigged but including some sprittles, e.g. *Intrepid* for himself in 1881 and *Emily* for Pauls in 1882. However, in amongst them he still managed to secure orders for deep-water craft: the barquentine *Lucy* for Hull owners in 1879 and the schooner *Grace*, of London, for the Newfoundland stockfish trade in 1883. When the *Grace* was launched the *Suffolk Chronicle* commented sadly, 'In these days a ship launch in Ipswich is a somewhat rare spectacle'. Finally, in 1885, the brigantine *Clementine*, of London, went down the ways at the St. Clement's Yard: she also was for the Newfoundland trade and she was the last round-bottomed trading vessel built in the town.[25]

One or two more ketch barges followed, and the firm built its last craft, the spritsail-rigged *Inflexible*, in 1889. Within a few weeks the yard closed and the chandlery was moved to other

Left: This workshop on St. Clement's yard, seen here in 1952, dated from the earliest days of the yard. Originally it probably contained the steam engine that powered the patent slip and the machine shop, but by 1912 it housed the smithy. A steam chest or kell for bending planks can be seen across the left hand end; by this time a small vertical boiler on the other side of the building supplied the steam for it. **Below:** The boiler for the steam chest, which can be seen towards the right. In the background is the *Riverview Hotel*, William Bayley's erstwhile home.

premises on the dockside. William Bayley, the head of the firm, died on 21st January, 1892, aged 73, and, sad to relate, his son William succumbed to illness only eight days later, at the age of 38.[26]

It is strange that not even the Cobbold family had a vessel built by the Bayleys after the death in 1857 of the elder William, with whom they had often been closely associated in their shipping activities. As we have seen, J.C. Cobbold built his *Adela* in his own yard next door; and his son, John Patteson Cobbold, took delivery of the family's last vessel, the brigantine *Constance*, in 1865. She was built by John Lambert, perhaps a former Cobbold employee, in a new yard called the Cliff Yard, which was opened on the south side of the brewery in that year.

John Lambert, in partnership with one Alfred of the same name, ran the yard for about five years. In addition to the *Constance*, they built the schooner-rigged barge *Edith* for themselves and others in 1867, and the schooner *Zenobia*, felted and yellow-metalled for warm seas, for Welsh owners in 1870. Among other vessels from the yard were the ketch barges *Kate* and *Emily*, the latter for the port of Maldon.[27]

In 1870 the Cliff Yard was briefly occupied by the Bayley

Dock End Shipyard in 1907. On the left the *Robert Powell* is being rebuilt as the *Wolsey*. The barge in the shed is the *Jock*, and in the centre we see the *Emily* under repair.

The remains of the barge *Inflexible* on Shotley Point about 1950. Launched in 1889, she was the last vessel built by the Bayley family of Ipswich.

brothers, but after James left the partnership it was taken over by William Curtis. The younger William Bayley also vacated the old Cobbold yard where the *Adela* had been built, and after it had stood empty for about three years this, too, was taken over by Curtis.

The name of William James Curtis first appeared in the rating assessments of the area round the shipyards in 1854, as the licensee of the *Ship Launch* public house that stood on the corner of Shiplaunch Road, which ran along the back of the St. Clement's Yard towards the lower dam of the dock. After a time, he began to build boats in a nearby shed before taking over the Cliff Yard. He retained the licence of the pub until 1876, which enabled him to provide a comprehensive service to the owners of vessels built in the yard, with celebratory dinners prepared under the supervision of Mrs. Curtis.[28]

Curtis soon installed a new patent slip in the yard and began repairing vessels.[29] The first that he built appear to be the sprittie *Deben* for Woodbridge, the dandy *Mystery* for Harwich and the ketch barge *Pioneer* for Maldon owners, all in 1874. Several other ketch barges followed: e.g. *Gazelle* (1877), *William* (1878) and

The ketch barge *Kate*, built by the Lamberts in 1867. She was sunk in a collision in the Thames in 1888, raised and repaired and then sold to a Faversham owner, eventually being broken up in 1909.

Reindeer (1879). In that year he also built the sprittie *Frederick William*, by which time the yard foreman was his nephew, William Harvey Orvis, who had 24 shares in the barge. Another 24 were owned by Frederick Fuller, later to be Orvis' partner for a time in their own shipbuilding firm; Fuller was described in the Register as a railway contractor's manager, of Notting Hill Gate in London. Curtis himself held the remaining 16 shares in the barge.

The ketch barge *Eliza Patience*, built by Curtis in 1883, seems to have linked the names of Mrs. Orvis (Orvis married twice) and Mrs. Patience Fuller. Orvis originally owned 32 of the shares and Fuller 16, while the remainder were taken by two of Fuller's associates in London.

Curtis also built the steam barge *Eaglet* in 1883. She was a little wooden vessel of only 21 tons gross (14 tons nett), fitted with a simple-expansion engine of 5 NHP from the Ipswich firm of E.R. & F. Turner. She was originally owned by Richard Blake, a miller and coal merchant of Bramford, and William Haste, her skipper. At first she plied up and down the Gipping but later, when owned at Sudbourne, she sailed between Orford and Ipswich, arriving at Ipswich with farm produce and departing with mixed cargoes of coke, paraffin, cattle feed, etc. In 1911 her name was changed to *Hycol* and she was sold away to Hull, where she was still working in 1935.

Curtis vacated the small former Cobbold yard, next to the St. Clement's Yard, about 1879: for the next couple of years it was recorded as 'empty' in the rate books and then it ceased to be mentioned. In 1885 Curtis retired and the Cliff Yard was taken over by William Orvis and Frederick Fuller, who also took over the St. Clement's Yard, empty since Bayley's time, in 1891, when Orvis moved into Bayley's old *River View* house on the premises. Fuller had retired from his post in London in 1889, and moved to Yarmouth. In a Register entry he described himself as a ship and barge builder at this time, but he was only a financial partner and not actively engaged in the business. He left the partnership in 1896, and Orvis continued with his son Ernest under the title of W.H. Orvis & Co.

Orvis & Fuller built two ketch, or boomie, barges for Ipswich owners, *Matilda Upton* (1887) and *Pearl* (1889), followed in 1891 by their last vessel of the type, *Lord Tennyson*, for Walker & Howard of London. The sritties they built included the *Stour* for

The Cliff Shipyard, a detail from an early-20th-century postcard of the old Stoke Bathing Place.

The *Ardwina*, launched from St. Clement's Yard in 1909, was the last of the many barges built in Ipswich.

Pauls and the *Petrel* for Masons – she was later owned by Cranfields for many years.

W.H. Orvis & Co launched a number of spritties, including *Spinaway C* (later with Cranfields) and, for Horlocks, *Vigilant*, winner of the Coasting Class in the 1928 Thames Barge Match. The very last sailing barge built in the town was the *Ardwina*, which went down the ways at St. Clement's at about the time William Orvis died in 1909; she was registered in London and for many years was owned by Goldsmiths of Grays.

At the same time, Orvis & Co left the Cliff Yard and this was taken over by the Dan Marine, Motor, Shipbuilding & Engineering Co. Ltd., a company which seems to have been a subsidiary of P. Jorgensens of Copenhagen, manufacturers of paraffin engines. Some of these engines were fitted into sailing craft as auxiliaries, and others into new vessels, some built in the Cliff Yard and others built elsewhere by sub-contractors. In its first couple of years the Dan Marine Co. is said to have built half a dozen new motor launches and fitted its engines to vessels of up to 70 tons. The workforce averaged 40, but at times up to 70 hands were employed.[30]

The company introduced steel shipbuilding to Ipswich, the first vessel being a motor barge of 20 nett registered tons, the *Eaglet*,

The boomie barge *Pearl*, built by Orvis & Fuller in 1889. She survived as a hulk until after the Second World War.

for Kenneth Clark of Sudbourne Hall in 1910. She replaced the wooden steamer of the same name already referred to, which was taken by the Dan Marine on a 'trade in' basis in part exchange. The new vessel was fitted with a twin cylinder Jorgensen engine of 50 brake h.p. which gave her a speed of 7 knots. Perhaps she was not entirely satisfactory, for in the following year her slightly raised forecastle was removed and a raised poop added: a water ballast tank was also installed. All this resulted in a small increase in her gross tonnage, to 44 tons. Clark retained her until November, 1918, when he sold her to an owner in Southampton. She remained registered at Ipswich and successively passed through several other hands, but nothing is recorded of her after 1922 – with ships, unlike motor vehicles, owners are under no obligation to inform the authorities of their demise.

Another Dan Marine vessel was the launch *Pin Mill*, whose wooden hull was built by the Whitstable Shipping Co. in 1910. For about a year she was chartered to Sir Thomas Lipton, the grocery magnate, who had a concession to provide canteen facilities for personnel in the warships stationed at Harwich. After this had expired the launch required repairs, and she was then offered to the G.E.R. Company for £400. The company purchased her in 1912

Opposite: A plan showing the shipyards outside the dock about 1875, based on the Parliamentary plan for the construction of the present lock, opened in 1881.

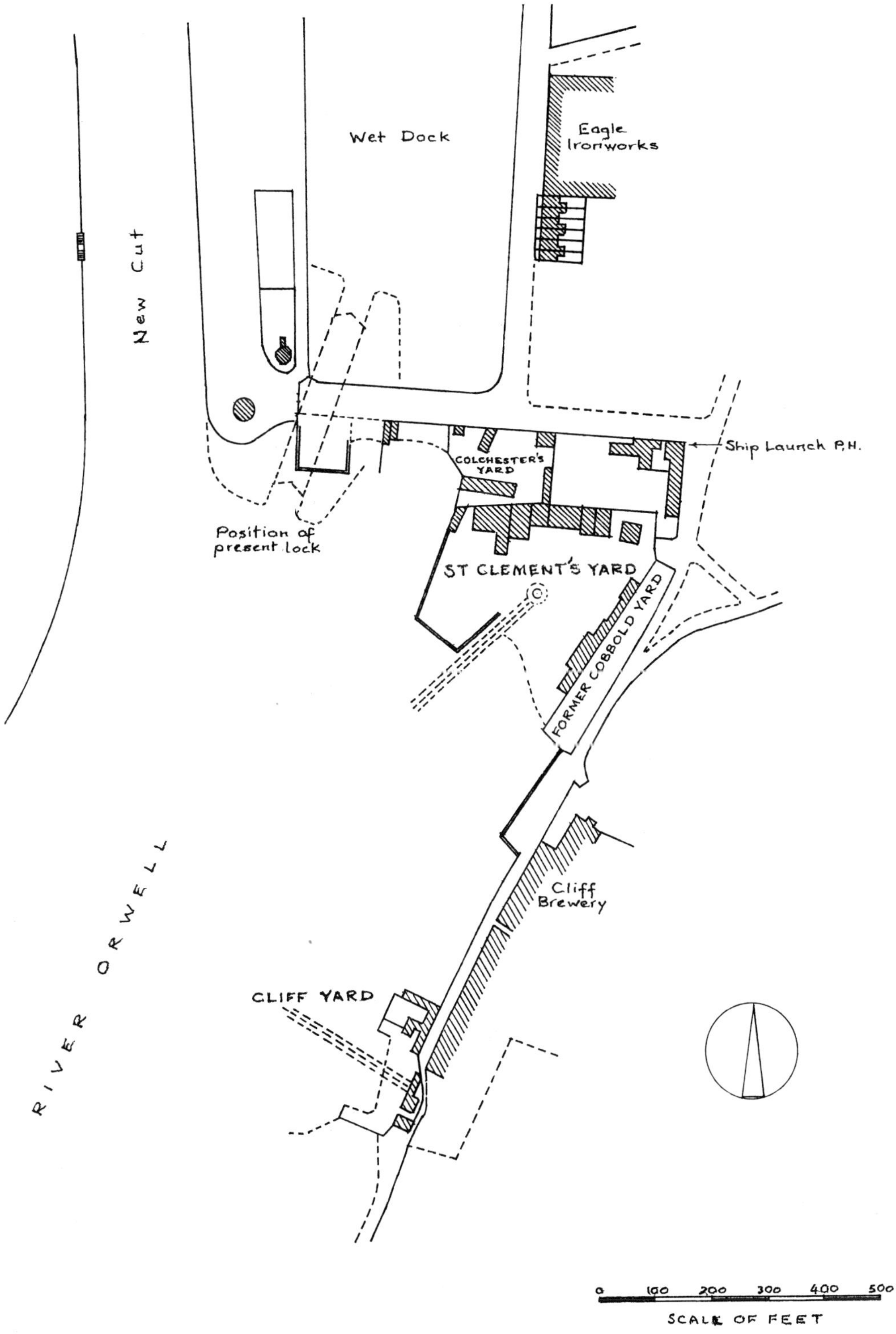
Wet Dock
Eagle Ironworks
New Cut
Ship Launch P.H.
COLCHESTER'S YARD
Position of present lock
ST CLEMENT'S YARD
FORMER COBBOLD YARD
RIVER ORWELL
Cliff Brewery
CLIFF YARD
0 100 200 300 400 500
SCALE OF FEET

and she remained in railway service for some 70 years,[31] and is still afloat at Ipswich.

The stories of these two vessels suggest possible losses for the Dan Marine Co. who may have been too generous in their efforts to popularise their vessels and engines. Certainly British fishing craft owners were slow to adopt auxiliary motors and preferred to invest in new steam vessels, while it was to be some years before the spritsail barge required auxiliary power to maintain her viability. The Royal Navy used boats with paraffin engines, but did not favour equipment unless spare parts were manufactured in this country. In both the naval and mercantile fields there were established British companies to compete with. There is evidence to suggest that the Dan Marine Co. was becoming financially embarrassed by June, 1913, and a year later it was in liquidation.[32] After the First World War, when the Dock Commission began the construction of Cliff Quay, a deep-water berth outside the Wet Dock, the Cliff Yard disappeared under its approaches.

As we have seen, William Colchester closed his yard in about 1884. The lease was taken over by George Percy Gildea, who built two ketch barges, *Southern Belle* and *Northern Belle*, in 1885 and three in the 'Lord' series – *Lord Shaftesbury* (1886), *Lord Hartingdon* (1887) and *Lord Iddesleigh* (1888) – all for London owners. Little else seems to be recorded about Gildea, who closed his yard soon afterwards and moved to Rochester.[33]

The yard was then taken over by Robert Peck and John Benstead (the latter presumably being Colchester's former employee), although all the barges they built were registered as built by Peck alone. These included the spritties *Gipping* and *Orwell* in 1889 and *Colne* in 1890, all for R. & W. Paul. When the *Flower of Essex* (later with Cranfields) was launched for Howard and Humphreys of Great Wakering, Essex, in 1890, Peck was able to provide credit terms for them in the shape of a £450 mortgage for a year, but then his fortunes declined.

He built the ketch barge *Ethel Edith* for himself in 1892 and was obliged to mortgage her immediately to provide working capital. She was followed by the *Ivy P* in 1893, the last boomie to be built in Ipswich, and she too was used to secure his credit. Horace Shrubsall, a member of a well-known barge-building family in Kent, had taken over the yard by May, 1895, but the two barges proved to be a profitable investment for Peck, and by 1904 they were free of debt. The *Ethel Edith* was then sold to a Kentish owner and in 1911, at the age of 67, Peck sold a half share in the

The ketch barge *Ethel Edith* and other coasters entering the Wet Dock about 1900. Built by Robert Peck in 1892, the *Ethel Edith* was owned by him until sold to a coal merchant in Kent in 1904. The pit for the railway swing bridge can be seen on the far side of the lock; it was part of the original design, but the bridge itself was not installed until 1904.

other barge and probably retired. He disposed of her remaining shares in 1916 and died in 1931.

When Shrubsall took over the yard he named it the Dock End Yard, and it became for a time the busiest in the port. The first barge that he built there was the *Rowland* in 1895 and over the next six years at least a dozen others went down the ways. Only one, the *Ethel Ada*, was for a local owner, for Eldred Watkins, the lime and cement merchant, in 1897. In that year Shrubsall opened a second yard at Limehouse, on the Thames, but early in 1901 he left Ipswich and concentrated all his business at East Greenwich.

R. & W. Paul Ltd. then took over the Dock End Yard, following a dispute with William Orvis who had previously maintained their barges. Pauls built several barges for themselves, and for many years they repaired and refitted their sizeable fleet themselves. It was common practice for an elderly barge to be sheathed with a complete extra layer of planking, and Pauls dealt with several of their craft in this way. However, after the *Tollesbury* had been sheathed in 1927, work of this kind was again carried out in the St.

Barges in the Wet Dock about 1953. The vessel on the right is the *Memory* of Ipswich, built at Harwich in 1904.

Clement's Yard next door; but Pauls carried on at the Dock End Yard as long as they owned barges in trade, and it finally closed in the early 1970s.

Orvis & Co. built no more vessels after the *Ardwina* until 1916, when they launched the steam barge *Trent River*. She seems to have been the very last trading craft to be built in the port: a wooden vessel of 22 tons gross, $13^1/_2$ tons nett, with a 20 indicated horse power compound engine by Plenty & Sons of Newbury.

Ernest Orvis left St. Clement's in 1927, and various repair companies worked the yard, with its patent slip, until 1951. For a time a large part of it was used for storing scrap metal, but at the time of writing the yard is again being used for ship repairs. It is the last to carry on a proud tradition which extends back for at least seven centuries.

Notes and References

Abbreviations

MM *The Mariner's Mirror*, Journal of the Society for Nautical Research
IJ *Ipswich Journal*
SC *Suffolk Chronicle*
SROI Suffolk Record Office, Ipswich branch

Preface

[1] Keith Wade, *The Origins of Ipswich* (Suffolk County Council, 1981), p.1 and p.10.

1 Ipswich ships 1700–1824

[1] MM 41, p.232. The Customs list did not include the port of London, but this source quotes London figures obtained from elsewhere.
[2] *Ibid*.
[3] IJ 29 Jan 1743.
[4] *Ipswich Gazette* 21 July 1733.
[5] F.H. af Chapman, *Architectura Navalis Mercatoria* (Stockholm, 1768). This work has been reprinted at least twice since 1957.
[6] IJ 1 Sept 1750.
[7] IJ 10 March 1810.
[8] IJ 17 Feb 1770.
[9] IJ 11 Feb, 22 April 1758.
[10] IJ 4 Jan 1777.
[11] Register of Woodbridge Ships, 1816/5 (SROI IG 2/4/1).
[12] IJ 20 Aug 1803. The 1816 Bill of Sale was in private hands when I saw it.
[13] IJ 28 April, 6 Oct 1753.
[14] IJ 16 Feb, 6 April 1754.
[15] IJ 14 Aug 1762.
[16] IJ 24 Jan, 16 May, 8 Aug 1767.
[17] IJ 30 May 1767.
[18] IJ 26 Dec 1767.
[19] IJ 20 Feb, 5 March, 12 Nov 1768.
[20] IJ 25 March 1769.
[21] IJ 21 Sept 1771; 26 June 1773.

[22] IJ 16 Aug 1777.
[23] IJ 21 Oct, 28 Oct, 4 Nov, 1780; 3 March, 7 July 1781.
[24] IJ 12 Nov, 31 Dec 1785.
[25] IJ 22 April, 18 Nov 1786; 22 March 1788.
[26] IJ 1 Aug 1789; 23 Oct 1802.
[27] IJ 12 Oct 1816.
[28] IJ 24 June, 1 Oct 1808; 15 Sept 1810.
[29] After Ipswich received its first charter in 1200, the town was presided over by two bailiffs until 1836, when a mayor took their place.
[30] IJ 1 Oct 1763.
[31] IJ 18 Aug 1764; 19 Jan, 8 June 1765.
[32] IJ 23 June 1744.
[33] IJ 18 Nov 1749.
[34] Bills of Sale, SROI Ref: W3/2/1; IJ 21 March 1778.
[35] IJ 5 March 1803, 16 May 1807.
[36] Register of Woodbridge Ships 1800/15.
[37] IJ 25 Oct 1794.
[38] IJ 20 Oct 1770.
[39] IJ 29 April 1780; 2 April 1796.
[40] IJ 27 March 1773.
[41] *Original Ipswich Journal* 29 May 1775 (Due to an ownership dispute there were two *Ipswich Journals* between 7 Jan 1775 and 22 March 1777, when publication of the *Original* ceased).
[42] IJ 5 Oct, 12 Oct 1782.
[43] IJ 6 Jan 1810.
[44] IJ 2 June 1798; 9 March 1805; SC 9 Nov 1811; IJ 18 Oct 1823.
[45] IJ 18 Nov 1809; SC 8 Aug 1817; IJ 9 Jan 1813.
[46] Shipping Arrivals and Sailings in IJ 17 Jan 17 Jan 1807.
[47] Nathaniel Bacon, *The Annals of Ipswich*, ed. W.H. Richardson (1884), p.482.
[48] G.R. Clarke, *The History and Description of the Town and Borough of Ipswich* (1830), p.307.
[49] *Ipswich Gazette* 28 Oct 1734.
[50] IJ 26 July, 2 Aug 1788.
[51] IJ 9 May 1807.
[52] IJ 8 May, 22 May 1819.
[53] IJ 14 Jan 1797; 17 May 1800; 12 Sept 1807.
[54] IJ 22 July 1826; 16 Nov 1844.
[55] Shipping Arrivals and Sailings in IJ 8 Nov 1817; 12 Oct 1822; 22 March 1828.

2 The Ipswich Whale Fishery

[1] IJ 24 Dec 1784.
[2] IJ 9 Dec 1786.
[3] IJ 3 Feb, 31 March 1787.
[4] IJ 28 July, 4 Aug 1787.
[5] IJ 11 Aug 1787.
[6] IJ 25 Aug 1787; J. Wodderspoon, *Memorials of the Ancient Town of Ipswich* (1850), p.218.

[7] IJ 18 Aug 1787.
[8] IJ 16 Feb, 23 Feb, 8 Mar 1788.
[9] IJ 1 March, 12 April 1788.
[10] IJ 8 March, 29 March 1788.
[11] IJ 30 Aug, 6 Sept 1788; Wodderspoon, p.219.
[12] IJ 9 May 1789.
[13] IJ 18 April 1789.
[14] IJ 11 July, 8 Aug 1789.
[15] IJ 1 Aug 1789.
[16] IJ 29 Aug 1789.
[17] IJ 9 Sept 1789; Wodderspoon, p.219.
[18] IJ 4 Aug 1798; *Lloyd's Register* 1823, 1842.
[19] IJ 9 Oct 1790.
[20] IJ 7 Aug 1790, 30 July 1791.
[21] IJ 2 March 1793, 1 Feb 1794.
[22] IJ 11 Jan, 1 Feb 1794.
[23] G.R. Clarke, *The History of the Town and Borough of Ipswich* (1830), p.406.

3 Ipswich ships 1824–1860

[1] Under the Act 4 Geo IV cap 41. Complete registers back to 1786 now survive for only 25 ports and former ports in England and Wales, including Colchester, Maldon and Woodbridge. Some early books for the port of London are still extant. See MM Vol. 55, p.3 *et seq*.
[2] Act 6 Geo IV capt 110.
[3] Veere on the island of Walcheren.
[4] IJ 19 Oct 1833.
[5] IJ 14 Jan 1854.
[6] The vessel was wrecked on the Point of Air in North Wales on 28 Nov 1833 (See IJ 7 Dec 1833). The Register just says 'Lost', with no details.
[7] SC 31 Aug 1850.
[8] IJ 26 Sept 1857.
[9] IJ 17 April 1847.
[10] IJ 16 Sept 1837.
[11] IJ 2 March 1850.
[12] IJ 24 May 1823.
[13] IJ 8 Dec, 20 April 1861.
[14] IJ 28 Jan 1860.
[15] IJ 15 Feb 1840.
[16] IJ16 March, 23 March, 20 April, 19 Oct 1844.
[17] R. Gardiner, *Sail's Last Century* (1993), p.80; IJ 21 Nov 1846.
[18] IJ 22 Jan 1842; Register of Woodbridge Ships 1839/5.
[19] IJ 3 Aug 1850. High water was at 3.31 a.m. (see IJ 27 July 1850).
[20] IJ 14 Sept, 9 Nov, 14 Dec 1850; 11 Jan 1851; Minutes of Committee of Management, Ipswich Dock Commission, 31 July, 24 Aug, 28 Dec 1850 (SROI Ref: EL1/4/4).

4 The First Steamers

[1] IJ 25 Sept 1813; SC 11 June 1814; IJ 13 Aug 1814.
[2] N.W. Kennedy, *Records of the Early British Steamships* (Liverpool, 1933); SC 5 Nov 1814; IJ 12 Aug 1815.
[3] IJ 21 Oct 1815.
[4] IJ 7 Aug 1824.
[5] G.R. Clarke, *History and Description of the Town and Borough of Ipswich* (1830), p.418; IJ 22 Jan, 25 May 1825; P. Banbury, *Shipbuilders of the Thames and Medway* (Newton Abbot, 1971), p.224.
[6] IJ 17 Sept, 19 Nov 1825; 18 March 1826.
[7] IJ 8 April 1826; SC 15 April 1826.
[8] IJ 23 Sept 1826 and *passim*.
[9] IJ 5 April 1828.
[10] SC 29 March 1828.
[11] SC 25 Sept 1830.
[12] IJ 29 May, 5 June 1830; SC 12 June 1830.
[13] IJ 10 April 1830.
[14] IJ 19 July 1834.
[15] SC 21 Nov 1835. I am indebted to the National Maritime Museum for information about the *Commerce* at Bristol and thereafter.
[16] MM 51, p.141.
[17] IJ and SC 26 May 1832.
[18] IJ 4 May 1833
[19] A.B. Randall, 'Betsey Thompson comes to Carmarthen', *Carmarthen Historian* Vol. 18. Betsey was the sister of Francis Thompson, the noted Woodbridge-born architect of early railway stations.
[20] IJ 13 Sept, 27 Sept 1834.
[21] IJ 17 Sept 1837.
[22] IJ 5 May 1838.
[23] IJ 12 May 1838; Kennedy, *op cit*.
[24] IJ 14 July 1838; SC 1 Sept 1838.
[25] IJ 17 April 1841. The figure for 1840 was 44,050.
[26] IJ 13 Oct 1838, 19 Jan, 30 Mar 1839.
[27] IJ 17 Aug, 14 Sept 1839.
[28] IJ 30 Nov, 21 Dec 1839; SC 7 March 1840.
[29] IJ 21 March, 25 April, 22 Aug, 31 Oct 1840.
[30] IJ 17 April 1841.
[31] IJ 11 April 1857.
[32] IJ 25 July 1857. The railway steamers sailed from the western side of the New Cut, where the E.U.R. had laid a short branch to Griffin Wharf.
[33] IJ 31 Oct 1857.
[34] IJ 24 July 1858.
[35] IJ 14 May, 25 June 1859.
[36] IJ 9 March 1861, 6 Sept 1862.
[37] IJ 8 Oct 1864.
[38] I am grateful to Mr J. Swieszkowski of the Great Eastern Railway Society for this information.
[39] IJ 24 July 1858, 8 Oct 1859, 11 Oct 1862, 23 Jan 1864.

[40] *East Anglian Daily Times* 27 Dec 1911.
[41] IJ 27 March, 3 July 1858, 23 April, 25 June 1859.
[42] IJ 22 March 1862.
[43] G.F. Burtt, *Steamers of the Thames and Medway* (1949).

5 Ipswich ships after 1860

[1] Gardiner, ed., *Sail's Last Century* (1993), pp.47-8.
[2] Register of Woodbridge Ships, 1798/5.
[3] IJ 15 Oct, 19 Oct, 22 Oct 1872.
[4] IJ 13 Oct 1860.
[5] IJ 24 Aug 1861.
[6] IJ 27 Feb 1875.
[7] IJ 5 Nov 1885.
[8] *Pigot's Commercial Directory of Norfolk & Suffolk* (1830); William White, *Directory of Suffolk* (1844).
[9] IJ 7 Nov 1840; 9 April 1853.
[10] William White, *Directory of Suffolk* (1855).
[11] William White, *Directory of Suffolk* (1874).
[12] Roger Finch, *A Cross in the Topsail* (1979), pp.10-12.
[13] The *Colchester* owned by Pauls was built at Blackwall in 1890, according to the Register. She was not the vessel whose details appear in Appendix 2 in *A Cross in the Topsail*, although her Official Number, 93977, is given correctly.
[14] Although it has been stated that the barges were sold to French owners, renamed and subsequently re-purchased (as Pauls' surviving records suggest), a time charter is the only possible explanation. Both barges were renamed and registered in London on 29 August 1906, where they remained recorded as owned by Pauls, until both were re-registered at Ipswich on 6 May 1912. The lump sum payments in 1906 and 1912 must have represented depreciation. Under a time charter the owners provide and pay the crew and insure and maintain the vessel. There is evidence to show that during this period the crews were British. The re-registrations in London may have been necessary to comply with French law.
[15] *The late Mr Edward Packard* (SROI S92/22865).
[16] SC 6 June, 20 June 1868.
[17] IJ 7 May, 10 May 1888.
[18] IJ 18 Oct 1890.
[19] IJ 5 Sept 1891.
[20] *Polar Record* Vol. 17, pp.375-381.
[21] Richard Smith, *Blue Water Sail at Ipswich* (1997).

6 Shipbuilding

[1] MM 59, pp.419 *et seq.*
[2] MM 51, pp.131 *et seq.*

7 The old St. Clement's yards

[1] W.G. Arnott, *Orwell Estuary* (1954), p.70.
[2] In SROI (Ref: HA49/6100, Box 21, bundle 3).
[3] In SROI (Ref: HS 6/1/1).
[4] H. Chamberlain, *Ipswich 200 Years Ago* (*c*.1880), p.21.
[5] MM 77, p.10.
[6] As 4 above.
[7] Daniel Defoe, *Tour Through the Whole Island of Great Britain* (1723).
[8] David Lyon, *The Sailing Navy List* (1993), p.25.
[9] John E. Barnard, *Building Britain's Wooden Walls* (1997), p.85.
[10] B.P. Grimsey, *Freemen of the Borough of Ipswich* (n.d.), p.80.
[11] Bills of Sale in SROI (Ref: W3/2/1-6; Boyd's Index of Suffolk Marriages in SROI.
[12] Song sheet, *The Launching of the Orwell, East-Indiaman, at Halifax Ship-Yard, Ipswich* (1817), in SROI (Ref: 782-42 LUA).
[13] As 11 above.
[14] IJ 21 June, 5 July 1740.
[15] IJ 7 Nov, 14 Nov 1741; Barnard, *op. cit.*, p.16.
[16] IJ 19 June 1742; Peter Goodwin, *The Bomb Vessel Granado 1742* (1989), p.9.
[17] *Lloyd's Register* 1764.
[18] IJ 28 Feb 1756.
[19] John Glyde, *Materials for a History of Ipswich* Vol 1, f.35 (SROI Ref: q S Ipswich 9).
[20] Barnard, *op. cit.*, p.14.
[21] Boyd's Index of Suffolk Marriages in SROI.
[22] IJ 2 March 1771.
[23] IJ 25 July1767.
[24] IJ 24 Nov 1759, 14 Nov 1761.
[25] *Lloyd's Register* 1764; IJ 21 Nov 1789.
[26] IJ 18 May 1771, 5 Dec 1863.
[27] IJ 25 Sept 1773.
[28] IJ 28 Nov 1778.
[29] IJ 16 April 1774.
[30] IJ 17 Aug 1765, 23 March 1776; *Original Ipswich Journal* 6 July 1776.
[31] *Original Ipswich Journal* 16 Sept, 7 Oct 1775.
[32] IJ 3 March 1781.
[33] IJ 22 Dec 1781, 26 April 1783.
[34] IJ 1 Nov 1788.
[35] IJ 9 Oct 1784.
[36] IJ 10 Aug 1793, 12 Aug 1797, 12 April 1800, 14 Nov 1801.
[37] IJ 23 April 1785, 21 April 1792.
[38] IJ 18 Oct 1806.
[39] IJ 18 Dec 1784.
[40] SC 16 May 1801; IJ 27 March, 31 July 1802, 5 Feb 1803, 23 March 1805.
[41] IJ 23 Dec 1786, 20 June 1789.
[42] IJ 25 June 1796.
[43] IJ 26 July 1800, 13 July 1811.

[44] IJ 21 Nov, 19 Dec 1818.
[45] MM 51, p.136.
[46] IJ 28 Aug 1824.
[47] IJ 19 Feb, 26 Feb 1825; *Lloyd's Register* 1843.
[48] IJ 19 Feb 1825.
[49] SC 13 Dec 1828, 16 Oct 1830; Robert Malster, *Lowestoft, east coast port* (1982), p.37.
[50] IJ 30 Oct 1830, 1 Jan 1831.
[51] H.R. Eyre, grangerised copy of G.R. Clarke's *History & Description of the Town and Borough of Ipswich* (1830), in five volumes in SROI, Vol 3, p.384.
[52] SC 2 April 1825.
[53] IJ 1 Sept 1832.
[54] SC 7 April, 6 Oct 1827; G.R. Clarke, *op. cit.*, p.458.
[55] Ipswich Dock Commissioners' Minutes, 28 Oct 1837 (SROI Ref: EL1/1/3/4); IJ 24 Dec 1841.
[56] IJ 15 Aug 1835.
[57] IJ 27 Aug 1836; drawings by Edward Caley (SROI Ref: EL1/7/3-6).
[58] IJ 8 July 1826.
[59] IJ 12 May 1827.
[60] *Pigot's Commercial Directory of Norfolk & Suffolk* (1830), p.111.
[61] IJ 23 April 1836; SC 12 March, 6 Aug, 1 Oct, 26 Nov 1836, 6 May 1837; IJ 28 July 1838, 14 Dec 1839.
[62] IJ 13 April 1839.
[63] IJ 29 Feb 1840.
[64] IJ 25 July 1840.
[65] IJ 24 April, 1 May 1841.
[66] IJ and SC 22 Feb 1851. The vessel's name was given to me from the company's engine register by a friend many years ago.

8 Yards on the Right Bank

[1] V.B. Redstone's extracts from the records of Ipswich Corporation (MS in SROI, Ref: S Ipswich 352), Vol. 23, p.7.
[2] eg. IJ 25 July 1789.
[3] Redstone's extracts, Vol. 23, pp.23 and 44.
[4] IJ 9 Nov 1765, 7 Feb 1767, 10 Nov 1770.
[5] IJ 10 April 1773, 13 April 1776, 18 Sept 1777, 4 April 1778.
[6] Pennington's map of Ipswich, 1778; IJ 20 March 1779.
[7] IJ 19 April 1783.
[8] MM 40, p.298n; IJ 17 Sept 1785.
[9] Redstone's extracts, Vol. 23, sec xi, p.113.
[10] IJ 4-11 July 1730.
[11] Ipswich Dock Commission records (SROI ELl/3/2).
[12] The rating assessments included 'Richard Montravers, for a Shop'. The accounts of the parish overseeers of the poor show that on 25 Sept 1752 he was paid £2 1s. 'for mending Henry Wright's boat'. (SROI FBA92/G1/1).
[13] IJ 5 Feb 1763.

[14] IJ 13 Aug, 15 Oct 1763, 24 Mar, 7 July, 15 Sept, 1 Dec 1764.
[15] IJ 25 Feb 1764.
[16] For a full account, see John E. Barnard, *Building Britain's Wooden Walls* (Oswestry, 1997).
[17] MM 51, p.131 *et seq*.
[18] IJ 30 March 1765; 20 Dec 1766.
[19] IJ 16 Dec 1769, 1 Dec 1770, 26 Oct, 16 Nov 1771, 16 May 1772.
[20] *Original Ipswich Journal* 25 May, 23 March 1776; IJ 12 April 1777, 2 May 1778, 22 May 1779.
[21] IJ 22 Dec 1781; Dock Commision records (SROI EL1/3/4).
[22] IJ 23 March 1782, 17 May 1783.
[23] Between Oct 1772 and Easter 1773 Teague was listed among the farmers in the parish of St. Mary Stoke and paid poor rate on land valued at £26 per annum. IJ 17 Jan 1784.
[24] MM 58, p.191.
[25] IJ 26 Mar 1785.
[26] MM 51, p.132.
[27] IJ 23 Feb 1788, 14 Nov, 21 Nov 1789, 9 April, 16 April 1791.
[28] IJ 9 March 1793, 12 April, 15 Nov 1794.
[29] Dock Commission records (SROI EL1/3/8 & 9).
[30] IJ 18 Mar 1797, 29 Nov 1800.
[31] IJ 5 June 1790; MM 51, p.132; IJ 16 Dec 1797.
[32] IJ 30 Nov 1799, 12 April, 6 Sept 1800.
[33] SC 20 Feb, 20 March, 27 March, 17 April 1802; IJ 27 March 1802.
[34] IJ 7 May 1803, 22 Sept 1804, 11 April 1807; MM 51, p.133.
[35] MM 51, p.133.
[36] IJ 19 July 1783, 24 Dec 1785.
[37] IJ 27 June 1795, 18 June 1803, 14 July 1821.
[38] IJ 15 Dec 1804; *Victoria County History of Suffolk*, Vol.2, p.245.
[39] IJ 13 Oct 1804.
[40] G.R. Clarke, *History & Description of the Town and Borough of Ipswich* (1830), p.407.
[41] MM 82, p.423.
[42] IJ 30 Nov 1805, 8 March 1806.
[43] *Dictionary of National Biography*; MM 51, p.133; Dock Commission records (SROI EL1/3/19 & 20.
[44] G.R. Clarke, *op. cit.*, p.407. If correct, the total tonnage cited must be for the merchant ships only; the figure for the naval vessels alone exceeded 9,000 tons.
[45] IJ 26 Jan, 16 March 1811; SC 16 March, 11 May 1811, 17 Sept 1814; IJ 29 April 1815, 27 July 1816; SC 27 July 1816.
[46] IJ 6 Dec 1845, 25 April 1807, 23 Sept 1815.
[47] MM 51, p.135; SC 20 April 1816.
[48] IJ 9 Aug, 30 Aug 1817.
[49] MM 51, p.135; SC 30 Aug 1817.
[50] IJ 19 Sept, 19 Dec 1818, 28 Aug, 11 Sept 1819; SC 11 Sept 1819.
[51] MM 51, p.137.
[52] IJ 15 Sept, 29 Sept 1821; SC 21 July 1821.
[53] IJ 7 April 1821.
[54] IJ 29 Sept 1821; SC 20 Jan 1821; IJ 28 Feb, 13 Nov, 18 Dec 1824, 22 April 1826, 24 March 1827.
[55] MM 51, p.134 *et seq*.; IJ 8 Sept 1821, 8 Jan 1825.

[56] IJ 12 Feb, 19 Feb, 5 March 1825; SC 24 Feb 1827.
[57] IJ 28 May 1825, 20 May 1826.
[58] Reports to the River Improvement Commissioners (SROI EL1/1/9/1/1, p.69 and p.84).
[59] River Improvement Commissioners' Minutes, 24 Sept 1805 *et seq*. (SROI EL1/1/3/1); Reports (as above), p.86.
[60] IJ 7 Dec 1811; SC 30 May, 19 Sept 1812.
[61] SC 27 June 1812; IJ 15 May 1813.
[62] IJ 3 Aug 1816, 28 June 1828, 17 March 1832.
[63] MM 51, p.137 *et seq*.; IJ 19 June, 4 Sept 1824, 15 June, 6 July 1833; *Lloyd's Register* 1843, 1884/5.
[64] SC 27 May, 8 July 1826.
[65] Clarke, *op. cit*., p.409; IJ 19 May 1827.
[66] MM 51, p.140; IJ 2 April 1831.
[67] IJ 1 Sept 1832; SC 31 March 1832; IJ 15 Sept 1832, 26 Jane 1833, 9 Aug 1834.
[68] IJ 27 Sept 1834; MM 51, p.134 and p.140; SC 30 May 1835.
[69] IJ 5 Sept 1835, 23 April, 2 July, 20 Aug 1836.
[70] SC 16 Dec 1837; IJ 3 Feb 1837.
[71] Dock Commissioners' Minutes, 23 Jan 1838 (SROI EL1/1/3/4).
[72] IJ 22 Oct 1836.
[73] IJ 25 Aug 1838.
[74] IJ 12 Jan, 21 Sept, 16 Nov 1839; SC 15 June 1839.
[75] SC 2 Nov 1839.
[76] IJ 25 April 1840.
[77] SC 31 Oct 1840.
[78] IJ 4 Dec 1841, 1 Jan 1842, 21 Sept 1844.
[79] A.G.H. Hollingsworth, *The History of Stowmarket* (1840), p.228; IJ and SC 23 Jun 1810.
[80] IJ 10 June 1843; Frank Hussey, *The Royal Harwich* (1972), p.13 *et seq*.
[81] IJ 8 June, 22 June 1844, 20 Sept 1845.
[82] Basil Greenhill, *The Merchant Schooners* (1957), Vol.2, p.45.
[83] IJ 20 Sept 1845, 14 Feb 1846, 29 May 1847; SC 14 Feb, 19 Sept 1846.
[84] IJ 15 May 1847, 16 June 1849.
[85] SC 3 June 1848.
[86] IJ 26 Jan, 4 May 1850. The year of the younger Thomas's birth was told to me by his son, the late Mr. F. Milton Harvey, who also pointed him out on the 1858 photograph of the yard.
[87] IJ 15 May 1852, 7 July 1855, 24 Dec 1859.
[88] IJ 20 Oct 1855, 29 March, 26 April 1856; J.J. Colledge, *Ships of the Royal Navy* (1970), Vol.2, pp.249-50; D.K. Brown, *Before the Ironclad* (1990), p.154.
[89] IJ 5 Jan 1856, 25 April 1857, 9 June 1860.
[90] IJ 6 Feb 1864; John Leather, *The Northseamen* (1971), p.283 *et seq*.

9 Yards round the Dock

[1] Ipswich Dock Commission records (SROI EL1/3/52).
[2] Dock Commissioners' Minutes, 8 Jan 1841 (SROI EL1/1/3/4).
[3] IJ 20 Nov 1841, 16 April 1842, 19 Aug 1848, 8 Sept 1849; SC 12 July 1845.
[4] IJ 31 May 1862.

[5] By Edward Caley, recording the condition of the old quay walls before the construction of the Wet Dock began (SROI EL1/7/12/3-6).
[6] Hervey Benham, *Down Tops'l* (1951), p.79.
[7] IJ 5 Jan 1850.
[8] IJ 2 March, 9 March, 27 July 1850.
[9] Basil Greenhill, *The Life and Death of the Merchant Sailing Ship* (1980), p.17. IJ 24 July 1852, 19 Feb 1853.
[10] IJ 10 Jan 1852.
[11] IJ 30 April 1853, 27 Jan 1855; *Lloyd's Register 1884/5*.
[12] IJ 18 Aug, 25 Aug, 1 Sept 1855; *Lloyd's Register 1857*.
[13] *East Anglian Daily Times* 27 Dec 1911.
[14] IJ 5 Sept 1857.
[15] IJ 23 April 1859, 4 Jan, 14 June 1862, 23 Jan 1864.
[16] Read's will (SROI IC/AA2/139/250). Robertson was the grandson of Read's sister-in-law.
[17] Codicil dated 7 Dec 1866 to Read's will. Also as 13 above.
[18] IJ 27 April, 4 May 1867; *Mercantile Navy List* 1890 and 1935.
[19] *Lloyd's Register* 1884/5.
[20] IJ 6 June, 27 June 1874.
[21] As 19 above.
[22] Robertson's will.
[23] William Bayley's will (SROI IC/AA2/128/156).
[24] IJ 2 July, 23 July 1859, 22 Sept 1860.
[25] IJ 5 Aug 1879; SC 23 June 1883; *Lloyd's Register* 1884/5.
[26] SC 23 Jan, 20 Jane 1870.
[27] IJ 15 July 1865, 22 Jan 1870.
[28] IJ 7 Feb 1874.
[29] Plan in SROI EL1/7/1/89.
[30] As 13 above.
[31] *Great Eastern Railway Society Journal Special No.2* (1979), p.24.
[32] Transfer of lease of foreshore from the Dan Marine Co. to the Dock Commission (SROI EL1/3/89).
[33] *Mercantile Navy List* 1890; Hervey Benham and Roger Finch, *The Big Barges* (1983), p.65.

Appendix one

Number of Vessels Registered at Ipswich

(excluding those owned in Woodbridge and Aldeburgh, and yachts.)

Sailing vessels

Rig	1830	1840	1850	1860	1870	1880	1890	1900
Barque	-	4	5	8	3	3	-	-
Barquentine	-	-	-	-	1	1	1	-
Brig	20	36	25	21	11	3	-	-
Brigantine	1	1	5	12	20	9	4	1
Snow	1	2	1	6	2	-	-	-
Schooner	31	67	74	72	65	32	10	3
Sloop	49	28	20	19	4	3	-	-
Ketch	-	2	6	4	6	11	22	17
Smack	24	28	20	10	13	4	1	-
Barge	4	9	19	17	10	9	5	5
Spritsail	-	1	2	15	24	36	46	54
Dandy	-	-	2	1	2	1	1	1
Yawl	4	1	-	1	1	1	-	-
Wherry	2	2	-	-	-	-	-	-
Totals	136	181	179	186	162	113	90	81

Steam Vessels

Paddle	2	4	6	6	10	8	4	2
Screw	-	-	-	-	1	-	9	10
Totals	2	4	6	6	11	8	13	12

Appendix two

Warships Built at Ipswich

By William Hubbard

Name	Type	Tonnage	Guns	Keel laid	Yard	Launched	Fate
MILFORD	Small Fifth Rate	385	32	-	St Clement's?	1695	Taken by the French, 1/1697. In French service as *Le Milford* until 1720
GREYHOUND	Large Fifth Rate	494	42	-	John's Ness	3/1703	Wrecked off Tynemouth, 26/8/1711.

By John Barnard

Name	Type	Tonnage	Guns	Keel laid	Yard	Launched	Fate
BIDDEFORD	Sixth Rate on Establishment of 1733.	443	24	11/1739	St Clement's	15/6/1740	Broken up 1754.
HAMPSHIRE	Fourth Rate on Establishment of 1733.	854	50	6/1740	John's Ness	13/11/1741	Broken up 1766.
GRANADO	Bomb Vessel (Ketch rigged).	267	10	11/1741	St Clement's?	22/6/1742	Sold 1763. Became mercantile *Prince Frederick*.
CORMORANT	*Swan* class ship sloop.	300	16	11/1775	Nova Scotia	21/5/1776	Taken by the French off Charleston, 24/8/1781.
ZEBRA	Ditto	300	16	7/1776	Ditto	8/4/1777	Wrecked in the Delaware River, 5/11/1778.
SAVAGE	Ditto	300	16	6/1777	Ditto	28/4/1778	Hulked 1803. Sold 1815.
CHAMPION	*Porcupine* class Sixth Rate	519	24	4/1778	John's Ness	17/5/1779	Hulked 1809. Sold 1816.

By Stephen Teague

Name	Type	Tonnage	Guns	Keel laid	Yard	Launched	Fate
SPITFIRE	*Tisiphone* class fire ship.	421	12	12/1780	Nova Scotia	19/3/1782	Sold 1825.
MEGAERA	Ditto	421	14?	-	Ditto	16/5/1783	Sold 1817.
CRUIZER	*Cruizer* class brig sloop.	382	18	2/1797	Halifax	20/12/1797	Sold 1819.

By Jabez Bayley

Name	Class	Tonnage	Guns	Keel laid	Yard	Launched	Fate
DARING	*Archer* class brig	178	12	6/1804	St Peter's	6/10/1804	Wrecked and blown up, Sierra Leone, 27/1/1813.
HEARTY	*Confounder* class brig	183	14	1/1805	Ditto	12/4/1805	Sold 1816.
IMOGEN	*Seagull* class brig	282	16	4/1805	Ditto	11/7/1805	Sold 1817.
ORESTES	Ditto	282	16	8/1805	Ditto	23/10/1805	Sold 1817.
JULIA	Ditto	282	16	10/1805	Ditto	4/2/1806	Wrecked off Tristan da Cuhna, 2/10/1817.
FAVOURITE	*Cormorant* class ship sloop	422	26	2/1806	Halifax	13/9/1806	Broken up 1821.
PEACOCK	*Cruizer* class brig sloop	382	18	4/1806	One in	9/12/1806	Sank after being taken by USS *Hornet*, 24/2/1813.
SAPPHO	Ditto	382	18	4/1806	each yard	15/12/1806	Laid up as defective 1825, broken up 1830.
BARRACOUTA	Ditto	382	18	1/1807		6/7/1807	Sold 1815.
JASPER	*Cherokee* class brig sloop	235	10	2/1808		27/5/1808	Wrecked in Plymouth Sound, 20/1/1817.
ONYX	Ditto	235	10	2/1808		8/7/1808	Sold 1819
HOPE	Ditto	235	10	4/1808		22/7/1808	Sold 1819.
TRANSIT	Advice boat	262	11	7/1808		3/3/1809	Shortened by 20 feet in 1809, sold 1815.
DRAKE	*Cherokee* class brig sloop	235	10	8/1808		3/11/1808	Wrecked off Newfoundland, 23/6/1822.
ROSARIO	Ditto	235	10	8/1808		7/12/1808	Sold 1832.
BEAVER	Ditto	235	10	10/1808		6/2/1809	Sold 1829.

Name	Class	Tonnage	Guns	Keel laid	Yard	Launched	Fate
NIMROD	*Cruizer* class brig sloop	382	18	11/1811	St Peter's	25/5/1812	Wrecked in Holyhead Bay, 14/1/1827.
ESPIEGLE	Ditto	382	18	1/1812	Ditto	10/8/1812	Sold 1832.
JASEUR	Ditto	382	18	8/1812	Ditto	2/2/1813	Sold 1845.
FLY	Ditto	382	18	6/1812	Ditto	16/2/1813	Sold 1828.
HARLEQUIN	Ditto	382	18	2/1813	Ditto	15/7/1813	Sold 1829.
HARRIER	Ditto	382	18	2/1813	Ditto	28/7/1813	Sold 1829.
ESK	*Cyrus* class ship sloop	454	20	3/1813	Halifax	11/10/1813	Sold 1827.
LEVEN	Ditto	454	20	3/1813	Ditto	23/12/1813	Hulked 1833, broken up 1848.
DEE	*Conway* class ship sloop	444	28	5/1813	Ditto	5/5/1814	Sold 1819.
DILIGENCE	Transport	313	-	10/1813		30/9/1814	Coal hulk 1862, sold 1904.
?	Sailing lighter	125	-	-		1807?	For Jamaica.
Two gunboats	'Commissioner Hamilton's' design	44?	3			1808?	
Six gunboats	'Commissioner Hamilton's' design	51?	3			1809?	
'Bailey No.1'	Stone vessel	112	-			1812	For the construction of Plymouth breakwater.

By Thomas Harvey and Sons

Name	Class	Tonnage	Guns	Keel laid	Yard	Launched	Fate
MV 45	Mortar vessel	166	1	-	Halifax	21/3/1856	Coastguard Watch Vessel No. 22. Broken up 1865.
MV 46	Mortar vessel	166	1	-	Halifax	21/4/1856	Watch Vessel No 10 in 1863. Sold for breaking up 1893.

Index

Entries in **bold type** refer to illustrations.